What's Where in the Apple?
An Atlas to the Apple Computer

MICRO INK Books on the Apple Computer

Edited by Ford Cavallari

What's Where in the Apple — An Atlas to the Apple Computer
by William F. Luebbert

August 1981

MICRO on the Apple Series — Works by various authors published in MICRO magazine, 1977-80

Volume 1 April 1981

Volume 2 Fall 1981

(Other volumes to follow)

What's Where in the Apple?

An Atlas to the Apple Computer

William F. Luebbert
Adjunct Professor of Engineering
Dartmouth College, Hanover, New Hampshire

MICRO INK, Inc.
34 Chelmsford Street
P.O. Box 6502
Chelmsford, Massachusetts 01824

Notice

Apple is a registered trademark of Apple Computer, Inc.
MICRO is a trademark of MICRO INK, Inc.

Every effort has been made to supply complete and accurate information. However, MICRO INK, Inc. assumes no responsibility for its use, nor for infringements of patents or other rights of third parties which would result.

What's Where in the Apple? ISBN: 0-938222-07-4
Printed in the United States of America
Printing 10 9 8 7 6 5 4 3 2 1

Acknowledgements

The information in this book has been accumulated over several years from a wide diversity of sources, including a variety of publications from Apple Computer, Inc., articles from many Apple user group publications and from many magazines, as well as from personal investigations triggered by one or more of these sources.

Unfortunately no record was made in the computer database at the time of original entry of the original source of each datum. Nevertheless the following persons, either through their writings or through personal contact, come to mind as particularly significant sources of information to whom I wish to extend my special gratitude:

Darrell Aldrich
Rick Auricchio
Bob Bishop
C. Bongers
John Crossley
William Dougherty
Andrew Eliason
Val Golding
Andy Hertzfeld
Donald Hyde
Peter Lechner
Lee Meador
C.K. Mesztenyi
Mark Pump
Lee Reynolds
William Reynolds
Lou Rivas
David Roe
Mike Rowe
Loy Spurlock
Dick Suitor
Don Worth
Steve Wozniak

I know that the moment this book goes to the printer, the names of several others who have been inadvertently omitted but who fully deserve to be on this list of those deserving special acknowledgement, will rise up out of my memory to weigh upon my conscience. To such worthy but unrecognized toilers in the orchard I offer, in advance, my sincere apologies.

William F. Luebbert
Hanover, N.H.
July 1981

Special thanks go to the Kiewit Computation Center, Dartmouth College, Hanover, New Hampshire, for assistance in producing the Atlas and Gazetteer output.

Contents

Introduction

You can get more out of an Apple — or any other computer with limited resources — by familiarizing yourself with its hardware and software environment.

When you graduate from simple programs to more ambitious programs involving careful control of man-machine interaction, analog to digital or digital to analog conversion, extensive use of computer grapics, the control of external devices, database management, sorting, or word processing, this knowledge becomes more important. When you get into real time programming, adding your own specialized interfaces, performing activities which require the absolute maximum speed, the information in this atlas becomes critical.

Not every serious programmer needs to become a machine language level programmer. However, good programmers know that when the computer is running their programs there is a lot of machine language code in the machine providing an operating environment for their programs. This operating environment typically includes the system monitor, a BASIC interpreter, and a disk operating system (DOS) and/or extra ROM packages.

When you look at interesting programs described in magazines and user group newsletters, you find that these programs often contain PEEKs, POKEs, and CALLs. These commands are extensions of BASIC (or other higher level languages). They allow you to interface with the computer hardware, operating environment software, and other machine language programs or subprograms.

PEEKs, POKEs, and CALLs all refer to memory locations which are identifiable by what they contain or what they do. PEEK examines the contents of a specified memory location and allows you to use that content in a program. POKE changes the content of a designated memory location to some specified value. It can be used to change parameters of the operating environment or to set up or change pieces of program or data. A CALL transfers program control to a particular memory location back to the CALLing routine in the user's program. Explanations and examples of how this can be done are given on pages 15 - 17.

Subroutines and other pieces of code from the Apple's firmware (i.e. its MONITOR and BASIC interpreter—Applesoft or Integer BASIC), and from its quasi-firmware (i.e. the DOS 3.2 or 3.3 disk operating system), can be accessed via CALLs to provide useful capabilities without writing any additional code. Some of the more powerful and deeply imbedded machine language routines will require the passing of paramters to and from them. This can usually be done by POKEs and PEEKs.

Usually the code you find built into the Apple system has been carefully written in machine language, optimized by good programmers, and takes less space or less computer time than the same function would require if programmed by the user.

Even in the most awkward cases, where deeply imbedded firmware requires the pre-setting of machine-level hardware registers, it is possible to perform the set-ups without doing any assembly or machine language coding by use of the PEEKs, POKEs, and CALLs to the register SAVE and RESTORE routines built into the system monitor. (There is another similar pair of SAVE/RESTORE routines also built into the Disk Operating System.)

Some users may find it more esthetically pleasing to perform the linkage directly by using machine language instructions such as LDA (LoaD Accumulator), LDX (LoaD X-register) or LDY (LoaD Y-register) to form a tiny machine language linkage program, load it into memory by means of POKEs or S.H. Lam's technique for dynamically entering and exiting the system monitor from a BASIC program. If this is your preference, you will find that it is neither necessary nor desirable to use an assembler for this process. It is easier to hand-code from the information in the Apple Reference Manual, perhaps using the disassembler in your Apple II or II+ (and/or the mini-assembler in the Apple II) to check your work.

Incidentally, there could hardly be an easier and less painful way to back gently into developing expertise for doing machine language/assembly language programming than by starting out with imbedding just a few machine language instructions into a predominately BASIC program.

A programming manual intended for serious programmers should supply some sort of memory map and information about the most important and frequently used PEEKs, POKEs, and CALLs. A good memory map can show the user where to get information from the computer, what potentially useful software is available but perhaps hidden away inside the computer, and where to find the "hooks" provided to perform a wide variety of functions by means of CALLs, POKEs and/or PEEKs. Once programmers begin using it as a source of information, they begin to wish for a more complete atlas which will let them find more and more information and guide them in their own explorations inside the computer and its software.

William F. Luebbert

User's Manual

The Apple II contains an address space of over 65,000 locations. Many areas of this space are shared by the user, the monitor, the DOS, and high-level languages. It is possible to write interesting and useful programs without regard to how the Apple memory space is used and managed. In fact, this is exactly how most BASIC and machine language programs are written. Yet a simple knowledge of how the Apple's memory is organized can simplify the task of writing most programs, and can help produce a more compact and efficient code.

Locked within the Apple are many permanently resident routines which can accomplish many common tasks. Most of these routines remain largely undocumented, and thus are difficult for the average Apple owner to use. While information is available here and there about some of these routines, there has been, up to now, no *one* reference source containing documentation on all these routines. The Atlas and Gazetteer which follow contain this information and more.

The *What's Where in the Apple* Atlas is the first complete memory map released for the Apple computer. Further, it is one of the most up-to-date references on the Apple monitor, the Integer and Applesoft BASIC interpreters, the Disk Operating Systems (3.1 - 3.3), and the hardware and I/O memory areas.

The numerically organized memory Atlas considers, in succession, each important memory location in the Apple. Starting with a detailed study of page zero, the Atlas documents each parameter location and vector, each software switch, all video buffer areas, and every data area, in addition to subroutine locations and entry points. The Gazetteer covers the same information, but is arranged in alphabetical order, and contains only those memory locations and areas with commonly used names (e.g. HIRESPG1). Armed with these two packages, any Apple user will be able to gain better performance from the Apple.

The memory maps presented here were not designed with only the machine language programmer in mind. On the contrary, most of the information is of even greater use to the BASIC programmer via PEEKs, POKEs, and CALLs. Thus, numerical memory locations are given in decimal as well as hexadecimal. Utilizing the "built-in" features of the Apple, both Applesoft and Integer BASIC can become much more flexible and powerful languages. Several examples of how the memory map information can improve BASIC programs are included for reference.

The Atlas and Gazetteer will also aid in understanding previously written BASIC programs which use POKEs and CALLs. Using the numerical Atlas, you can easily check just which routine is being CALLed or which vectors or parameters are being POKEd.

One common complaint with a language interpreter such as Applesoft is that it tends to be very slow when compared to machine language. Directly accessing many of the subroutines embedded within the Applesoft or Integer BASIC interpreter or the monitor may significantly decrease execution time. An example of this would be POKEing information directly to the video screen instead of repeatedly using TABs, VTABs, and PRINTs from BASIC. Another example would be to directly access the Applesoft high-resolution plotting routines via POKEs and CALLs.

The Atlas also points out locations which are of general interest to all Apple users. Examples of such locations include SPDBYT, the address which controls the output speed, PADDL0, the hardware address which contains the paddle 0 position readout, MOTORON, the location which turns on the disk drive motor, or the Applesoft mystery parameter at $D6 (see the Atlas to find out what this one does!). Various characteristics of the Apple, ranging from video output format to DOS command names, can be changed by simple POKEs to the right addresses.

The *What's Where in the Apple* Atlas and Gazetteer also should be of great use to any machine language programmer who sees the value of tightening up code by using existing Apple firmware subroutines. For instance, 16 and 32 bit divisions can become a problem in 6502 machine code. However, using the already existing routine for division in the Applesoft interpreter can simplify this problem tremendously. The only key necessary is the knowledge of how to use the routine. The Atlas can provide that knowledge.

Countless other uses exist for the Atlas and Gazetteer; you are limited only by your imagination. With enough digging through these pages, you should be able to find information which can help in almost any problem. The examples which follow will illustrate both the different levels of use (BASIC vs. machine language environment, for instance) and some specific application-oriented examples. While going through the examples, you should be able to think up more without too much difficulty. Then it will be time for you to leaf through the Atlas, and find out exactly *What's Where in the Apple*.

Overview of Apple Memory Organization

A few words about the organization of Apple memory may help you find your way around this memory map.

First, even if you don't know a hexadecimal number from a hole in the ground, it is usually more convenient to use the $ plus 4-character hexadecimal abbreviation for memory addresses when you are looking for information. Its first two characters specify which of the 256 memory pages is being used and its last two characters specify which of the 256 locations within that page. Since the machine language instructions of the machine depend upon this structure, you will find that the utilization of memory and software tends to group related functions on related pages. Thus, instead of a group of oddly sized decimal numbers which seem initially to make no sense at all, you can deal with easy-to-remember 4-character blocks which almost immediately develop a clear and logical structure.

For example, as you go up the memory from page zero towards page 256 you'll find:

Page 0 ($00xx): Used for frequently accessed parameters

Since the parameters most likely to be used time and time again in running programs are those in the system monitor, the BASIC interpreter and the Disk Operating System, this page is dominated by these uses. (Several important hardware instructions run much faster or only run when memory locations in page zero are used.)

Page 1 ($01xx): Used for the System Stack

This is a special area used primarily for subroutine returns (both machine language and BASIC), interrupts, and parameters used in re-entrant coding. Only the most careful and experienced programmers should ever fool with this area.

Page 2 ($02xx): Keyboard and General-Purpose Input Buffer

Characters inputted from the keyboard are stored here. Normally they go no further until an end-of-line carriage-return releases them for further processing.

Page 3 ($03xx): Linkage Vector Page

Except during DOS booting most of this page is unused except for the extreme top which contains jump commands and linkage vectors to key locations in firmware (e.g. $03D0 is the start of the familiar 3D0G linkage which you use to return from the system monitor level to BASIC). During normal operations after disk booting, the otherwise vacant lower sections of this page are a favorite location for short, user-created machine language programs.

Pages 4-7 ($04xx-$07xx): Text and Lo-Res Graphics Display Buffer

The 1024 locations on these 4 pages contain 960 locations which correspond one-to-one with the 960 (40 × 24) possible text character positions on the Apple's display screen. The space is organized into 8 macro-lines of 128 bytes, each of which contains 3 text lines (one on the top ⅓ of the screen, one in the same relative position in the middle ⅓, and the last in the same relative position in the bottom ⅓ of the screen). The remaining 8 bytes are not displayed but are reserved for use by the Apple's special peripheral slots — one location for each slot 0 through 7. These locations are the specific locations involved (s = 0 for slot 0; s = 1 for slot 1;...s = 7 for slot 7): $0478 + s, $04F8 + s, $0578 + s, $05F8 + s, $0678 + s, $06F8 + s, $0778 + s, and $07F8 + s.

In text mode, each character is represented in memory by a single byte (8 bits) of memory. The character displayed is determined by Apple's own special adaptation of the ASCII (American Standard Code for Information Interchange). The actual on-screen display is by a 8 high by 7 wide (including blank margins) array of dots.

In low-resolution graphics mode each 8-bit byte is treated as two 4-bit nibbles. The 2^4 = 16 possible values of each nibble becomes 16 different color combinations, and the output is displayed as two colored blocks, one over the other. The color is controlled by a single nibble. Since there are 24 rows of characters this means there are 48 possible rows (vertical positions) for low resolution color blocks.

Pages 8-11 (Pages $08xx-$0Bxx): Lo-Res and Graphics Secondary Video Display Buffer

This area is seldom used as an alternate text display area. Layout is the same as the primary page, but is seldom used because there is no easy way to print the text here. (It must be POKEd in or moved from page 1.)

Pages 8 upward ($08xx upward): Default Applesoft BASIC Program and Data Space or Default Integer BASIC Data Space

Note: Unless an overt use of LOMEM by the user alters the situation, user BASIC programs or data start at $0800 (unless RAM Applesoft is in use).

Set LOMEM to start at $1200 if Text/Lo-Res graphics page 2 is used. Start after the RAM version of Applesoft if you're using Applesoft without either an Apple with a language card, an Apple II+, or an Apple II with an Applesoft card.

Warning: If RAM Applesoft is used it extends far enough upward in memory to interfere with the use of Hi-Res Graphics Video Display Page 1. If Integer BASIC is used data starts here and works its way upward in memory.

If Applesoft BASIC is used, this space is normally occupied by Applesoft programs and data, with program statements on the bottom, data above the program and linkages to strings and arrays above that.

Warning: Note that as the program size increases, the data is pushed upward. $1FFF is not the top limit of the program. It can expand upward until it meets the string data which expands downward from HIMEM (usually the beginning of the DOS), but after $1FFF this program-related material begins to intrude upon the high-resolution graphics display space making it unusable for graphics purposes.

Pages 32-63 (Pages $20xx-$3Fxx): High-Resolution Graphics Primary Video-Display (HGR pg1)

It is conventional to describe the high resolution graphics video-display area as a bit-mapped area 280 dots wide by 192 dots high in which each possible dot position represents one bit in these pages of memory.

Since there are 280 × 192 = 53760 dot positions we must somehow map the 53,760 dot positions into 53760 bits of the 8K (32 pages of 256-bytes of 8 bits each) = 65,536 bits on these memory pages.

At first the mapping seems absurdly scrambled. If you are perceptive, you may finally detect an assignment pattern which is closely related to the mapping pattern used by text/low-resolution graphics.

This area, though eight times the size of the text screen buffer area, is organized in a conceptually similar fashion. It contains 8 text macrolines each 128 'standardized' characters long which break into 3 screen lines (top ⅓, middle ⅓, bottom ⅓) plus 8 character positions leftover for allocation to peripheral slots.

However, in high-resolution graphics a 'standardized' character position is not represented by a single ASCII character. Instead it is an array 7 dot positions wide by 8 dot positions high, i.e. 8 slices each containing 7 dot positions stacked one over another.

Thus the 40 'standardized' character positions also represent 7 × 40 = 280 dot positions. Each 'slice' of 7 dot positions is associated with one byte of memory, one dot/no-dot position per bit, with the eighth bit (the most significant bit) being a 'color bit'.

Note: On a black-and-white monitor a change in the color bit causes any dot within that byte of memory to shift ½ position left or ½ position right. This creates 560 distinguishable dot-positions across the screen and makes black-and-white plotting possible at a horizontal resolution of 560 bits — providing you program for it and don't use Apple's line-drawing software.

On a color monitor, a dot moving across the 560 distinguishable positions will change color in cycles of 4 colors: violet, blue, green, red/orange. This means that there are only 140 possible bit-mapped green dot positions, so the maximum, resolution for plotting in green (or any other color than black-and-white on a black-and-white monitor) is 140 dot positions across the screen.

On a color monitor if two adjacent colored dots are turned on simultaneously they will merge into a single larger, white-ish dot. The plotting technique used by Apple software uses this technique for plotting the color 'white'. Since there are 280 possible positions for these double-width dots, Apple's standard plotting technique achieves a 280 dot resolution across the width of the screen.

The individual 'slices' which make up a 'standardized' high-resolution character space are located 4 memory pages apart. Thus for the character at the top left corner of the screen, the topmost slice is represented by the byte at location $2000, the next slice by the byte at $2400, the next at $2800, etc.

Since there are 8 slices (8 bytes of memory) stacked one above another per displayed 'standardized' high resolution graphics character, there are 8 × 24 = 192 lines of dots possible on the high-resolution graphics screen, so the screen display checks as 192 dots high by 280 dots wide.

It is from this pattern that we derive the initially scrambled order of memory positions for the left edges of the individual lines of screen display which starting at the top line, goes as follows: $2000, $2400, $2800,..., $3800, $3C00, $2808, $2480, $2C80,... $2380, $2780, $2B80, $2F80, $3380, $3780, $3F80, $2128, $2528,..., $24A8, $27A8, $2AA8, $2EA8, $2050, $2450,..., $24D0, $28D0, $2CD0, $2FD0.

Pages 64-95 (Pages $40xx-$5Fxx): Hi-Resolution Graphics Secondary Display Page (HGR pg2)

The interior layout is the same as HGR pg1 but $2000 higher.

Pages before 150 (before Page $96xx): Applesoft Strings or Integer BASIC Program

Unless an overt setting of HIMEM is used to override it, Applesoft strings work downward from $BFFF if DOS not used or from the beginning of DOS if DOS is used. In a default case (when DOS is using 3 buffers) $9600 is the beginning of DOS so strings work downward from here.

Unless an overt setting of HIMEM is used to override it, Integer BASIC puts its program in this same area with the end of the program at $95FF and the beginning of the program pushing downward as far as necessary.

Pages 150-191 (Pages $96xx-$BFxx): Disk Operating System

When the Disk Operating System is booted on a 48K Apple it occupies locations $9600-$BFFF in the default case. In an Apple with less memory, the start of the DOS moves down by the amount of the reduction of memory. E.g., in a 32K Apple, the DOS would start at $5600.

Warning: Note the interference with Hi-Resolution graphics page 2.

If DOS Maxfiles are set to a value other than the default value of 3, buffers added to or deleted from DOS will alter this boundary point. With maxfiles = 6, DOS extends downward to $8F57; with maxfiles = 1, DOS extends downward only to $9AA6.

DOS buffers normally occupy $9600-$9D00; the main body of DOS routine from $9D00-$AAC9; the file manager or I/O section of the DOS from $AAC9 to $B600; and the RWTS (Read-Write Track-Sector) routines from $B600-$C000.

Pages 192-207 ($C0xx-$CFxx): Special Hardware I-O Area

This area is reserved for Input/Output and 'slot' (peripheral) operations. It divides naturally into four sub-areas:

$C000-$C07F	Built-In I/O Locations
$C080-$C0FF	Peripheral Card I/O Space
$C100-$C7FF	Peripheral Card ROM Space
$C800-$CFFF	Expansion ROM Space (Allocated to Currently Active Peripheral Slot).

Page 192 ($C0xx) is divided into two half pages. The $C000-$C07F half-page contains special data and flag inputs (such as the keyboard, cassette pushbutton and game-control/joystick). It also contains strobe functions which activate special I/O activities and program-controllable 'soft-switches' and 'toggle-switches' which control such alternatives as video display of text vs. display of graphics; Lo-Res vs. Hi-Res graphics, Primary vs. Secondary video display page being displayed, all full page graphic display or mixed text-graphics display.

The $C080-$C0FF half-page is divided into 8, 16-byte chunks, each of which is assigned to one of the 8 peripheral slots (0-7) for use as Input/Output space for that peripheral.

Pages 193-199 ($C1-$C7) are allocated one page to each peripheral slot (1-7, but not slot 0) for its exclusive use by its own on-board PROM (Programmable Read Only Memory).

Pages 202-207 ($C8-$CF) is a 2K (8 page) area reserved for use by memory (usually a ROM) on a peripheral card. Only that memory on the card whose slot is currently active has access to the central machine.

Please note that the peripheral cards also have assigned to them additional individual bytes of RAM memory from the 'breakage' at the end of each line of the video display buffer areas.

Pages 208-255 ($D0xx-$FFxx): Used for Monitor and Interpreter ROM

Note: When the language card is used, ROM may be replaced by RAM Into which firmware may be read and then protected against accidental writing to make it a de-facto ROM equivalent after initial loading.

The topmost part of this, pages 248-255 ($F8-$FF), are assigned to the monitor, which may appear in either of two forms: the (old) monitor ROM or the (new) autostart monitor ROM. The major differences between them are that the autostart version has had the autostart features added and has had the mini-assembler and single-step trace capabilities removed to make space for the additions.

In the Apple II+, the remainder of this area, pages 208-247 ($D0-F7), is occupied by the Applesoft BASIC interpreter.

In the Apple II, the Integer BASIC, rather than the Applesoft BASIC, is built, and it occupies a smaller area, pages 240-255 ($E0-$FF). The remaining space, pages 208-239, is available for other ROMs such as the Integer BASIC 'Programmer's Aid #1'.

Examples

Using a Monitor Routine from Applesoft

```
1   REM  ******************************
2   REM  *                            *
3   REM  *       CASE STUDY NO. 1     *
5   REM  * WHAT'S WHERE IN THE APPLE  *
6   REM  * ------ ----- -- --- -----  *
7   REM  *                            *
8   REM  ******************************
9   REM
10   HOME : VTAB 7: PRINT "ENTER DECIMAL NUMBER";: INPUT N
15   HOME : VTAB 7: PRINT " DEC= ";N
20 MSP =  INT (N / 256): POKE 0,MSP: REM  MSP => LOCATION 0
30 LSP = N - 256 *  INT (N / 256): POKE 1,LSP: REM  LSP => LOCATION 1
40   POKE 60,0: POKE 61,0: REM  0 => PARAMETER A1
50   POKE 62,1: POKE 63,0: REM  1 => PARAMETER A2
60   CALL  - 589: REM  ROUTINE TO HEX PRINT MEMORY FROM A1 TO A2 (0-1)
70   POKE 1064,160: POKE 1065,200: POKE 1066,197: POKE 1067,216
80   POKE 1068,189: POKE 1069,160: REM  POKE TO SCREEN "HEX = "
90   VTAB 11: PRINT "PRESS ANY KEY TO CONTINUE";: GET R$: GOTO 10
```

Analysis:

The best way to start is to look up the memory locations involved in the Programmers' Atlas:

1. Locations 0 and 1 seem to be usable for several different purposes.
2. Locations 60 and 61 are often used together as a two-byte general-usage 'Parameter A1' for many monitor subroutines.
3. Locations 62 and 63 are often similarly used as two-byte general-usage 'Parameter A2' for many monitor subroutines.
4. Location −589 contains a subroutine which outputs a block of memory in hex format using parameters A1 and A2 to specify the starting and ending addresses of the block.
5. Locations 1064 through 1069 are located in the middle of text page 1. Anything POKEd to them should appear as text on the screen of the Apple.

Now down to detailed analysis of the program:

1. Line 10 clears the screen, tabs part way down, and asks for and accepts as input a decimal number. It then reclears the screen and prints out ' DEC= ' and the value of the number accepted.
2. Lines 20 and 30 do a computation we have seen before. They break the integer value of the number into two byte-sized pieces and put the more significant part (MSP) into location 0 and the less significant part (LSP) into location 1.
3. Lines 40 and 50 respectively put the address 0 into parameter A1 and the address 1 into parameter A2.
4. Line 60 calls the hexadecimal print subroutine used by the monitor for printout of the contents of any desired portion of memory. Parameter A1 tells it to start at location 0 (where the MSP of the number is located) and to print the hexadecimal contents of memory locations through that specified by parameter A2, which turns out to be only through location 1 (where the LSP of the number is located). Thus, only two locations are printed: that containing the MSP and that containing the LSP. These two locations contain the number which was to be printed in hexadecimal form.
5. Unfortunately the subroutine at −589 also prints the starting memory location for the group of values that it prints out. This is unnecessary and confusing in the context of this use. The problem is resolved by having line 70 overprint the location on the screen where this undesired '0000 −' is printed with the identification ' HEX= '. Thus the Apple screen now shows ' DEC= ' and the decimal value and immediately below it

' HEX= ' with the corresponding hexadecimal equivalent.

6. Line 80 freezes the output on the screen by stopping the program until the user presses some key, then goes back to the beginning of the program to repeat the process.

Several comments are in order. First, the choice of memory locations 0-1 was purely arbitrary. They weren't being used for anything else and were easy to remember and POKE.

Second, the POKEd output onto the screen in line 70 might better be replaced by a BASIC 'PRINT '' DEC= ''' with appropriate prepositioning by TAB commands. However, this made a nice illustration of the direct POKE output onto the screen, so why not use it?

Finally, the monitor subroutine at –589 was not designed to do exactly what was wanted. It did something more which had to be undone by the overprinting operation.

Creating a Machine Language Program from Applesoft

```
1   REM ******************************
2   REM *                            *
3   REM *      CASE STUDY NO. 2      *
4   REM * WHAT'S WHERE IN THE APPLE*
5   REM * ------ ----- -- --- -----*
6   REM *                            *
7   REM ******************************
8   REM
10   POKE 768,216: POKE 769,160: POKE 770,0: POKE 771,76: POKE 772,44: POKE 773,254
20   POKE 60,BEG -  INT (BEG / 256) * 256: POKE 61, INT (BEG / 256)
30   POKE 62,EN -  INT (EN / 256) * 256: POKE 63, INT (EN / 256)
40   POKE 66,DEST -  INT (DEST / 256) * 256: POKE 67, INT (DEST / 256)
50   CALL 768
```

Analysis:

In a quick overview we note the following:

1. The first line POKEs information into memory locations 768-773.
2. The next 3 lines each do similar computations of the type we have seen before: breaking a number down into two bytes — a more significant part, the quotient of an integer division by 256, and less significant part, the remainder of integer division by 256. First the computation is done on the value of BEG (the BEGinning of the block to be moved); next it is done on the value of EN (the ENd of the block to be moved); and finally it is done on the value of DEST (the DESTination of the block to be moved).
3. The results of these computations are POKEd into memory locations 60,61 - 62,63 and 66,67. Finally,
4. The last line CALLs (transfers control to) memory location –768, the first location into which something was POKEd at the beginning of the program. Since the last line transferred control to it we may suspect that what was POKEd into location 768, and the locations following it, was a tiny piece of program.

Now let's begin our normal analysis using the Programmers' Atlas:

1. At memory location 768 in the Atlas, we find the indication that the block of memory starting at that location is often used as a convenient location for user-written programs. The suspicion is reinforced as a working hypothesis, but not fully confirmed.
2. Locations 60 and 61 are listed together as a pair of 8-bit bytes: A1L and A1H. The L denotes the Low (or Least Significant Byte — LSB) and the H denotes the High (or Most Significant Byte — MSB) of two bytes normally used together to form the two-byte (16-bit) parameter A1. The Programmer's Atlas describes A1 as follows: ''Monitor general-usage subroutine parameter A. Many uses include source pointer for monitor move subroutine.'' (A 'pointer' is an address which 'points' to a given location in memory.)

3. Line 20 uses variable BEG (for BEGinning) to compute the address of the beginning of the block of memory to be transferred, and puts it into the same memory locations as those used for general-usage parameter A1.

4. Line 30 performs similar computations on EN (the ENd address of the block of memory to be moved and puts the results into the same location used by monitor general-usage subroutine parameter A2.

5. Line 40 does the same again with DEST (the DESTination address) and puts the results into monitor general-usage subroutine parameter A4.

6. Could the MOVE subroutine, which is present as part of the monitor any time the Apple is running, be at the heart of the 'FAST MOVE' capability? Again we have preliminary suspicions, but lack confirmation. However, there is only one more line to the program. It does not call location 65068 or anything readily associated with −468, or with the 'MOVE' routine, wherever that may be. Instead it calls location 768, the first of such locations into which we POKEd something. Too bad! You can't win them all! However, let's not be too discouraged.

7. A CALL is a subroutine-type transfer of control to a piece of machine language code, so let's see what happens if we interpret the POKEs in line 10 which begin with a POKE to location as machine language. This involves a conversion from decimal format to machine language format. Perhaps they will make sense as a program, even though it seems unlikely that a program so short could accomplish block move.

8. The POKEs in line 10 do indeed describe a machine language program, beginning at hex location $300. For those interested in the mechanics of this program, enter the monitor (call −151) and disassemble starting at location $300 (300L).

Checking Software Locations from within a Program

```
10   REM ******************************
20   REM *                            *
30   REM *      CASE STUDY NO. 3      *
40   REM * WHAT'S WHERE IN THE APPLE*
50   REM * ------ ----- -- --- -----*
60   REM *                            *
70   REM ******************************
80   REM
100  SPD = 256 -  PEEK (241): REM  PRINTING SPEED
110  LEFT =  PEEK (32): REM  SAVE LEFT MARGIN
120  RIGHT =  PEEK (32) +  PEEK (33): REM  SAVE RIGHT MARGIN
130  TP =  PEEK (34): REM  SAVE TOP MARGIN
140  BOT =  PEEK (35): REM  SAVE BOTTOM MARGIN
150  :
160   TEXT : HOME : REM  RESET SCREEN
170   REM  PRINT OUT SCREEN AND STATUS
180   PRINT "SPEED = ";SPD
190   PRINT "LEFT = ";LEFT
200   PRINT "RIGHT = ";RIGHT
210   PRINT "TOP = ";TP
220   PRINT "BOTTOM = ";BOT
230  :
240   REM  SET SCREEN BACK
250   POKE 241, - (SPD - 256): REM  LOAD PRINTING SPEED
260   POKE 32,LEFT: REM  LOAD LEFT MARGIN
270   POKE 33,RIGHT - LEFT: REM  LOAD RIGHT MARGIN
280   POKE 34,TP: REM  LOAD TOP MARGIN
290   POKE 35,BOT: REM  LOAD BOTTOM MARGIN
300  :
310   END
```

Analysis: Left as an exercise for the reader!

Useful Tables

Zero Page Usage

Decimal	Hex	0 $0	1 $1	2 $2	3 $3	4 $4	5 $5	6 $6	7 $7	8 $8	9 $9	10 $A	11 $B	12 $C	13 $D	14 $E	15 $F
0	$00	AS	AS	AS	AS	AS	AS	S	S	S	S	AS	AS	AS	AS	AS	AS
16	$10	AS	AS	AS	AS	AS	AS	AS	AS	AS	S	S	S	S	S	S	S
32	$20	M	M	M	M	M	M	MD	MD	M	M	MD	MD	MD	MD	MD	MD
48	$30	M	M	M	M	M	MD	MD	MD	MD	MD	M	M	M	M	MD	MD
64	$40	MD	MD	MD	MD	MD	MD	MD	MD	MD	M	DI	DI	DI	DI	M	M
80	$50	MA	MA	MA	MA	MA	MAI	AI	AI	AI	AI	AI	AI	AI	AI	AI	AI
96	$60	AI	AI	AI	AI	AI	AI	AI	DAI	DAI	DAI	AI	AI	AI	AI	AI	DAI
112	$70	DAI	AI	AI	AI	AI	AI	AI	AI	AI	AI	AI	AI	AI	AI	AI	AI
128	$80	AI	AI	AI	AI	AI	AI	AI	AI	AI	AI	AI	AI	AI	AI	AI	AI
144	$90	AI	AI	AI	AI	AI	AI	AI	AI	AI	AI	AI	AI	AI	AI	AI	AI
160	$A0	AI	AI	AI	AI	AI	AI	AI	AI	AI	AI	AI	AI	AI	AI	AI	DAI
176	$B0	DAI	AI	AI	AI	AI	AI	AI	AI	AI	AI	AI	AI	AI	AI	AI	AI
192	$C0	AI	AI	AI	AI	AI	AI	AI	AI	AI	AI	DAI	DAI	DAI	DAI	AI	AI
208	$D0	AI	AI	AI	AI	AI	AI	I	I	DAI	AI	AI	AI	AI	AI	AI	AI
224	$E0	A	A	A		A	A	A	A	A	A	A					
240	$F0	A	A	A	A	A	A	A	A	A							

A = Used by Applesoft   I = Used by Integer BASIC   S = Used by Sweet-16 Interpreter
D = Used by DOS   M = Used by Monitor

Apple ASCII Representation

		Inverse				Flashing				Normal							
										(Control)						(Lower C)	
Decimal		000	016	032	048	064	080	096	112	128	144	160	176	192	208	224	240
	Hex	$00	$10	$20	$30	$40	$50	$60	$70	$80	$90	$A0	$B0	$C0	$D0	$E0	$F0
00	$0	@	P		0	@	P		0	@	P		0	@	P		0
01	$1	A	Q	!	1	A	Q	!	1	A	Q	!	1	A	Q	!	1
02	$2	B	R	"	2	B	R	"	2	B	R	"	2	B	R	"	2
03	$3	C	S	#	3	C	S	#	3	C	S	#	3	C	S	#	3
04	$4	D	T	$	4	D	T	$	4	D	T	$	4	D	T	$	4
05	$5	E	U	%	5	E	U	%	5	E	U	%	5	E	U	%	5
06	$6	F	V	&	6	F	V	&	6	F	V	&	6	F	V	&	6
07	$7	G	W	'	7	G	W	'	7	G	W	'	7	G	W	'	7
08	$8	H	X	(	8	H	X	(	8	H	X	(	8	H	X	(	8
09	$9	I	Y	)	9	I	Y	)	9	I	Y	)	9	I	Y	)	9
10	$A	J	Z	*	:	J	Z	*	:	J	Z	*	:	J	Z	*	:
11	$B	K	[	+	;		[	+	;	K	[	+	;	K	[	+	;
12	$C	L		,		-		,		L		,		L		,	
13	$D	M	]	-	=	M	]	-	=	M	]	-	=	M	]	-	=
14	$E	N		.		N		.		N		.		N		.	
15	$F	O	-	/	?	O	-	/	?	O	-	/	?	O	-	/	?

Apple Text Screen Organization

Memory Layout of Text "Super-Line"

```
. . . First 40 characters . . . . . Second 40 characters . .  . . Third 40 characters . .   . . . . . 8 . . . . .
      (Top ⅓ of screen)             (Middle ⅓ of screen)         (Bottom ⅓ of screen)            'slot'
                                                                                                  bytes
```

Logical Organization of Text Display Area

```
. . . . . Super-Line 0 (SL00) - 120 displayable characters + 8 non-displayable scratchpad bytes .
. . . . . Super-Line 1 (SL01) . . . . . . . . . . . . . . . . . . . . . . . . . . . . . . . . . . .
. . . . . Super-Line 2 (SL02) . . . . . . . . . . . . . . . . . . . . . . . . . . . . . . . . . . .
. . . . . Super-Line 3 (SL03) . . . . . . . . . . . . . . . . . . . . . . . . . . . . . . . . . . .
. . . . . Super-Line 4 (SL04) . . . . . . . . . . . . . . . . . . . . . . . . . . . . . . . . . . .
. . . . . Super-Line 5 (SL05) . . . . . . . . . . . . . . . . . . . . . . . . . . . . . . . . . . .
. . . . . Super-Line 6 (SL06) . . . . . . . . . . . . . . . . . . . . . . . . . . . . . . . . . . .
. . . . . Super-Line 7 (SL07) . . . . . . . . . . . . . . . . . . . . . . . . . . . . . . . . . . .
```

Screen Display Layout of "Super-Line"

```
00 - - - - - - - - - - - - - - - - First 40 characters - - - - - - - - - - - - - - - -
01 . . . . . . . . . . . . . . . . . . . . . . . . . . . . . . . . . . . . . . . .
02 . . . . . . . . . . . . . . . . . . . . . . . . . . . . . . . . . . . . . . . .
03 . . . . . . . . . . . . . . . . . . . . . . . . . . . . . . . . . . . . . . . .
04 . . . . . . . . . . . . . . . . . . . . . . . . . . . . . . . . . . . . . . . .
05 . . . . . . . . . . . . . . . . . . . . . . . . . . . . . . . . . . . . . . . .
06 . . . . . . . . . . . . . . . . . . . . . . . . . . . . . . . . . . . . . . . .
07 . . . . . . . . . . . . . . . . . . . . . . . . . . . . . . . . . . . . . . . .
08 - - - - - - - - - - - - - - - - Second 40 characters - - - - - - - - - - - - - - -
09 . . . . . . . . . . . . . . . . . . . . . . . . . . . . . . . . . . . . . . . .
10 . . . . . . . . . . . . . . . . . . . . . . . . . . . . . . . . . . . . . . . .
11 . . . . . . . . . . . . . . . . . . . . . . . . . . . . . . . . . . . . . . . .
12 . . . . . . . . . . . . . . . . . . . . . . . . . . . . . . . . . . . . . . . .
13 . . . . . . . . . . . . . . . . . . . . . . . . . . . . . . . . . . . . . . . .
14 . . . . . . . . . . . . . . . . . . . . . . . . . . . . . . . . . . . . . . . .
15 . . . . . . . . . . . . . . . . . . . . . . . . . . . . . . . . . . . . . . . .
16 - - - - - - - - - - - - - - - - Third 40 characters - - - - - - - - - - - - - - - -
17 . . . . . . . . . . . . . . . . . . . . . . . . . . . . . . . . . . . . . . . .
18 . . . . . . . . . . . . . . . . . . . . . . . . . . . . . . . . . . . . . . . .
19 . . . . . . . . . . . . . . . . . . . . . . . . . . . . . . . . . . . . . . . .
20 . . . . . . . . . . . . . . . . . . . . . . . . . . . . . . . . . . . . . . . .
21 . . . . . . . . . . . . . . . . . . . . . . . . . . . . . . . . . . . . . . . .
22 . . . . . . . . . . . . . . . . . . . . . . . . . . . . . . . . . . . . . . . .
23 . . . . . . . . . . . . . . . . . . . . . . . . . . . . . . . . . . . . . . . .
```

ATLAS

```
$0000~$FFFF (0~-1) \HB\              ADDRESS RANGE OF APPLE II ($0000~$FFFF SIGNED DECIMAL EQUIV IS 0~32767 FOLLOWED BY
                                     -32768~-1)
$0000~$BFFF (0~-16385) \HB\          RAM ADDRESS RANGE OF APPLE II (NOT INCLUDING RAM IN LANGUAGE CARD IF PRESENT)
$0000~$00FF (0~255) \HB\             HARDWARE PAGE ZERO
$0000~$001F (0~31) [(R0-R15)] \PB\'SWEET-16' REGISTERS R0 THRU R15 OF 'SWEET-16' (16-BIT INTERPRETER IN MONITOR)
$0000~$0002 (0~2) \SE\               APPLESOFT SOFT REENTRY (0G IS EQUIVALENT TO CTRL~C)
$0000~$0001 (0~1) [R0L~R0H] \P2\     'SWEET-16' REGISTER R0 (IN 16-BIT PSEUDOMACHINE IN APPLE SYSTEM MONITOR)
$0000 (0) [LOC0] \P1\                MONITOR MEMORY LOCATION 'LOC0'. PRESET TO $4C (JMP) - (JUMP ADDRESS IN $001~$002)
$0001~$0002 (1~2) [LOC1] \P2\        MONITOR MEMORY LOCATION 'LOC1' - POINTER PRESET TO ADDRESS OF APPLESOFT SOFT ENTRY
$0002~$0003 (2~3) [(R1)] \P2\        'SWEET-16' REGISTER R1 (IN 16-BIT PSEUDOMACHINE IN APPLE SYSTEM MONITOR)
$0003~ $0005\SE\                     APPLESOFT JUMP COMMAND TO $F128 (HARD ENTRY?)
$0004~$0005 (4~5) [(R2)] \P2\        'SWEET-16' REGISTER R2 (IN 16-BIT PSEUDOMACHINE IN APPLE SYSTEM MONITOR)
$0006~$0007 (6~7) [(R3)] \P2\        'SWEET-16' REGISTER R3 (IN 16-BIT PSEUDOMACHINE IN APPLE SYSTEM MONITOR)
$0008~$0009 (8~9) [(R4)] \P2\        'SWEET-16' REGISTER R4 (IN 16-BIT PSEUDOMACHINE IN APPLE SYSTEM MONITOR)
$000A~$0016 (10~22) [(A/S RESVD)] \PB\APPLESOFT RESERVED BLOCK IN PAGE ZERO
$000A~$000C (10~12) \SI\             APPLESOFT LOCN FOR USR FUNCTION'S JUMP INSTRUCTION
$000A~$000B (10~11) [(R5)] \P2\      'SWEET-16' REGISTER R5 (IN 16-BIT PSEUDOMACHINE IN APPLE SYSTEM MONITOR)
$000C~$000D (12~13) [(R6)] \P2\      'SWEET-16' REGISTER R6 (IN 16-BIT PSEUDOMACHINE IN APPLE SYSTEM MONITOR)
$000D (13) [CHARAC]                  APPLESOFT - USED BY STRLT2 STRING UTILITY
$000D~$0016 (13~22) \PB\             GENERAL PURPOSE COUNTERS/FLAGS FOR APPLESOFT
$000E~$000F (14~15) [(R7)] \P2\      'SWEET-16' REGISTER R7 (IN 16-BIT PSEUDOMACHINE IN APPLE SYSTEM MONITOR)
$000E (14) [ENDCHR]                  APPLESOFT - USED BY STRLT2 STRING UTILITY
$0010~$0011 (16~17) [(R8)] \P2\      'SWEET-16' REGISTER R8 (IN 16-BIT PSEUDOMACHINE IN APPLE SYSTEM MONITOR)
$0011 (17) [VALTYP]                  APPLESOFT FLAG FOR LAST FAC (FLOATING ACCUMULATOR) OPERATION: $00 = NUMBER; $FF=STRING
$0012~$0013 (18~19) [(R9)] \P2\      'SWEET-16' REGISTER R9 (IN 16-BIT PSEUDOMACHINE IN APPLE SYSTEM MONITOR)
$0014~$0015 (20~21) [(R10)] \P2\     'SWEET-16' REGISTER R10 (IN 16-BIT PSEUDOMACHINE IN APPLE SYSTEM MONITOR)
$0014 (20) [SUBFLG]                  APPLESOFT SUBSCRIPT FLAG: $00= SUBSCRIPTS ALLOWED;$80= SUBSCRIPTS NOT ALLOWED
$0016~$0017 (22~23) [(R11)] \P2\     'SWEET-16' REGISTER R11 (IN 16-BIT PSEUDOMACHINE IN APPLE SYSTEM MONITOR)
$0016 (22) [(COMPRTYP)] \P1\         APPLESOFT~- PARAMETER TO CONTROL TYPE OF COMPARISON MADE BY FLOATING POINT COMPARISON
                                     ROUTINE AT $DF6A (1:> ;2:= ;3:>= ;4:< ;5:<> ;6:<=)
$0018~$0019 (24~25) [(R12)] \P2\     'SWEET-16' REGISTER R12 (IN 16-BIT PSEUDOMACHINE IN APPLE SYSTEM MONITOR)
$001A~$001B (26~27) [(R13)] \P2\     'SWEET-16' REGISTER R13 (IN 16-BIT PSEUDOMACHINE IN APPLE SYSTEM MONITOR)
$001A~$001B (26~27) [SHAPEL~SHAPEH] \P2\HI-RES POINTER TO SHAPE LIST (ON-THE-FLY SHAPE POINTER)
$001C~$001D (28~29) [(R14)] \P2\     'SWEET-16' REGISTER R14 (IN 16-BIT PSEUDOMACHINE IN APPLE SYSTEM MONITOR)
$001C (28) [HCOLOR1] \P1\            HI-RES RUNNING COLOR MASK (ON-THE-FLY COLOR BYTE)
$001D (29) [COUNTH] \P1\             HI-RES GRAPHICS HIGH-ORDER BYTE OF STEP COUNT FOR LINE
$001E~$001F (30~31) [R15L~R15H] \P2\'SWEET-16' REGISTER R15 (USED AS PROGRAM COUNTER IN 16-BIT PSEUDOMACHINE IN APPLE
                                     SYSTEM MONITOR) (REG-R15 )
$0020~$0055 (32~85) [(MONITOR RESVD)] \PB\APPLE II SYSTEM MONITOR RESERVED LOCATIONS ($0050~$0055 USED ONLY BY
                                     MULTIPLY-DIVIDE ROUTINES AND THUS AVAILABLE IN MANY SITUATIONS)
$0020~$004F (32~79) [(AUTOSTART RESVD)] \PB\AUTOSTART MONITOR RESERVED LOCATIONS
$0020 (32) [WNDLFT] \P1\             LEFT COLUMN OF SCROLL WINDOW: RANGE 0-39 OR $0~$27. USED ONLY IN VTABZ.
$0021 (33) [WNDWDTH] \P1\            WIDTH OF THE SCROLL WINDOW: RANGE:1 TO 40-(WNDLFT) OR $1 TO $28 - (WNDLFT)
$0022 (34) [WNDTOP] \P1\             TOP LINE OF SCROLL WINDOW: RANGE 0-22($16) FOR FULL TEXT SCREEN 20-22($14~$16) FOR
                                     MIXED SCREEN
$0023 (35) [WNDBTM] \P1\             BOTTOM LINE OF SCROLL WINDOW: RANGE (WNDTOP)+1 TO 24($18).
$0024 (36) [CH] \P1\                 CURSOR HORIZONTAL DISPLACEMENT FROM WNDLFT: RANGE 0 TO (WNDWDTH)-1
$0025 (37) [CV] \P1\                 CURSOR VERTICAL POSITION RELATIVE TO TOP OF SCREEN: RANGE 0-23 ($0~$17)
$0026~$0027 (38~39) \P2\             PAGE ZERO LOCATIONS USED BY DOS
$0026~$0027 (38~39) [GBASL~GBASH] \P2\MEMORY ADDRESS OF LEFT END POINT OF DESIRED LINE FOR LO-RES PLOT (SET BY GBASCALC)
$0026~$0027 (38~39) [HBASL~HBASH] \P2\HI-RES GRAPHICS ON-THE-FLY BASE ADDRESS (LEFT END POINT OF DESIRED LINE FOR
                                     HI-RES PLOT)
```

```
$0026~$0027 (38~39)                USED AS SCRATCH BY DOS
$0028~$0029 (40~41) [BASL~BASH] \P2\MEMORY ADDRESS FOR LEFT END CHARACTER POS'N OF CURRENT TEXT LINE
$002A~$002F (42~47) \PB\           PAGE ZERO LOCATIONS USED BY DOS
$002A~$002B (42~43) \P2\           USED AS SCRATCH BY DOS
$002A~$002B (42~43) [BAS2L~BAS2H] \P2\USED DURING SCROLLING AS DESTINATION LINE POINTER AS EACH LINE IS MOVED TO
                                   POSITION ABOVE CURRENT
$002C~$002D (44~45) [RTNL~RTNH] \P2\MONITOR RETURN POINTER (POINTS TO SAVE AREA USED BY INSTRUCTION TRACE ROUTINE)
$002C~$002D (44~45) [LMNEM~RMNEM] \P2\ADDRESS POINTER USED BY DISASSEMBLER FOR INDEX TO MNEMONICS TABLE
$002C~$002D (44~45) [TEMP] \P2\    DOS RWTS (READ-WRITE TRACK-SECTOR TEMPORARY STORAGE FOR ADDRESS INFORMATION
$002C (44) [COUNT - CSUM] \P1\     DOS RWTS (READ-WRITE TRACK-SECTOR) PARAMETER (RETURNS CHECKSUM)
$002C (44) [H2] \P1\               RIGHT END POINT OF A HORIZONTAL LINE BEING DRAWN BY HLINE: RANGE 0-39 ($0~$27)
$002D (45) [V2] \P1\               BOTTOM PT OF LO-RES VERT LINE DRAWN BY VLINE. RANGE: 0-19(~$21) FOR MIXED SCR;
                                   0-23(~$17) FOR FULL SCR
$002D (45) [SECT] \P1\             DOS RWTS (READ-WRITE TRACK-SECTOR) PARAMETER FOR CURRENT DISK SECTOR
$002E (46) [CHKSUM] \P1\           LOCN WHERE CHECKSUM IS ACCUMULATED DURING CASSETTE TAPE READ
$002E (46) [FORMAT] \P1\           USED BY MINIASSEMBLER & DISASSEMBLER TO SPECIFY FORMAT OF INSTRUCTION FOR DISPLAY
                                   PURPOSES
$002E (46) [MASK] \P1\             LOW-RES COLOR GRAPHICS MASK. $0F OR $F0 TO SELECT HIGH OR LOW NIBBLE TO SPECIFY WHICH
                                   OF 2 PLOT LINES REP BY GBASL~H POINTER
$002E (46) [TRACK - TRKN] \P1\     DOS RWTS (READ-WRITE TRACK-SECTOR) TRACK NUMBER
$002F (47) [LASTIN] \P1\           USED IN CASSETTE INPUT BY RDBIT AS WORK AREA TO DETERMINE WHETHER INPUT HAS CHANGED
$002F (47) [LENGTH] \P1\           USED BY DISASSEMBLER TO INDICATE LENGTH OF THE INSTRUCTION. ALSO BY TRACE
$002F (47) [SIGN] \P1\             $01 BIT SET AFTER CALL TO MULPM OR DIVPM (SIGNED 16 BIT MULT OR DIV) TO SPECIFY
                                   WHETHER COMPLEMENT NEEDED (NOTE MULPM & DIVPM IN OLD MONITOR ONLY ~ NOT IN AUTOSTART)
$002F (47) [VOLUME] \P1\           DOS RWTS (READ-WRITE TRACK-SECTOR) DISK VOLUME NUMBER
$0030 (48) [COLOR] \P1\            LOW-RES COLOR GRAPHICS COLOR CODE (FOR PLOT/HLIN/VLIN FUNCTIONS) - CONTAINS SELECTED
                                   COLOR VALUES FOR TWO LOW-RES GRAPHICS 'LINES' ONE IN EACH NIBBLE OF BYTE
$0030 (48) [HMASK] \P1\            HI-RES GRAPHICS ON-THE-FLY BIT MASK
$0031 (49) [MODE] \P1\             USED BY MONITOR COMMAND PROCESSING TO INDICATE DISPOSITION OF HEX INFO IN THE INPUT
                                   LINE
$0032 (50) [INVFLG] \P1\           VIDEO FORMAT CONTROL: 255($FF)=NORMAL;127($7F)=FLASHING;63($3F)=INVERSE
$0033 (51) [PROMPT] \P1\           PROMPT CHARACTER WRITTEN TO SCREEN WHENEVER A LINE OF INPUT IS CALLED FOR BY GETLN
                                   ROUTINE
$0034 (52) [YSAV] \P1\             USED BY MONITOR COMMAND PROCESSOR TO SAVE CONTENTS OF Y-REGISTER DURING PROCESSOR
                                   {Y-REGISTER SAVE LOCN FOR MONITOR}
$0035~$0039 (53~57) \PB\           PAGE ZERO LOCATIONS USED BY DOS FOR INTERFACE (DRIVENO CSW & KSW)
$0035 (53) [YSAV1] \P1\            USED TO SAVE CONTENTS OF Y-REGISTER ACROSS A CALL TO SCREEN OUTPUT ROUTINES.
                                   {Y-REGISTER SAVE LOCN FOR COUT1}
$0035 (53) [L] \P1\                MINIASSEMBER MEMORY LOCATION 'L'
$0035 (53) [DRIVENO] \P1\          DOS DISK DRIVE NO
$0036~$0039 (54~57) [(I/O HOOK TBLS)] \PB\MONITOR OUTPUT & INPUT HOOKS (VECTORS TO DOS OUTPUT & INPUT ROUTINES)
$0036~$0037 (54~55) [CSWL~CSWH] \P2\MONITOR OUTPUT REG & OUTPUT HOOK TO DOS; I.E. ADDRESS OF ROUTINE WHICH IS TO
                                   RECEIVE AND DISPOSE OF OUTPUT CHARACTERS. RESET 0 CTRL-P & PR#0 SET THIS LOCN TO
                                   $FDF0 (MONITOR OUTPUT TO SCREEN); S CTRL-P & PR#S SET THIS LOCN TO $CS00 (SLOT S ROM)
$0038~$0039 (56~57) [KSWL~KSWH] \P2\DOS INPUT HOOK; I.E. ADDRESS OF THE USER INPUT ROUTINE. CONTROLLED BY CURRIN PORT
                                   IN# & KEYIN. RESET ~ 0 CTRL-K & IN#0 SET THIS LOCN TO $FD1B (MONITOR KEYBOARD INPUT
                                   ROUTINE); S CTRL-K &IN#S SET THIS LOCN TO $CS00(SLOT S ROM) {MONITOR INPUT REG}
$003A~$003B (58~59) [PCL~PCH] \P2\SAVE AND CONTROL AREA FOR PROGRAM COUNTER. USED IN BREAK PROCESSING AND
                                   MINIASSEMBLER. SET BY MONITOR CMDS L G S &T {PC SAVED HERE BY MONITOR}
$003C~$0043 (60~67) [XQT/XQTNZ] \PB\8 BYTE WORK AREA FOR INSTRUCTION STEP/TRACE. NEXT INSTRUCTION SOMETIMES MOVED HERE
$003C~$003D (60~61) [A1L-A1H] \P2\MONITOR GENERAL USAGE SUBROUTINE PARAMETER A1. MANY USES INCLUDE SOURCE POINTER
                                   DURING MONITOR MOVE
```

```
HEX LOCN (DEC LOCN) [NAME]  \USE-TYPE\ - DESCRIPTION
-------------------------------------------------------------------------------------------------------

$003C~$003D (60~61) [DEVCTBL] \P2\DOS RWTS  DEVICE IN READ-WRITE TRACK-SECTOR PARAMETER POINTING TO DEVICE TABLE.
                              PRESET TO 'PTRSDEST' = POINTER TO DESTINATION  DEVICE IN DEVICE TABLE. NOT A SYNONYM
                              FOR BUFPTR
$003C~$003D (60~61) [DEVCTBL] DOS RWTS (READ-WRITE TRACK-SECTOR) DEVICE TABLE ~ SYNONYM FOR BUFPTR
$003E~$003F (62~63) [BUFPTR] \P2\DOS RWTS (READ-WRITE TRACK-SECTOR) PARAMETER 'BUFPTR' (POINTS TO DATA BUFFER IN RWTS)
$003E~$003F (62~63) [A2L-A2H] \P2\MONITOR GENERAL USAGE SUBROUTINE PARAMETER A2. USED IN CALLING LIST OF MANY MONITOR
                              SUBROUTINES SUCH AS MOVE & CASSETTE ROUTINES
$0040~$0048 (64~72)           PAGE ZERO LOCATIONS USED BY DOS
$0040~$0041 (64~65) [A3L-A3H] \P1\MONITOR GENERAL USAGE SUBROUTINE PARAMETER A3. USED IN CALLING LIST OF MOST MONITOR
                              SUBROUTINES
$0040~$0041 (64~65) [FCBFOP ZPGWRK V NPE] DOS - USED AS GENERAL POINTER BY 1ST LEVEL (COMMAND DECODE) ROUTINES IN DOS
$0041 (65) [TRKCNT] \P1\      DOS DISK SYSTEM FORMATTER SPECIAL TRACK COUNTER
$0042~$0043 (66~67) [A4L-A4H] \P2\MONITOR GENERAL USAGE SUBROUTINE PARAMETER A4.  USED IN CALLING LIST OF SOME MONITOR
                              SUBROUTINES
$0043~$0043 (67~67) [ZPGBM3 ZPGFCB] DOS - USED AS GENERAL PURPOSE POINTER BY SECOND-LEVEL DOS ROUTINES
$0044~$0045 (68~69) [A5L-A5H] \P2\MONITOR GENERAL USAGE SUBROUTINE PARAMETER A5. USED MOSTLY BY SINGLE-CYLCLE & TRACE
$0044~$0045 (68~69) [CNUM]    DOS - POINTS TO AVAILABLE BUFFER IN OPEN. ALSO USED AS ARITHMETIC REGISTER BY DOS FIRST &
                              SECOND LEVEL ROUTINES
$0044 (68) [FMT] \P1\         MINIASSEMBLER MEMORY LOCATION 'FMT'
$0045 (69) [ACC] \P1\         USER A-REG SAVED HERE ON BRK TO MONITOR & DURING TRACE
$0046 (70) [XREG] \P1\        USER X-REG SAVED HERE ON BRK TO MONITOR & DURING TRACE
$0046 (70) [MONTIME] \P1\     DOS RWTS (READ-WRITE TRACK-SECTOR) PARAMETER 'MONTIME'
$0046 (70) [EXCNT] \P1\       DOS DISK SYSTEM FORMATTER GENERAL COUNTER
$0047 (71) [YREG] \P1\        USER Y-REG SAVED HERE ON BRK TO MONITOR & DURING TRACE (Y-REG SAVED HERE ON BRK)
$0047 (71) [YCNT] \P1\        DOS DISK SYSTEM FORMATTER NYBBLE COUNTER (ALSO COUNTER FOR DISK-DRIVE MOTOR-ON TIME?)
$0048~$0049 (72~73) [IOBPL~H] \P2\DOS READ-WRITE-TRACK-SECTOR (RWTS)  'IOBPL~H' (INPUT-OUTPUT CONTROL BLOCK POINTER)
$0048 (72) [STATUS] \P1\      USER STATUS REGISTER (P-REGISTER) SAVED HERE ON BRK TO MONITOR & DURING TRACE. WARNING:
                              INITIALIZE BEFORE G FUNCTION TO AVOID DECIMAL MODE IF DOS HAS BEEN USED
$0049 (73) [SPNT] \P1\        USER STACK POINTER (S-REGISTER) SAVED HERE BY MONITOR 'SAVE' ROUTINE  ON BRK & DURING
                              TRACE
$004A~$00DF (74~223) \PB\      PAGE ZERO LOCATIONS USED BY INTEGER BASIC (GAP AT $004E~$0054)
$004A~$004D (74~77)            PAGE ZERO LOCATIONS USED BY DOS
$004A~$0043 (74~75) [LOMEML~LOMEMH] \P2\POINTER TO LOMEM (CONTAINS 'START OF BASIC VARIABLES' FOR INTEGER BASIC - START
                               OF PROGRAM FOR APPLESOFT BASIC)
$004A (74) [A] \P1\            DOS DISK SYSTEM FORMATTER DUMMY LOCATION FOR TIMING PURPOSES AND SCRATCH. DOS WILL
                               REPAIR IN INIT COMMAND; USER MUST REPAIR IF RWTS FORMATTER CALLED DIRECTLY
$004B (75) [FILLCNT - SCTR] \P1\DOS DISK SYSTEM FORMATTER GENERAL COUNTER & SECTOR NUMBER
$004C~$004D (76~77) [HIMEML~HIMEMH] \P2\ADDRESS POINTER TO HIMEM (INTEGER BASIC - END OF BASIC PROGRAM)(APPLESOFT -
                               START OF STRING DATA)
$004E~$004F (78~79) [RNDL~RNDH] \P2\16 BIT NO. RANDOMIZED WITH EACH KEY ENTRY DONE BY MONITOR KEYIN ROUTINE (AND BY
                               MANY OTHER ROUTINES SUCH AS SERIAL & COMM CARD WHICH ARE USED TO REPLACE KEYIN).
                               RANDOMIZATION ACCOMPLISHED BY CONTINUOUSLY INCREMENTING WHILE AWAITING KEYBOARD
                               INPUT. HIGH ORDER BYTE $4F
$0050~$00F8 (80~248)           APPLESOFT - PAGE ZERO LOCATIONS USED (GAPS AT  $00D7 $00E3 & $00EB~$00EF)
$0050~$0061 (80~97) [(A/S POINTERS)] \PB\GENERAL PURPOSE POINTERS FOR APPLESOFT {PB}
$0050~$0057 (80~87) [NOUNSTKL] \P8\INTEGER BASIC MEMORY LOCATION 'NOUNSTKL'
$0050~$0055 (80~85) \P6\       MONITOR/INTEGER BASIC MULTIPLY-DIVIDE WORKAREA
$0050~$0053 (80~83) [AC] \P4\  32-BIT EXTENDED ACCUMULATOR USED IN MONITOR 16-BIT MULT & DIVIDE
$0050~$0051 (80~81) [LINNUM] \P2\APPLESOFT GENERAL PURPOSE 16 BIT NUMBER LOCATION (USES INCLUED LOCATION FOR LINE
                               NUMBER)
$0050~$0051 (80~81) [ACL~ACH] \P2\OLD MONITOR (NOT AUTOSTART). USED BY 16 BIT MULT & DIVIDE ROUTINES AS
                               PSEUDO-ACCUMULATOR
-------------------------------------------------------------------------------------------------------
```

```
$0050~$0051 (80~81) [DXL~DXH] \P2\HI-RES GRAPHICS DELTA-X FOR HLIN SHAPE
$0051 (81) [SHAPEX] \P1\        HI-RES GRAPHICS SHAPE TEMP.
$0052~$0053 (82~83) [XTNDL~XTNDH] \P2\OLD MONITOR (NOT AUTOSTART) - USED IN 16-BIT MULT & DIVIDE AS ACCUMULATOR
                                EXTENSION (TO 32 BITS)
$0052 (82) [TEMPPT] \P1\        APPLESOFT TEMPORARY POINT - LAST USED TEMPORARY STRING DESCRIPTOR (SEE DSCTMP)
$0052 (82) [DY] \P1\            HI-RES GRAPHICS DELTA-Y FOR HLIN SHAPE
$0053 (83) [LASTPT] \P1\        APPLESOFT LAST USED TEMPORARY STRING POINTER
$0053 (83) [QDRNT] \P1\         HI-RES GRAPHICS QDRNT: 2 LSB'S ARE ROTATION QUADRANT FOR DRAW
$0054~$0055 (84~85) [AUXL~AUXH] \P2\OLD MONITOR (NOT AUTOSTART) - USED FOR 16-BIT MULT & DIVIDE AS AUXILLIARY REGISTER
$0054~$0055 (84~85) [EL~EH] \P2\HI-RES GRAPHICS ERROR FOR HLIN
$0055 (85)                      APPLESOFT - START OF STRING SCRATCH AREA (LENGTH UNKNOWN - AT LEAST 3 BYTES)
$0058 (88) [SYNSTKH]            INTEGER BASIC MEMORY LOCATION 'SYNSTKH'
$005E~$005F (94~95) [INDEX] \P2\APPLESOFT TEMPORARY (STACK) POINTER FOR MOVING STRINGS
$0060~$0061 (96~97) \P2\        APPLESOFT PARAMETER STORAGE SPACE FOR FLOATING POINT COMPARE ROUTINES
$0062~$0066 (98~102) \P5\       RESULT OF LAST MULTIPLY/DIVIDE (APPLESOFT)
$0067~$006A (103~106) \PB\       PAGE ZERO LOCATIONS USED BY DOS
$0067~$0068 (103~104) [TEXTTAB] \P2\APPLESOFT TEXT TABLE POINTER (POINTS TO TO BEGINNING OF PROGRAM TEXT . DEFAULT
                                 VALUE $0801
$0069~$006A (105~106) [VARTAB:] \P2\APPLESOFT VARIABLE TABLE POINTER - POINTS TO TO START OF SIMPLE VARIABLE SPACE (AT
                                 END OF APPLESOFT PROGRAM TEXT)
$006B~$006C (107~108) [ARYTAB] \P2\APPLESOFT ARRAY TABLE POINTER (POINTS TO BEGINNING OF ARRAY SPACE)
$006D~$006E (109~110) [STREND] \P2\APPLESOFT STORAGE END POINTER (POINTS TO TOP OF ARRAY STORAGE I.E. TO END OF NUMERIC
                                 STORAGE IN USE)
$006F~$0070 (111~112) \PB\       PAGE ZERO LOCATIONS USED BY DOS
$006F~$0070 (111~112) [FRETOP] \P2\APPLESOFT POINTER TO END OF STRING STORAGE OR TOP OF USER-AVAILABLE FREE SPACE.
                                 DEFAULTS TO HIMEM - USUALLY $BFFF FOR 48K APPLE)
$0071~$0072 (113~114) [FRESPC] \P2\APPLESOFT TEMPORARY POINTER FOR STRING-STORAGE ROUTINES
$0073~$0074 (115~116) [MEMSIZE] \P2\APPLESOFT HIMEM (HIGHEST LOC IN MEM AVAIL + 1). INIT TO HIGHEST RAM - $BFFF FOR 48K
                                 APPLE IF DOS NOT ACTIVE BEGINNING OF DOS IF DOS ACTIVE
$0075~$0076 (117~118) [CURLIN] \P2\APPLESOFT - LINE # OF LINE CURRENTLY BEING EXECUTED NOTE: HI BYTE OF CURLIN TESTED
                                 BY DOS FOR DIRECT-DEFERRED MODE USAGE - BYTE SET TO $FF IN DIRECT. IF CONTENTS OF
                                 $AAB6<>0 AND IF PROMPT=']' OR IF THIS LOCN CONTAINS $FF DOS ASSUMES DIRECT MODE AND
                                 WILL NOT DO OPEN OR OTHER DIRECT MODE COMMANDS
$0077~$0078 (119~120) [OLDLIN] \P2\APPLESOFT - LAST LINE EXECUTED -  LINE # AT WHICH EXECUTION INTERRUPED BY CTRL-C
                                 STOP ETC.
$0078~$0097 (120~151) [NOUNSTKH] INTEGER BASIC MEMORY LOCATION 'NOUNSTKH' (NOUN STACK HI BYTE)
$0079~$007A (121~122) [(OLD TEXT PTR)] \P2\APPLESOFT OLD TEXT PTR. PTS TO LOC IN MEM FOR NEXT STMT TO BE EXE
$007B~$007C (123~124) [DATLIN] \P2\APPLESOFT CURRENT LINE # FROM WHICH DATA IS BEING READ
$007D~$007E (125~126) [DATPTR] \P2\POINTS TO ABS LOC IN MEM FROM WHICH DATA IS BEING READ BY APPLESOFT
$007F~$0080 (127~128) [(INP SOURCE PTR)] \P2\APPLESOFT - PTR TO CURRENT SOURCE OF INPUT. $201 DURING INPUT STATEMENT IF
                                 STANDARD BUFFER IN USE
$0080~$009F (128~159) [SYNSTKL] INTEGER BASIC MEMORY LOCATION 'SYNSTKL' (SYNTAX STACK LOCATION)
$0081~$0082 (129~130) [(LAST VBL NAME)] \P2\APPLESOFT - HOLDS LAST-USED VARIABLE'S NAME
$0083~$0084 (131~132) [VARPNT] \P2\APPLESOFT POINTER TO THE LAST-USED VARIABLE'S VALUE (USED BY PTRGET)
$0085~$009C (133~156) \PB\       APPLESOFT GENERAL USAGE
$0085~$0086 (133~134) [FORPNT] \P2\APPLESOFT GENERAL POINTER. SEE COPY SUBROUTINE FOR EXAMPLE
$008A~$008E (138~142) [TEMP3] \P5\APPLESOFT REGISTER TEMP3 FOR FLOATING POINT MATH PACKAGE (PACKED 5-BYTE FORMAT)
$0090 (144)                      INITIALIZED TO $4C (JMP)
$0093~$0097 (147~151) [TEMP1] \P5\APPLESOFT REGISTER TEMP1 FOR FLOATING POINT MATH PACKAGE (PACKED 5-BYTE FORMAT)
$0094~$0095 (148~149) [HIGHDS] \P2\USED BY BLOCK TRANSFER UTILITY (BLTU) AS HIGH DESTINATION
$0096~$0097 (150~151) [HIGHTR] \P2\APPLESOFT - USED BY BLOCK TRANSFER UTILITY (BLTU) AS HIGH END OF BLOCK TO BE
                                 TRANSFERRED
```

```
$0098-$009C (152-156) [TEMP2] \P5\APPLESOFT FLOATING POINT MATH PACKAGE REGISTER TEMP2 (PACKED 5-BYTE FORMAT)
$009B-$009C (155-156) [LOWTR] \P2\APPLESOFT GENERAL PURPOSE REGISTER USED BY GETARYPT-FNDLN-BLTU (E.G. LOW END OF BLOCK
                              TO BE TRANSFERRED IN BLTU)
$009D-$00A3 (157-163) [FAC] \P6\APPLESOFT MAIN FLOATING-POINT ACCUMULATOR (USES 6-BYTE UNPACKED MATH PACKAGE FORMAT
                              DESCRIBED BELOW)
$009D-$009F (157-159) [DSCTMP] \P3\APPLESOFT TEMPORARY STRING DESCRIPTOR (SEE VALTYP & TEMPPT)
$009D (157) [FACEXP] \P1\     EXPONENT BYTE OF FAC. SIGNED NUMBER IN EXCESS $80 FORM (SIGNED VALUE HAS $80 ADDED)
$009E-$00A1 (158-161) \P4\    FOUR BYTE MANTISSA OF FAC. BINARY POINT ASSUMED TO RIGHT OF MSB. NAMES OF BYTES IN MATH
                              PACKAGE HO-MOH-MO-LO RESPECTIVELY.
$009E (158) [FACHO] \P1\      HIGH ORDER BYTE OF MANTISSA OF FAC
$009F (159) [FACMOH] \P1\     MIDDLE ORDER HIGH BYTE OF MANTISSA OF FAC
$00A0-$00BF (160-191) [NOUNSTKC] INTEGER BASIC MEMORY LOCATION 'NOUNSTKC' (NOUN STACK COUNTER)
$00A0-$00A1 (160-161) [FACMO-FACLO] \P2\POINTER TO STRING DESCRIPTOR USED IN STRING UTILITIES
$00A0 (160) [FACMO] \P1\      MIDDLE ORDER BYTE OF MANTISSA OF FAC
$00A1 (161) [FACLO] \P1\      LOW ORDER BYTE OF MANTISSA OF FAC
$00A2 (162) [(FACSIGN)] \P1\  SINGLE BYTE SIGN OF FAC. WHILE IN MATH PKG SIGN IS KEPT IN SGN WHERE ONLY BIT 7 IS
                              SIGNIFICANT
$00A4 (164)                   GENERAL USE IN FLOATING POINT MATH ROUTINES
$00A5-$00AA (165-170) [ARG] \PB\APPLESOFT SECONDARY FLOATING POINT ACCUMULATOR (USES 6-BYTE UNPACKED MATH PACKAGE
                              FORMAT DESCRIBED BELOW)
$00A5 (165) [ARGEXP] \P1\     EXPONENT PART OF ARG. SINGLE BYTE SIGNED NUMBER IN EXCESS $80 FORM (SIGNED VALUE HAS
                              $80 ADDED TO IT)
$00A6-$00A9 (166-169) \P4\    FOUR BYTE MANTISSA PART OF ARG. BINARY POINT ASSUMED TO RIGHT OF MSB. NAMES OF BYTES IN
                              MATH PACKAGE HO-MOH-MO-LO RESPECITVELY.
$00A8-$00C7 (168-199) [TXTNDXSTK] INTEGER BASIC MEMORY LOCATION 'TXTNDXSTK' (TEXT INDEX STACK)
$00AA (170) \P1\              SIGN BYTE OF ARG (UNPACKED FORMAT). BYTE NAMED SGN
$00AB-$00AC (171-172) [STRNG1] \P2\APPLESOFT POINTER TO A STRING USED IN 'MOVINS' STRING UTILITY
$00AC-$00AE (172-174) \PB\    APPLESOFT GENERAL USAGE FLAGS/POINTERS
$00AD-$00AE (173-174) [STRNG2] \P2\APPLESOFT POINTER TO A STRING USED IN STRLT2 STRING UTILITY
$00AF-$00B0 (175-176)         PAGE ZERO LOCATIONS USED BY DOS
$00AF-$00B0 (175-176) [PRGEND] \P2\APPLESOFT POINTER TO END OF PROGRAM. NOT CHANGED BY LOMEM:
$00B1-$00C8 (177-200) [CHRGET] \SB\APPLESOFT CHRGET ROUTINE. CALLED WHEN WANTS ANOTHER CHARACTER (X- Y-REGS NOT ALTERED)
$00B1 (177) [CHRGET] \SE\     APPLESOFT CHRGET S/R CALL - GETS NEXT SEQUENTIAL CHR OR TOKEN - LOADS A-REG FROM LOCN
                              SPECIFIED BY TXTPTR($00B8-$00B9 & INCREMENTS TXTPTR. CARRY IS RESET TO ZERO IF
                              CHARACTER IS A DIGIT OTHERWISE IT IS SET; ZERO FLAT SET IF CHAR =0 (END OF LINE SIGN)
                              OR $3A (END OF STATEMENT SIGN ':') OTHERWISE RESET (X- Y-REGS NOT ALTERED)
$00B7 (183) [CHRGOT] \SE\     APPLESOFT CHRGOT S/R CALL. CHRGET INCREMENTS TXTPTR. CHRGOT DOES NOT
$00B8-$00B9 (184-185) [(LAST CHAR PTR)] \P2\APPLESOFT PTR TO LAST CHAR OBTAINED THRU CHRGET ROUTINE
$00B8-$00B9 (184-185) [TXTPTR] \P2\TXTPTR - POINTS AT NEXT CHAR OR TOKEN FROM PROG (C/A DEC 78)
$00C8 (200) [OUTVAL]          INTEGER BASIC MEMORY LOCATION 'OUTVAL' (OUTPUT VALUE TEMPORARY)
$00C8 (200) [TXTNDX]          INTEGER BASIC MEMORY LOCATION 'TXTNDX' (TEXT INDEX VALUE)
$00C9-$00CD (201-205) [RND] \P5\APPLESOFT FLOATING POINT RANDOM NUMBER (5-BYTE FLOATING POINT PACKED FORMAT C9=EXP
                              CA-CD=MANTISSA)
$00C9 (201) [LEADBL]          INTEGER BASIC MEMORY LOCATION 'LEADBL' (LEADING BLANKS INDEX)
$00C9 (201) [YTEMP]           INTEGER BASIC MEMORY LOCATION 'YTEMP' (TEMPORARY STORAGE FOR Y-REGISTER)
$00CA-$00CD (202-205) \PB\    PAGE ZERO LOCATIONS USED BY DOS
$00CA-$00C3 (202-203) [PPL-PPH] \P2\INTEGER BASIC PROGRAM POINTER (START-OF-PROGRAM EQUAL TO HIMEM IF NO PROGRAM)
$00CC-$00CD (204-205) [PVL-PVH] \P2\INTEGER BASIC CURRENT VARIABLE POINTER (END OF CURRENT VARIABLE EQUAL TO LOMEM IF
                              NO ACTIVE CURRENT VARIABLE )
$00CE-$00CF (206-207) [ACL-ACH] \P2\INTEGER BASIC MAIN ACCUMULATOR
$00CE-$00CF (206-207) [-VALGETL-VALGETH-] \P2\INTEGER BASIC PRIMARY EVALUATOR TEMPORARY LOCATION
```

```
HEX LOCN (DEC LOCN) [NAME]  \USE-TYPE\ - DESCRIPTION
----------------------------------------------------------------------------------------------------

$00CE~$00CF (206~207) [~VALL~VALH~] \P2\INTEGER BASIC 16-BIT TEMPORARY VALUE FOR MATHEMATICAL OPERATIONS
$00D0~$00DF (208~223) \PB\       ONERR POINTERS/SCRATCH
$00D0~$00D1 (208~209) [SRCHL~SRCHH] \P2\INTEGER BASIC MEMORY LOCATION 'SRCHL' (POINTER TO SEARCH VARIABLE TABLE)
$00D0 (208) [ERRFLG] \P1\        ERROR FLAG. ON IF BIT 7 SET (PEEK(216)>127). POKE 0 TO CLEAR.
$00D1~$00F0 (209~240) [TOKNDXSTK] INTEGER BASIC MEMORY LOCATION 'TOKNDXSTK' ('TOKEN INDEX STACK?)
$00D2~$00D3 (210~211) \P2\       IF ONERR GOTO OCCURS CONTAINS ADDRESS OF LINE # OF STMT WHERE ERROR OCCURED
$00D2~$00D3 (210~211) [SRCH2L~SRCH2H] \P2\INTEGER BASIC MEMORY LOCATION 'SRCH2L' (SECOND VARIABLE SEARCH POINTER)
$00D4 (212) [IFSKIP] \P1\        INTEGER BASIC MEMORY LOCATION 'IFSKIP' (IF\THEN FAIL FLAG)
$00D5 (213) [CRFLAG] \P1\        INTEGER BASIC MEMORY LOCATION 'CRFLAG' (CARRIAGE RETURN FLAG)
$00D6 (214) [VERBNOW] \P1\       INTEGER BASIC MEMORY LOCATION 'VERBNOW' (VERB CURRENTLY IN USE)
$00D6 (214) \P1\                 APPLESOFT MYSTERY PARAMETER. IF SET TO $80 MAKES ALL COMMANDS = RUN
$00D7 (215) [PRINOW] \P1\        INTEGER BASIC MEMORY LOCATION 'PRINOW' (PRINT IT NOW FLAG)
$00D8 (216)                      PAGE ZERO LOCATION USED BY DOS (INFO FROM DCT RELATED TO MOTOR-ON TIME-REQUIREMENT?)
$00D8 (216) [ERRFLG] \P1\        APPLESOFT ERROR FLAG: $80 IF ONERR ACTIVE. SET TO 0 TO DISABLE 'ONERR GOTO'
$00D8 (216) [XSAVE] \P1\         INTEGER BASIC MEMORY LOCATION 'XSAVE' (TEMPORARY STORAGE FOR CONTENTS OF X-REGISTER)
$00D9 (217) [RUNMODE] \P1\       USED BY DOS TO TEST FOR DIRECT-DEFERRED MODE USAGE. IF $AAB6 CONTAINS 0 AND BIT 7 OF
                                 THIS LOCATION IS CLEAR DOS ASSUMES DIRECT MODE AND WILL NOT DO OPEN OR OTHER DIRECT
                                 MODE COMMANDS
$00D9 (217) [RUNMODE] \P1\       INTEGER BASIC MEMORY LOCATION 'RUNMODE' USED AS RUN MODE FLAG BYTE
$00DA~$00DB (218~219) [AUXL~AUXH] \P2\INTEGER BASIC MEMORY LOCATIONS 'AUXL~AUXH' (AULILIARY COUNTER)
$00DA~$00DB (218~219) [ERRLIN] \P2\APPLESOFT LINE # WHERE ERROR OCCURED
$00DC~$00DD (220~221) [ERRPOS] \P2\APPLESOFT TEXPTR SAVE FOR HNDLERR SUBROUTINE
$00DC~$00DD (220~221) [PRL~PRH] \P2\INTEGER BASIC MEMORY LOCATIONS 'PRL~PRH' (CURRENT LINE VALUE)
$00DE~$00DF (222~223) [PNL~PNH] \P2\INTEGER BASIC MEMORY LOCATIONS 'PNL~PNH' (CURRENT NOUN POINTER)
$00DE (222) [ERRNUM] \P1\        APPLESOFT - WHEN ERROR OCCURS~ TYPE-OF-ERROR CODE APPEARS HERE - SEE MANUAL FOR CODE
                                 NUMBER MEANINGS
$00DF (223) [ERRSTK] \P1\        APPLESOFT STACK POINTER VALUE BEFORE ERROR OCCURED
$00E0~$00E1 (224~225) [PXL~PXH] \P2\INTEGER BASIC MEMORY LOCATIONS 'PXL~PXH' (CURRENT VERB POINTER)
$00E0~$00E1 (224~225) \P2\       HIGH-RES GRAPHICS X-COORDINATE
$00E2 (226) \P1\                 HIGH-RES GRAPHICS Y-COORDINATE
$0032~$00E3 (50~227) [P1L~P1H] \P2\INTEGER BASIC MEMORY LOCATIONS 'P1L~P1H' (AUXILIARY POINTER ONE)
$00E2~$00E3 (226~227) [DELL~DELH] \P2\INTEGER BASIC MEMORY LOCATIONS 'DELL~DELH' (DELETE LINE POINTER)
$00E4~$00E5 (228~229) [LNAL~LNAH] \P2\INTEGER BASIC MEMORY LOCATIONS 'LNAL~LNAH' (LINE NUMBER ADDRESS)(NEXT LINE NUMBER)
$00E4~$00E5 (228~229) [P2L~P2H] \P2\INTEGER BASIC MEMORY LOCATIONS 'P2L~P2H' (AUXILIARY POINTER TWO)
$00E4 (228) \P1\                 HI-RES GRAPHICS COLOR BYTE
$00E4 (228) [FLAG]               INTEGER BASIC MEMORY LOCATION 'FLAG' (GENERAL FLAG BYTE)
$00E5~$00E7 (229~231) \PB\       GENERAL USAGE FOR HI-RES GRAPHICS
$00E5 (229) \P1\                 HI-RES GRAPHICS HORIZONTAL BYTE INDEX FOR CURRENT POSITION(?)
$00E6~$00E7 (230~231) [NXTL~NXTH] \P2\INTEGER BASIC MEMORY LOCATIONS 'NXTL~NXTH' (NEXT POINTER)
$00E6~$00E7 (230~231) [P3L~P3H] \P2\INTEGER BASIC MEMORY LOCATIONS 'P3L~P3H' (AUXILIARY POINTER THREE)
$00E6 (230) [HPAG] \P1\          HI-RES PAGE TO PLOT ON REGARDLESS OF WHICH PAGE BEING DISPLAYED - $20 FOR PG1; $40 FOR
                                 PG2
$00E7 (231) [SCALE] \P1\         HI-RES GRAPHICS SCALE FACTOR
$00E8~$00E9 (232~233) \P2\       HI-RES GRAPHICS POINTER TO BEGINNING OF SHAPE TABLE
$00EA (234) \P1\                 COLLISION COUNTER FOR HI-RES GRAPHICS
$00F0~$00F3 (240~243) \PB\       GENERAL USE FLAGS
$00F0 (240) [FIRST] \P1\         APPLESOFT - USED BY UTILITY PLOTFNS FOR DESTINATION OF FIRST NUMBER OF LO-RES PLOT
                                 COORDINATES
$00F1 (241) [SPDBYT] \P1\        USED FOR SPEED CONTROL OF OUTPUT & DISPLAY. SPEED 0-255 ($00-$FF) CONTROLS INSERTED
                                 DELAY)
$00F1 (241) [TOKNDX] \P1\        INTEGER BASIC MEMORY LOCATION 'TOKNDX' (TOKEN INDEX VALUE)
----------------------------------------------------------------------------------------------------
```

```
$00F2~$00F3 (242~243) [CONL~CONH] \P2\INTEGER BASIC MEMORY LOCATIONS 'CONL~CONH' (CONTINUE POINTER)
$00F3 (243) [ORMASK] \P1\        MASK FOR OUTPUT CONTROL: NORMAL/FLASHING/INVERSE
$00F3 (243) [SIGN] \P1\          MONITOR & FLOATING POINT ROUTINES MEMORY LOC 'SIGN'
$00F4~$00F8 (244~248) \PB\       ONERR POINTERS
$00F4~$00F7 (244~247) [FP1] \P4\MONITOR & FLOATING POINT ROUTINES FLOATING POINT ACCUMULATOR 2 (CONTAINS X2 & M2)
$00F4~$00F5 (244~245) [AUTOINCL~AUTOINCH] \P2\INTEGER BASIC MEMORY LOCATIONS 'AUTOINCL~AUTOINCH' (CURRENT AUTO LINE
                                 NUMBER VALUE)
$00F4 (244) [X2] \P1\            MONITOR & OLD (NON-APPLESOFT) FLOATING POINT ROUTINES FLOATING POINT ACCUMULATOR 2
                                 MEMORY LOC 'X2' (EXPONENT)
$00F5~$00F7 (245~247) [M2] \P3\ MONITOR & OLD (NON-APPLESOFT) FLOATING POINT ACCUMULATOR 2 MEMORY LOC 'M2' (MANTISSA -
                                 3 BYTES)
$00F6~$00F7 (246~247) [AUTOLNL~AUTOLNH] \P2\INTEGER BASIC MEMORY LOCATIONS 'AUTOLNL~AUTOLNH'
$00F7 (247) [S16PAG] \P\         SWEET-16 MEMORY LOCATION 'S16PAG'
$00F8~$00FE (248~254) [FP1] \P6\OLD (NON-APPLESOFT) FLOATING POINT ROUTINES FLOATING POINT ACCUMULATOR FP1 (CONTAINS X1
                                 M1 AND E (EXTENSION))
$00F8 (248) [AUTCMCDE] \P1\      INTEGER BASIC MEMORY LOCATION 'AUTOMODE' (THE AUTOMODE FLAG)
$00F8 (248) [X1]                 OLD (NON-APPLESOFT) FLOATING POINT ROUTINES FLOATING POINT ACCUMULATOR FP1 MEMORY LOC
                                 'X1' (EXPONENT)
$00F8 (248) [REMSTK] \P1\        APPLESOFT STACK POINTER SAVED BEFORE EACH STATEMENT
$00F9~$00FB (249~251) [M1] \P3\ FLOATING POINT ROUTINES FLOATING POINT ACCUMULATOR FP1 MEMORY LOC 'M1' (MANTISSA)
$00F9 (249) [CHAR] \P1\          INTEGER BASIC MEMORY LOCATION 'CHAR' (CURRENT CHARACTER)
$00F9 (249) [COUNT] \P1\         INTEGER BASIC MEMORY LOCATION 'COUNT'
$00FA (250) [LEAD2R] \P1\        INTEGER BASIC MEMORY LOCATION 'LEADZR' (LEADING ZEROS INDEX)
$00FB (251) [FORNDX] \P1\        INTEGER BASIC MEMORY LOCATION 'FORNDX' (FOR-NEXT LOOP INDEX)
$00FC~$00FE (252~254) [E] \P3\  MONITOR & FLOATING POINT ROUTINES MEMORY LOC 'E' (3 BYTE MANTISSA EXTENTION OF FP
                                 ACCUMULATOR 1)
$00FC (252) [GOSUBNDX] \P1\      INTEGER BASIC MEMORY LOCATION 'GOSUBNDX' (GOSUB INDEX)
$00FD (253) [SYNSTKDX] \P1\      INTEGER BASIC MEMORY LOCATION 'SYNSTKDX' (SYNTAX STACK INDEX VALUE)
$00FE~$00FF (254~255) [SYNPAGL~SYNPAGH] INTEGER BASIC SYNTAX PAGE POINTER. IF $00FF NOT ZERO THEN ERROR CONDITION EXISTS
$0100~$01FF (256~511) \HB\       APPLE SYSTEM STACK. MANY USES INCLUDING SUBROUTINE RETURN STACK
$0100~$01FF (256~511)            THIS PAGE IS THE STACK USED BY DOS 3.2 TO GET THE SLOTNUMBER IN WHICH THE BOOT DISK IS
                                 LOCATED
$0100~$0110 (256~272) [FOUT] \PB\FOUT BUFFER
$0200~$02FF (512~767) [BUF INBUFF] \HB\KEYIN (CHARACTER INPUT) BUFFER (MONITOR~INTEGER BASIC~APPLESOFT BASIC)
$0200 (512) [IN]                 MONITOR & MINIASSEMBLER MEMORY LOCATION 'IN'
$0300~$03FF (768~1023) \HB\       MEMORY PAGE 3 (MONITOR VECTOR MEMORY PAGE - BUT MONITOR VECTORS ONLY IN $03F0~$0EFF)
$0300~$03E7 (768~999) \HB\        BLOCK OFTEN AVAILABLE AS FREE SPACE FOR USER PROGRAMS.  NOTE CONSTRAINTS & COMPETING
                                  USES
$0300~$03FF (768~1023) \HB\       FIRST STAGE OF DOS 3.2 BOOT USES THIS AREA FOR PART 1 OF THE NIBBLE BUFFER. THEN LATER
                                  DOS 3.2 BOOT USES IT FOR CODE. AREA CLOBBERED BY EITHER MASTER OR SLAVE DISKETTE BOOT.
                                  READS DATA FROM TRACK 0; SECTORS 0-9 INTO MEMORY AT $B600~$BFFF (48K MACHINE) SLAVE
                                  DISKETTE OR $3600~$3FFF FOR A MASTER DISKETTE
$0300~$03AF (768~943) \SB\        EXAMPLE: DECWRITER PRINTER OUTPUT FOR SERIAL COMMUNICATIONS CARD (BLOADED FROM DISK)
$0301 (769) \SE\                  DOS 3.2 BOOT PROCESS JUMPS HERE AFTER ROM BOOT IS FINISHED. TRANSFER (ENTRY) POINT FOR
                                  ENTRY TO PART 2 OR STAGE 2 OF DOS 3.2 BOOT. READS IN RWTS & ITS SUBPROGRAMS
$0320~$0321 (800~801) [XOL~XOH] \P2\HI-RES GRAPHICS- PRIOR X-COORD SAVE AFTER HLIN OR HPLOT
$0322 (802) [YO] \P1\             HI-RES GRAPHICS YO - MOST RECENT Y-COORDINATE
$0323 (803) [BXSAV]               HI-RES GRAPHICS 'BXSAV'
$0324 (804) [HCOLOR] \P1\         HI-RES GRAPHICS COLOR FOR HPLOT~ HPOSN
$0325 (805) [HNDX] \P1\           HI-RES  ON-THE-FLY BYTE INDEX FROM BASE ADDRESS TO CURRENT PLOT BYTE (FUNCTION OF
                                  CURRENT X-COORD)
```

```
$0326 (806) [HPAG] \P1\          HI-ORDER BYTE OF START ADDR OF CURRENT HI-RES DISPLAY MEM PG (POKE 32 FOR HI-RES PG1 ~
                                 64 FOR PG2)
$0326 (806) [HPAG] \P1\          HI-RES GRAPHICS MEM PAGE FOR PLOTTING GRAPHICS $20 FOR PG1 ~$40 FOR PG2
$0327 (807) [SCALE] \P1\         ON-THE-FLY SCALE FACTOR FOR DRAW~ SHAPE~ MOVE
$0328~$0329 (808~809) [SHAPXL~SHAPXH] \P2\START-OF-SHAPE-TABLE POINTER
$032A (810) [COLLSN] \P1\        COLLISION COUNT FROM DRAW~DRAW1
$0399 (921)                      DOS 3.2 OFFSET IN THE 1ST NIBBLE BUFFER USED IN RECONSTRUCTING THE REAL DATA
$03CC (972)                      DOS 3.2 OFFSET IN THE FIRST NIBBLE BUFFER USED IN RECONSTRUCTING THE REAL DATA
$03D0~$03E0 (976~992) \SB\       BLOCK OF COMMANDS ETC. COPIED FROM $9E50~$9E80 ON DOS 3.2 BOOT TO CONTROL TRANSFERS TO
                                 SOFT ENTRY~ HARD ENTRY~ I-O PKG~ RWTS AND TO GET END OF SYSTEM BUFFER~ IOB ADDRESS~
                                 AND TO UPDATE I-O HOOKS~ AND DO JUMP TRANSFERS TO AUTO BRK ENTRY~ CTRL~Y ENTRY~ NMI
                                 ENTRY AND PROVIDE IRQ ADDRESS
$03D0 (976) [(3D0G)] \SE\        DOS 3.2 SOFT-ENTRY POINT; I.E. RE-ENTRY POINT (3D0G) FOR RE-INITIALIZATION SAVING ALL
                                 VARIABLES & DATA OF CURRENT BASIC PROGRAM (JMP $9DBF)
$03D3 (979) \SE\                 DOS 3.1/3.2 HARD ENTRY POINT; I.E. RE-INITIALIZATION DESTROYS ALL INFORMATION RELATING
                                 TO CURRENT BASIC PROGRAM (JMP $9D84)
$03D6 (982) \SE\                 DOS 3.1~3.2 ENTRY POINT FOR I~O PACKAGE (JMP $AAFD)
$03D9 (985) \SE\                 DOS 3.1~3.2 ENTRY POINT FOR RWTS (JMP $B7B5)
$03DC (988) \SE\                 DOS 3.1~3.2 ENTRY POINT TO LOAD Y~A WITH ADDRESS AT END OF SYS BUFFER
$03E3 (995) [995] \SE\           DOS 3.1~3.2 ENTRY POINT TO LOAD Y~A WITH ADDRESS OF IOBLK
$03EA (1002) [1002] \SE\         DOS 3.2 ENTRY POINT FOR ROUTINE THAT UPDATES I/O HOOK TABLES IN $0036~$0039. (JMP
                                 $A851 - SAVES ADDRESSES OF CHARACTER INPUT & OUTPUT ROUTINES CURRENTLY IN USE AND
                                 RECONNECTS DOS I/O)
$03EA (1002) [(LOAD DOS 3.2 REGS)] \SE\RECONNECT DOS 3.2 VIA APPLE MONITOR REGS. PREVIOUS CONTENTS OF MONITOR I/O REGS
                                 ($0036~$0039) TO DOS 3.2 INPUT & OUTPUT REGS (DOS 3.2 REGS ALTERED)
$03F0~$03F1 (1008~1009) [BRKV] \P2\AUTOSTART ROM BREAK VECTOR - DEFAULT VALUE $FA59
$03F2~$03F3 (1010~1011) [SOFTEV] \P2\AUTOSTART ROM RESET VECTOR USED FOR SOFT ENTRY TO LANGUAGE IN USE - DEFAULT VALUE
                                  $E003 FOR APPLESOFT
$03F4 (1012) [PWREDUP] \P1\       AUTOSTART ROM POWER UP MASK. SET BY SETPWRC TO EXCLUSIVE 'OR' OF $03F3 & $00A5
$03F5~$03F7 (1013~1015) [AMPERV]  APPLESOFT - HOLDS JMP (JUMP) INSTRUCTION TO S/R WHICH HANDLES & COMMANDS.  DEFAULT
                                  $4C $58 $FF (JUMP TO $FF58)
$03F8~$03FA (1016~1018)           HOLDS JMP (JUMP) INSTRUCTION TO S/R WHICH HANDLES 'USER' COMMANDS (E.G. CTRL-Y)
$03F8 (1016) [USRADR]             IN MONITOR MODE KEYBOARD ENTRY OF CTL-Y WILL CAUSE JSR HERE
$03FB~$03FD (1019~1021)           HOLDS JMP (JUMP) INSTRUCTION TO S/R WHICH HANDLES NON-MASKABLE INTERRUPTS
$03FB (1019) [NMI]                NMI'S VECTORED TO THIS LOCATION
$03FE~$03FF (1022~1023) [IRQADR~IRQLOC] \P2\IRQ'S VECTORED BY POINTER HERE TO SUBROUTINE TO HANDLE INTERRUPT REQUESTS
$0400~$07FF (1024~2047) \HB\      SCREEN BUFFER (MEMORY PAGES 4-7)(LOW-RES GRAPHICS & TEXT PAGE 1); CONSISTS OF 8
                                  SUBPAGES: EACH CONTAINING 3 TEXT LINES OF 40 ($27) CHARACTERS EACH FOLLOWED BY 8
                                  BYTES WHICH ARE USED AS INPUT-OUTPUT PARAMETERS - ONE BYTE FOR EACH SLOT (0-7). LINES
                                  ARE INTERLACED DOWN PAGE: I.E. FIRST SUBPAGE CONTAINS LINES 1~9~17 & FIRST BLOCK OF
                                  I-O BYTES; SECOND SUBPAGE CONTAINS LINES 2~10~18 & SECOND BLOCK OF I-O BYTES; THIRD
                                  SUBPAGE CONTAINS LINES 3~11~19 & THIRD BLOCK OF I-O BYTES ETC.
$0400~$0477 (1024~1143) [(MACROLINE0)] \HB\TEXT VIDEO SCREEN DISPLAY PAGE 1 - MACROLINE ORSUBPAGE CONSISTING OF LINES 0
                                  ~ 8 & 16
$0400-$0427[(LO-RESLNS0/1)] \BB\  VIDEO SCREEN BUFFER LO-RES LINES 0 AND 1
$0400-$0427[(TEXTLN0)] \BB\       VIDEO SCREEN BUFFER TEXT LINE 0
$0428-$044F[(LO-RESLNS16/17)] \BB\VIDEO SCREEN BUFFER LO-RES LINES 16 AND 17
$0428-$044F[(TEXTLN8)] \BB\       VIDEO SCREEN BUFFER TEXT LINE 8
$0450-$0477[(LO-RESLNS32/33)] \BB\VIDEO SCREEN BUFFER LO-RES LINES 32 AND 33
$0450-$0477[(TEXTLN16)] \BB\      VIDEO SCREEN BUFFER TEXT LINE 16
$0478+S (1144+S) \P1\             SCRATCHPAD MEMORY BYTE FOR PERIPHERAL IN SLOT #S
```

```
$0478+S (1144+S) [BRATE] \P1\      EXAMPLE: SERIAL INTERFACE BAUD QUANTUM RATE. $1= 19200 BAJD;$40=300 BAUD
$0478+S (1144+S) [DVOTRK] \P1\     EXAMPLE:'DRVOTRAK'= DISK DRIVE 0 CURRENT TRACK (VALUE = 2*TRACK#); DOS 3.2 PARAMETER
                                   FOR DISK IN SLOT #S
$0478 (1144) [CURTRK] \P1\         DOS 3.2 RWTS (READ-WRITE TRACK-SECTOR) PARAMETER CURRENT TRACK (LAST TRACK 'SEEK'-ED)
$0478~$047F (1144~1151)            SCRATCHPAD BYTES FOR I/O PERIPHERALS - ONE BYTE FOR EACH PERIPHERAL 'SLOT' 0 THRU 7
$0479 (1145) \P1\                  SCRATCHPAD MEMORY BYTE FOR PERIPHERAL IN SLOT #1
$047A (1146) \P1\                  SCRATCHPAD MEMORY BYTE FOR PERIPHERAL IN SLOT #2
$047B (1147) \P1\                  SCRATCHPAD MEMORY BYTE FOR PERIPHERAL IN SLOT #3
$047C (1148) \P1\                  SCRATCHPAD MEMORY BYTE FOR PERIPHERAL IN SLOT #4
$047D (1149) \P1\                  SCRATCHPAD MEMORY BYTE FOR PERIPHERAL IN SLOT #5
$047E (1150) \P1\                  SCRATCHPAD MEMORY BYTE FOR PERIPHERAL IN SLOT #6
$047F (1151) \P1\                  SCRATCHPAD MEMORY BYTE FOR PERIPHERAL IN SLOT #7
$0480-$04A7[(LO-RESLNS2/3)] \BB\   VIDEO SCREEN BUFFER LO-RES LINES 2 AND 3
$0480-$04A7[(TEXTLN1)] \BB\        VIDEO SCREEN BUFFER TEXT LINE 1
$0480~$04F7 (1152~1271) [(MACROLINE1)] \HB\TEXT PAGE 1 - MACROLINE OR SUBPAGE CONSISTING OF 3 TEXT LINES OF 40 BYTES
                                   (CHARACTERS) EACH PLUS A BLOCK OF 8 I-O PERIPHERAL BYTES. SUBSEQUENT
                                   MACROLINES WILL BE OMITTED FROM DATABASE
$04A8-$04CF[(LO-RESLNS18/19)] \BB\VIDEO SCREEN BUFFER LO-RES LINES 18 AND 19
$04A8-$04CF[(TEXTLN9)] \BB\        VIDEO SCREEN BUFFER TEXT LINE 9
$04D0-$04F7[(LO-RESLNS34/35)] \BB\VIDEO SCREEN BUFFER LO-RES LINES 34 AND 35
$04D0-$04F7[(TEXTLN17)] \BB\       VIDEO SCREEN BUFFER TEXT LINE 17
$04F8+S (1272+S) \P1\              SCRATCHPAD MEMORY BYTE FOR PERIPHERAL IN SLOT #S
$04F8+S (1272+S) [DRV1TRK] \P1\    EXAMPLE: 'DRV1TRK' = DISK DRIVE 1 CURRENT TRACK (VALUE = 2*TRACK#); DOS 3.2 PARAMETER
                                   FOR DISK IN SLOT #S
$04F8+S (1272+S) [STBITS] \P1\     EXAMPLE: APPLE SERIAL INTERFACE IN SLOT #S: CONTAIN NUMBER OF STOP BITS (INCLUDING 1
                                   PARITY BIT)
$04F8 (1272) \P1\                  SCRATCHPAD MEMORY BYTE USED BY DOS 3.2 (SHARED BY ALL PERIPHERAL CARDS)
$04F8~$04FF (1272~1279) \HB\       TEXT PAGE 1 - BLOCK OF 8 I-O PERIPHERAL BYTES ONE FOR EACH SLOT (0-7)
$04F9 (1273) \P1\                  SCRATCHPAD MEMORY BYTE FOR PERIPHERAL IN SLOT #1
$04FA (1274) \P1\                  SCRATCHPAD MEMORY BYTE FOR PERIPHERAL IN SLOT #2
$04FB (1275) \P1\                  SCRATCHPAD MEMORY BYTE FOR PERIPHERAL IN SLOT #3
$04FB (1275) [SEEKCNT] \P1\        DOS 3.2 RWTS (READ-WRITE TRACK-SECTOR) SEEK COUNTER PARAMETER
$04FC (1276) \P1\                  SCRATCHPAD MEMORY BYTE FOR PERIPHERAL IN SLOT #4
$04FD (1277) \P1\                  SCRATCHPAD MEMORY BYTE FOR PERIPHERAL IN SLOT #5
$04FE (1278) \P1\                  SCRATCHPAD MEMORY BYTE FOR PERIPHERAL IN SLOT #6
$04FF (1279) \P1\                  SCRATCHPAD MEMORY BYTE FOR PERIPHERAL IN SLOT #7
$0500-$0527[(LO-RESLNS4/5)] \BB\   VIDEO SCREEN BUFFER LO-RES LINES 4 AND 5
$0500-$0527[(TEXTLN2)] \BB\        VIDEO SCREEN BUFFER TEXT LINE 2
$0500~$0577 (1280~1399) [(TEXTMACROLINE2)] \HB\TEXTVIDEO DISPLAY - SUBPAGE 2. CONSISTS OF TEXT LINES 2~ 10 & 18
                                   FOLLOWED BY AN 8-BYTE BLOCK FOR I-O PERIPHERALS
$0528-$054F[(LO-RESLNS20/21)] \BB\VIDEO SCREEN BUFFER LO-RES LINES 20 AND 21
$0528-$054F[(TEXTLN10)] \BB\       VIDEO SCREEN BUFFER TEXT LINE 10
$0550-$0577[(LO-RESLNS36/37)] \BB\VIDEO SCREEN BUFFER LO-RES LINES 36 AND 37
$0550-$0577[(TEXTLN18)] \BB\       VIDEO SCREEN BUFFER TEXT LINE 18
$0578+S (1400+S) \P1\              EXAMPLE APPLE PARALLEL PRINTER INTERFACE IN SLOT #S: CARRIAGE WIDTH. E.G. POKE
                                   1400+S~80 FOR 80 COLUMN PRINT WIDTH
$0578+S (1400+S) \P1\              SCRATCHPAD MEMORY BYTE FOR PERIPHERAL IN SLOT#S
$0578+S (1400+S) [STATUS] \P1\     EXAMPLE: APPLE SERIAL INTERFACE IN SLOT #S: PARITY CHECKSUM OPTIONS (SEE MANUAL)
$0578 (1400) \P1\                  SCRATCHPAD MEMORY BYTE USED BY DOS 3.2 (SHARED BY ALL PERIPHERAL CARDS)
$0578~$057F (1400~1407) \HB\       BLOCK OF SCRATCH PAD BYTES FOR PERIPHERALS IN SLOTS 0-7
$0579 (1401) \P1\                  SCRATCHPAD MEMORY BYTE FOR PERIPHERAL IN SLOT #1
```

```
$057A (1402) \P1\                    SCRATCHPAD MEMORY BYTE FOR PERIPHERAL IN SLOT #2
$057B (1403) \P1\                    SCRATCHPAD MEMORY BYTE FOR PERIPHERAL IN SLOT #3
$057C (1404) \P1\                    SCRATCHPAD MEMORY BYTE FOR PERIPHERAL IN SLOT #4
$057D (1405) \P1\                    SCRATCHPAD MEMORY BYTE FOR PERIPHERAL IN SLOT #5
$057E (1406) \P1\                    SCRATCHPAD MEMORY BYTE FOR PERIPHERAL IN SLOT #6
$057F (1407) \P1\                    SCRATCHPAD MEMORY BYTE FOR PERIPHERAL IN SLOT #7
$0580-$05A7[(LO-RESLNS6/7)] \BB\     VIDEO SCREEN BUFFER LO-RES LINES 6 AND 7
$0580-$05A7[(TEXTLN3)] \BB\          VIDEO SCREEN BUFFER TEXT LINE 3
$05A8-$05CF[(LO-RESLNS22/23)] \BB\VIDEO SCREEN BUFFER LO-RES LINES 22 AND 23
$05A8-$05CF[(TEXTLN11)] \BB\         VIDEO SCREEN BUFFER TEXT LINE 11
$05D0-$05F7[(LO-RESLNS38/39)] \BB\VIDEO SCREEN BUFFER LO-RES LINES 38 AND 39
$05D0-$05F7[(TEXTLN19)] \BB\         VIDEO SCREEN BUFFER TEXT LINE 19
$05F8+S (1528+S) \P1\                EXAMPLE: APPLE PARALLEL PRINTER INTERFACE IN SLOT #S - CHARACTER COUNTER. E.G. POKE
                                     1528+S~0 TO RESET COUNT TO ZERO
$05F8+S (1528+S) \P1\                SCRATCHPAD MEMORY BYTE FOR PERIPHERAL IN SLOT #S
$05F8+S (1528+S) [SLOT] \P1\         DOS READ-WRITE-TRACK-SECTOR (RWTS) 'SLOT' = HOLDS SLOT NUMBER USED
$05F8 (1528) [(BOOT DISK #)] \P1\ CONTAINS SLOT # OF DISK CONTROLLER CARD FROM WHICH ANY ACTIVE DOS 3.2 WAS BOOTED
$05F8 (1528) \P1\                    SCRATCHPAD MEMORY BYTE USED BY DOS 3.2 (SHARED BY ALL PERIPHERAL CARDS)
$05F9 (1529) \P1\                    SCRATCHPAD MEMORY BYTE FOR PERIPHERAL IN SLOT #1
$05FA (1530) \P1\                    SCRATCHPAD MEMORY BYTE FOR PERIPHERAL IN SLOT #2
$05FB (1531) \P1\                    SCRATCHPAD MEMORY BYTE FOR PERIPHERAL IN SLOT #3
$05FC (1532) \P1\                    SCRATCHPAD MEMORY BYTE FOR PERIPHERAL IN SLOT #4
$05FD (1533) \P1\                    SCRATCHPAD MEMORY BYTE FOR PERIPHERAL IN SLOT #5
$05FE (1534) \P1\                    SCRATCHPAD MEMORY BYTE FOR PERIPHERAL IN SLOT #6
$05FF (1535) \P1\                    SCRATCHPAD MEMORY BYTE FOR PERIPHERAL IN SLOT #7
$0600-$0627[(LO-RESLNS8/9)] \BB\     VIDEO SCREEN BUFFER LO-RES LINES 8 AND 9
$0600-$0627[(TEXTLN4)] \BB\          VIDEO SCREEN BUFFER TEXT LINE 4
$0628-$064F[(LO-RESLNS24/25)] \BB\VIDEO SCREEN BUFFER LO-RES LINES 24 AND 25
$0628-$064F[(TEXTLN12)] \BB\         VIDEO SCREEN BUFFER TEXT LINE 12
$0678+S (1656+S) \P1\                EXAMPLE: APPLE PARALLEL PRINTER INTERFACE CARD IN SLOT #S - CHARACTER COUNTER. E.G.
                                     POKE 1656+S~0 TO RESET CHARACTER COUNT TO ZERO
$0678+S (1656+S) \P1\                SCRATCHPAD MEMORY BYTE FOR PERIPHERAL IN SLOT #S
$0678+S (1656+S) [BYTE]              EXAMPLE: APPLE SERIAL INTERFACE IN SLOT #S INPUT OUTPUT BUFFER
$0678 (1656) \P1\                    SCRATCHPAD MEMORY BYTE USED BY DOS 3.2 (SHARED BY ALL PERIPHERAL CARDS)
$0679 (1657) \P1\                    SCRATCHPAD MEMORY BYTE FOR PERIPHERAL IN SLOT #1
$067A (1658) \P1\                    SCRATCHPAD MEMORY BYTE FOR PERIPHERAL IN SLOT #2
$067B (1659) \P1\                    SCRATCHPAD MEMORY BYTE FOR PERIPHERAL IN SLOT #3
$067C (1660) \P1\                    SCRATCHPAD MEMORY BYTE FOR PERIPHERAL IN SLOT #4
$067D (1661) \P1\                    SCRATCHPAD MEMORY BYTE FOR PERIPHERAL IN SLOT #5
$067E (1662) \P1\                    SCRATCHPAD MEMORY BYTE FOR PERIPHERAL IN SLOT #6
$067F (1663) \P1\                    SCRATCHPAD MEMORY BYTE FOR PERIPHERAL IN SLOT #7
$0680-$06A7[(LO-RESLNS10/11)] \BB\VIDEO SCREEN BUFFER LO-RES LINES 10 AND 11
$0680-$06A7[(TEXTLN5)] \BB\          VIDEO SCREEN BUFFER TEXT LINE 5
$06=0-$0677[(LO-RESLNS40/41)] \BB\VIDEO SCREEN BUFFER LO-RES LINES 40 AND 41
$06=0-$0677[(TEXTLN20)] \BB\         VIDEO SCREEN BUFFER TEXT LINE 20
$06A8-$06CF[(LO-RESLNS26/27)] \BB\VIDEO SCREEN BUFFER LO-RES LINES 26 AND 27
$06A8-$06CF[(TEXTLN13)] \BB\         VIDEO SCREEN BUFFER TEXT LINE 13
$06D0-$06F7[(LO-RESLNS42/43)] \BB\VIDEO SCREEN BUFFER LO-RES LINES 42 AND 43
$06D0-$06F7[(TEXTLN21)] \BB\         VIDEO SCREEN BUFFER TEXT LINE 21
$06F8+S (1784+S) [PWDTH] \P1\        EXAMPLE:APPLE SERIAL INTERFACE CARD IN SLOT #S - PRINTER WIDTH ('PWDTH')
$06F8+S (1784+S) \P1\                EXAMPLE:APPLE PARALLEL PRINTER INTERFACE CARD IN SLOT #S - COMMAND PREFIX. E.G. POKE
                                     1784+S~137 TO USE CTRL-L (ASCII 137) AS COMMAND PREFIX
```

```
$06F8+S (1784+S) \P1\       SCRATCHPAD MEMORY BYTE FOR PERIPHERAL IN SLOT #S
$06F8 (1784) \P1\           SCRATCHPAD MEMORY BYTE USED BY DOS (SHARED BY ALL PERIPHERAL CARDS)
$06F9 (1785) \P1\           SCRATCHPAD MEMORY BYTE FOR PERIPHERAL IN SLOT #1
$06FA (1786) \P1\           SCRATCHPAD MEMORY BYTE FOR PERIPHERAL IN SLOT #2
$06FB (1787) \P1\           SCRATCHPAD MEMORY BYTE FOR PERIPHERAL IN SLOT #3
$06FC (1788) \P1\           SCRATCHPAD MEMORY BYTE FOR PERIPHERAL IN SLOT #4
$06FD (1789) \P1\           SCRATCHPAD MEMORY BYTE FOR PERIPHERAL IN SLOT #5
$06FE (1790) \P1\           SCRATCHPAD MEMORY BYTE FOR PERIPHERAL IN SLOT #6
$06FF (1791) \P1\           SCRATCHPAD MEMORY BYTE FOR PERIPHERAL IN SLOT #7
$0700-$0727[(LO-RESLNS12/13)] \BB\VIDEO SCREEN BUFFER LO-RES LINES 12 AND 13
$0700-$0727[(TEXTLN6)] \BB\VIDEO SCREEN BUFFER TEXT LINE 6
$0728-$074F[(LO-RESLNS28/29)] \BB\VIDEO SCREEN BUFFER LO-RES LINES 28 AND 29
$0728-$074F[(TEXTLN14)] \BB\VIDEO SCREEN BUFFER TEXT LINE 14
$0750-$0777[(LO-RESLNS44/45)] \BB\VIDEO SCREEN BUFFER LO-RES LINES 44 AND 45
$0750-$0777[(TEXTLN22)] \BB\VIDEO SCREEN BUFFER TEXT LINE 22
$0778+S (1912+S) \P1\       EXAMPLE: APPLE COMMUNICATIONS INTERFACE CARD IN SLOT #S - VIDEO ECHO (SEE ACIC MANUAL PAGE
                            17). E.G. POKE 1912+S~0 FOR NO VIDEO ECHO
$0778+S (1912+S) \P1\       EXAMPLE: APPLE PARALLEL PRINTER INTERFACE CARD IN SLOT #S - VIDEO & LINEFEED STATUS (HIGH
                            BIT CONTROLS VIDEO; LOW BIT CONTROLS L.F.). E.G. POKE 1912+S~1 FOR NO~VIDEO LF~ENABLE. POKE
                            1912+S~128 FOR VIDEO~ENABLE NO~LF. (CENTRONICS VERSION OF APPI DOES NOT HAVE LF OPTIONS
                            ACTIVATED)
$0778+S (1912+S) \P1\       SCRATCHPAD MEMORY BYTE FOR PERIPHERAL IN SLOT #S
$0778+S (1912+S) [NBITS] \P1\EXAMPLE: APPLE SERIAL INTERFACE IN SLOT #S NUMBER OF DATA BITS PLUS 1 FOR START BIT
$0778 (1912) \P1\           SCRATCHPAD MEMORY BYTE USED BY DOS 3.2 (SHARED BY ALL PERIPHERAL CARDS)
$0779 (1913) \P1\           SCRATCHPAD MEMORY BYTE FOR PERIPHERAL IN SLOT #1
$077A (1914) \P1\           SCRATCHPAD MEMORY BYTE FOR PERIPHERAL IN SLOT #2
$077B (1915) \P1\           SCRATCHPAD MEMORY BYTE FOR PERIPHERAL IN SLOT #3
$077C (1916) \P1\           SCRATCHPAD MEMORY BYTE FOR PERIPHERAL IN SLOT #4
$077D (1917) \P1\           SCRATCHPAD MEMORY BYTE FOR PERIPHERAL IN SLOT #5
$077E (1918) \P1\           SCRATCHPAD MEMORY BYTE FOR PERIPHERAL IN SLOT #6
$077F (1919) \P1\           SCRATCHPAD MEMORY BYTE FOR PERIPHERAL IN SLOT #7
$0780-$07A7[(LO-RESLNS14/15)] \BB\VIDEO SCREEN BUFFER LO-RES LINES 14 AND 15
$0780-$07A7[(TEXTLN7)] \BB\VIDEO SCREEN BUFFER TEXT LINE 7
$07A8-$07CF[(LO-RESLNS30/31)] \BB\VIDEO SCREEN BUFFER LO-RES LINES 30 AND 31
$07A8-$07CF[(TEXTLN15)] \BB\VIDEO SCREEN BUFFER TEXT LINE 15
$07D0-$07F7[(LO-RESLNS46/47)] \BB\VIDEO SCREEN BUFFER LO-RES LINES 46 AND 47
$07D0-$07F7[(TEXTLN23)] \BB\VIDEO SCREEN BUFFER TEXT LINE 23
$07F8+S (2040+S) \P1\       INTERRUPT RETURN MEMORY BYTE FOR PERIPHERAL IN SLOT #S (LOAD WITH $00CS)
$07F8+S (2040+S) [FLAGS] \P1\EXAMPLE: APPLE SERIAL INTERFACE IN SLOT #S OPERATION MODE
$07F8+S (2040+S) [STAT] \P1\APPLE COMMUNICATIONS INTERFACE CARD IN SLOT #S - STATUS (SEE ACIC MANUAL PG 17). E.G. POKE
                            2040+S~17
$07F8 (2040) [(SLOT #)]     CONTAINS SLOT NUMBER (IN THE FORMAT $CS) OF THE PERIPHERAL CARD CURRENTLY ACTIVE - PRINT
                            PEEK(2040)-192 YIELDS SLOT # IN DECIMAL FORMAT
$07F8 (2040) \P1\           SCRATCHPAD MEMORY BYTE USED BY DOS 3.2 (SHARED BY ALL PERIPHERAL CARDS)
$07F9 (2041) \P1\           SCRATCHPAD MEMORY BYTE FOR PERIPHERAL IN SLOT #1
$07FA (2042) \P1\           SCRATCHPAD MEMORY BYTE FOR PERIPHERAL IN SLOT #2
$07FB (2043) \P1\           SCRATCHPAD MEMORY BYTE FOR PERIPHERAL IN SLOT #3
$07FC (2044) \P1\           SCRATCHPAD MEMORY BYTE FOR PERIPHERAL IN SLOT #4
$07FD (2045) \P1\           SCRATCHPAD MEMORY BYTE FOR PERIPHERAL IN SLOT #5
$07FE (2046) \P1\           SCRATCHPAD MEMORY BYTE FOR PERIPHERAL IN SLOT #6
$07FF (2047) \P1\           SCRATCHPAD MEMORY BYTE FOR PERIPHERAL IN SLOT #7
```

```
$0800-$C000 (2048--16384)         RANGE OF POSSIBLE SETTINGS FOR HIMEM (DEPENDING UPON MEM SIZE- DOS 3.2 ETC.)
$0800-$3003 (2048-12291)          APPLESOFT - AREA OCCUPIED BY RAM VERSION (AS OPPOSED TO ROM OR LANGUAGE PACK
                                  VERSION) - MOST LOCATIONS IN ATLAS ARE GIVEN AT ROM LOCATIONS. USE OFFSET TO
                                  TRANSFER TO RAM LOCATIONS
$0800-$0BFF (2048-3071) [(LO-RES PAGE 2)] \HB\SECONDARY SCREEN BUFFER (TEXT & LOW-RES GRAPHICS PAGE 2)
$0800-$0BFF (2048-3071) \SB\      NORMAL LOCATION FOR HI-RES SUBROUTINES (INTEGER BASIC)
$0800-$09FF (2048-2559) \HB\      'NIBBLE' BUFFER AREA FOR PART 2 OF DOS 3.2 BOOT. CLOBBERED BY ANY DOS 3.2 BOOT.
$0800-LOMEM                       PROGRAM STORAGE FOR ROM VERSION OF  APPLESOFT
$0800 (2048)                      DEFAULT INTEGER BASIC LOMEM
$0801-$084C (2049-2124) \SB\      DOS 3.3 - PHASE 2 OF BOOT FROM SECTOR ZERO ON TRACK ZERO - FIRST RAM BOOTSTRAP
                                  LOADER (BOOT1). THIS ROUTINE LOADS THE SECOND RAM LOADER; BOOT 2 INCLUDING RWTS;
                                  INTO MEMORY AND JUMPS TO IT. USES $081F FOR SLOT#;$08FE FOR BOOT2 MEM PG;$08FE FOR
                                  BOOT2 LENGTH
$081F (2079) \SE\                 DOS 3.3 - PHASE 2 OF BOOT - FIRST RAM BOOTSTRAP LOADER. GETS SECTOR TO READ. IF
                                  ZERO GOTO $0839. TRANSLATES THEORETICAL SECTOR NUMBER INTO PHYSICAL SECTOR NUMBER
                                  BY INDEXING INTO SKEWING TABLE AT $084D. DECREMENTS $08FF (THEORETICAL SECTOR #).
                                  SETS UP PARAMETERS FOR ROM S/R $C65C ND JUMPS TO IT. (IT RETURNS TO $0801 WHEN
                                  SECTOR READ
$0839 (2105) \SE\                 DOS 3.3 - PHASE 2 OF BOOT - FIRST RAM BOOTSTRAP LOADER (BOOT1). ADJUSTS PAGE NUMBER
                                  AT $08FE TO LOCATE ENTRY POINT OF BOOT2. INITIALIZES MONITOR (TEXT MODE - STD
                                  WINDOW ETC.). GOTO BOOT2 ($3700 FOR A MASTER DISK;$B700 IN ITS FINAL RELOCATED
                                  LOCN)
$08A0 (2208) \SB\                 DURING DOS 3.2 BOOT AREA STARTING HERE HOLDS THE DISK ->NIBBLE TRANSLATE TABLE
$0C00-$1FFF (3072-8191) \HB\      OFTEN FREE SPACE UNLESS RAM\DISK APPLESOFT IN USE)
$0C00 (3072) \HB\                 DEFAULT LOCATION FOR START OF SHAPE TABLE AS SET BY HI-RES SHAPE LOAD S/R
$0C3C (3132) \SE\                 DOS 3.2\APPLESOFT TRANSFER POINT TO RAM APPLESOFT (DISK AS OPPOSED TO ROM OR
                                  LANGUAGE PACK VERSION) USED BY DOS 3.2 FOR SOFT ENTRY
$0CF2 (3314) \SE\                 APPLESOFT - SET (OR RESET) POINTERS & LINKAGES FOR RAM APPLESOFT STORED AT
                                  $0800-$3003 (2048-12291)
$0CF2 (3314) \SE\                 APPLESOFT - TO CNVRT A/S PROG FROM FIRMWARE (ROM OR LANGUAGE CARD) TO RAM (A/S
                                  STORED IN $0800-$3003): LOAD PROG- CALL 3314-LIST-SAVE
$1067 (4199) \SE\                 DOS 3.2\APPLESOFT TRANSFER POINT USED BY DOS 3.2 INTO RAM (DISK AS OPPOSED TO ROM
                                  OR LANGUAGE PACK) VERSION OF APPLESOFT WHEN PROCESSING ERRORS
$1B00-$3FFF (6912-16383) \SB\     THIS REGION OF MEMORY IS CLOBBERED BY A SLAVE DISKETTE BOOT
$1B00-$3FFF (6912-16383) \SB\     TEMP LOCATION OF RAWDOS 3.2 DURING DOS 3.2 BOOT
$1B00-$1CFF (6912-7423) [SB]      TEMPORARY LOCATION OF DOS 3.2 RELOCATION CODE DURING DOS 3.2 BOOT (SB)
$1DBF (7615) \SE\                 ROUTINE TO RECONNECT DOS 3.2 IF PAGE 3 MONITOR LINKAGES OVERWRITTEN (16K APPLE ONLY)
$2000-$3FFF (8192-16383) [(HI-RES P1)] \HB\HI-RES GRAPHICS PAGE 1
$2000-$2027 (8192-8231) [(HIRES P1L000)] \HB\HI-RES GRAPHICS: PAGE 1 - LINE #000
$2028-$204F (8232-8271) [(HIRES P1L064)] \HB\HI-RES GRAPHICS: PAGE 1 - LINE #064
$2050-$2077 (8272-8311) [(HIRES P1L128)] \HB\HI-RES GRAPHICS: PAGE 1 - LINE #128
$2080-$20A7 (8320-8359) [(HIRES P1L008)] \HB\HI-RES GRAPHICS: PAGE 1 - LINE #008
$20A8-$20CF (8360-8399) [(HIRES P1L072)] \HB\HI-RES GRAPHICS: PAGE 1 - LINE #072
$20D0-$20E7 (8400-8423) [(HIRES P1L136)] \HB\HI-RES GRAPHICS: PAGE 1 - LINE #136
$2100-$2127 (8448-8487) [(HIRES P1L016)] \HB\HI-RES GRAPHICS: PAGE 1 - LINE #016
$2128-$214F (8488-8527) [(HIRES P1L80)] \HB\HI-RES GRAPHICS: PAGE 1 - LINE #80
$2150-$217F (8528-8575) [(HIRES P1L144)] \HB\HI-RES GRAPHICS: PAGE 1 - LINE #144
$2180-$21A7 (8576-8615) [(HIRES P1L024)] \HB\HI-RES GRAPHICS: PAGE 1 - LINE #024
$21A8-$21CF (8616-8655) [(HIRES P1L088)] \HB\HI-RES GRAPHICS: PAGE 1 - LINE #088
$21D0-$21F7 (8656-8695) [(HIRES P1L152)] \HB\HI-RES GRAPHICS: PAGE 1 - LINE #152
$2200-$2227 (8704-8743) [(HIRES P1L032)] \HB\HI-RES GRAPHICS: PAGE 1 - LINE #032
```

```
$2228-$224F (8744-8783) [(HIRES P1L096)] \HB\HI-RES GRAPHICS: PAGE 1 - LINE #096
$2250-$2277 (8784-8823) [(HIRES P1L160)] \HB\HI-RES GRAPHICS: PAGE 1 - LINE #160
$2280-$22A7 (8832-8871) [(HIRES P1L040)] \HB\HI-RES GRAPHICS: PAGE 1 - LINE #040
$22A8-$22CF (8872-8911) [(HIRES P1L104)] \HB\HI-RES GRAPHICS: PAGE 1 - LINE #104
$22D0-$22F7 (8912-8951) [(HIRES P1L168)] \HB\HI-RES GRAPHICS: PAGE 1 - LINE #168
$2300-$2327 (8960-8999) [(HIRES P1L048)] \HB\HI-RES GRAPHICS: PAGE 1 - LINE #048
$2328-$234F (9000-9039) [(HIRES P1L112)] \HB\HI-RES GRAPHICS: PAGE 1 - LINE #112
$2350-$237F (9040-9087) [(HIRES P1L176)] \HB\HI-RES GRAPHICS: PAGE 1 - LINE #176
$2380-$23A7 (9088-9127) [(HIRES P1L056)] \HB\HI-RES GRAPHICS: PAGE 1 - LINE #056
$23A8-$23CF (9128-9167) [(HIRES P1L120)] \HB\HI-RES GRAPHICS: PAGE 1 - LINE #120
$23D0-$23F7 (9168-9207) [(HIRES P1L184)] \HB\HI-RES GRAPHICS: PAGE 1 - LINE #184
$2400-$2427 (9216-9255) [(HIRES P1L001)] \HB\HI-RES GRAPHICS: PAGE 1 - LINE #001
$2428-$244F (9256-9295) [(HIRES P1L065)] \HB\HI-RES GRAPHICS: PAGE 1 - LINE #065
$2450-$2477 (9296-9335) [(HIRES P1L129)] \HB\HI-RES GRAPHICS: PAGE 1 - LINE #129
$2480-$24A7 (9344-9383) [(HIRES P1L009)] \HB\HI-RES GRAPHICS: PAGE 1 - LINE #009
$24A8-$24CF (9384-9423) [(HIRES P1L073)] \HB\HI-RES GRAPHICS: PAGE 1 - LINE #073
$24D0-$24E7 (9424-9447) [(HIRES P1L137)] \HB\HI-RES GRAPHICS: PAGE 1 - LINE #137
$2500-$2527 (9472-9511) [(HIRES P1L017)] \HB\HI-RES GRAPHICS: PAGE 1 - LINE #017
$2528-$254F (9512-9551) [(HIRES P1L081)] \HB\HI-RES GRAPHICS: PAGE 1 - LINE #081
$2550-$257F (9552-9599) [(HIRES P1L145)] \HB\HI-RES GRAPHICS: PAGE 1 - LINE #145
$2580-$25A7 (9600-9639) [(HIRES P1L025)] \HB\HI-RES GRAPHICS: PAGE 1 - LINE #025
$25A8-$25CF (9640-9679) [(HIRES P1L089)] \HB\HI-RES GRAPHICS: PAGE 1 - LINE #089
$25D0-$25F7 (9680-9719) [(HIRES P1L153)] \HB\HI-RES GRAPHICS: PAGE 1 - LINE #153
$2600-$2627 (9728-9767) [(HIRES P1L033)] \HB\HI-RES GRAPHICS: PAGE 1 - LINE #033
$2628-$264F (9768-9807) [(HIRES P1L097)] \HB\HI-RES GRAPHICS: PAGE 1 - LINE #097
$2650-$2677 (9808-9847) [(HIRES P1L161)] \HB\HI-RES GRAPHICS: PAGE 1 - LINE #161
$2680-$26A7 (9856-9895) [(HIRES P1L041)] \HB\HI-RES GRAPHICS: PAGE 1 - LINE #041
$26A8-$26CF (9896-9935) [(HIRES P1L105)] \HB\HI-RES GRAPHICS: PAGE 1 - LINE #105
$26D0-$26F7 (9936-9975) [(HIRES P1L169)] \HB\HI-RES GRAPHICS: PAGE 1 - LINE #169
$2700-$2727 (9984-10023) [(HIRES P1L049)] \HB\HI-RES GRAPHICS: PAGE 1 - LINE #049
$2728-$274F (10024-10063) [(HIRES P1L113)] \HB\HI-RES GRAPHICS: PAGE 1 - LINE #113
$2750-$277F (10064-10111) [(HIRES P1L177)] \HB\HI-RES GRAPHICS: PAGE 1 - LINE #177
$2780-$27A7 (10112-10151) [(HIRES P1L057)] \HB\HI-RES GRAPHICS: PAGE 1 - LINE #057
$27A8-$27CF (10152-10191) [(HIRES P1L121)] \HB\HI-RES GRAPHICS: PAGE 1 - LINE #121
$27D0-$47F7 (10192-18423) [(HIRES P1L185)] \HB\HI-RES GRAPHICS: PAGE 1 - LINE #185
$2800-$2827 (10240-10279) [(HIRES P1L002)] \HB\HI-RES GRAPHICS: PAGE 1 - LINE #002
$2828-$284F (10280-10319) [(HIRES P1L066)] \HB\HI-RES GRAPHICS: PAGE 1 - LINE #066
$2850-$2877 (10320-10359) [(HIRES P1L130)] \HB\HI-RES GRAPHICS: PAGE 1 - LINE #130
$2880-$28A7 (10368-10407) [(HIRES P1L010)] \HB\HI-RES GRAPHICS: PAGE 1 - LINE #010
$28A8-$28CF (10408-10447) [(HIRES P1L074)] \HB\HI-RES GRAPHICS: PAGE 1 - LINE #074
$28D0-$28E7 (10448-10471) [(HIRES P1L138)] \HB\HI-RES GRAPHICS: PAGE 1 - LINE #138
$2900-$2927 (10496-10535) [(HIRES P1L018)] \HB\HI-RES GRAPHICS: PAGE 1 - LINE #018
$2928-$294F (10536-10575) [(HIRES P1L082)] \HB\HI-RES GRAPHICS: PAGE 1 - LINE #082
$2950-$297F (10576-10623) [(HIRES P1L146)] \HB\HI-RES GRAPHICS: PAGE 1 - LINE #146
$2980-$29A7 (10624-10663) [(HIRES P1L026)] \HB\HI-RES GRAPHICS: PAGE 1 - LINE #026
$29A8-$29CF (10664-10703) [(HIRES P1L090)] \HB\HI-RES GRAPHICS: PAGE 1 - LINE #090
$29D0-$29F7 (10704-10743) [(HIRES P1L154)] \HB\HI-RES GRAPHICS: PAGE 1 - LINE #154
$2A00-$2A27 (10752-10791) [(HIRES P1L034)] \HB\HI-RES GRAPHICS: PAGE 1 - LINE #034
$2A28-$2A4F (10792-10831) [(HIRES P1L098)] \HB\HI-RES GRAPHICS: PAGE 1 - LINE #098
$2A50-$2A77 (10832-10871) [(HIRES P1L162)] \HB\HI-RES GRAPHICS: PAGE 1 - LINE #162
$2A80-$2AA7 (10880-10919) [(HIRES P1L042)] \HB\HI-RES GRAPHICS: PAGE 1 - LINE #042
```

```
$2AA8~$2ACF (10920~10959) [(HIRES P1L106)] \HB\HI-RES GRAPHICS: PAGE 1 - LINE #106
$2AD0~$2AF7 (10960~10999) [(HIRES P1L170)] \HB\HI-RES GRAPHICS: PAGE 1 - LINE #170
$2B00~$2B27 (11008~11047) [(HIRES P1L050)] \HB\HI-RES GRAPHICS: PAGE 1 - LINE #050
$2B28~$362F (11048~13871) [(HIRES P1L114)] \HB\HI-RES GRAPHICS: PAGE 1 - LINE #114
$2B50~$2B7F (11088~11135) [(HIRES P1L178)] \HB\HI-RES GRAPHICS: PAGE 1 - LINE #178
$2B80~$2BA7 (11136~11175) [(HIRES P1L058)] \HB\HI-RES GRAPHICS: PAGE 1 - LINE #058
$2BA8~$2BCF (11176~11215) [(HIRES P1L122)] \HB\HI-RES GRAPHICS: PAGE 1 - LINE #122
$2BD0~$2BF7 (11216~11255) [(HIRES P1L186)] \HB\HI-RES GRAPHICS: PAGE 1 - LINE #186
$2C00~$2C27 (11264~11303) [(HIRES P1L003)] \HB\HI-RES GRAPHICS: PAGE 1 - LINE #003
$2C28~$2C4F (11304~11343) [(HIRES P1L067)] \HB\HI-RES GRAPHICS: PAGE 1 - LINE #067
$2C50~$2C77 (11344~11383) [(HIRES P1L131)] \HB\HI-RES GRAPHICS: PAGE 1 - LINE #131
$2C80~$2CA7 (11392~11431) [(HIRES P1L011)] \HB\HI-RES GRAPHICS: PAGE 1 - LINE #011
$2CA8~$2CCF (11432~11471) [(HIRES P1L075)] \HB\HI-RES GRAPHICS: PAGE 1 - LINE #075
$2CD0~$2CE7 (11472~11495) [(HIRES P1L139)] \HB\HI-RES GRAPHICS: PAGE 1 - LINE #139
$2D00~$2D27 (11520~11559) [(HIRES P1L019)] \HB\HI-RES GRAPHICS: PAGE 1 - LINE #019
$2D28~$2D4F (11560~11599) [(HIRES P1L083)] \HB\HI-RES GRAPHICS: PAGE 1 - LINE #083
$2D50~$2D7F (11600~11647) [(HIRES P1L147)] \HB\HI-RES GRAPHICS: PAGE 1 - LINE #147
$2D80~$2DA7 (11648~11687) [(HIRES P1L027)] \HB\HI-RES GRAPHICS: PAGE 1 - LINE #027
$2DA8~$2DCF (11688~11727) [(HIRES P1L091)] \HB\HI-RES GRAPHICS: PAGE 1 - LINE #091
$2DD0~$2DF7 (11728~11767) [(HIRES P1L155)] \HB\HI-RES GRAPHICS: PAGE 1 - LINE #155
$2E00~$2E27 (11776~11815) [(HIRES P1L035)] \HB\HI-RES GRAPHICS: PAGE 1 - LINE #035
$2E28~$2E4F (11816~11855) [(HIRES P1L099)] \HB\HI-RES GRAPHICS: PAGE 1 - LINE #099
$2E50~$2E77 (11856~11895) [(HIRES P1L163)] \HB\HI-RES GRAPHICS: PAGE 1 - LINE #163
$2E80~$2EA7 (11904~11943) [(HIRES P1L043)] \HB\HI-RES GRAPHICS: PAGE 1 - LINE #043
$2EA8~$2ECF (11944~11983) [(HIRES P1L107)] \HB\HI-RES GRAPHICS: PAGE 1 - LINE #107
$2ED0~$2EF7 (11984~12023) [(HIRES P1L171)] \HB\HI-RES GRAPHICS: PAGE 1 - LINE #171
$2F00~$2F27 (12032~12071) [(HIRES P1L051)] \HB\HI-RES GRAPHICS: PAGE 1 - LINE #051
$2F28~$2F4F (12072~12111) [(HIRES P1L115)] \HB\HI-RES GRAPHICS: PAGE 1 - LINE #115
$2F50~$2F7F (12112~12159) [(HIRES P1L179)] \HB\HI-RES GRAPHICS: PAGE 1 - LINE #179
$2F80~$2FA7 (12160~12199) [(HIRES P1L059)] \HB\HI-RES GRAPHICS: PAGE 1 - LINE #059
$2FA8~$2FCF (12200~12239) [(HIRES P1L123)] \HB\HI-RES GRAPHICS: PAGE 1 - LINE #123
$2FD0~$2FF7 (12240~12279) [(HIRES P1L187)] \HB\HI-RES GRAPHICS: PAGE 1 - LINE #187
$3000-LOMEM\SB\                            APPLESOFT - PROGRAM STORAGE FOR RAM VERSION
$3000~$3027 (12288~12327) [(HIRES P1L004)] \HB\HI-RES GRAPHICS: PAGE 1 - LINE #004
$3003 (12291)                              APPLESOFT - DISKETTE APPLESOFT FP SETS LOMEM TO THIS VALUE
$3028~$304F (12328~12367) [(HIRES P1L068)] \HB\HI-RES GRAPHICS: PAGE 1 - LINE #068
$3050~$3077 (12368~12407) [(HIRES P1L132)] \HB\HI-RES GRAPHICS: PAGE 1 - LINE #132
$3080~$30A7 (12416~12455) [(HIRES P1L012)] \HB\HI-RES GRAPHICS: PAGE 1 - LINE #012
$30A8~$30CF (12456~12495) [(HIRES P1L076)] \HB\HI-RES GRAPHICS: PAGE 1 - LINE #076
$30D0~$30E7 (12496~12519) [(HIRES P1L140)] \HB\HI-RES GRAPHICS: PAGE 1 - LINE #140
$3100~$3127 (12544~12583) [(HIRES P1L020)] \HB\HI-RES GRAPHICS: PAGE 1 - LINE #020
$3128~$314F (12584~12623) [(HIRES P1L084)] \HB\HI-RES GRAPHICS: PAGE 1 - LINE #084
$3150~$317F (12624~12671) [(HIRES P1L148)] \HB\HI-RES GRAPHICS: PAGE 1 - LINE #148
$3180~$31A7 (12672~12711) [(HIRES P1L028)] \HB\HI-RES GRAPHICS: PAGE 1 - LINE #028
$31A8~$31CF (12712~12751) [(HIRES P1L092)] \HB\HI-RES GRAPHICS: PAGE 1 - LINE #092
$31D0~$31F7 (12752~12791) [(HIRES P1L156)] \HB\HI-RES GRAPHICS: PAGE 1 - LINE #156
$3200~$3227 (12800~12839) [(HIRES P1L036)] \HB\HI-RES GRAPHICS: PAGE 1 - LINE #036
$3228~$324F (12840~12879) [(HIRES P1L100)] \HB\HI-RES GRAPHICS: PAGE 1 - LINE #100
$3250~$3277 (12880~12919) [(HIRES P1L164)] \HB\HI-RES GRAPHICS: PAGE 1 - LINE #164
$3280~$32A7 (12928~12967) [(HIRES P1L044)] \HB\HI-RES GRAPHICS: PAGE 1 - LINE #044
$32A8~$32CF (12968~13007) [(HIRES P1L108)] \HB\HI-RES GRAPHICS: PAGE 1 - LINE #108
```

```
$32D0~$32F7 (13008~13047) [(HIRES P1L172)] \HB\HI-RES GRAPHICS: PAGE 1 - LINE #172
$3300~$3327 (13056~13095) [(HIRES P1L045)] \HB\HI-RES GRAPHICS: PAGE 1 - LINE #045
$3328~$334F (13096~13135) [(HIRES P1L116)] \HB\HI-RES GRAPHICS: PAGE 1 - LINE #116
$3350~$337F (13136~13183) [(HIRES P1L180)] \HB\HI-RES GRAPHICS: PAGE 1 - LINE #180
$3380~$33A7 (13184~13223) [(HIRES P1L060)] \HB\HI-RES GRAPHICS: PAGE 1 - LINE #060
$33A8~$33CF (13224~13263) [(HIRES P1L124)] \HB\HI-RES GRAPHICS: PAGE 1 - LINE #124
$33D0~$33F7 (13264~13303) [(HIRES P1L188)] \HB\HI-RES GRAPHICS: PAGE 1 - LINE #188
$3400~$3427 (13312~13351) [(HIRES P1L005)] \HB\HI-RES GRAPHICS: PAGE 1 - LINE #005
$3428~$344F (13352~13391) [(HIRES P1L069)] \HB\HI-RES GRAPHICS: PAGE 1 - LINE #069
$3450~$3477 (13392~13431) [(HIRES P1L133)] \HB\HI-RES GRAPHICS: PAGE 1 - LINE #133
$3480~$34A7 (13440~13479) [(HIRES P1L013)] \HB\HI-RES GRAPHICS: PAGE 1 - LINE #013
$34A8~$34CF (13480~13519) [(HIRES P1L077)] \HB\HI-RES GRAPHICS: PAGE 1 - LINE #077
$34D0~$34E7 (13520~13543) [(HIRES P1L141)] \HB\HI-RES GRAPHICS: PAGE 1 - LINE #141
$3500~$3527 (13568~13607) [(HIRES P1L021)] \HB\HI-RES GRAPHICS: PAGE 1 - LINE #021
$3528~$354F (13608~13647) [(HIRES P1L085)] \HB\HI-RES GRAPHICS: PAGE 1 - LINE #085
$3550~$357F (13648~13695) [(HIRES P1L149)] \HB\HI-RES GRAPHICS: PAGE 1 - LINE #149
$3580~$35A7 (13696~13735) [(HIRES P1L029)] \HB\HI-RES GRAPHICS: PAGE 1 - LINE #029
$35A8~$35CF (13736~13775) [(HIRES P1L093)] \HB\HI-RES GRAPHICS: PAGE 1 - LINE #093
$35D0~$35F7 (13776~13815) [(HIRES P1L157)] \HB\HI-RES GRAPHICS: PAGE 1 - LINE #157
$3600~$3627 (13824~13863) [(HIRES P1L037)] \HB\HI-RES GRAPHICS: PAGE 1 - LINE #037
$3628~$364F (13864~13903) [(HIRES P1L101)] \HB\HI-RES GRAPHICS: PAGE 1 - LINE #101
$3650~$3677 (13904~13943) [(HIRES P1L165)] \HB\HI-RES GRAPHICS: PAGE 1 - LINE #165
$3680~$36A7 (13952~13991) [(HIRES P1L045)] \HB\HI-RES GRAPHICS: PAGE 1 - LINE #045
$36A8~$36CF (13992~14031) [(HIRES P1L109)] \HB\HI-RES GRAPHICS: PAGE 1 - LINE #109
$36D0~$36F7 (14032~14071) [(HIRES P1L173)] \HB\HI-RES GRAPHICS: PAGE 1 - LINE #173
$3700 (14080)                       DOS 3.3 - START OF BOOT2 AREA FOR A MASTER DISK
$3700~$3727 (14080~14119) [(HIRES P1L053)] \HB\HI-RES GRAPHICS: PAGE 1 - LINE #053
$3728~$374F (14120~14159) [(HIRES P1L117)] \HB\HI-RES GRAPHICS: PAGE 1 - LINE #117
$3750~$377F (14160~14207) [(HIRES P1L181)] \HB\HI-RES GRAPHICS: PAGE 1 - LINE #181
$3780~$37A7 (14208~14247) [(HIRES P1L061)] \HB\HI-RES GRAPHICS: PAGE 1 - LINE #061
$37A8~$37CF (14248~14287) [(HIRES P1L125)] \HB\HI-RES GRAPHICS: PAGE 1 - LINE #125
$37D0~$37F7 (14288~14327) [(HIRES P1L189)] \HB\HI-RES GRAPHICS: PAGE 1 - LINE #189
$3800~$3827 (14336~14375) [(HIRES P1L006)] \HB\HI-RES GRAPHICS: PAGE 1 - LINE #006
$3828~$384F (14376~14415) [(HIRES P1L070)] \HB\HI-RES GRAPHICS: PAGE 1 - LINE #070
$3850~$3877 (14416~14455) [(HIRES P1L134)] \HB\HI-RES GRAPHICS: PAGE 1 - LINE #134
$3880~$38A7 (14464~14503) [(HIRES P1L014)] \HB\HI-RES GRAPHICS: PAGE 1 - LINE #014
$38A8~$38CF (14504~14543) [(HIRES P1L078)] \HB\HI-RES GRAPHICS: PAGE 1 - LINE #078
$38D0~$38E7 (14544~14567) [(HIRES P1L142)] \HB\HI-RES GRAPHICS: PAGE 1 - LINE #142
$3900~$3927 (14592~14631) [(HIRES P1L022] \HB\HI-RES GRAPHICS: PAGE 1 - LINE #022
$3928~$394F (14632~14671) [(HIRES P1L086)] \HB\HI-RES GRAPHICS: PAGE 1 - LINE #086
$3950~$397F (14672~14719) [(HIRES P1L150)] \HB\HI-RES GRAPHICS: PAGE 1 - LINE #150
$3980~$39A7 (14720~14759) [(HIRES P1L030)] \HB\HI-RES GRAPHICS: PAGE 1 - LINE #030
$39A8~$39CF (14760~14799) [(HIRES P1L094)] \HB\HI-RES GRAPHICS: PAGE 1 - LINE #094
$39D0~$39F7 (14800~14839) [(HIRES P1L158)] \HB\HI-RES GRAPHICS: PAGE 1 - LINE #158
$3A00~$3A27 (14848~14887) [(HIRES P1L038)] \HB\HI-RES GRAPHICS: PAGE 1 - LINE #038
$3A28~$3A4F (14888~14927) [(HIRES P1L102)] \HB\HI-RES GRAPHICS: PAGE 1 - LINE #102
$3A50~$3A77 (14928~14967) [(HIRES P1L166)] \HB\HI-RES GRAPHICS: PAGE 1 - LINE #166
$3A80~$3AA7 (14976~15015) [(HIRES P1L046)] \HB\HI-RES GRAPHICS: PAGE 1 - LINE #046
$3AA8~$3ACF (15016~15055) [(HIRES P1L110)] \HB\HI-RES GRAPHICS: PAGE 1 - LINE #110
$3AD0~$3AF7 (15056~15095) [(HIRES P1L174)] \HB\HI-RES GRAPHICS: PAGE 1 - LINE #174
$3B00~$3B27 (15104~15143) [(HIRES P1L054)] \HB\HI-RES GRAPHICS: PAGE 1 - LINE #054
```

```
$3B28~$362F (15144~13871) [(HIRES P1L118)] \HB\HI-RES GRAPHICS: PAGE 1 - LINE #118
$3B50~$3B7F (15184~15231) [(HIRES P1L182)] \HB\HI-RES GRAPHICS: PAGE 1 - LINE #182
$3B80~$3BA7 (15232~15271) [(HIRES P1L062)] \HB\HI-RES GRAPHICS: PAGE 1 - LINE #062
$3BA8~$3BCF (15272~15311) [(HIRES P1L126)] \HB\HI-RES GRAPHICS: PAGE 1 - LINE #126
$3BD0~$3BF7 (15312~15351) [(HIRES P1L190)] \HB\HI-RES GRAPHICS: PAGE 1 - LINE #190
$3C00~$3C27 (15360~15399) [(HIRES P1L007)] \HB\HI-RES GRAPHICS: PAGE 1 - LINE #007
$3C28~$3C4F (15400~15439) [(HIRES P1L071)] \HB\HI-RES GRAPHICS: PAGE 1 - LINE #071
$3C50~$3C77 (15440~15479) [(HIRES P1L135)] \HB\HI-RES GRAPHICS: PAGE 1 - LINE #135
$3C80~$3CA7 (15488~15527) [(HIRES P1L015)] \HB\HI-RES GRAPHICS: PAGE 1 - LINE #015
$3CA8~$3CCF (15528~15567) [(HIRES P1L079)] \HB\HI-RES GRAPHICS: PAGE 1 - LINE #079
$3CD0~$3CE7 (15568~15591) [(HIRES P1L143)] \HB\HI-RES GRAPHICS: PAGE 1 - LINE #143
$3D00~$3D27 (15616~15655) [(HIRES P1L023)] \HB\HI-RES GRAPHICS: PAGE 1 - LINE #023
$3D00~$3E93 (15616~16027) [RWTS] \SB\DOS 3.1/3.2 RWTS SUBROUTINE
$3D00 (15616) [RWTS] \SE\          DOS 3.1/3.2 READ\WRITE A TRACK & SECTOR. UPON ENTRY A- & Y-REGS POINT AT I/O
                                   CONTROL BLOCK (IOB)
$3D1E (15646) [STILLON] \SL\       DOS 3.2 RWTS (READ-WRITE TRACK-SECTOR) INTERIOR LABEL STARTS CODE WHICH SENSES IF
                                   MOTOR STILL ON
$3D23 (15651) [NOTSURE] \SL\       DOS 3.2 RWTS (READ-WRITE TRACK-SECTOR) INTERIOR LABEL - AT THIS POINT PROGRAM NOT
                                   SURE WHETHER MOTOR IS RUNNING (STABLE LONG ENOUGH)
$3D28~$3D4F (15656~15695) [(HIRES P1L087)] \HB\HI-RES GRAPHICS: PAGE 1 - LINE #087
$3D2D (15661) [SAMESLOT] \SL\      DOS 3.2 RWTS (READ-WRITE TRACK-SECTOR) INTERIOR LABEL - STARTS CODE TO DETERMINE IF
                                   SAME SLOT BEING USED
$3D44 (15684) [PTRMOV] \SL\        DOS 3.2 RWTS (READ-WRITE TRACK-SECTOR) INTERIOR LABEL - STARTS CODE TO MOVE OUT ALL
                                   POINTERS FROM IOB (IN-OUT-BLOCK) TO ZERO PAGE
$3D50~$3D7F (15696~15743) [(HIRES P1L151)] \HB\HI-RES GRAPHICS: PAGE 1 - LINE #151
$3D5E (15710) [OK] \SL\            DOS 3.2 RWTS (READ-WRITE TRACK-SECTOR) INTERIOR LABEL - STARTS CODE THAT IT IS OKAY
                                   TO CONTINUE
$3D67 (15719) [DRVSEL] \SL\        DOS 3.2 RWTS (READ-WRITE TRACK-SECTOR) INTERIOR LABEL
$3D7D (15741) [MOTOF] \SL\         DOS 3.2 RWTS (READ-WRITE TRACK-SECTOR INTERIOR LABEL - STARTSCODE TO DELAY UNTIL
                                   MOTOR UP TO SPEED
$3D7F (15743) [CONWAIT] \SL\       DOS 3.2 RWTS (READ-WRITE TRACK-SECTOR INTERIOR LABEL - STARTS CONSTANT WAIT DELAY
                                   LOOP RETURN POINT
$3D80~$3DA7 (15744~15783) [(HIRES P1L031)] \HB\HI-RES GRAPHICS: PAGE 1 - LINE #031
$3D8A (15754) [TRYTRK] \SL\        DOS 3.2 RWTS (READ-WRITE TRACK-SECTOR INTERIOR LABEL - TRY DISK TRACK AS PART OF
                                   LOCATING CORRECT SECTOR FOR READ
$3D9B (15771) [TRYTRK2] \SL\       DOS 3.2 RWTS (READ-WRITE TRACK-SECTOR INTERIOR LABEL 'TRYTRK2'
$3DA0 (15776) [TRYADR] \SL\        DOS 3.2 RWTS (READ-WRITE TRACK SECTOR) INTERIOR LABEL 'TRYADR'
$3DA8~$3DCF (15784~15823) [(HIRES P1L095)] \HB\HI-RES GRAPHICS: PAGE 1 - LINE #095
$3DA8 (15784) [TRYADR2] \SL\       DOS 3.2 RWTS (READ-WRITE TRACK SECTOR) INTERIOR LABEL 'TRYADR2
$3DC1 (15809) [GOCAL] \SL\         DOS 3.2 RWTS (READ-WRITE TRACK-SECTOR) INTERIOR LABEL - GO CALCULATE CORRECT TRACK
$3DC7 (15815) [RDRIGHT] \SL\       DOS 3.2 RWTS (READ-WRITE TRACK-SECTOR) INTERIOR LABEL WHICH STARTS CODE TO
                                   DETERMINE IF ONE IS READING CORRECT TRACK SECTOR AND VOLUME
$3DD0~$3DF7 (15824~15863) [(HIRES P1L159)] \HB\HI-RES GRAPHICS: PAGE 1 - LINE #159
$3DDE (15838) [DRVERR] \SL\        DOS 3.2 RWTS (READ-WRITE TRACK-SECTOR) INTERIOR LABEL - STARTS CODE FOR CLEANUP
                                   WHEN DRIVE ERROR DETECTED
$3DE1 (15841) [JMPTO1] \SL\        DOS 3.2 RWTS (READ-WRITE TRACK-SECTOR) INTERIOR LABEL 'JMPTO1'
$3DE2 (15842) [JMPTOERR] \SL\      DOS 3.2 RWTS (READ-WRITE TRACK-SECTOR) INTERIOR LABEL 'JMPTOERR' (JUMP TO ERROR
                                   HANDING ROUTINE HNDLERR)
$3DF0 (15856) [RTTRK] \SL\         DOS 3.2 RWTS (READ-WRITE TRACK-SECTOR INTERIOR LABEL WHICH ASSUMES RIGHT TRACK
                                   SELECTED AND BEGINS CHECK OF CORRECT VOLUME NUMBER ON DISKETTE
$3E00~$3E27 (15872~15911) [(HIRES P1L039)] \HB\HI-RES GRAPHICS: PAGE 1 - LINE #039
```

```
$3E06 (15878) [CORRECTVOL] \SL\     DOS 3.2 RWTS (READ-WRITE TRACK-SECTOR) INTERIOR LABEL WHICH ASSUMES CORRECT VOLUME
                                    HAS BEEN DETECTED AND CHECKS FOR SECTOR SELECTION
$3E15 (15893) [JJTOER] \SL\         DOS 3.2 RWTS (READ-WRITE TRACK-SECTOR) INTERIOR LABEL 'JJTOER'
$3E17 (15895) [CORRECTSECT] \SL\    DOS 3.2 RWTS (READ-WRITE TRACK-SECTOR) INTERIOR LABEL AT START OF CODE WHICH ASSUME
                                    SECTOR CORRECTLY CHOSEN AND JUMPS TO APPROPRIATE SUBROUTINE TO READ OR WRITE
$3E27 (15911) [ALLDONE] \SL\        DOS 3.2 RWTS (READ-WRITE TRACK-SECTOR) INTERIOR LABEL 'ALLDONE'
$3E28~$3E4F (15912~15951) [(HIRES P1L103)] \HB\HI-RES GRAPHICS: PAGE 1 - LINE #103
$3E29 (15913) [HNDLERR] \SL\        DOS 3.2 RWTS (READ-WRITE TRACK-SECTOR) INTERIOR LABEL AT START OF ERROR HANDLING
                                    MODULE
$3E32 (15922) [WRIT] \SL\           DOS 3.2 RWTS (READ-WRITE TRACK-SECTOR) INTERIOR LABEL AT START OF CODE TO WRITE
                                    NIBBLES TO DISK IF NOT WRITE PROTECTED
$3E3B (15931) [MYSEEK] \SE\         DOS 3.2 RWTS (READ-WRITE TRACK-SECTOR) INTERIOR LABEL AT START OF ROUTINE WHICH
                                    SEEKS TRACK 'N' IN SLOT #X/$10. (IF DRIVENO IS - THEN DRIVE 0;IF DRIVENO IS + THEN
                                    DRIVE 1
$3E4C (15948) [SEEK] \SE\           DOS 3.2 RWTS (READ-WRITE TRACK-SECTOR) INTERIOR LABEL AT SOFT ENTRY POINT OF SEEK
                                    SUBROUTINE
$3E50~$3E77 (15952~15991) [(HIRES P1L167)] \HB\HI-RES GRAPHICS: PAGE 1 - LINE #167
$3E67 (15975) [ESDFO] \SL\          DOS 3.2 RWTS (READ-WRITE TRACK-SECTOR INTERIOR LABEL 'WASDO'
$3E75 (15989) [ISDRVO] \DL\         DOS 3.2 RWTS (READ-WRITE TRACK-SECTOR) INTERIOR LABEL 'ISDRVO'
$3E78 (15992) [GOSEEK] \DL\         DOS 3.2 RWTS (READ-WRITE TRACK-SECTOR) INTERIOR LABEL 'GOSEEK'
$3E7B (15995) [XTOY] \DL\           DOS 3.2 RWTS (READ-WRITE TRACK-SECTOR) INTERIOR LABEL 'XTOY'
$3E80~$3EA7 (16000~16039) [(HIRES P1L047)] \HB\HI-RES GRAPHICS: PAGE 1 - LINE #047
$3E82 (16002) [SETTRK] \SM\         DOS 3.2 RWTS (READ-WRITE TRACK-SECTOR) INTERIOR LABEL - CODE SETS THE
                                    SLOT-DEPENDENT TRACK LOCATION
$3E8F (16015) [SETTRK2] \SM\        DOS 3.2 RWTS (READ-WRITE INTERIOR LABEL 'SETTRK2'
$3E9B (16027) [ONDRVO] \DL\         DOS 3.2 RWTS (READ-WRITE TRACK-SECTOR) INTERIOR LABEL 'ONDRVO'
$3E9C~$3FD4 (16028~16340) [DSKFORM] \SB\DOS 3.2 DISK FORMATTER PACKAGE
$3E9C~$3ED9 (16028~16089) [DSKFORM] \SB\DOS 3.2 DISK FORMATTER MODULE TO FILL TRACK WITH SYNC
$3E9C (16028) [DSKFORM] \SE\        DOS 3.2 DISK FORMATTER ENTRY POINT - TURN MOTOR ON & FILL TRACK WITH SYNC
$3EA8~$3ECF (16040~16079) [(HIRES P1L111)] \HB\HI-RES GRAPHICS: PAGE 1 - LINE #111
$3EAB (16043) [DSKF2] \SL\          DOS 3.2 DISK FORMATTER LABEL AT POINT WHERE MOTOR IS RUNNING AND ON TRACK 0. BEGINS
                                    CODE WHICH FORMATS THIS TRACK
$3EAE (16046) [TRKFRM] \SL\         DOS 3.2 DISK FORMATTER LABEL AT POINT WHERE TRACK FORMATTING BEGINS
$3EC4 (16068) [WRTRK] \SL\          DOS 3.2 DISK FORMATTER - LABEL AT POINT WHERE WRITE OF FORMATTING INFO ONTO TRACK
                                    BEGINS -- A HIGHLY TIMING-SENSITIVE AREA OF CODE
$3ECA (16074) [CONSYNC] \SL\        DOS 3.2 DISK FORMATTER - LABEL AT POINT WHERE CONSTRUCTION OF SYNC BEGINS
$3ED0~$3EF7 (16080~16119) [(HIRES P1L175)] \HB\HI-RES GRAPHICS: PAGE 1 - LINE #175
$3ED6 (16086) [NXTPRT] \SL\         DOS 3.2 DISK FORMATTER - LABEL AT POINT WHERE CHECK IS MADE TO SEE IF TRACK DONE
$3EDA~$3F72 (16090~16242) \SB\      DOS 3.2 DISK FORMATTER BLOCK OF CODE TO DO SECTOR-BY-SECTORFORMATTING ON TRACK
                                    ALREADY FILLED WITH SELF-SYNC
$3EDE (16094) [RGTIM] \SL\          DOS 3.2 DISK FORMATTER INTERIOR LABEL 'RGTIM'
$3EE0 (16096) [FRMWSYNC] \SL\       DOS 3.2 DISK FORMATTER INTERIOR LABEL 'FRMWSYNC'
$3EE2 (16098) [WRIT2] \SL\          DOS 3.2 DISK FORMATTER INTERIOR LABEL 'WRIT2'
$3EE6 (16102) [WRITSF] \SL\         DOS 3.2 DISK FORMATTER INTERIOR LABEL 'WRITSF'
$3EE7 (16103) [WRIT3] \SL\          DOS 3.2 DISK FORMATTER INTERIOR LABEL 'WRIT3'
$3F00~$3F27 (16128~16167) [(HIRES P1L055)] \HB\HI-RES GRAPHICS: PAGE 1 - LINE #055
$3F28~$3F4F (16168~16207) [(HIRES P1L119)] \HB\HI-RES GRAPHICS: PAGE 1 - LINE #119
$3F40 (16192) [FAKESCT] \SL\        DOS 3.2 DISK FORMATTER INTERIOR LABEL 'FAKESCT' AT BEGINNING OF CODE TO WRITE FAKE
                                    SECTOR
$3F46 (16198) [INTOIT] \SL\         DOS 3.2 DISK FORMATTER INTERIOR LABEL 'INTOIT'
$3F50~$3F7F (16208~16255) [(HIRES P1L183)] \HB\HI-RES GRAPHICS: PAGE 1 - LINE #183
```

```
$3F50 (16208) [NXTTRY] \SL\          DOS 3.2 DISK FORMATTER INTERIOR LABEL 'NXTTRY'
$3F80~$3FA7 (16256~16295) [(HIRES P1L063)] \HB\HI-RES GRAPHICS: PAGE 1 - LINE #063
$3FC6 (16326) [CHGIT] \SL\           DOS 3.2 DISK FORMATTER INTERIOR LABEL 'CHGIT'
$3F73~$3FD4 (16243~16340) [TRKDON] \SB\DOS 3.2 DISK FORMATTER CHECK TRACK FORMATTING ROUTINE
$EF73 (-4237) [TRKDON] \SE\          DOS 3.2 DISK FORMATTER INTERIOR LABEL AT POINT WHERE TRACK FORMATTING IS DONE AND
                                     CHECKING OF THAT FORMATTING BEGINS
$3F80 (16256) [WLOOP] \SL\           DOS 3.2 DISK FORMATTER INTERIOR LABEL AT BEGINNING OF 26 MICROSECOND WAIT LOOP
$3F94 (16276) [NOGOOD] \SL\          DOS 3.2 DISK FORMATTER INTERIOR LABEL AT BEGINNING OF CLEAN UP IF NOGOOD CONDITION
                                     DETECTED
$3F9E (16286) [ITSGOOD] \SL\         DOS 3.2 DISK FORMATTER INTERIOR LABEL AT BEGINNING OF CONTINUATION IF GOOD
                                     CONDITION DETECTED
$3FA8~$3FCF (16296~16335) [(HIRES P1L127)] \HB\HI-RES GRAPHICS: PAGE 1 - LINE #127
$3FB3 (16307) [DRIVERR] \SL\         DOS 3.2 DISK FORMATTER INTERIOR LABEL AT BEGINNING OF CLEANUP IF DRIVE ERROR IS
                                     DETECTED
$3FB8 (16312) [DONEDSK] \SL\         DOS 3.2 DISK FORMATTER INTERIOR LABEL AT POINT WHERE DISK IS COMPLETED AND NO
                                     ERRORS HAVE BEEN DETECTED
$3FBB (16315) [WBYTE] \SL\           DOS 3.2 DISK FORMATTER INTERIOR LABEL AT BEGINNING OF TIGHT TIMING ROUTINE
$3FCA (16330) [WNIBLA] \SL\          DOS 3.2 DISK FORMATTER INTERIOR LABEL 'WNIBLA'
$3FCB (16331) [WINBLB2] \SL\         DOS 3.2 DISK FORMATTER INTERIOR LABEL 'WINBLB2'
$EFCD (-4147) [WINBLC] \SL\          DOS 3.2 DISK FORMAT INTERIOR LABEL 'WINBLC'
$EFCE (-4146) [WRNIBL] \SL\          DOS 3.2 DISK FORMAT INTERIOR LABEL 'WRNIBL'
$3FD0~$3FF7 (16336~16375) [(HIRES P1L191)] \HB\HI-RES GRAPHICS: PAGE 1 - LINE #191
$4000~$5FFF (16384~24575) [(HI-RES PAGE 2)] \HB\HI-RES GRAPHICS PAGE 2
$4000~$4520 (16384~17696) \PB\       NORMAL LOCATION FOR MANY HI RES TEXT SETS - E.G. KAPOR'S
$4000~$4027 (16384~16423) [(HIRES P2L000)] \HB\HI-RES GRAPHICS: PAGE 2 - LINE #000
$4028~$404F (16424~16463) [(HIRES P2L064)] \HB\HI-RES GRAPHICS: PAGE 2 - LINE #064
$4050~$4077 (16464~16503) [(HIRES P2L128)] \HB\HI-RES GRAPHICS: PAGE 2 - LINE #128
$4080~$40A7 (16512~16551) [(HIRES P2L008)] \HB\HI-RES GRAPHICS: PAGE 2 - LINE #008
$40A8~$40CF (16552~16591) [(HIRES P2L072)] \HB\HI-RES GRAPHICS: PAGE 2 - LINE #072
$40D0~$40E7 (16592~16615) [(HIRES P2L136)] \HB\HI-RES GRAPHICS: PAGE 2 - LINE #136
$4100~$4127 (16640~16679) [(HIRES P2L016)] \HB\HI-RES GRAPHICS: PAGE 2 - LINE #016
$4128~$414F (16680~16719) [(HIRES P2L080)] \HB\HI-RES GRAPHICS: PAGE 2 - LINE #080
$4150~$417F (16720~16767) [(HIRES P2L144)] \HB\HI-RES GRAPHICS: PAGE 2 - LINE #144
$4180~$41A7 (16768~16807) [(HIRES P2L024)] \HB\HI-RES GRAPHICS: PAGE 2 - LINE #024
$41A8~$41CF (16808~16847) [(HIRES P2L088)] \HB\HI-RES GRAPHICS: PAGE 2 - LINE #088
$41D0~$41F7 (16848~16887) [(HIRES P2L152)] \HB\HI-RES GRAPHICS: PAGE 2 - LINE #152
$4200~$4227 (16896~16935) [(HIRES P2L032)] \HB\HI-RES GRAPHICS: PAGE 2 - LINE #032
$4228~$424F (16936~16975) [(HIRES P2L096)] \HB\HI-RES GRAPHICS: PAGE 2 - LINE #096
$4250~$4277 (16976~17015) [(HIRES P2L160)] \HB\HI-RES GRAPHICS: PAGE 2 - LINE #160
$4280~$42A7 (17024~17063) [(HIRES P2L040)] \HB\HI-RES GRAPHICS: PAGE 2 - LINE #040
$42A8~$42CF (17064~17103) [(HIRES P2L104)] \HB\HI-RES GRAPHICS: PAGE 2 - LINE #104
$42D0~$42F7 (17104~17143) [(HIRES P2L168)] \HB\HI-RES GRAPHICS: PAGE 2 - LINE #168
$4300~$4327 (17152~17191) [(HIRES P2L048)] \HB\HI-RES GRAPHICS: PAGE 2 - LINE #048
$4328~$434F (17192~17231) [(HIRES P2L112)] \HB\HI-RES GRAPHICS: PAGE 2 - LINE #112
$4350~$437F (17232~17279) [(HIRES P2L176)] \HB\HI-RES GRAPHICS: PAGE 2 - LINE #176
$4380~$43A7 (17280~17319) [(HIRES P2L056)] \HB\HI-RES GRAPHICS: PAGE 2 - LINE #056
$43A8~$43CF (17320~17359) [(HIRES P2L120)] \HB\HI-RES GRAPHICS: PAGE 2 - LINE #120
$43D0~$43F7 (17360~17399) [(HIRES P2L184)] \HB\HI-RES GRAPHICS: PAGE 2 - LINE #184
$4400~$4427 (17408~17447) [(HIRES P2L001)] \HB\HI-RES GRAPHICS: PAGE 2 - LINE #001
$4428~$444F (17448~17487) [(HIRES P2L065)] \HB\HI-RES GRAPHICS: PAGE 2 - LINE #065
$4450~$4477 (17488~17527) [(HIRES P2L129)] \HB\HI-RES GRAPHICS: PAGE 2 - LINE #129
```

```
$4480-$44A7 (17536-17575) [(HIRES P2L009)] \HB\HI-RES GRAPHICS: PAGE 2 - LINE #009
$44A8-$44CF (17576-17615) [(HIRES P2L073)] \HB\HI-RES GRAPHICS: PAGE 2 - LINE #073
$44D0-$44E7 (17616-17639) [(HIRES P2L137)] \HB\HI-RES GRAPHICS: PAGE 2 - LINE #137
$4500-$4527 (17664-17703) [(HIRES P2L017)] \HB\HI-RES GRAPHICS: PAGE 2 - LINE #017
$4528-$454F (17704-17743) [(HIRES P2L081)] \HB\HI-RES GRAPHICS: PAGE 2 - LINE #081
$4550-$457F (17744-17791) [(HIRES P2L145)] \HB\HI-RES GRAPHICS: PAGE 2 - LINE #145
$4580-$45A7 (17792-17831) [(HIRES P2L025)] \HB\HI-RES GRAPHICS: PAGE 2 - LINE #025
$45A8-$45CF (17832-17871) [(HIRES P2L089)] \HB\HI-RES GRAPHICS: PAGE 2 - LINE #089
$45D0-$45F7 (17872-17911) [(HIRES P2L153)] \HB\HI-RES GRAPHICS: PAGE 2 - LINE #153
$4600-$4627 (17920-17959) [(HIRES P2L033)] \HB\HI-RES GRAPHICS: PAGE 2 - LINE #033
$4628-$464F (17960-17999) [(HIRES P2L97)] \HB\HI-RES GRAPHICS: PAGE 2 - LINE #97
$4650-$4677 (18000-18039) [(HIRES P2L161)] \HB\HI-RES GRAPHICS: PAGE 2 - LINE #161
$4680-$46A7 (18048-18087) [(HIRES P2L041)] \HB\HI-RES GRAPHICS: PAGE 2 - LINE #041
$46A8-$46CF (18088-18127) [(HIRES P2L105)] \HB\HI-RES GRAPHICS: PAGE 2 - LINE #105
$46D0-$46F7 (18128-18167) [(HIRES P2L169)] \HB\HI-RES GRAPHICS: PAGE 2 - LINE #169
$4700-$4727 (18176-18215) [(HIRES P2L049)] \HB\HI-RES GRAPHICS: PAGE 2 - LINE #049
$4728-$474F (18216-18255) [(HIRES P2L113)] \HB\HI-RES GRAPHICS: PAGE 2 - LINE #113
$4750-$477F (18256-18303) [(HIRES P2L177)] \HB\HI-RES GRAPHICS: PAGE 2 - LINE #177
$4780-$47A7 (18304-18343) [(HIRES P2L057)] \HB\HI-RES GRAPHICS: PAGE 2 - LINE #057
$47A8-$47CF (18344-18383) [(HIRES P2L121)] \HB\HI-RES GRAPHICS: PAGE 2 - LINE #121
$47D0-$47F7 (18384-18423) [(HIRES P2L185)] \HB\HI-RES GRAPHICS: PAGE 2 - LINE #185
$4800-$4827 (18432-18471) [(HIRES P2L002)] \HB\HI-RES GRAPHICS: PAGE 2 - LINE #002
$4828-$484F (18472-18511) [(HIRES P2L066)] \HB\HI-RES GRAPHICS: PAGE 2 - LINE #066
$4850-$4377 (18512-18551) [(HIRES P2L130)] \HB\HI-RES GRAPHICS: PAGE 2 - LINE #130
$4880-$48A7 (18560-18599) [(HIRES P2L010)] \HB\HI-RES GRAPHICS: PAGE 2 - LINE #010
$48A8-$48CF (18600-18639) [(HIRES P2L074)] \HB\HI-RES GRAPHICS: PAGE 2 - LINE #074
$48D0-$48E7 (18640-18663) [(HIRES P2L138)] \HB\HI-RES GRAPHICS: PAGE 2 - LINE #138
$4900-$4927 (18688-18727) [(HIRES P2L018)] \HB\HI-RES GRAPHICS: PAGE 2 - LINE #018
$4928-$494F (18728-18767) [(HIRES P2L082)] \HB\HI-RES GRAPHICS: PAGE 2 - LINE #082
$4950-$497F (18768-18815) [(HIRES P2L146)] \HB\HI-RES GRAPHICS: PAGE 2 - LINE #146
$4980-$49A7 (18816-18855) [(HIRES P2L026)] \HB\HI-RES GRAPHICS: PAGE 2 - LINE #026
$49A8-$49CF (18856-18895) [(HIRES P2L090)] \HB\HI-RES GRAPHICS: PAGE 2 - LINE #090
$49D0-$49F7 (18896-18935) [(HIRES P2L154)] \HB\HI-RES GRAPHICS: PAGE 2 - LINE #154
$4A00-$4A27 (18944-18983) [(HIRES P2L034)] \HB\HI-RES GRAPHICS: PAGE 2 - LINE #034
$4A28-$4A4F (18984-19023) [(HIRES P2L098)] \HB\HI-RES GRAPHICS: PAGE 2 - LINE #098
$4A50-$4A77 (19024-19063) [(HIRES P2L162)] \HB\HI-RES GRAPHICS: PAGE 2 - LINE #162
$4A80-$4AA7 (19072-19111) [(HIRES P2L042)] \HB\HI-RES GRAPHICS: PAGE 2 - LINE #042
$4AA8-$4ACF (19112-19151) [(HIRES P2L106)] \HB\HI-RES GRAPHICS: PAGE 2 - LINE #106
$4AD0-$4AF7 (19152-19191) [(HIRES P2L170)] \HB\HI-RES GRAPHICS: PAGE 2 - LINE #170
$4B00-$4B27 (19200-19239) [(HIRES P2L050)] \HB\HI-RES GRAPHICS: PAGE 2 - LINE #050
$4B28-$562F (19240-22063) [(HIRES P2L114)] \HB\HI-RES GRAPHICS: PAGE 2 - LINE #114
$4B50-$4B7F (19280-19327) [(HIRES P2L178)] \HB\HI-RES GRAPHICS: PAGE 2 - LINE #178
$4B80-$4BA7 (19328-19367) [(HIRES P2L058)] \HB\HI-RES GRAPHICS: PAGE 2 - LINE #058
$4BA8-$4BCF (19368-19407) [(HIRES P2L122)] \HB\HI-RES GRAPHICS: PAGE 2 - LINE #122
$4BD0-$4BF7 (19408-19447) [(HIRES P2L186)] \HB\HI-RES GRAPHICS: PAGE 2 - LINE #186
$4C00-$4C27 (19456-19495) [(HIRES P2L003)] \HB\HI-RES GRAPHICS: PAGE 2 - LINE #003
$4C28-$4C4F (19496-19535) [(HIRES P2L067)] \HB\HI-RES GRAPHICS: PAGE 2 - LINE #067
$4C50-$4C77 (19536-19575) [(HIRES P2L131)] \HB\HI-RES GRAPHICS: PAGE 2 - LINE #131
$4C80-$4CA7 (19584-19623) [(HIRES P2L011)] \HB\HI-RES GRAPHICS: PAGE 2 - LINE #011
$4CA8-$4CCF (19624-19663) [(HIRES P2L075)] \HB\HI-RES GRAPHICS: PAGE 2 - LINE #075
$4CD0-$4CE7 (19664-19687) [(HIRES P2L139)] \HB\HI-RES GRAPHICS: PAGE 2 - LINE #139
```

```
HEX LOCN (DEC LOCN) [NAME]  \USE-TYPE\ - DESCRIPTION
------------------------------------------------------------------------------------------

$4D00-$4D27 (19712-19751) [(HIRES P2L019)] \HB\HI-RES GRAPHICS: PAGE 2 - LINE #019
$4D28-$4D4F (19752-19791) [(HIRES P2L083)] \HB\HI-RES GRAPHICS: PAGE 2 - LINE #083
$4D50-$4D7F (19792-19839) [(HIRES P2L147)] \HB\HI-RES GRAPHICS: PAGE 2 - LINE #147
$4D80-$4DA7 (19840-19879) [(HIRES P2L027)] \HB\HI-RES GRAPHICS: PAGE 2 - LINE #027
$4DA8-$4DCF (19880-19919) [(HIRES P2L091)] \HB\HI-RES GRAPHICS: PAGE 2 - LINE #091
$4DD0-$4DF7 (19920-19959) [(HIRES P2L155)] \HB\HI-RES GRAPHICS: PAGE 2 - LINE #155
$4E00-$4E27 (19968-20007) [(HIRES P2L035)] \HB\HI-RES GRAPHICS: PAGE 2 - LINE #035
$4E28-$4E4F (20008-20047) [(HIRES P2L099)] \HB\HI-RES GRAPHICS: PAGE 2 - LINE #099
$4E50-$4E77 (20048-20087) [(HIRES P2L163)] \HB\HI-RES GRAPHICS: PAGE 2 - LINE #163
$4E80-$4EA7 (20096-20135) [(HIRES P2L043)] \HB\HI-RES GRAPHICS: PAGE 2 - LINE #043
$4EA8-$4ECF (20136-20175) [(HIRES P2L107)] \HB\HI-RES GRAPHICS: PAGE 2 - LINE #107
$4ED0-$4EF7 (20176-20215) [(HIRES P2L171)] \HB\HI-RES GRAPHICS: PAGE 2 - LINE #171
$4F00-$4F27 (20224-20263) [(HIRES P2L051)] \HB\HI-RES GRAPHICS: PAGE 2 - LINE #051
$4F28-$4F4F (20264-20303) [(HIRES P2L115)] \HB\HI-RES GRAPHICS: PAGE 2 - LINE #115
$4F50-$4F7F (20304-20351) [(HIRES P2L179)] \HB\HI-RES GRAPHICS: PAGE 2 - LINE #179
$4F80-$4FA7 (20352-20391) [(HIRES P2L059)] \HB\HI-RES GRAPHICS: PAGE 2 - LINE #059
$4FA8-$4FCF (20392-20431) [(HIRES P2L123)] \HB\HI-RES GRAPHICS: PAGE 2 - LINE #123
$4FD0-$4FF7 (20432-20471) [(HIRES P2L187)] \HB\HI-RES GRAPHICS: PAGE 2 - LINE #187
$5000-$5027 (20480-20519) [(HIRES P2L004)] \HB\HI-RES GRAPHICS: PAGE 2 - LINE #004
$5028-$504F (20520-20559) [(HIRES P2L068)] \HB\HI-RES GRAPHICS: PAGE 2 - LINE #068
$5050-$5077 (20560-20599) [(HIRES P2L132)] \HB\HI-RES GRAPHICS: PAGE 2 - LINE #132
$5080-$50A7 (20608-20647) [(HIRES P2L012)] \HB\HI-RES GRAPHICS: PAGE 2 - LINE #012
$50A8-$50CF (20648-20687) [(HIRES P2L076)] \HB\HI-RES GRAPHICS: PAGE 2 - LINE #076
$50D0-$50E7 (20688-20711) [(HIRES P2L140)] \HB\HI-RES GRAPHICS: PAGE 2 - LINE #140
$5100-$5127 (20736-20775) [(HIRES P2L020)] \HB\HI-RES GRAPHICS: PAGE 2 - LINE #020
$5128-$514F (20776-20815) [(HIRES P2L084)] \HB\HI-RES GRAPHICS: PAGE 2 - LINE #084
$5150-$517F (20816-20863) [(HIRES P2L148)] \HB\HI-RES GRAPHICS: PAGE 2 - LINE #148
$5180-$51A7 (20864-20903) [(HIRES P2L028)] \HB\HI-RES GRAPHICS: PAGE 2 - LINE #028
$51A8-$51CF (20904-20943) [(HIRES P2L092)] \HB\HI-RES GRAPHICS: PAGE 2 - LINE #092
$51D0-$51F7 (20944-20983) [(HIRES P2L156)] \HB\HI-RES GRAPHICS: PAGE 2 - LINE #156
$5200-$5227 (20992-21031) [(HIRES P2L036)] \HB\HI-RES GRAPHICS: PAGE 2 - LINE #036
$5228-$524F (21032-21071) [(HIRES P2L100)] \HB\HI-RES GRAPHICS: PAGE 2 - LINE #100
$5250-$5277 (21072-21111) [(HIRES P2L164)] \HB\HI-RES GRAPHICS: PAGE 2 - LINE #164
$5280-$52A7 (21120-21159) [(HIRES P2L044)] \HB\HI-RES GRAPHICS: PAGE 2 - LINE #044
$52A8-$52CF (21160-21199) [(HIRES P2L108)] \HB\HI-RES GRAPHICS: PAGE 2 - LINE #108
$52D0-$52F7 (21200-21239) [(HIRES P2L172)] \HB\HI-RES GRAPHICS: PAGE 2 - LINE #172
$5300-$5327 (21248-21287) [(HIRES P2L045)] \HB\HI-RES GRAPHICS: PAGE 2 - LINE #045
$5328-$534F (21288-21327) [(HIRES P2L116)] \HB\HI-RES GRAPHICS: PAGE 2 - LINE #116
$5350-$537F (21328-21375) [(HIRES P2L180)] \HB\HI-RES GRAPHICS: PAGE 2 - LINE #180
$5380-$53A7 (21376-21415) [(HIRES P2L060)] \HB\HI-RES GRAPHICS: PAGE 2 - LINE #060
$53A8-$53CF (21416-21455) [(HIRES P2L124)] \HB\HI-RES GRAPHICS: PAGE 2 - LINE #124
$53D0-$53F7 (21456-21495) [(HIRES P2L188)] \HB\HI-RES GRAPHICS: PAGE 2 - LINE #188
$5400-$5427 (21504-21543) [(HIRES P2L005)] \HB\HI-RES GRAPHICS: PAGE 2 - LINE #005
$5428-$544F (21544-21583) [(HIRES P2L069)] \HB\HI-RES GRAPHICS: PAGE 2 - LINE #069
$5450-$5477 (21584-21623) [(HIRES P2L133)] \HB\HI-RES GRAPHICS: PAGE 2 - LINE #133
$5480-$54A7 (21632-21671) [(HIRES P2L013)] \HB\HI-RES GRAPHICS: PAGE 2 - LINE #013
$54A8-$54CF (21672-21711) [(HIRES P2L077)] \HB\HI-RES GRAPHICS: PAGE 2 - LINE #077
$54D0-$54E7 (21712-21735) [(HIRES P2L141)] \HB\HI-RES GRAPHICS: PAGE 2 - LINE #141
$5500-$5527 (21760-21799) [(HIRES P2L021)] \HB\HI-RES GRAPHICS: PAGE 2 - LINE #021
$5528-$554F (21800-21839) [(HIRES P2L085)] \HB\HI-RES GRAPHICS: PAGE 2 - LINE #085
$5550-$557F (21840-21887) [(HIRES P2L149)] \HB\HI-RES GRAPHICS: PAGE 2 - LINE #149
------------------------------------------------------------------------------------------
```

```
$5580-$55A7 (21888-21927) [(HIRES P2L029)] \HB\HI-RES GRAPHICS: PAGE 2 - LINE #029
$55A8-$55CF (21928-21967) [(HIRES P2L093)] \HB\HI-RES GRAPHICS: PAGE 2 - LINE #093
$55D0-$55F7 (21968-22007) [(HIRES P2L157)] \HB\HI-RES GRAPHICS: PAGE 2 - LINE #157
$5600-$8000 (22016-32768) \SB\      DOS (32K APPLE ONLY) - DISK OPERATING SYSTEM
$5600-$5627 (22016-22055) [(HIRES P2L037)] \HB\HI-RES GRAPHICS: PAGE 2 - LINE #037
$5628-$564F (22056-22095) [(HIRES P2L101)] \HB\HI-RES GRAPHICS: PAGE 2 - LINE #101
$5650-$5677 (22096-22135) [(HIRES P2L165)] \HB\HI-RES GRAPHICS: PAGE 2 - LINE #165
$5680-$56A7 (22144-22183) [(HIRES P2L045)] \HB\HI-RES GRAPHICS: PAGE 2 - LINE #045
$56A8-$56CF (22184-22223) [(HIRES P2L109)] \HB\HI-RES GRAPHICS: PAGE 2 - LINE #109
$56D0-$56F7 (22224-22263) [(HIRES P2L173)] \HB\HI-RES GRAPHICS: PAGE 2 - LINE #173
$5700-$5727 (22272-22311) [(HIRES P2L053)] \HB\HI-RES GRAPHICS: PAGE 2 - LINE #053
$5728-$574F (22312-22351) [(HIRES P2L117)] \HB\HI-RES GRAPHICS: PAGE 2 - LINE #117
$5750-$577F (22352-22399) [(HIRES P2L181)] \HB\HI-RES GRAPHICS: PAGE 2 - LINE #181
$5780-$57A7 (22400-22439) [(HIRES P2L061)] \HB\HI-RES GRAPHICS: PAGE 2 - LINE #061
$57A8-$57CF (22440-22479) [(HIRES P2L125)] \HB\HI-RES GRAPHICS: PAGE 2 - LINE #125
$57D0-$57F7 (22480-22519) [(HIRES P2L189)] \HB\HI-RES GRAPHICS: PAGE 2 - LINE #189
$5800-$5827 (22528-22567) [(HIRES P2L006)] \HB\HI-RES GRAPHICS: PAGE 2 - LINE #006
$5828-$584F (22568-22607) [(HIRES P2L070)] \HB\HI-RES GRAPHICS: PAGE 2 - LINE #070
$5850-$5877 (22608-22647) [(HIRES P2L134)] \HB\HI-RES GRAPHICS: PAGE 2 - LINE #134
$5880-$58A7 (22656-22695) [(HIRES P2L014)] \HB\HI-RES GRAPHICS: PAGE 2 - LINE #014
$58A8-$58CF (22696-22735) [(HIRES P2L078)] \HB\HI-RES GRAPHICS: PAGE 2 - LINE #078
$58D0-$58E7 (22736-22759) [(HIRES P2L142)] \HB\HI-RES GRAPHICS: PAGE 2 - LINE #142
$5900-$5927 (22784-22823) [(HIRES P2L022] \HB\HI-RES GRAPHICS: PAGE 2 - LINE #022
$5928-$594F (22824-22863) [(HIRES P2L086)] \HB\HI-RES GRAPHICS: PAGE 2 - LINE #086
$5950-$597F (22864-22911) [(HIRES P2L150)] \HB\HI-RES GRAPHICS: PAGE 2 - LINE #150
$5980-$59A7 (22912-22951) [(HIRES P2L030)] \HB\HI-RES GRAPHICS: PAGE 2 - LINE #030
$59A8-$59CF (22952-22991) [(HIRES P2L094)] \HB\HI-RES GRAPHICS: PAGE 2 - LINE #094
$59D0-$59F7 (22992-23031) [(HIRES P2L158)] \HB\HI-RES GRAPHICS: PAGE 2 - LINE #158
$5A00-$5A27 (23040-23079) [(HIRES P2L038)] \HB\HI-RES GRAPHICS: PAGE 2 - LINE #038
$5A28-$5A4F (23080-23119) [(HIRES P2L102)] \HB\HI-RES GRAPHICS: PAGE 2 - LINE #102
$5A50-$5A77 (23120-23159) [(HIRES P2L166)] \HB\HI-RES GRAPHICS: PAGE 2 - LINE #166
$5A80-$5AA7 (23168-23207) [(HIRES P2L046)] \HB\HI-RES GRAPHICS: PAGE 2 - LINE #046
$5AA8-$5ACF (23208-23247) [(HIRES P2L110)] \HB\HI-RES GRAPHICS: PAGE 2 - LINE #110
$5AD0-$5AF7 (23248-23287) [(HIRES P2L174)] \HB\HI-RES GRAPHICS: PAGE 2 - LINE #174
$5B00-$5B27 (23296-23335) [(HIRES P2L054)] \HB\HI-RES GRAPHICS: PAGE 2 - LINE #054
$5B28-$562F (23336-22063) [(HIRES P2L118)] \HB\HI-RES GRAPHICS: PAGE 2 - LINE #118
$5B50-$5B7F (23376-23423) [(HIRES P2L182)] \HB\HI-RES GRAPHICS: PAGE 2 - LINE #182
$5B80-$5BA7 (23424-23463) [(HIRES P2L062)] \HB\HI-RES GRAPHICS: PAGE 2 - LINE #062
$5BA8-$5BCF (23464-23503) [(HIRES P2L126)] \HB\HI-RES GRAPHICS: PAGE 2 - LINE #126
$5BD0-$5BF7 (23504-23543) [(HIRES P2L190)] \HB\HI-RES GRAPHICS: PAGE 2 - LINE #190
$5C00-$5C27 (23552-23591) [(HIRES P2L007)] \HB\HI-RES GRAPHICS: PAGE 2 - LINE #007
$5C28-$5C4F (23592-23631) [(HIRES P2L071)] \HB\HI-RES GRAPHICS: PAGE 2 - LINE #071
$5C50-$5C77 (23632-23671) [(HIRES P2L135)] \HB\HI-RES GRAPHICS: PAGE 2 - LINE #135
$5C80-$5CA7 (23680-23719) [(HIRES P2L015)] \HB\HI-RES GRAPHICS: PAGE 2 - LINE #015
$5CA8-$5CCF (23720-23759) [(HIRES P2L079)] \HB\HI-RES GRAPHICS: PAGE 2 - LINE #079
$5CD0-$5CE7 (23760-23783) [(HIRES P2L143)] \HB\HI-RES GRAPHICS: PAGE 2 - LINE #143
$5D00-$5D27 (23808-23847) [(HIRES P2L023)] \HB\HI-RES GRAPHICS: PAGE 2 - LINE #023
$5D28-$5D4F (23848-23887) [(HIRES P2L087)] \HB\HI-RES GRAPHICS: PAGE 2 - LINE #087
$5D50-$5D7F (23888-23935) [(HIRES P2L151)] \HB\HI-RES GRAPHICS: PAGE 2 - LINE #151
$5D80-$5DA7 (23936-23975) [(HIRES P2L031)] \HB\HI-RES GRAPHICS: PAGE 2 - LINE #031
$5DA8-$5DCF (23976-24015) [(HIRES P2L095)] \HB\HI-RES GRAPHICS: PAGE 2 - LINE #095
```

```
$5DD0~$5DF7 (24016~24055) [(HIRES P2L159)] \HB\HI-RES GRAPHICS: PAGE 2 - LINE #159
$5E00~$5E27 (24064~24103) [(HIRES P2L039)] \HB\HI-RES GRAPHICS: PAGE 2 - LINE #039
$5E28~$5E4F (24104~24143) [(HIRES P2L103)] \HB\HI-RES GRAPHICS: PAGE 2 - LINE #103
$5E50~$5E77 (24144~24183) [(HIRES P2L167)] \HB\HI-RES GRAPHICS: PAGE 2 - LINE #167
$5E80~$5EA7 (24192~24231) [(HIRES P2L047)] \HB\HI-RES GRAPHICS: PAGE 2 - LINE #047
$5EA8~$5ECF (24232~24271) [(HIRES P2L111)] \HB\HI-RES GRAPHICS: PAGE 2 - LINE #111
$5ED0~$5EF7 (24272~24311) [(HIRES P2L175)] \HB\HI-RES GRAPHICS: PAGE 2 - LINE #175
$5F00~$5F27 (24320~24359) [(HIRES P2L055)] \HB\HI-RES GRAPHICS: PAGE 2 - LINE #055
$5F28~$5F4F (24360~24399) [(HIRES P2L119)] \HB\HI-RES GRAPHICS: PAGE 2 - LINE #119
$5F50~$5F7F (24400~24447) [(HIRES P2L183)] \HB\HI-RES GRAPHICS: PAGE 2 - LINE #183
$5F80~$5FA7 (24448~24487) [(HIRES P2L063)] \HB\HI-RES GRAPHICS: PAGE 2 - LINE #063
$5FA8~$5FCF (24488~24527) [(HIRES P2L127)] \HB\HI-RES GRAPHICS: PAGE 2 - LINE #127
$5FD0~$5FF7 (24528~24567) [(HIRES P2L191)] \HB\HI-RES GRAPHICS: PAGE 2 - LINE #191
$6884 (26756) [(COMMAND TBL)] \PB\   DOS 3.2 COMMAND TABLE (32K APPLE ONLY!)
$6974 (26996) [(DOS 3.2 ERR MSGS)] \PB\DOS 3.2 ERROR MESSAGES (32K APPLE ONLY!)
$6996~$6A53 (27030~27219) \PB\       DOS 3.2 COUT AND OTHER HOOKS (32K APPLE ONLY! - SEE $A996~$AA53 FOR MORE
                                     DESCRIPTION BASED ON 48K APPLE)
$6A60 (27232) \P2\                   LENGTH OF MOST RECENTLY BLOADED PROGRAM OR DATA (32K APPLE ONLY)
$6A72 (27250) \P2\                   STARTING ADDRESS OF MOST RECENTLY BLOADED PROGRAM OR DATA (32K APPLE ONLY)
$8F57~$91B9 (-28841~-28231) \PB\      SPACE NORMALLY AVAILABLE FOR USER USE. HOWEVER IF DOS MAXFILES >=6 THIS AREA
                                      BECOMES DOS FILE BUFFER #6
$91B9~$940C (-28231~-27636) \PB\      SPACE NORMALLY AVAILABLE FOR USER USE. HOWEVER IF DOS MAXFILES >=5 THIS AREA
                                      BECOMES DOS FILE BUFFER #5
$940D~$95FF (-27635~-27137) \PB\      SPACE NORMALLY AVAILABLE FOR USER USE. HOWEVER IF DOS MAXFILES >=4 THIS AREA
                                      BECOMES DOS FILE BUFFER #4
$95FF (-27137)                        DEFAULT (MAXFILES = 3) END OF USER RAM WHEN DOS ACTIVE (HIMEM=49151)
$9600~$9CF8 (-27136~-25352) \HB\      3 DOS FILE BUFFERS (DEFAULT CASE) - APPLICABLE TO ALL VERSIONS
                                      (3.1~3.2~3.2.1~3.3) 48K
$9600~$9853 (-27136~-26541) \HB\      DOS FILE BUFFER #3. NOTE: THIS IS DEFAULT FIRST BUFFER USED BY DOS. IF MAXFILES>3
                                      ADDITIONAL BUFFERS WILL BE PLACED BELOW $9600 AND HIGHEST NUMBER BUFFER WILL BE
                                      USED DEFAULT FIRST
$9600~$9700 (-27136~-26880) \HB\      DOS FILE BUFFER #3 - SECTION 1: DATA BUFFER. RECEIVES CONTENTS OF CURRENT DATA
                                      SECTOR
$9600 (-27136)                        HIMEM VALUE (+1) SET HERE WHEN USING DOS 3.1~3.2~3.2.1~3.3 OR 3.2 IN DEFAULT CASE
                                      (MAXFILES=3)
$9701~$9800 (-26879~-26624) \PB\      DOS FILE BUFFER #3 - SECTION 2: TRACK & SECTOR BUFFER. RECEIVES THE CURRENT
                                      TRACK+SECTOR LIST (TSL) SECTOR
$9801~$9853 (-26623~-26541) \PB\      DOS FILE BUFFER #3 - FILE NAME & MISC DATA
$9CF8~$9CFF (-25352~-25345) \HB\      7-BYTE VACANT AREA NOT USED BY DOS 3.23.2
$982D (-26579)                        DOS FILE BUFFER #3 - START OF NAME OF FILE
$984B~$984C (-26549~-26548)           DOS FILE BUFFER #3 - ADDRESS OF START OF MISC INFO SECTION (SECTION 3)  ( DEFAULT
                                      CONTENTS =  $9800)
$984D~$984E (-26547~-26546)           DOS FILE BUFFER #3 - ADDRESS OF START OF TRACK & SECTOR SECTION (SECTION 2)
                                      (DEFAULT CONTENTS =  $9700)
$984F~$9850 (-26545~-26544)           DOS FILE BUFFER #3 - ADDRESS OF START OF DATA SECTION (SECTION 1)  (DEFAULT
                                      CONTENTS =  $9600)
$9851~$9852 (-26543~-26542)           DOS FILE BUFFER #3 - ADDRESS OF START OF NAME BUFFER FOR NEXT FILE ($0000 = NO
                                      MORE FILES)
$9853 (-26541)                        START OF DOS (=HIMEM+1) FOR MAXFILES=2
$9853~$9952 (-26541~-26286)           DOS FILE BUFFER #2 - SECTION 1: DATA BUFFER
$9953~$9A52 (-26285~-26030)           DOS FILE BUFFER #2 - SECTION 2: TRACK & SECTOR BUFFER
```

```
$9A53 (-26029)                           DOS FILE BUFFER #2 - SECTION 3: START OF MISCELLANEOUS INFO BUFFER
$9A80 (-25984)                           DOS FILE BUFFER #2 - NAME
$9A9E-$9A9F (-25954--25953)              DOS FILE BUFFER #2 - ADDRESS OF START OF SECTION 3- MISCELLANEOUS INFO BUFFER
                                         ($9A53)
$9AA0-$9AA1 (-25952--25951)              DOS FILE BUFFER #2 - ADDRESS OF START OF SECTION 2- TRACK AND SECTOR BUFFER
                                         ($9953)
$9AA2-$9AA3 (-25950--25949)              DOS FILE BUFFER #2 - ADDRESS OF START OF SECTION 1- DATA BUFFER ($9853)
$9AA4-$9AA5 (-25948--25947)              DOS FILE BUFFER #2 - ADDRESS OF START OF NAME BUFFER OF NEXT FILE DOWN ($982D)
$9AA6 (-25946)                           START OF DOS (=HIMEM+1) WHEN MAXFILES=1
$9AA6-$9BA5 (-25946--25691)              DOS FILE BUFFER #1 - SECTION 1- DATA BUFFER
$9BA6-$9CA5 (-25690--25435)              DOS FILE BUFFER #1 - SECTION 2- & SECTOR BUFFER
$9CA6 (-25434)                           DOS FILE BUFFER #1 - SECTION 3- START OF MISC INFO BUFFER ($53 BYTES)
$9CD3 (-25389)                           DOS FILE BUFFER #1 - NAME
$9CF1-$9CF2 (-25359--25358)              DOS FILE BUFFER #1 - ADDRESS OF SECTION 3- OF MISC INFO BUFFER ($9CA6)
$9CF3-$9CF4 (-25357--25356)              DOS FILE BUFFER #1 - ADDRESS OF START OF SECTION 2- TRACK & SECTOR BUFFER ($9BA6)
$9CF5-$9CF6 (-25355--25354)              DOS FILE BUFFER #1 - ADDRESS OF START OF SECTION 1- DATA BUFFER ($9AA6)
$9CF7-$9CF8 (-25353--25352)              DOS FILE BUFFER #1 - ADDRESS OF START OF NAME BUFFER OF NEXT FILE DOWN ($9A80)
$9CF9-$9CFF (-25351--25345)              DOS 3.2 UNUSED
$9D00-$BFFF (-25344--16385) \SB\         DOS 3.2/3.3 (NOT INCLUDING ANY BUFFERS)
$9D00-$9D83 (-25344--25213) \SB\         DOS 3.2/3.3 ADDRESS TABLE (LIST OF TWO-BYTE ADDRESS CONSTANTS USED BY DOS)
$9D00-$9D01 (-25344--25343) \P2\         ADDRESS OF DOS 3.2/3.3 FILE BUFFER #1 AT ITS FILE NAME FIELD ($9CD3)
$9D02-$9D03 (-25342--25341) \P2\         ADDRESS OF DOS 3.2/3.3 INPUT CHARACTER (KEYBOARD INTERCEPT) ROUTINE ($9E81)
$9D04-$9D05 (-25340--25339) \P2\         ADDRESS OF DOS 3.2/3.3 OUTPUT CHARACTER (VIDEO INTERCEPT) ROUTINE ($9EBD)
$9D06-$9D07 (-25338--25337) \P2\         ADDRESS OF DOS 3.2/3.3 FILE NAME FOR BUFFER #1 (PRIMARY FILE NAME) ($AA75)
$9D08-$9D09 (-25336--25335) \P2\         ADDRESS OF DOS 3.2/3.3 FILE NAME FOR BUFFER #2 (SECONDARY OR 'RENAME' FILE NAME)
                                         ($AA93)
$9D0A-$9D0B (-25334--25333) \P2\         ADDRESS POINTS TO PARAMETER SECTION FOR FIRST LEVEL OF DOS 3.2/3.3 - SEE NEXT
                                         ITEM FOR FIRST ENTRY IN SECTION
$9D0A-$9D0B (-25334--25333) \P2\         ADDRESS OF DOS 3.2/3.3 LENGTH OF LOAD ($AA60)
$9D0C-$9D0D (-25332--25331) \P2\         ADDRESS OF DOS 3.2/3.3 LOAD ADDRESS - I.E. BEGINNING OF DOS ($9D00)
$9D0E-$9D0F (-25330--25329) \P2\         DOS 3.2/3.3 ADDRESS POINTS TO PARAMETER SECTION FOR FILE MANAGER - I.E. SECOND
                                         (I/O ROUTINE) LEVEL OF DOS
$9D0E-$9D0F (-25330--25329) \P2\         ADDRESS OF DOS 3.2/3.3 END OF SYSTEM BUFFERS ($B5BB)
$9D10-$9D1C (-25328--25316) \SB\         DOS VIDEO (CSWL) INTERCEPT'S STATE HANDLER ADDRESS TABLE; I.E. TABLE OF ADDRESSES
                                         USED IN STATE MACHINE THAT ROUTES OUTPUT CHARACTERS. USED FROM $9EC0 TO $9ED0.
                                         $AA52 IS USED TO CHOOSE WHICH ONE
$9D10-$9D11 (-25328--25327) \P2\         ADDRESS OF DOS 3.2/3.3 STATE MACHINE CONDITION #0 CODE ($9EEB-1)
$9D12-$9D13 (-25326--25325) \P2\         ADDRESS OF DOS 3.2/3.3 STATE MACHINE CONDITION #1CODE ($9F12-1)
$9D14-$9D15 (-25324--25323) \P2\         ADDRESS OF DOS 3.2/3.3 STATE MACHINE CONDITION #2 CODE ($9F23-1)
$9D16-$9D17 (-25322--25321) \P2\         ADDRESS OF DOS 3.2/3.3 STATE MACHINE CONDITION #3 CODE ($9F2F-1)
$9D18-$9D19 (-25320--25319) \P2\         ADDRESS OF DOS 3.2/3.3 STATE MACHINE CONDITION #4 CODE ($9F52-1)
$9D1A-$9D1B (-25318--25317) \P2\         ADDRESS OF DOS 3.2/3.3 STATE MACHINE CONDITION #5 CODE ($9F61-1)
$9D1C-$9D1D (-25316--25315) \P2\         ADDRESS OF DOS 3.2/3.3 STATE MACHINE CONDITION #6 CODE ($9F71-1)
$9D1E-$9D55 (-25314--25259) \SB\         DOS 3.2/3.3 COMMAND DECODER TABLE OF SUBROUTINE ADDRESSES (EXPRESSED IN VALUE-1
                                         FORM TO SIMPLIFY CALLING)
$9D1E-$9D1F (-25314--25313) \P2\         DOS 3.2/3.3/3.3 ADDRESS-1 OF CODE FOR 'INIT' COMMAND ($A54F-1)
$9D20-$9D21 (-25312--25311) \P2\         DOS 3.2/3.3 ADDRESS-1 OF CODE FOR 'LOAD' COMMAND ($A413-1)
$9D22-$9D23 (-25310--25309) \P2\         DOS 3.2/3.3 ADDRESS-1 OF CODE FOR 'SAVE' COMMAND ($A397-1)
$9D24-$9D25 (-25308--25307) \P2\         DOS 3.2/3.3 ADDRESS-1 OF CODE FOR 'RUN' COMMAND ($A4D1-1)
$9D26-$9D27 (-25306--25305) \P2\         DOS 3.2/3.3 ADDRESS-1 OF CODE FOR 'CHAIN' COMMAND ($A4F0-1)
$9D28-$9D29 (-25304--25303) \P2\         DOS 3.2/3.3 ADDRESS-1 OF CODE FOR 'DELETE' COMMAND ($A263-1)
```

```
$9D2A~$9D2B (-25302~-25301) \P2\    DOS 3.2/3.3 ADDRESS-1 OF CODE FOR 'LOCK' COMMAND ($A271-1)
$9D2C~$9D2D (-25300~-25299) \P2\    DOS 3.2/3.3 ADDRESS-1 OF CODE FOR 'UNLOCK' COMMAND ($A275-1)
$9D2E~$9D2F (-25298~-25297) \P2\    DOS 3.2/3.3 ADDRESS-1 OF CODE FOR 'CLOSE' COMMAND ($A2EA-1)
$9D30~$9D31 (-25296~-25295) \P2\    DOS 3.2/3.3 ADDRESS-1 OF CODE FOR 'READ' COMMAND ($A51B-1)
$9D32~$9D33 (-25294~-25293) \P2\    DOS 3.2/3.3 ADDRESS-1 OF CODE FOR 'EXEC' COMMAND ($A5C6-1)
$9D34~$9D35 (-25292~-25291) \P2\    DOS 3.2/3.3 ADDRESS-1 OF CODE FOR 'WRITE' COMMAND ($A510-1)
$9D36~$9D37 (-25290~-25289) \P2\    DOS 3.2/3.3 ADDRESS-1 OF CODE FOR 'POSITION' COMMAND ($A5DD-1)
$9D38~$9D39 (-25288~-25287) \P2\    DOS 3.2/3.3 ADDRESS-1 OF CODE FOR 'OPEN' COMMAND ($A2A3-1)
$9D3A~$9D3B (-25286~-25285) \P2\    DOS 3.2/3.3 ADDRESS-1 OF CODE FOR 'APPEND' COMMAND ($A298-1)
$9D3C~$9D3D (-25284~-25283) \P2\    DOS 3.2/3.3 ADDRESS-1 OF CODE FOR 'RENAME' COMMAND ($A281-1)
$9D3E~$9D3F (-25282~-25281) \P2\    DOS 3.2/3.3 ADDRESS-1 OF CODE FOR 'CATALOG' COMMAND ($A56E-1)
$9D40~$9D41 (-25280~-25279) \P2\    DOS 3.2/3.3 ADDRESS-1 OF CODE FOR 'MON' COMMAND ($A233-1)
$9D42~$9D43 (-25278~-25277) \P2\    DOS 3.2/3.3 ADDRESS-1 OF CODE FOR 'NOMON' COMMAND ($A23D-1)
$9D44~$9D45 (-25276~-25275) \P2\    DOS 3.2/3.3 ADDRESS-1 OF CODE FOR 'PR#' COMMAND ($A229-1)
$9D46~$9D47 (-25274~-25273) \P2\    DOS 3.2/3.3 ADDRESS-1 OF CODE FOR 'IN#' COMMAND ($A22E-1)
$9D48~$9D49 (-25272~-25271) \P2\    DOS 3.2/3.3 ADDRESS-1 OF CODE FOR 'MAXFILES' COMMAND ($A251-1)
$9D4A~$9D4B (-25270~-25269) \P2\    DOS 3.2/3.3 ADDRESS-1 OF CODE FOR 'FP' COMMAND ($A57A-1)
$9D4C~$9D4D (-25268~-25267) \P2\    DOS 3.2/3.3 ADDRESS-1 OF CODE FOR 'INT' COMMAND ($A59E-1)
$9D4E~$9D4F (-25266~-25265) \P2\    DOS 3.2/3.3 ADDRESS-1 OF CODE FOR 'BSAVE' COMMAND ($A331-1)
$9D50~$9D51 (-25264~-25263) \P2\    DOS 3.2/3.3 ADDRESS-1 OF CODE FOR 'BLOAD' COMMAND ($A35D-1)
$9D52~$9D53 (-25262~-25261) \P2\    DOS 3.2/3.3 ADDRESS-1 OF CODE FOR 'BRUN' COMMAND ($A38E-1)
$9D54~$9D55 (-25260~-25259) \P2\    DOS 3.2/3.3 ADDRESS-1 OF CODE FOR 'VERIFY' COMMAND ($A27D-1)
$9D56~$9D83 (-25258~-25213) \SB\    FOUR TABLES OF VECTORS USED BY DOS 3.2/3.3 TO INTERFACE WITH THE VARIOUS
                                    SUPPORTED LANGUAGES. DOS USES THESE ADDRESSES TO JUMP INTO THE LANGUAGE WHEN
                                    RUNNING (OR CHAINING IN THE CASE OF INTEGER BASIC) A NEW PROGRAM OR WHEN
                                    PROCESSING ERRORS
$9D56~$9D61 (-25258~-25247) \SB\    TABLE OF VECTORS USED BY DOS 3.2/3.3 TO INTERFACE WITH CURRENT LANGUAGE
$9D56~$9D57 (-25258~-25257) \P2\    DOS 3.2/3.3 CURRENT LANGUAGE ENTRY-VECTOR TO 'CHAIN'
$9D58~$9D59 (-25256~-25255) \P2\    DOS 3.2/3.3 CURRENT LANGUAGE ENTRY-VECTOR TO 'RUN'
$9D5A~$9D5B (-25254~-25253) \P2\    DOS 3.2/3.3 CURRENT LANGUAGE ENTRY-VECTOR TO 'ERROR'
$9D5C~$9D5D (-25252~-25251) \P2\    DOS 3.2/3.3 CURRENT LANGUAGE ENTRY-VECTOR TO 'HARD ENTRY'
$9D5E~$9D5F (-25250~-25249) \P2\    DOS 3.2/3.3 CURRENT LANGUAGE ENTRY-VECTOR TO 'SOFT ENTRY'
$9D60~$9D61 (-25248~-25247) \P2\    DOS 3.2/3.3 CURRENT LANGUAGE ENTRY-VECTOR TO 'RECOMPUTE LINKS' FOR APPROPRIATE
                                    LOCATION OF APPLESOFT BASIC (APPLESOFT ONLY)
$9D62~$9D6B (-25246~-25237) \SB\    IMAGE OF THE ENTRY POINT VECTOR FOR INTEGER BASIC; I.E. TABLE OF VECTORS USED BY
                                    DOS 3.2/3.3 TO INTERFACE WITH INTEGER BASIC. MOVED INTO $9D56~$9D59 WHEN INTEGER
                                    BASIC IS CURRENT LANGUAGE
$9D62~$9D63 (-25246~-25245) \P2\    DOS 3.2/3.3 ENTRY-VECTOR TO INTEGER BASIC 'CHAIN'  ($E839)
$9D64~$9D65 (-25244~-25243) \P2\    DOS 3.2/3.3 ENTRY-VECTOR TO INTEGER BASIC 'RUN'  ($A4E5)
$9D66~$9D67 (-25242~-25241) \P2\    DOS 3.2/3.3 ENTRY-VECTOR TO INTEGER BASIC 'ERROR'  ($E3E3)
$9D68~$9D69 (-25240~-25239) \P2\    DOS 3.2/3.3 ENTRY-VECTOR TO INTEGER BASIC - 'CONTROL-B' OR 'COLD' OR 'HARD' ENTRY
                                     ($E000)
$9D6A~$9D6B (-25238~-25237) \P2\    DOS 3.2/3.3 ENTRY-VECTOR TO INTEGER BASIC 'SOFT ENTRY'  ($E003)
$9D6C~$9D6D (-25236~-25235)         NOT USED
$9D6C~$9D77 (-25236~-25225) \PB\    DOS 3.2/3.3 - IMAGE OF THE ENTRY POINT VECTOR FOR APPLESOFT (ROM VERSION) I.E.
                                    TABLE OF INTERFACE VECTORS MOVED INTO $9D56~$9D61 WHEN ROM APPLESOFT IS CURRENT
                                    LANGUAGE
$9D6C~9D6D\P2\                      DOS 3.2/3.3 ENTRY-VECTOR TO APPLESOFT (ROM VERSION) 'CHAIN' (REALLY RUN)  ($A4FC)
$9D6E~$9D6F (-25234~-25233) \P2\    DOS 3.2/3.3 ENTRY-VECTOR TO APPLESOFT (ROM VERSION) 'RUN'  ($A4FC)
$9D70~$9D71 (-25232~-25231) \P2\    DOS 3.2/3.3 ENTRY-VECTOR TO APPLESOFT (ROM VERSION) 'ERROR'  ($D865)
$9D72~$9D73 (-25230~-25229) \P2\    DOS 3.2/3.3 ENTRY-VECTOR TO APPLESOFT (ROM VERSION) - 'CONTROL-B' OR 'COLD' OR
                                    'HARD' ENTRY  ($E000)
```

HEX LOCN (DEC LOCN) [NAME] \USE-TYPE\	- DESCRIPTION
$9D73¯$A7DF (-25229¯-22561) \SB\	SYSTEM SECTION OF DOS 3.1 (48K APPLE)
$9D74¯$9D75 (-25228¯-25227) \P2\	DOS 3.2/3.3 ENTRY-VECTOR TO APPLESOFT (ROM VERSION) 'SOFT ENTRY' ($D43C)
$9D76¯$9D77 (-25226¯-25225) \P2\	DOS 3.2/3.3 ENTRY-VECTOR TO APPLESOFT (ROM VERSION) 'RECOMPUTE LINKS' ($D4F2)
$9D78¯$9D83 (-25224¯-25213) \PB\	DOS 3.2/3.3 APPLESOFT (RAM OR DISK VERSION) INTERFACE VECTORS (MOVED INTO $9D56¯$9D61 WHEN RAM OR DISK APPLESOFT IS CURRENT LANGUAGE)
$9D84¯$A883 (-25212¯-22397)	DOS 3.2/3.3 (48K) SYSTEM CODE SECTION
$9D84¯$9DBE (-25212¯-25154) \SB\	DOS 3.2/3.3 COLDSTART ENTRY ROUTINE
$9D84 (-25212) \SE\	LOCATION TO WHICH DOS 3.2/3.3 JUMPS (ON A CTRL-B OR 3D3G) FOR CODE TO IMPLEMENT A HARD ENTRY TO RAM (DISK AS OPPOSED TO ROM OR LANGUAGE PACK) VERSION OF APPLESOFT
$9D78¯$9D79 (-25224¯-25223) \P2\	DOS 3.2/3.3 ENTRY-VECTOR TO APPLESOFT (RAM OR DISK) 'CHAIN' ($A506)
$9D7A¯$9D7B (-25222¯-25221) \P2\	DOS 3.2/3.3 ENTRY-VECTOR TO APPLESOFT (RAM OR DISK) 'RUN' ($A506)
$9D7C¯$9D7D (-25220¯-25219) \P2\	DOS 3.2/3.3 ENTRY-VECTOR TO APPLESOFT (RAM OR DISK) 'ERROR' ($1067)
$9D7E¯$9D7F (-25218¯-25217) \P2\	DOS 3.2/3.3 ENTRY-VECTOR TO APPLESOFT (RAM OR DISK) 'HARD ENTRY' ($9D84)
$9D80¯$9D81 (-25216¯-25215) \P2\	DOS 3.2/3.3 ENTRY-VECTOR TO APPLESOFT (RAM OR DISK) 'SOFT ENTRY' ($0C3C)
$9D82¯$9D83 (-25214¯-25213) \P2\	DOS 3.2/3.3 ENTRY-VECTOR TO APPLESOFT (RAM OR DISK) 'RECOMPUTE LINKS' ($0CF2)
$9D84 (-25212) \SE\	DOS 3.2/3.3 HARD ENTRY POINT. BOOTSTRAP ROUTINE AT $B700 AND $03D3G BOTH JUMP HERE
$9DB9 (-25159) \SE\	INITIALIZE OR RE-INITIALIZE DOS 3.2/3.3 IF PAGE 3 LINKAGES DESTROYED. OBSOLETE (DOS 3.1 ONLY?)
$9DBF-$9DE9\SB\	DOS 3.2/3.3 WARMSTART ENTRY ROUTINE. GETS REMEMBERED BASIC TYPE AND SETS ROM CARD AS NECESSARY CALLING $A5B2
$9DBF (-25153) \SE\	DOS 3.2/3.3 (48K) SOFT ENTRY POINT. $03D0G AND RESET WITH AUTOSTART ROM BOTH JUMP HERE. (RECONNECTS DOS 3.2 IF PAGE 3 MONITOR LINKAGES OVERWRITTEN)
$9DD1 (-25135)	DOS 3.2/3.3 PARAMETER TO REMEMBER WHETHER ENTRY IS COLDSTART OR WARMSTART
$9DEA (-25110) \SE\	DOS 3.2/3.3 (48K) BLOCK OF CODE WHICH INITS DOS BUFFERS AND SETS VECTORS FOR RAM APPLESOFT. RESTORES $03D0¯$03FF FROM $9E51¯$9E80. CALLED BY KEYIN IF APPLESOFT MUST COME FROM DISK
$9DEA-$9E50\SB\	DOS 3.2/3.3 FIRST ENTRY PROCESSING ROUTINE CALLED BY KEYBOARD INTERCEPT HANDLER WHEN FIRST KEYBOARD INPUT REQUEST MADE BY BASIC AFTER A DOS COLDSTART
$9E4D (-25011) \SE\	ROUTINE WHICH HANDLES DOS 3.1 INPUT HOOK
$9E50¯$9E80 (-25008¯-24960) \SB\	BLOCK OF COMMANDS ETC. COPIED INTO $03D0¯$03E0 ON DOS 3.2/3.3 BOOT TO CONTROL TRANSFERS TO SOFT ENTRY¯ HARD ENTRY¯ I-O PKG¯ RWTS AND TO GET END OF SYSTEM BUFFER¯ IOB ADDRESS¯ AND TO UPDATE I-O HOOKS¯ AND DO JUMP TRANSFERS TO AUTO BRK ENTRY¯ CTRL¯Y ENTRY¯ NMI ENTRY AND PROVIDE IRQ ADDRESS
$9E51¯$9E7F (-25007¯-24961)	DOS 3.3 IMAGE OF 3-PAGE JUMP VECTOR WHICH ROUTINE AT $9DEA COPIES TO $3D0-$3FF
$9E7E (-24962) \SE\	ROUTINE WHICH HANDLES DOS 3.1 OUTPUT HOOK
$9E81¯$9EB9 (-24959¯-24903) \SE\	DOS 3.2/3.3 (48K) KEYBOARD INTERCEPT (INPUT CHARACTER) ROUTINE. CALLS $9ED1 AND MAY CALL $9E9E¯$A626 AND¯OR $9DEA. DOS COMES HERE FOR EVERY BASIC INPUT STATEMENT OR EVERY LINE TYPED TO THE BASIC PROMPT (E.G.] OR >) OR EVERY TIME PROGRAM USES JSR $FD18 OR $FD0C
$9EBA¯$9EBC (-24902¯-24900)	DOS 3.2/3.3 JUMP TO THE TRUE KSWL HANDLER ROUTINE
$9EBD¯$9EEA (-24899¯-24854) \SB\	DOS 3.2/3.3 (48K) DOS COMMAND DECODER -- PART 3. OUTPUT STATE MACHINE AND DEVICE SELECTION CODE
$9EBD¯$9ED0 (-24899¯-24880)	DOS 3.2/3.3 DOS VIDEO INTERCEPT ROUTINE. CALLS $9ED1 TO SAVE REGISTERS AT ENTRY TO DOS. GETS VIDEO INTERCEPT STATE AND USING IT AS INDEX TO STATE HANDLER TABLE ($9D10) GOES TO PROPER HANDLER ROUTINE & PASSES IT THE CHARACTER TO BE PRINTED
$9EBD (-24899) \SE\	DOS 3.2/3.3 OUTPUT ROUTINE. IF DOS ACTIVE OUTPUT HOOK POINTS HERE & EVERY CHAR TO BE OUTPUTTED PUT INTO ACCUMULATOR FOR DISPOSAL BY CALLING THIS ROUTINE. IT PUSHES ADDRESS FROM STATE MACHINE TABLE ONTO STACK AND THEN RTS'S TO JUMP TO THAT ADDRESS+1
$9ED1-$9EEA	DOS 3.2/3.3 COMMON INTERCEPT SAVE REGISTERS ROUTINE. SAVES A¯X¯Y AND S-REGISTERS AT $AA59-$AA5C. WHILE IN DOS RESTOR TRUE I/O HANDLERS TO $0036¯$0039

HEX LOCN (DEC LOCN) [NAME] \USE-TYPE\	DESCRIPTION
$9ED1 (-24879) \SE\	ENTRY POINT TO ABOVE ROUTINE WHICH RESTORES KEYBOARD AND PRINT HOOKS
$9EEB˜$9F11 (-24853˜-24815) \SB\	DOS 3.2/3.3 STATE 0 OUTPUT HANDLER
$9EEB (-24853) \SE\	DOS 3.2/3.3 STATE MACHINE ENTRY DOS#0 ($AA52=0). DEFAULT VALUE ON DOS ENTRY (SET AT $9DDA) AND ALSO USED AT FRONT OF LINE OUTPUTTED FROM A PROGRAM. CHECKS FOR A VARIETY OF SPECIAL CASES
$9F12˜$9F22 (-24814˜-24798) \SB\	DOS 3.2/3.3 STATE 1 OUTPUT HANDLER. FUNCTION: COLLECT DOS COMMAND
$9F12 (-24814) \SE\	DOS 3.2/3.3 (48K) STATE MACHINE ENTRY DOS#1 ($AA52=1). USED WHEN OUTPUTTING CTRL-D LINE (DOS COMMAND) FROM PROGRAM SO DOS MUST COLLECT THE LINE FOR DECODING
$9F23˜$9F2E (-24797˜-24786) \SB\	DOS 3.2/3.3 STATE 2 OUTPUT HANDLER. FUNCTION: NON-DOS COMMAND TO BE IGNORED
$9F23 (-24797) \SE\	DOS 3.2/3.3 (48K) STATE MACHINE ENTRY DOS#2 ($AA52=2). USED FOR OUTPUTTING NORMAL LINE FROM PROGRAM SO DOS MUST ROUTE TO OUTPUT DEVICE
$9F2F (-24785) \SB\	DOS 3.2/3.3 (48K) STATE 3 OUTPUT HANDLER. FUNCTION: INPUT STATEMENT HANDLER
$9F2F (-24785) \SE\	DOS 3.2/3.3 (48K) STATE MACHINE ENTRY DOS#3 ($AA52=3). COME HERE TO OUTPUT A CHARACTER BEING ECHOED FROM THE INPUT ROUTINE (KEYBOARD OR EXEC FILE)
$9F52˜$9F60 (-24750˜-24736) \SB\	DOS 3.2/3.3 (48K) STATE 4 OUTPUT HANDLER. FUNCTION: WRITE DATA TO A FILE
$9F52 (-24750) \SE\	DOS 3.2/3.3 (48K) STATE MACHINE ENTRY DOS#4 ($AA52=4). STATES DOS#4 & DOS#5 WORK TOGETHER TO OUTPUT TO THE DISK UNTIL A LINE COMES ALONG WITH A CTRL-D ON THE FRONT. DOS#4 - WRITE IS ACTIVE˜ MIDDLE OF LINE
$9F61 (-24735) \SB\	DOS 3.2/3.3 (48K) STATE 5 OUTPUT HANDLER. FUNCTION: START OF WRITE DATA LINE
$9F61 (-24735) \SE\	DOS 3.2/3.3 (48K) STATE MACHINE ENTRY DOS#5 ($AA52=5). SEE $9F52 FOR EXPLANATION. DOS#5 - WRITE IS ACTIVE˜ FRONT OF LINE
$9F71˜$9F77 (-24719˜-24713) \SB\	DOS 3.2/3.3 (48K) STATE 6 OUTPUT HANDLER. FUNCTION: SKIP PROMPT CHARACTER. SETS STATE TO 0 AND EXITS VIA $9F9D (ECHO IF MON I)
$9F71 (-24719) \SE\	DOS 3.2/3.3 (48K) STATE MACHINE ENTRY DOS#6 ($AA52=6). CONDITION WHEN ECHOING INPUT FROM 'READ' FILE. DOS IGNORES CHARACTERS FOR DOS COMMAND PURPOSES. USED BY THE EXEC COMMAND
$9F78˜$9F82 (-24712˜-24702)	DOS 3.2/3.3 (48K) FINISHES RUN COMMAND INTERRUPTED BY APPLESOFT RAM LOAD. RESETS 'RUN INTERRUPTED' FLAG; CALLS $A851 TO REPLACE DOS CSWL/KSWL INTERCEPTS AND GOES TO $A4DC TO COMPLETE THE RUN COMMAND
$9F83˜$9F94 (-24701˜-24684)	DOS 3.2/3.3 (48K) COMMAND SCANNER EXIT TO BASIC ROUTINE. IF 1ST CHAR OF COMMAND LINE IS CONTROL-D GO TO ECHO EXIT ($9F75); OTHERWISE SET THINGS UP SO BASIC WON'T SEE THE DOS COMMAND (BY PASSING A ZERO-LENGTH LINE I.E. ONLY A CARRIAGE RETURN) AND FALL THRU TO ECHO EXIT
$9F95˜$9FB0 (-24683˜-24656)	DOS 3.2/3.3 (48K) ROUTINE TO ECHO CHARACTER ON SCREEN (CONDITIONALLY) AND EXIT DOS. ($9F95 ECHO ONLY IF MON C SET; OTHERWISE GOTO $9FBE. $9F99 ECHO ONLY IF MON O SET; OTHERWISE GO TO $9FB3. $9F9D ECHO ONLY IF MON I SET; OTHERWISE GOTO $9FB3. $9FA4 ALWAYS ECHO CHARACTER.) CALLS $9FBA EXIT DOS $9FC5
$9FB3˜$9FC4 (-24653˜-24636)	DOS 3.2/3.3 (48K) EXIT ROUTINE AND REGISTER RESTORE. CALLS $A851 TO PUT BACK DOS KSWL/CSWL INTERCEPTS. RESTORES S-REGISTER FROM ENTRY TO DOS.
$9FBA (-24646)	DOS 3.2/3.3 (48K) DOS REGISTER RESTORE SUBROUTINE. RESTORES REGISTERS FROM FIRST ENTRY TO DOS AND RETURNS TO CALLER
$9FC5-$9FC7	DOS 3.2/3.3 (48K) JUMP TO THE TRUE CSWL ROUTINE
$9FC8˜$9FCC (-24632˜-24628)	DOS 3.2/3.3 (48K) SKIP A LINE ON THE SCREEN BY LOADING A CARRIAGE RETURN INTO THE A REGISTER AND CALLING $9FC5 TO PRINT IT
$9FCD˜$A179 (-24627˜-24199) \SB\	DOS 3.2/3.3 (48K) DOS COMMAND PARSE ROUTINE
$9FCD (-24627)	START OF SECTION OF CODE THAT ATTEMPTS TO MATCH TO A COMMAND AND GET ALL INFO NEEDED & ALL OPERATIONAL INFO GIVEN. CHECKS SYNTAX AND RANGES BEFORE EXECUTION
$A095 (-24427)	DOS 3.2/3.3 (48K) SUBROUTINE TO BLANK BOTH FILENAME BJFFERS
$A0D1 (-24367)	DOS 3.2/3.3 (48K) SETS DEFAULTS FOR THE KEYWORD OPERANDS (V=0˜L=0˜B=0)
$A0E8 (-24344)	DOS 3.2/3.3 (48K) GET THE LINE OFFSET INDEX AND FLUSH TO THE NEXT NON-BLANK SKIPPING ANY COMMAS FOUND. IF NOT YET TO END OF LINE GOTO $A10C. CHECK TO SEE IF ANY KEYWORDS WERE GIVEN WHICH WERE NOT ALLOWED BY THIS COMMAND

$A10C (-24308)	DOS 3.2/3.3 (48K) LOOKUP THE KEYWORD FOUND ON THE COMMAND LINE IN THE TABLE OF VALID KEYWORDS ($A941). SAVE VALUE OF KEYWORD IN KEYWORD VALUES TABLE STARTING AT $AA66. GO PARSE NEXT KEYWORD. GOTO $A0E8
$A164 (-24220)	DOS 3.2/3.3 (48K) INDICATE C˜I OR O KEYWORDS WERE PARSED. UPDATE MONN VALUE IN KEYWORD VALUE TABLE APPROPRIATELY. GOT PARSE THE NEXT KEYWORD. GOTO $A0E8
$A180˜$A192 (-24192˜-24174)	DOS 3.2/3.3 (48K) DO COMMAND. RESET VIDEO INTERCEPT STATE TO ZERO;CLEAR FILE MANAGER PARAMETER LIST. USING COMMAND INDEX GET ADDRESS OF THE COMMAND HANDLING ROUTINE FROM THE COMMAND HANDLER ROUTINE TABLE AT $9D1E AND GO TO IT. COMMAND HANDLER WILL EXIT TO CALLER OF THIS ROUTINE
$A193˜$A1A3 (-24173˜-24157)	DOS 3.2/3.3 (48K) GET NEXT CHARACTER ON COMMAND LINE AND CHECK TO SEE IF IT IS A C/R OR A COMMA
$A1A4˜$A1AD (-24156˜-24147)	DOS 3.2/3.3 (48K) FLUSHES COMMAND LINE CHARACTERS UNTIL A NON-BLANK IS FOUND
$A1AE˜$A1B3 (-24146˜-24136)	DOS 3.2/3.3 (48K) CLEAR FILE MANAGER PARAMETER LIST AT $B5BB TO ZEROS
$A1B4 (-24140)	DOS 3.1 (48K) ENTRY POINT FOR CODE TO IMPLEMENT 'PR#' COMMAND
$A1B9 (-24135) \SE\	DOS 3.1 (48K) ENTRY POINT FOR CODE TO IMPLEMENT 'IN#' COMMAND
$A1BE (-24130) \SE\	DOS 3.1 (48K) ENTRY POINT FOR CODE TO IMPLEMENT 'MON' COMMAND
$A1DC (-24100) \SE\	DOS 3.1 (48K) ENTRY POINT FOR CODE TO IMPLEMENT 'MAXFILES' COMMAND
$A1EE (-24082) \SE\	DOS 3.1 (48K) ENTRY POINT FOR CODE TO IMPLEMENT 'DELETE' COMMAND
$A1FC (-24068) \SE\	DOS 3.1 (48K) ENTRY POINT FOR CODE TO IMPLEMENT 'LOCK' COMMAND
$A200 (-24064) \SE\	DOS 3.1 (48K) ENTRY POINT FOR CODE TO IMPLEMENT 'BSAVE' COMMAND
$A200 (-24064) \SE\	DOS 3.1 (48K) ENTRY POINT FOR CODE TO IMPLEMENT 'UNLOCK' COMMAND
$A208 (-24056) \SE\	DOS 3.1 (48K) ENTRY POINT FOR CODE TO IMPLEMENT 'VERIFY' COMMAND
$A20C (-24052) \SE\	DOS 3.1 (48K) ENTRY POINT FOR CODE TO IMPLEMENT 'RENAME' COMMAND
$A223 (-24029) \SE\	DOS 3.1 (48K) ENTRY POINT FOR CODE TO IMPLEMENT 'APPEND' COMMAND
$A229˜$A60D (-24023˜-23027) \SB\	DOS 3.2/3.3 (48K) - BLOCK OF CODE TO HANDLE INDIVIDUAL DOS COMMANDS
$A229 (-24023) \SE\	DOS 3.2/3.3 (48K) ENTRY POINT OF CODE TO IMPLEMENT 'PR#' COMMAND
$A22E (-24018) \SE\	DOS 3.2/3.3 (48K) ENTRY POINT OF CODE TO IMPLEMENT 'IN#' COMMAND
$A233 (-24013) \SE\	DOS 3.2/3.3 (48K) ENTRY POINT OF CODE TO IMPLEMENT 'MON' COMMAND
$A236 (-24010) \SE\	DOS 3.1 (48K) ENTRY POINT FOR CODE TO IMPLEMENT 'OPEN' COMMAND
$A23D (-24003) \SE\	DOS 3.2/3.3 (48K) ENTRY POINT OF CODE TO IMPLEMENT 'NOMON' COMMAND
$A251 (-23983) \SE\	DOS 3.2/3.3 (48K) ENTRY POINT OF CODE TO IMPLEMENT 'MAXFILES' COMMAND
$A263 (-23965) \SE\	DOS 3.2/3.3 (48K) ENTRY POINT OF CODE TO IMPLEMENT 'DELETE' COMMAND
$A271 (-23951) \SE\	DOS 3.2/3.3 (48K) ENTRY POINT OF CODE TO IMPLEMENT 'LOCK' COMMAND
$A275 (-23947) \SE\	DOS 3.2/3.3 (48K) ENTRY POINT OF CODE TO IMPLEMENT 'UNLOCK' COMMAND
$A278 (-23944) \SE\	DOS 3.1 (48K) ENTRY POINT FOR CODE TO IMPLEMENT 'CLOSE' COMMAND
$A27D (-23939) \SE\	DOS 3.2/3.3 (48K) ENTRY POINT OF CODE TO IMPLEMENT 'VERIFY' COMMAND
$A281 (-23935) \SE\	DOS 3.2/3.3 (48K) ENTRY POINT OF CODE TO IMPLEMENT 'RENAME' COMMAND
$A298 (-23912) \SE\	DOS 3.2/3.3 (48K) ENTRY POINT OF CODE TO IMPLEMENT 'APPEND' COMMAND
$A2A3 (-23901) \SE\	DOS 3.2/3.3 (48K) ENTRY POINT OF CODE TO IMPLEMENT 'OPEN' COMMAND
$A2EA (-23830) \SE\	DOS 3.2/3.3 (48K) ENTRY POINT OF CODE TO IMPLEMENT 'CLOSE' COMMAND
$A2EC (-23828) \SE\	DOS 3.1 (48K) ENTRY POINT FOR CODE TO IMPLEMENT 'BLOAD' COMMAND
$A327 (-23769) \SE\	DOS 3.1 (48K) ENTRY POINT FOR CODE TO IMPLEMENT 'BRUN' COMMAND
$A330 (-23760) \SE\	DOS 3.1 (48K) ENTRY POINT FOR CODE TO IMPLEMENT 'SAVE' COMMAND
$A331 (-23759) \SE\	DOS 3.2/3.3 (48K) ENTRY POINT OF CODE TO IMPLEMENT 'BSAVE' COMMAND
$A35D (-23715) \SE\	DOS 3.2/3.3 (48K) ENTRY POINT OF CODE TO IMPLEMENT 'BLOAD' COMMAND
$A38E (-23666) \SE\	DOS 3.2/3.3 (48K) ENTRY POINT OF CODE TO IMPLEMENT 'BRUN' COMMAND
$A397 (-23657) \SE\	DOS 3.2/3.3 (48K) ENTRY POINT OF CODE TO IMPLEMENT 'SAVE' COMMAND
$A3A5 (-23643) \SE\	DOS 3.1 (48K) ENTRY POINT FOR CODE TO IMPLEMENT 'LOAD' COMMAND
$A413 (-23533) \SE\	DOS 3.2/3.3 (48K) ENTRY POINT OF CODE TO IMPLEMENT 'LOAD' COMMAND
$A476 (-23434) \SE\	DOS 3.1 (48K) ENTRY POINT FOR CODE TO IMPLEMENT 'RUN' COMMAND
$A48D (-23411) \SE\	DOS 3.1 (48K) ENTRY POINT FOR CODE TO IMPLEMENT 'CHAIN' COMMAND

A39C LDA $06

```
HEX LOCN (DEC LOCN) [NAME]  \USE-TYPE\ - DESCRIPTION
------------------------------------------------------------------------------------------------
$A4A5 (-23387) \SE\                  DOS 3.1 (48K) ENTRY POINT FOR CODE TO IMPLEMENT 'WRITE' COMMAND
$A4B0 (-23376) \SE\                  DOS 3.1 (48K) ENTRY POINT FOR CODE TO IMPLEMENT 'READ' COMMAND
$A4D1 (-23343) \SE\                  DOS 3.2/3.3 (48K) ENTRY POINT OF CODE TO IMPLEMENT 'RUN' COMMAND
$A4E4 (-23324) \SE\                  DOS 3.1 (48K) ENTRY POINT FOR CODE TO IMPLEMENT 'INIT' COMMAND
$A4E5 (-23323) \SE\                  DOS 3.2/3.3 (48K) ENTRY POINT TO WHICH DOS TRANSFERS TO RUN A NEW INTEGER BASIC
                                     PROGRAM
$A4F0 (-23312) \SE\                  DOS 3.2/3.3 (48K) ENTRY POINT OF CODE TO IMPLEMENT 'CHAIN' COMMAND
$A4FC (-23300) \SE\                  DOS 3.2/3.3\APPLESOFT TRANSFER POINT USED BY DOS 3.2 TO JUMP INTO EITHER CHAIN OR
                                     RUN OF AN APPLESOFT (ROM) PROGRAM
$A501 (-23295) \SE\                  DOS 3.1 (48K) ENTRY POINT FOR CODE TO IMPLEMENT 'NOMON' COMMAND
$A506 (-23290) \SE\                  DOS 3.2/3.3\APPLESOFT TRANSFER POINT USED BY DOS 3.2 TO JUMP INTO EITHER CHAIN OR
                                     RUN OF AN APPLESOFT (RAM OR DISK VERSION) PROGRAM
$A50D (-23283) \SE\                  DOS 3.1 (48K) ENTRY POINT FOR CODE TO IMPLEMENT 'FP' COMMAND
$A510 (-23280) \SE\                  DOS 3.2/3.3 (48K) ENTRY POINT OF CODE TO IMPLEMENT 'WRITE' COMMAND
$A51B (-23269) \SE\                  DOS 3.2/3.3 (48K) ENTRY POINT OF CODE TO IMPLEMENT 'READ' COMMAND
$A531 (-23247) \SE\                  DOS 3.1 (48K) ENTRY POINT FOR CODE TO IMPLEMENT 'INT' COMMAND
$A54F (-23217) \SE\                  DOS 3.2/3.3 (48K) ENTRY POINT OF CODE TO IMPLEMENT 'INIT' COMMAND
$A54F (-23217) \SE\                  DOS 3.1 (48K) ENTRY POINT FOR CODE TO IMPLEMENT 'EXEC' COMMAND
$A566 (-23194) \SE\                  DOS 3.1 (48K) ENTRY POINT FOR CODE TO IMPLEMENT 'POSITION' COMMAND
$A56E (-23186) \SE\                  DOS 3.2/3.3 (48K) ENTRY POINT OF CODE TO IMPLEMENT 'CATALOG' COMMAND
$A57A (-23174) \SE\                  DOS 3.2/3.3 (48K) ENTRY POINT OF CODE TO IMPLEMENT 'FP' COMMAND
$A59E (-23138) \SE\                  DOS 3.2/3.3 (48K) ENTRY POINT OF CODE TO IMPLEMENT 'INT' COMMAND
$A5C6 (-23098) \SE\                  DOS 3.2/3.3 (48K) ENTRY POINT OF CODE TO IMPLEMENT 'EXEC' COMMAND
$A5DD (-23075) \SE\                  DOS 3.2/3.3 (48K) ENTRY POINT OF CODE TO IMPLEMENT 'POSITION' COMMAND
$A60E (-23026)                       DOS 3.2/3.3 - CODE WHICH STARTS THE READ PROCESS
$A626 (-23002)                       DOS 3.2/3.3 - CODE WHICH STARTS THE WRITE PROCESS
$A644 (-22972)                       DOS 3.2/3.3 - CODE WHICH STORES DATA COMING FROM TEXT FILE INTO KEYBOARD BUFFER.
                                     USED BY EXEC COMMAND
$A679 (-22919)                       DOS 3.2/3.3 - CODE TO CLOSE FILES AND EXIT DOS
$A69D (-22883)                       DOS 3.2/3.3 - CODE TO SET UP ADDRESS OF NAME SECTION OF NEXT FILE
$A6AB (-22869)                       DOS 3.2/3.3 - CODE TO CLOSE THE BUFFER LAST USED
$A6C4 (-22844)                       DOS 3.2/3.3 - PRINTS 'SYNTAX ERROR'
$A6C8 (-22840)                       DOS 3.2/3.3 - PRINT 'NO BUFFERS AVAILABLE'
$A6CC (-22836)                       DOS 3.2/3.3 - PRINTS 'PROGRAM TOO LARGE'
$A6D0 (-22832)                       DOS 3.2/3.3 - PRINTS 'FILE TYPE MISMATCH'
$A6D2 (-22830)                       DOS 3.2/3.3 - START OF ERROR PROCESSING ROUTINE. ENTER WITH ERROR NUMBER IN A-REG
$A6D5 (-22827)                       DOS 3.2/3.3 - PRINTS OTHER ERROR MESSAGES BY MESSAGE NUMBER CONTAINED IN $AA5C
$A702 (-22782)                       DOS 3.2/3.3 - ANOTHER PART OF ROUTINE THAT PRINTS APPROPRIATE DOS ERROR MESSAGES
                                     (?)
$A743 (-22717)                       DOS 3.2/3.3 - MOVES NAME FROM THE NAME BUFFER TO THE NAME SECTION OF THE FILE
                                     BUFFER
$A764 (-22684)                       DOS 3.2/3.3 - ATTEMPTS TO FIND A FILE BUFFER ALREADY IN USE BY THE NAME GIVEN
$A7C4 (-22588)                       DOS 3.2/3.3 - CHECKS FILE TYPE
$A7D4 (-22572)                       DOS 3.2/3.3 - SETS UP FILE BUFFERS AND ADDRESSES (USED BY MAXFILES)
$A7E0~$A863 (-22560~-22429) [(DOS 3.1 COMMAND TBL)] \PB\DOS 3.1 COMMAND TABLE (DOS 3.1 - 48K APPLE ONLY!)
$A851 (-22447)                       DOS 3.2/3.3 - RESTORES DOS HOOKS (SAVE ADDRESSES OF CHARACTER INPUT AND OUTPUT
                                     ROUTINES CURRENTLY IN USE AND RECONNECT DOS)
$A884~$AAFC (-22396~-21764)          DOS 3.2/3.3 (48K) PARAMETER AREA FOR SYSTEM SECTION
$A884~$A908 (-22396~-22264) [(DOS 3.2/3.3 COMMAND TBL)] \PB\DOS 3.2 (48K) COMMAND NAME TABLE OF DOS COMMAND DECODER
                                     (TABLE-DRIVEN COMMAND PARSER). CONTAINS NAMES OF DOS
                                     COMMANDS WITH LAST BYTE OF EACH NAME HAVING HIGH (7TH) BIT
                                     SET; OTHER BYTES HAVE IT CLEAR. THIS PERMITS CLOSE PACKING
                                     FOR SEQUENTIAL SEARCH. EOT IS $00 BYTE
------------------------------------------------------------------------------------------------
```

```
$A909~$A970 (-22263~-22160) \PB\      DOS 3.2/3.3 (48K) PARAMETER VALIDITY TABLE OF DOS COMMAND DECODER. USED TO CHECK
                                      VALIDITY OF VARIOUS PARAMETERS AGAINST USABILITY WITH VARIOUS COMMANDS. USES
                                      2-BYTE MASKS. ONE BYTE USED TO DETERMINED WHAT TYPE(S) OF EXTRA DATA ARE NEEDED
                                      BY A COMMAND; THE OTHER FOR WHAT FILE TYPE TO CREATE OR LOOK FOR
$A941 (-22207)                        DOS 3.2/3.3 -TABLE CONTAINING THE LETTERS V~D~S~L~R~B~A~C. THESE ARE USED AS
                                      SINGLE-CHARACTER KEYWORDS WHICH MAY APPEAR ON DOS COMMANDS. USED WHEN CHECKING
                                      FOR THIS OPTIONAL DATA
$A94B~$A954 (-22197~-22188)           DOS 3.2/3.3 -TABLE OF BYTES FOR. TABLE CONTAINS OPERAND MASKS ASSOCIATED WITH
                                      EACH OPERAND. IF HIGH ORDER BIT IS CLEAR IT INDICATES A NUMERIC ASSOCIATED WITH
                                      IT DETERMINING WHAT TYPE OF OPTIONAL DATA TO LOOK FOR. TABLE CONTAINS OPERAND
                                      MASKS ASSOCIATED WITH EACH OPERAND. IF HIGH ORDER BIT IS CLEAR IT INDICATES A
                                      NUMERIC ASSOCIATED WITH IT
$A955~$A970 (-22187~-22160)           DOS 3.2/3.3 -TABLE OF MINIMUM AND MAXIMUM RANGES FOR V~D~S~L~R~B~A
$A971~$AA3E (-22159~-21954) \PB\      DOS 3.2/3.3 (48K) ERROR MESSAGE TABLE (TEXT OF MESSAGES) NOTE: $AA3F~$AA4F IS
                                      INDEX TABLE FOR SELECTION OF SPECIFIC MESSAGE FROM THIS BLOCK
$AA3F~$AA4F (-21953~-21937) \PB\      DOS 3.2/3.3 (48K) INDEX TABLE FOR ERROR MESSAGES AT $A971
$A8CD~$A980 (-22323~-22144) [(DOS 3.1 ERROR MSGS)] \PB\DOS 3.1 ERROR MSG TABLE (DOS 3.1 - 48K APPLE ONLY!)
$A971~$AA3E (-22159~-21954) [(DOS 3.2/3.3 ERROR MSGS)] \PB\DOS 3.2/3.3 ERROR MESSAGES (DOS 3.2/3.3 - 48K APPLE ONLY!)
$A996~$A997 (-22122~-22121) [COUT] \P2\DOS 3.1 INTERNAL HOOK ENTRY ADDRESS TO OUTPUT A CHARACTER
$A998~$A999 (-22120~-22119) [CIN] \P2\DOS 3.1  INTERNAL HOOK ENTRY ADDRESS TO INPUT A CHARACTER
$A9A3~$A9A4 (-22109~-22108) \P2\      LENGTH OF MOST RECENTLY BLOADED FILE (DOS 3.1 ONLY - 48K)
$A9B5~$A9B6 (-22091~-22090) \P2\      STARTING ENTRY ADDRESS OF BLOADED FILE (DOS 3.1 ONLY - 48K)
$AA0B (-22005)                        START OF LIST OF POINTERS TO SECTIONS OF DOS 3.1 I/O PACKAGES
$AA3F~$B2CE (-21953~-19762) \SB\      DOS 3.1 I/O PACKAGE (48K APPLE) (SEE $AAFD FOR CORRESPONDING PKG DOS
                                      3.2~3.2.1~3.3)
$AA42~$AAC8 (-21950~-21816) \PB\      DOS 3.2/3.3 (48K) BLOCK OF IMPORTANT VARIABLES (PARAMETERS)
$AA4F~$AA50 (-21937~-21936) \P2\      DOS 3.2/3.3 (48K) CURRENT FILE BUFFER POINTER
$AA51 (-21935) \P1\                   DOS 3.2/3.3 STATE-MACHINE INPUT-STATE CONTROL PARAMETER
$AA52 (-21934) \P1\                   DOS 3.2/3.3 (48K) STATE-MACHINE OUTPUT-STATE-CONTROL PARAMETER (0-7)
$AA53~$AA54 (-21933~-21932) \P2\      DOS 3.2/3.3 (48K) OUTPUT HOOK - I.E. ADDRESS OF CHARACTER OUTPUT ROUTINE WHICH
                                      WAS IN CONTROL WHEN DOS WAS RECONNECTED (DEFAULT $FDF0)
$AA55~$AA56 (-21931~-21930) \P2\      DOS 3.2/3.3 (48K) INPUT HOOK - I.E. ADDRESS OF CHARACTER INPUT ROUTINE WHICH WAS
                                      IN CONTROL WHEN DOS WAS RECONNECTED (DEFAULT $FD1B)
$AA57 (-21929) \P1\                   DOS 3.2/3.3 (48K) CURRENT NUMBER OF DOS BUFFERS. DEFAULT=3; CHANGED BY SETTING
                                      MAXFILES
$AA59 (-21927) \P1\                   DOS 3.2/3.3 (48K) TEMPORARY DOS STORAGE FOR S-REGISTER
$AA5A (-21926) \P1\                   DOS 3.2/3.3 (48K) TEMPORARY DOS STORAGE FOR X-REGISTER
$AA5B (-21925) \P1\                   DOS 3.2/3.3 (48K) TEMPORARY DOS STORAGE FOR Y-REGISTER
$AA5C (-21924) \P1\                   DOS 3.2/3.3 (48K) TEMPORARY DOS STORAGE FOR A-REGISTER
$AA5C (-21924) \P1\                   DOS 3.2/3.3 (48K) UPON ENCOUNTERING A DOS ERROR CONTAINS DOS ERROR CODE USED AS
                                      INDEX INTO TABLE AT $AA3F OUTPUT OF WHICH IS USED AS INDEX TO ERROR TEXT TABLE AT
                                      $A971
$AA5D (-21923) \P1\                   DOS 3.2/3.3 (48K) LINE BUFFER INDEX (DISPLACEMENT)
$AA5E (-21922) \P1\                   DOS 3.2/3.3 (48K) MON-NOMON STATUS PARAMETERS MASK
$AA5F (-21921) \P1\                   DOS 3.2/3.3 (48K) COMMAND NUMBER
$AA60~$AA61 (-21920~-21919) \P2\      DOS 3.2/3.3 (48K) BLOCK LENGTH (FOUND L$ FROM A 'BLOAD')
$AA60~$AA61 (-21920~-21919) \P2\      DOS 3.2/3.3 (48K) - CONTAINS LENGTH OF LOADED BASIC PROGRAM
$AA62 (-21918) \P1\                   DOS 3.2/3.3 (48K) STORES COMMAND NUMBER
$AA63 (-21917) \P1\                   DOS 3.2/3.3 (48K) TEMP 1A
$AA64 (-21916) \P1\                   DOS 3.2/3.3 (48K) TEMP 2A
$AA65 (-21915) \P1\                   DOS 3.2/3.3 (48K) COMMAND INPUT OPTIONS
```

```
$AA66~$AA74 (-21914~-21900)          DOS 3.2/3.3 (48K) KEYWORD VALUES PARSED FROM COMMAND AND/OR DEFAULTED
$AA66~$AA67 (-21914~-21913) \P2\     DOS 3.2/3.3 (48K) COMMAND (OR DEFAULT) VOLUME
$AA68~$AA69 (-21912~-21911) \P2\     DOS 3.2/3.3 (48K) COMMAND (OR DEFAULT) DRIVE
$AA6A~$AA6B (-21910~-21909) \P2\     DOS 3.2/3.3 (48K) COMMAND (OR DEFAULT) SLOT
$AA6C~$AA6D (-21908~-21907) \P2\     DOS 3.2/3.3 (48K) COMMAND L-VALUE (LENGTH)
$AA6E~$AA6F (-21906~-21905) \P2\     DOS 3.2/3.3 (48K) COMMAND R-VALUE (RECORD NUMBER)
$AA70~$AA71 (-21904~-21903) \P2\     DOS 3.2/3.3 (48K) COMMAND B-VALUE (BYTE NUMBER)
$AA72~$AA73 (-21902~-21901) \P2\     DOS 3.2/3.3 (48K) COMMAND A-VALUE (ADDRESS)
$AA72~$AA73 (-21902~-21901) \P2\     CONTAINS START ADDRESS OF MOST RECENTLY BLOAD-ED PROGRAM OR DATA (DOS 3.2/3.3 -
                                     48K APPLE)
$AA74 (-21900) \P1\                  DOS 3.2/3.3 (48K) DOS 'C' 'I' & 'O' BITS
$AA75~$AA92 (-21899~-21870) \PB\     DOS 3.2/3.3 (48K) START OF LAST FILE NAME USED IN A DOS COMMAND. THIS IS NORMALLY
                                     FILE NAME OF BUFFER #3. IF RUN COMMAND USED WITHOUT FILE NAME THIS FIELD IS SET
                                     TO BLANKS. AT BOOT THIS AREA CONTAINS THE NAME OF THE GREETING PROGRAM
$AA93~$AAB0 (-21869~-21840) \PB\     DOS 3.2/3.3 (48K) START OF FILE NAME - BUFFER #2
$AAB1 (-21839) \P1\                  DOS 3.2/3.3 (48K) DEFAULT NUMBER OF FILE BUFFERS (3)
$AAB2 (-21838) \P1\                  DOS 3.2/3.3 (48K) COMMAND CHARACTER (CTRL-D)
$AAB3 (-21837) \P1\                  DOS 3.2/3.3 (48K) EXEC FILE STATE (DIRECT~ DEFERRED ETC.)
$AAB4~$AAB5 (-21836~-21835) \P2\     DOS 3.2/3.3 (48K) EXEC FILE BUFFER POINTER
$AAB6 (-21834) \P1\                  DOS 3.2/3.3 (48K) APPLESOFT-INTEGER BASIC SWITCH ($00=INTEGER BASIC;$40=ROM
                                     APPLESOFT;$80=RAM APPLESOFT)
$AAB7 (-21833) \P1\                  DOS 3.2/3.3 (48K) APPLESOFT - BEGIN RUN SWITCH ($00=NO;$40 OR $80=YES)
$AAB8~$AAC0 (-21832~-21824) \PB\     TEXT WORD 'APPLESOFT' (NAME OF DOS 3.2/3.3 FP FILE USED TO GET DISK APPLESOFT)
$AAC1~$AAC2 (-21823~-21822) \P2\     DOS 3.2/3.3 (48K) ADDRESS POINTER TO IOB (RWTS BUFFER) NOTE: THIS IS LOADED INTO
                                     Y & A-REGS WHEN $03E3 IS BRANCHED TO
$AAC3~$AAC4 (-21821~-21820) \P2\     DOS 3.2/3.3 (48K) ADDRESS POINTER TO VTOC BUFFER (BUFFER FOR TRACK/SECTOR LIST -
                                     USED BY RWTS
$AAC5~$AAC6 (-21819~-21818) \P2\     DOS 3.2/3.3 (48K) ADDRESS POINTER TO SYS BUFFER (BUFFER FOR DATA - USED BY RWTS)
$AAC7~$AAC8 (-21817~-21816) \P2\     DOS 3.2/3.3 (48K) ADDRESS POINTER TO TOP OF RAM+1
$AAC9~$AAFC (-21815~-21764) \SB\     DOS 3.2/3.3 (48K)  I/O PACKAGE COMMANDS FUNCTIONAL-CODE LOOK-UP TABLE. THIS TABLE
                                     IS USED AT $AB14 TO $AB1E TO JUMP TO CORRECT I-O ROUTINE. $B5BB IS USED TO CHOOSE
                                     WHICH I-O ROUTINE WILL BE CALLED
$AAC9~$AACA (-21815~-21814) \P2\     DOS 3.2/3.3 (48K) I-O PKG ADDRESS FOR 'GOOD RETURN' ($B37F-1)
$AACB~$AACC (-21813~-21812) \P2\     DOS 3.2/3.3 (48K) I-O PKG ADDRESS FOR 'OPEN FILE' ($AB22-1)
$AACD~$AACE (-21811~-21810) \P2\     DOS 3.2/3.3 (48K) I-O PKG ADDRESS FOR 'CLOSE FILE' ($AC06-1)
$AACF~$AAD0 (-21809~-21808) \P2\     DOS 3.2/3.3 (48K) I-O PKG ADDRESS FOR 'READ FROM FILE' ($$AC58-1)
$AAD1~$AAD2 (-21807~-21806) \P2\     DOS 3.2/3.3 (48K) I-O PKG ADDRESS FOR 'WRITE TO FILE' ($AC70-1)
$AAD3~$AAD4 (-21805~-21804) \P2\     DOS 3.2/3.3 (48K) I-O PKG ADDRESS FOR 'DELETE FILE' ($AD2B-1)
$AAD5~$AAD6 (-21803~-21802) \P2\     DOS 3.2/3.3 (48K) I-O PKG ADDRESS FOR 'PRINT CATALOG' ($AD98-1)
$AAD7~$AAD8 (-21801~-21800) \P2\     DOS 3.2/3.3 (48K) I-O PKG ADDRESS FOR 'LOCK A FILE' ($ACEF-1)
$AAD9~$AADA (-21799~-21798) \P2\     DOS 3.2/3.3 (48K) I-O PKG ADDRESS FOR 'UNLOCK A FILE' ($ACF6-1)
$AADB~$AADC (-21797~-21796) \P2\     DOS 3.2/3.3 (48K) I-O PKG ADDRESS FOR 'RENAME FILE' ($AC3A-1)
$AADD~$AADE (-21795~-21794) \P2\     DOS 3.2/3.3 (48K) I-O PKG ADDRESS FOR 'POSITION FILE' ($AD12-1)
$AADF~$AAE0 (-21793~-21792) \P2\     DOS 3.2/3.3 (48K) I-O PKG ADDRESS FOR 'FORMAT DISK (INIT)' ($AE8E-1)
$AAE1~$AAE2 (-21791~-21790) \P2\     DOS 3.2/3.3 (48K) I-O PKG ADDRESS FOR 'VERIFY FILE' ($AD18)
$AAE3~$AAE4 (-21789~-21788) \P2\     DOS 3.2/3.3 (48K) I-O PKG ADDRESS FOR GOOD RETURN ($B37F-1) [DUMMY ENTRY IN
                                     TABLE?]
$AAE5~$AAF0 (-21787~-21776) \PB\     DOS 3.2/3.3 (48K) I-O PKG READ COMMAND ENTRY-VECTOR TABLE. THIS TABLE USED AT
                                     $AC58 TO $AC69 TO JUMP TO CORRECT READ ROUTINE. THE VALUE OF $B5BC IS USED TO GET
                                     THE CORRECT ENTRY AND A JUMP IS MADE TO THERE
$AAE5~$AAE6 (-21787~-21786) \P2\     DOS 3.2/3.3 (48K) I-O PKG READ COMMAND ENTRY-VECTOR FOR 'GOOD RETURN' ($B37F-1)
```

$AAE7~$AAE8 (-21785~-21784) \P2\	DOS 3.2/3.3 (48K) I-O PKG READ COMMAND ENTRY-VECTOR FOR 'READ NEXT BYTE' ($AC8A-1)
$AAE9~$AAEA (-21783~-21782) \P2\	DOS 3.2/3.3 (48K) I-O PKG READ COMMAND ENTRY-VECTOR FOR 'READ NEXT BLOCK' ($AC96-1)
$AAEB~$AAEC (-21781~-21780) \P2\	DOS 3.2/3.3 (48K) I-O PKG READ COMMAND ENTRY-VECTOR FOR 'READ SPECIFIC BYTE' ($AC93-1)
$AAED~$AAEE (-21779~-21778) \P2\	DOS 3.2/3.3 (48K) I-O PKG READ COMMAND ENTRY-VECTOR FOR 'READ SPECIFIC BLOCK' ($AC93-1)
$AAEF~$AAF0 (-21777~-21776) \P2\	DOS 3.2/3.3 (48K) I-O PKG READ COMMAND ENTRY-VECTOR FOR 'GOOD RETURN' (DUMMY??)($B37F-1)
$AAF1~$AAFC (-21775~-21764) \PB\	DOS 3.2/3.3 (48K) I-O PKG WRITE COMMAND ENTRY-VECTOR TABLE. THIS TABLE IS USED AT $AC70 TO $AC86 TO JUMP TO THE CORRECT WRITE ROUTINE. THE VALUE OF $B5BC IS USED TO SPECIFY WHICH ROUTINE WILL BE JUMPED TO
$AAF1~$AAF2 (-21775~-21774) \P2\	DOS 3.2/3.3 (48K) I-O PKG WRITE COMMAND ENTRY-VECTOR FOR 'GOOD RETURN' ($B37F-1)
$AAF3~$AAF4 (-21773~-21772) \P2\	DOS 3.2/3.3 (48K) I-O PKG WRITE COMMAND ENTRY-VECTOR FOR 'WRITE NEXT BYTE' ($ACBE-1)
$AAF5~$AAF6 (-21771~-21770) \P2\	DOS 3.2/3.3 (48K) I-O PKG WRITE COMMAND ENTRY-VECTOR FOR 'WRITE NEXT BLOCK' ($ACCA-1)
$AAF7~$AAF8 (-21769~-21768) \P2\	DOS 3.2/3.3 (48K) I-O PKG WRITE COMMAND ENTRY-VECTOR FOR 'WRITE SPECIFIC BYTE' ($ACBB-1)
$AAF9~$AAFA (-21767~-21766) \P2\	DOS 3.2/3.3 (48K) I-O PKG WRITE COMMAND ENTRY-VECTOR FOR 'WRITE SPECIFIC BLOCK' ($ACC7-1)
$AAFB~$AAFC (-21765~-21764) \P2\	DOS 3.2/3.3 (48K) I-O PKG WRITE COMMAND ENTRY-VECTOR FOR 'GOOD RETURN' ($BE7F-1) [DUMMY ENTRY IN TABLE?]
$AAFD~$B5FF (-21763~-18945) \SB\	DOS 3.2/3.3 (48K) FILE MANAGER I-O PACKAGE (INCLUDING PARAMETER & SYSTEM BUFFER AREAS). CONTAINS CODE TO PERFORM FUNCTIONS LIKE OPEN~ CLOSE~ RENAME~ DELETE~ WRITE BYTES TO A FILE~ READ BYTES FROM A FILE ETC. NOTE: REFERENCED FROM PAGE 3 BY BRANCH FROM $03D6
$AAFD~$B395 (-21763~-19562) \SB\	DOS 3.2/3.3 (48K) FILE MANAGER (I-O PACKAGE) CODE (LESS PARAMETER & SYSTEM BUFFER AREAS)
$AAFD (-21763) \SE\	DOS 3.2/3.3 FILE MANAGER (I-O PACKAGE) ENTRY POINT. REFERENCED FROM PAGE 3 BY A BRANCH FROM $03D6
$AB22 (-21726) \SE\	DOS 3.2/3.3 (48K) I-O PKG ROUTINE TO OPEN FILE
$AB28 (-21720)	DOS 3.2/3.3 (48K). READS VTOC & DIRECTORY ATTEMPTING TO FIND AN ENTRY WITH SAME NAME AS THAT GIVEN. IF NOT FOUND CHECKS TABLE OF MASKS TO SEE IF IT IS ALLOWED TO CREATE A FILE. IF IT IS ALLOWED IT DOES SO; IF NOT EXITS WITH 'FILE NOT FOUND' OR 'LANGUAGE NOT AVAILABLE'
$ABDC (-21540)	DOS 3.2/3.3 (48K) - CLEARS MISCELLANEOUS INFO HARDWARE BUFFER;SETS VOLUME NUMBER DRIVE NUMBER AND SLOT NUMBER
$AC06 (-21498) \SE\	DOS 3.2/3.3 (48K) I-O PKG ROUTINE TO CLOSE FILE (UPDATES VTOC~ TRACK BIT MAP AND SECTOR COUNT OF DIRECTORY ENTRY AS NEEDED)
$AC3A (-21446) \SE\	DOS 3.2/3.3 (48K) I-O PKG ROUTINE TO RENAME FILE (FINDS DIRECTORY ENTRY~ STORES NEW NAME IN ENTRY~ THEN WRITES THAT DIRECTORY SECTOR BACK TO DISK)
$AC58 (-21416) \SE\	DOS 3.2/3.3 (48K) I-O PKG ROUTINE TO READ FROM FILE
$AC70 (-21392) \SE\	DOS 3.2/3.3 (48K) I-O PKG ROUTINE TO WRITE TO FILE
$AC87 (-21369) \SE\	DOS 3.2/3.3 (48K) I-O PKG ROUTINE TO READ SPECIFIC BYTE
$AC8A (-21366) \SE\	DOS 3.2/3.3 (48K) I-O PKG ROUTINE TO READ NEXT BYTE
$AC93 (-21357) \SE\	DOS 3.2/3.3 (48K) I-O PKG ROUTINE TO READ SPECIFIC BLOCK
$ACBB (-21317) \SE\	DOS 3.2/3.3 (48K) I-O PKG ROUTINE TO WRITE SPECIFIC BYTE
$AC96 (-21354) \SE\	DOS 3.2/3.3 (48K) I-O PKG ROUTINE TO READ NEXT BLOCK
$ACBE (-21314) \SE\	DOS 3.2/3.3 (48K) I-O PKG ROUTINE TO WRITE NEXT BYTE
$ACC7 (-21305) \SE\	DOS 3.2/3.3 (48K) I-O PKG ROUTINE TO WRITE SPECIFIC BLOCK

```
$ACCA (-21302) \SE\            DOS 3.2/3.3 (48K) I-O PKG ROUTINE TO WRITE NEXT BLOCK
$ACEF (-21265) \SE\            DOS 3.2/3.3 (48K) I-O PKG ROUTINE TO LOCK A FILE
$ACF6 (-21258) \SE\            DOS 3.2/3.3 (48K) I-O PKG ROUTINE TO UNLOCK A FILE
$AD12 (-21230) \SE\            DOS 3.2/3.3 (48K) I-O PKG ROUTINE TO POSITION FILE
$AD18 (-21224) \SE\            DOS 3.2/3.3 (48K) I-O PKG ROUTINE TO VERIFY FILE
$AD2B (-21205) \SE\            DOS 3.2/3.3 (48K) I-O PKG ROUTINE TO DELETE FILE
$AD54 (-21164)                 DOS 3.2/3.3 (48K) PART OF DELETE ROUTINE WHICH FREES SECTORS USED BY DELETED FILE
$AD98 (-21096) \SE\            DOS 3.2/3.3 (48K) I-O PKG ROUTINE TO PRINT CATALOG
$AE39 (-20935)                 DOS 3.2/3.3 (48K) PART OF CATALOG ROUTINE RESPONSIBLE FOR PAUSING DURING A
                               CATALOG LISTING. TO DISABLE THIS INSTRUCTION SIMPLY PATCH OVER IT WITH 3 NOP'S
$AE42 (-20926)                 DOS 3.2/3.3 (48K) PART OF CATALOG ROUTINE WHICH PRINTS THE NUMBER IN $0044 AS 3
                               DIGIT ASCII
$AE6A (-20886)                 DOS 3.2/3.3 (48K) MOVES MISCELLANEOUS INFO FROM THE FILE BUFFER TO THE I-O PKG
                               BUFFER
$AE7E (-20866)                 DOS 3.2/3.3 (48K) MOVES MISCELLANEOUS INFO FROM THE FILE BUFFER TO THE I-O PKG
                               BUFFER
$AE8E (-20850) \SE\            DOS 3.2/3.3 (48K) I-O PKG ROUTINE TO FORMAT A DISK (INIT)
$AF1D (-20707)                 DOS 3.2/3.3 (48K)  WRITES DATA SECTION OF FILE BUFFER TO DISK
$AF34 (-20684)                 DOS 3.2/3.3 (48K)  WRITES TRACK/SECTOR LIST SECTION OF FILE BUFFER TO DISK
$AF4B (-20661)                 DOS 3.2/3.3 (48K)  SETS HARDWARE POINTER TO THE TRACK AND SECTOR LIST SECTION OF
                               THE FILE BUFFER BEING USED
$AF5E (-20642)                 DOS 3.2/3.3 (48K)  CHECKS POSITION IN FILE. IF OUT OF CURRENT SECTOR READS/WRITES
                               NEXT SECTOR~ UPDATES VTOC BUFFER~ UPDATES TRACK/SECTOR LIST SECTION OF FILE
                               BUFFER IF IN WRITE MODE
$AFDC (-20516)                 DOS 3.2/3.3 (48K)  READS FROM DISK INTO DATA SECTION OF FILE BUFFER
$AFE4 (-20508)                 DOS 3.2/3.3 (48K)  SETS HARDWARE POINTERS TO DATA SECTION OF FILE BUFFER BEING
                               USED
$AFF7 (-20489)                 DOS 3.2/3.3 (48K)  READS VTOC TO ITS BUFFER ($B3BB~$B4BA)
$AFFB (-20485)                 DOS 3.2/3.3 (48K)  WRITES VOTC FROM ITS BUFFER ($B3BB~$B4BA)
$B011 (-20463)                 DOS 3.2/3.3 (48K)  READS A DIRECTORY SECTOR INTO ITS BUFFER ($B4BB~$B5BA).
                               INITIALLY READS SECTOR A. SUCCESSIVE ENTRIES INTO THIS SUBROUTINE READ SUCCESSIVE
                               SECTORS FROM DISK. WHEN ALL SECTORS READ AND SUBROUTINE CALLED AGAIN IT MAY EXIT
                               WITH CARRY SET
$B037 (-20425)                 DOS 3.2/3.3 (48K)  WRITES CURRENT DIRECTORY SECTOR FROM BUFFER TO DISK
$B052 (-20398)                 DOS 3.2/3.3 (48K)  SETS UP IOB FOR DIRECTORY SECTORS; GOES TO RWTS
$B0A0 (-20320)                 DOS 3.2/3.3 (48K)  NO ERROR EXIT TO $B052
$B0A1 (-20319)                 DOS 3.2/3.3 (48K)  START OF ERROR-HANDING ROUTINE FOR $B052
$B0B6 (-20298)                 DOS 3.2/3.3 (48K)  CHECKS POSITION IN FILE; READS/WRITES NEXT SECTOR AS NEEDED
$B134 (-20172)                 DOS 3.2/3.3 (48K)  INITIALIZES DATA SECTION OF FILE BUFFER TO ALL ZEROES
$B15B (-20133)                 DOS 3.2/3.3 (48K)  SETS NEXT POSITION IN FILE
$B194 (-20076)                 DOS 3.2/3.3 (48K)  INCREMENTS POSITION IN FILE
$B1A2 (-20062)                 DOS 3.2/3.3 SETS NEXT RAM ADDRESS
$B1B5 (-20043)                 DOS 3.2/3.3 CALCULATES HOW MUCH RAM IS LEFT
$B1C9~$B213 (-20023~-19941)    DOS 3.3 - LOCATE OR ALLOCATE A DIRECTORY ENTRY IN THE CATALOG; READ THE VTOC
                               SECTOR ($AFF7); SET $0042~$0043 TO POINT TO FILE NAME BEING LOOKED FOR; SET PAGE
                               NUMBER TO 1 (LOCATE FILE).
$B1C9 (-20023)                 DOS 3.2/3.3 READS VTOC (VOLUME TABLE OF CONTENTS) AND SUCCESSIVE ENTRIES
                               ATTEMPTING TO FIND SPECIFIED FILE NAME
$B21C~$B22F (-19940~-19921)    DOS 3.3 - COPY FILE NAME TO DIRECTORY ENTRY. ADVANCE INDEX TO FILE NAME FIELD IN
                               DIRECTORY ENTRY; COPY 30 BYTE FILENAME TO DIRECTORY ENTRY; RELOAD DIRECTORY INDEX
                               AND RETURN TO CALLER
```

$B21E (-19938)	DOS 3.2/3.3 PUTS NAME OF FILE INTO DIRECTORY
$B224 (-19932)	DOS 3.2/3.3 SETS NEXT SECTOR; UPDATES VTOC BUFFER
$B230 (-19920)	DOS 3.3 ADVANCE INDEX TO NEXT DIRECTORY ENTRY IN SECTOR; ADD 35 (LENGTH OF ENTRY) TO INDEX; TEST FOR END OF SECTOR AND RETURN TO CALLER
$B23A~$B243 (-19910~-19901)	DOS 3.3 SWITCH TO SECOND PASS IN DIRECTORY SCAN. IF ON PASS ONE~ SWITHC TO PASS 2 AND GOTO $B1D8; IF ON PASS TWO EXIT FILE MANAGER WITH 'DISK FULL' ERROR
$B244~$B2C2 (-19900~-19774)	DOS 3.3 ALLOCATE A DISK SECTOR
$B2C3~$B2DC (-19773~-19748)	DOS 3.3 RELEASE PRE-ALLOCATED SECTORS IN CURRENT TRACK AND CHECKPOINT THE VTOC.
$B2C3 (-19773)	DOS 3.2/3.3 UPDATES VTOC
$B2DD~$B2FF (-19747~-19713)	DOS 3.3 (48K) - FREE ONE OR MORE SECTORS BY SHIFTING MASK IN FILE MANAGER'S ALLOACTION AREA BACK INTO VTOC BIT MAP
$B2DD (-19747)	DOS 3.2/3.3 CALCULATES TRACK BIT MAP FOR VTOC
$B300~$B35E (-19712~-19618)	DOS 3.3 (48K) - CALCULATE FILE POSITION
$B35F~$B37D (-19617~-19587)	DOS 3.3 (48K) - ERROR EXISTS
$B35F (-19617)	DOS 3.3 (48K) - RC=1 "LANGUAGE NOT AVAILABLE"
$B363 (-19613)	DOS 3.3 (48K) - RC=2 "RANGE ERROR" (BAD OPCODE)
$B367 (-19609)	DOS 3.3 (48K) - RC=3 "RANGE ERROR" (BAD SUBCODE)
$B36B (-19605)	DOS 3.3 (48K) - RC=4 "WRITE PROTECTED"
$B36F (-19601)	DOS 3.3 (48K) - RC=5 "END OF DATA"
$B373 (-19597)	DOS 3.3 (48K) - RC=6 "FILE NOT FOUND"
$B37B (-19589)	DOS 3.3 (48K) - RC=A "FILE LOCKED"
$B37F~$B396 (-19585~-19562)	EXIT FILE MANAGER
$B37F (-19585) \SE\	DOS 3.2/3.3 (48K) FILE MANAGER (I-O) PKG GOOD RETURN (RETURN CODE =0; CLEAR CARRY FLAG AND GO TO $B386)
$B385 (-19579)	DOS 3.3 (48K) - EXIT SETTING CARRY FLAG TO INDICATE ERROR
$B386 (-19578)	DOS 3.3 (48K) - SAVE RETURN CODE IN PARAMLIST; CLEAR MONITOR STATUS REGISTER; SAVE FILE MANAGER WORKAREA TO FILE BUFFER ($AE7E); RESTORE PROCESSOR STATUS AND STACK REGISTER; EXIT TO ORIG CALLER OF FILE MANAGER
$B397~$B6FF (-19561~-18689)	DOS 3.2/3.3 (48K) FILE MANAGER (I-O PACKAGE) DATA AREA (PARAMETERS & SYSTEM BUFFER)
$B397~$B3A3 (-19561~-19549)	DOS 3.3 FILE MANAGER (I-O PACKAGE) SCRATCH SPACE
$B397 (-19561) \P2\	DOS 3.2/3.3 (48K) CONTAINS TRACK AND SECTOR ADDRESS OF MOST RECENTLY READ DIRECTORY (CATALOG) SECTOR
$B39B (-19557)	DOS 3.3 FILE MANAGER S-REGISTER SAVE AREA
$B39C (-19556)	DOS 3.3 FILE MANAGER DIRECTORY INDEX
$B39D (-19555)	DOS 3.3 FILE MANAGER CATALOG LINE COUNTER~ DIRECTOR LOOKUP FLAG ~ ETC
$B39E (-19554)	DOS 3.3 (48K) LOCK/UNLOCK MASK~ ALLOCATION FLAG ETC.
$B3A0 (-19552)	DOS 3.3 (48K) FOUR BYTE MASK USED BY INIT TO FREE AN ENTIRE TRACK IN THE VTOC BIT MAP
$B3A4~$B3A6 (-19548~-19546)	DOS 3.3 (48K) DECIMAL CONVERSION TABLE (1~10~100)
$B3A7~$B3AE (-19545~-19538)	DOS 3.3 (48K) FILE TYPE NAME TABLE USED BY CATALOG. FILE TYPES ARE T~I~A~B~S~R~A~B CORRESPONDING TO HEX VALUES OF $00~$02$04~$08~$10~$20 AND $40 RESPECTIVELY
$B3A7 (-19545)	DOS 3.2 (48K) CONTAINS 4 FILETYPE CHARACTERS T~ I~ A~ AND B
$B3AF~$B3BA (-19537~-19526)	DOS 3.2/3.3 (48K) CONTAINS CHARACTER STRING 'DISK VOLUME' FOR CATALOG COMMAND (IN REVERSE ORDER)
$B3BB~$B4BA (-19525~-19270)	DOS 3.2/3.3 (48K) VTOC SECTOR BUFFER PART OF SYSTEM BUFFER - CONTAINS THE MASTER TRACK/SECTOR BIT MAP SECTOR OR VOLUME TABLE OF CONTENTS
$B3BC (-19524)	TRACK~SECTOR OF FIRST DIRECTOR SECTOR
$B3BE (-19522)	DOS RELEASE NUMBER (1~2 OR 3 FOR 3.1~3.2 OR 3.3)
$B3C1 (-19519)	VOLUME NUMBER OF DISKETTE

```
$B3E2 (-19486)                      NUMBER OF ENTRIES IN EACH TRACK~SECTOR LIST SECTOR
$B3EB (-19477)                      TRACK TO ALLOCATE NEXT
$B3EC (-19476)                      DIRECTION OF TRACK ALLOCATION (+1 OR -1)
$B3EF (-19473) \P1\                 NUMBER OF TRACKS ON A DISK
$BEF0 (-16656) \P1\                 NUMBER OF SECTORS ON A DISK
$BEF1 (-16655) \P2\                 SECTOR SIZE IN BYTES
$B3F3~$B47B (-19469~-19333)         ARRAY OF 34 TRACK BIT MAPS
$B3F3 (-19469)                      TRACK 0 BIT MAP
$B3F4 (-19468)                      TRACK 1 BIT MAP
$B3F5 (-19467)                      TRACK 2 BIT MAP
$B3F6 (-19466)                      TRACK 3 BIT MAP
$B47A (-19334)                      TRACK 33 BIT MAP
$B47B (-19333)                      TRACK 34 BIT MAP
$B3EF~$B642 (-19473~-18878) \HB\    DOS 3.1 (48K) SYSTEM BUFFER (FOR CATALOG ETC.)(SEE $B4BB FOR DOS 3.2~3.2.1~3.3)
$B4BB~$B5BA (-19269~-19014)         DOS 3.2/3.3 DIRECTORY SECTOR BUFFER PART OF SYSTEM BUFFER. CONTAINS LAST ACCESSED
                                    DIRECTORY SECTORY SECTOR (ACCESS BY A CATALOG COMMAND OR ANY OTHER DOS COMMAND
                                    REQUIRING A DIRECTORY SECTORY SEARCH)
$B4BC (-19268)                      TRACK~SECTOR OF NEXT DIRECTORY SECTOR
$B4C6 (-19258)                      FIRST DIRECTORY ENTRY AND TRACK OF TRACK-SECTOR LIST
$B4C7 (-19257)                      SECTOR OF TRACK-SECTOR LIST
$B4C8 (-19256)                      FILE TYPE AND LOCK BIT
$B4C9 (-19255)                      FILENAME FIELD (30 BYTES)
$B4E7 (-19225)                      SIZE OF FILE IN SECTORS (INCLUDING TRACK~SECTOR LIST(S))
$B5BB~$B5D0 (-19013~-18992)         DOS 3.2/3.3 (48K) FILE MANAGER PARAMETER LIST
$B5BB (-19013)                      1ST BYTE BEYOND SYSTEM BUFFER. PAGE 3 ROUTINE AT $03DC LOADS Y-REG & A-REG TO
                                    POINT HERE
$B5BB (-19013) \P\                  DOS 3.2/3.3 (48K) I-O PKG 'OPCODE' PARAMETER USED TO CHOOSE WHICH I-O PKG
                                    'OPCODE' ROUTINE WILL BE CALLED
$B5BC (-19012)                      DOS 3.2/3.3 (48K) I-O PKG 'SUBCODE' PARAMETER USED TO CHOOSE WHICH READ OR WRITE
                                    OPTION IS TO BE USED
$B5BD~$B5C4 (-19011~-19004)         DOS 3.2/3.3 (48K) EIGHT BYTES OF PARAMETERS. PARAMETERS VARY ACCORDING TO
                                    'OPCODE' PARAMETER IN $B5BB
$B5C5 (-19003)                      DOS 3.2/3.3 FILE MANAAGER PARAMETER LIST RETURN CODE
$B5C7 (-19001)                      DOS 3.2/3.3 ADDRESS OF FILE MANAGER WORK AREA BUFFER
$B5C9 (-18999)                      DOS 3.2/3.3 ADDRESS OF TRACK/SECTOR LIST SECTOR BUFFER
$B5CB (-18997)                      DOS 3.2/3.3 (48K) ADDRESS OF DATA SECTOR BUFFER
$B5CD (-18995)                      DOS 3.2/3.3 (48K) ADDRESS OF NEXT DOS BUFFER ON CHAIN (NOT USED)
$B5D1~$B5FD (-18991~-18947)         DOS 3.2/3.3 FILE MANAGER WORK AREA
$B5D1 (-18991)                      FIRST TRACK-SECTOR LIST SECTOR'S TRACK & SECTOR
$B5D3 (-18989)                      CURRENT TRACK-SECTOR LIST SECTOR'S TRACK & SECTOR
$B5D5 (-18987)                      FLAGE: 80=T~S LIST NEEDS CHECKPOINT;40=DATA SECTOR NEEDS CHECKPOINT;20=VTOC
                                    SECTOR NEEDS CHECKPOINT;02 LAST OPERATION WAS WRITE
$B5D6 (-18986)                      CURRENT DATA SECTOR'S TRACK~SECTOR
$B5D8 (-18984)                      DIRECTORY SECTOR INDEX FOR FILE ENTRY
$B5D9 (-18983)                      INDEX INTO DIRECTORY SECTOR TO DIRECTORY ENTRY FOR FILE
$B5DA (-18982)                      NUMBER OF SECTORS DESCRIBED BY ON TRACK~SECTOR LIST
$B5DC (-18980)                      RELATIVE SECTOR NUMBER OF FIRST SECTOR IN LIST
$B5DE (-18978)                      RELATIVE SECTOR NUMBER +1 OF LAST SECTOR IN LIST
$B5E0 (-18976)                      RELATIVE SECTOR NUMBER OF LAST SECTOR READ
$B5E2 (-18974)                      SECTOR LENGTH IN BYTES
$B5E4 (-18972)                      FILE POSITION (3 BYTES); SECTOR OFFSET;BYTE OFFSET INTO THAT SECTOR
```

HEX LOCN (DEC LOCN) [NAME] \USE-TYPE\	DESCRIPTION
$B5E8 (-18968)	RECORD LENGTH FROM 'OPEN'
$B5EA (-18966)	RECORD NUMBER
$B5EC (-18964)	BYTE OFFSET INTO RECORD.
$B5EE (-18962)	NUMBER OF SECTORS IN FILE
$B5F0 (-18960)	SECTOR ALLOCATION AREA (6 BYTES). NEXT SECTOR TO ALLOCATE (SHIFT COUNT);TRACK BEING ALLOCATED;FOUR BYTE BIT MAP OF TRACK BEING ALLOCATED~ ROTATED TO NEXT SECTOR TO ALLOCATE
$B5F6 (-18954)	FILE TYPE
$B5F7 (-18953)	SLOT NUMBER *16
$B5F8 (-18952)	DRIVE NUMBER
$B5F9 (-18951)	VOLUME NUMBER (IN COMPLEMENT FORM)
$B5FA (-18950)	TRACK NUMBER
$B5FE~$B5FF (-18946~-18945)	DOS 3.2/3.3 NOT USED
$B600~$B6FF (-18944~-18689)	DOS 3.2/3.3 BOOT SECTOR BUFFER; I.E. BOOT 2 RWTS (READ-WRITE TRACK-SECTOR) IMAGE
$B600 (-18944)	DOS 3.3 (48K) START OF PHASE 2 (BOOT 1) IMAGE WHICH CAN BE WRITTEN TO INIT'ED DISKS ON TRACK 0 SECTOR 0
$B65D (-18851)	DOS 3.3 (48K) PATCH AREA STARTS HERE WITH APPEND PATCH
$B65E (-18850)	DOS 3.3 (48K) ANOTHER APPEND PATCH STARTS HERE
$B686 (-18810)	DOS 3.3 (48K) VERIFY PATCH
$B692 (-18798)	DOS 3.3 (48K) ANOTHER APPEND PATCH STARTS HERE
$B6FE (-18690)	DOS 3.3 (48K) PAGE ADDRESS OF FIRST PAGE IN PHASE 3 (BOOT 2)
$B6FF (-18689)	DOS 3.3 (48K) NUMBER OF SECTORS (PAGES) IN PHASE 3 (BOOT 2)
$B700 (-18688)	DOS 3.2 BOOTSTRAP LOADER FOR PHASE 3 (BOOT 2) OF DOS BOOT (PHASE 1 IN DISK CONTROLLER ROM; PHASE 2 IN PAGE 3 [$300-$3FF]). READS DRIVE1 CURRENT SLOT $B1 SECTORS AND TRACK 0 SECTOR A INTO RAM STARTING AT $1B00
$B700~$B749 (-18688~-18615)	DOS 3.3 BOOTSTRAP LOADER FOR PHASE 3 (BOOT 2) OF DOS BOOT (PHASE 2 IN $0800-$08FF). SETS RWTS PARAMETER LIST TO READ DOS FROM DISK; CALLS READ~WRITE GROUPP OF PAGES ($B793) & CREATES NEW STACK. ALSO CALLS $FE93 (SETVID) AND $FE89 (SETKBD) AND EXITS TO COLDSTART AT $9D84
$B74A~$B78C (-18614~-18548)	DOS 3.3 (48K) - WRITES DOS ONTO TRACKS 0-2. SETS RWTS PARAMETER LIST TO READ DOS FROM DISK; CALLS READ/WRITE GROUP OF PAGES ($B793); EXITS TO CALLER
$B74A (-18614)	DOS 3.2 (48K) - WRITES $0A SECTORS STARTING FROM $B600~ THEN $1B SECTORS STARTING AT $1B00 BEGINNING AT TRACK 0 SECTOR 0
$B78D~$B792 (-18547~-18542)	DOS 3.3 (48K) UNUSED
$B793~$B7B4 (-18541~-18508) \SB\	DOS 3.3 (48K) READ/WRITE A GROUP OF PAGES. CALLS RWTS THROUGH EXTERNAL ENTRY POINT $B7B5 & EXITS TO CALLER
$B793 (-18541)	DOS 3.2~3.2.1~3.3 ROUTINE TO STORE A BLOCK OF CONSECUTIVE SECTORS. LOADS COMMAND BYTE ($B7FC);NUMBER OF SECTORS IN $B7E1; DOS 3.2 INCREMENTS - SET UP IOBLK TO 1ST SECTOR; DOS 3.3 DECREMENTS - SET UP IOBLK TO LAST SECTOR
$B793 (-18541)	DOS 3.2 (48K) - INCREMENTS OR DECREMENTS TRACK/SECTOR AS NEEDED AND DATA ADDRESS FOR $B700 & $B793 ROUTINES
$B7B5~$B7C1 (-18507~-18495)	DOS 3.3 (48K) DISABLE INTERRUPTS AND CALL RWTS
$B7B5 (-18507)	DOS 3.2 (48K) START OF RWTS-IN-ENVIRONMENT ROUTINE. DISABLES INTERRUPTS; CALLS RWTS (LOCATED AT $BD00); RE-ENABLES INTERRUPS AND PASSES BACK RETURN CODE FROM RWTS IN FORM OF CARRY FLAG
$B7C2~$B7D5 (-18494~-18475)	DOS 3.3 (48K) SET RWTS PARAMETERS FOR WRITING DOS
$B7C2 (-18494)	DOS 3.2 (48K) SETS ADDRESS OF DATA BUFFER AND SETS EXPECTED VOLUME NUMBER
$B7D6~$B7DE (-18474~-18466)	DOS 3.3 (48K) ZERO CURRENT BUFFER (256 BYTES POINTED TO BY $0042~$0043) AND EXIT TO CALLER
$B7DB (-18469)	DOS 3.2 (48K) STORES ZEROES IN ONE PAGE STARTING AT ADDRESS IN $0042~$0043
$B7DF~$B7E7 (-18465~-18457)	DOS 3.3 (48K) DOS PHASE 3 (BOOT 2) BOOT LOADER PARAMETER LIST

```
$B7DF (-18465)                     DOS 3.3 (48K) UNUSED
$B7E0 (-18464)                     DOS 3.3 (48K) NUMBER OF PAGES IN 2ND DOS LOAD (PHASE 3)
$B7E1 (-18463)                     DOS 3.3 NUMBER OF SECTORS TO READ/WRITE
$B7E2 (-18462)                     DOS 3.3 NUMBER OF PPAGES IN 1ST DOS LOAD (PHASE 2)
$B7E3 (-18461)                     DOS 3.3 INIT DOS PAGE COUNTER
$B7E4~$B7E5 (-18460~-18459)        DOS 3.3 POINTER TO RWTS PARAMETER LIST
$B7E6~$B7E7 (-18458~-18457)        DOS 3.3 POINTER TO 1ST STAGE BOOT LOCATION
$B7E8~$B7F8 (-18456~-18440)        DOS 3.2/3.3 (48K) RWTS PARAMETER LIST OR SYSTEM IOB. THIS IOB SET UP ACCORDING TO
                                   LAST DOS OPERATION THAT OCCURED
$B7E8 (-18456)                     DOS 3.2/3.3 (48K) - TABLE TYPE. MUST BE $01
$B7E9 (-18455)                     DOS 3.2/3.3 (48K) - SLOT NUMBER * 16
$B7EA (-18454)                     DOS 3.2/3.3 (48K) - DRIVE NUMBER ($01 OR $02)
$B7EB (-18453)                     DOS 3.2/3.3 (48K) - VOLUME NUMBER  (NOTE: 0 MATCHES ANY VOLUME.)
$B7EC (-18452)                     DOS 3.2/3.3 (48K) - TRACK NUMBER ($00~$22)
$B7ED (-18451)                     DOS 3.2/3.3 (48K) - SECTOR NUMBER (DOS 3.2 $0~$C;DOS 3.3 $0~$F)
$B7EE~$B7EF (-18450~-18449)        DOS 3.2/3.3 - POINTER TO DCT (DEVICE CHARACTERISTICS TABLE)
$B7F0~$BFF1 (-18448~-16399)        DOS 3.2/3.3 - POINTER TO USER DATA BUFFER FOR READ/WRITE
$B7F2 (-18446)                     DOS 3.2/3.3 - UNUSED
$B7F3 (-18445)                     DOS 3.2/3.3 - BYTE COUNTER FOR PARTIAL SECTOR; USE $00 FOR  FULL 256 BYTES
$B7F4 (-18444)                     DOS 3.2/3.3 - COMMAND CODE: 0=SEEK; 1=READ; 2=WRITE; 4=FORMAT.
$B7F5 (-18443)                     DOS 3.2/3.3 - ERROR CODE (VALID IF CARRY SET): $10=WRITE PROTECT;$20=VOLUME
                                   MISMATCH; $40=DRIVE ERROR; $08=INIT ERROR.
$B7F6 (-18442)                     DOS 3.2/3.3 - VOLUME NUMBER FOUND
$B7F7 (-18441)                     DOS 3.2/3.3 - SLOT NUMBER FOUND
$B7F8 (-18440)                     DOS 3.2/3.3 - DRIVE NUMBER FOUND
$B7F9~B7FA                         DOS 3.3 (48K) UNUSED
$B7FB~$B7FE (-18437~-18434)        DOS 3.2/3.3 (48K) - DEVICE CHARACTERISTICS TABLE (DCT) ASSOCIATED WITH SYSTEM
                                   IOB. NOTE: IOB CONTAINS DETAILED DEVICE CHARACTERISTICS TABLE AS DOCUMENTED FOR
                                   RWTS IN WOZPACK
$B7FB (-18437)                     DOS 3.2/3.3 (48K) - DEVICE TYPE (SHOULD BE $00)
$B7FC (-18436)                     DOS 3.3 (48K) - PHASES PER TRACK (SHOULD BE $01)
$B7FD~$B7FE (-18435~-18434)        DOS 3.3 (48K) - MOTOR ON TIME COUNT (SHOULD BE $EF & $D8)
$B7FF (-18433)                     DOS 3.3 (48K) - UNUSED.
$B800~$B869 (-18432~-18327) [PRENIBL-PRENIB16] \SB\DOS 3.1~3.2~3.3 RWTS (READ-WRITE TRACK-SECTOR) PRENIBL MODULE.
                                   CONVERTS A PAGE OF 256 OF REAL BYTES TO A SECTOR OF 410 ($19A) RIGHT
                                   JUSTIFIED 5 BIT NIBBLES (EXCEPT DOS 3.3 CONVERTS TO 342 6 BIT
                                   NIBBLES OF THE FORM 00XXXXXX). POINTER TO PAGE TO CONVERT AT
                                   $003E~$003F; DATA STORED AT PRIMARY XXX) SECONDARY BUFFERS; ON EXIT
                                   X-REG XXX) Y-REG CONTAIN $FF & CARRY SET.
$B82A~$B8B7 (-1839C~-18249) [WRITE16 (DOS 3.3)] \SB\DOS 3.3 'WRITE'. WRITES PRENIBBILIZED DATA FROM PRIMARY & SECONDARY
                                   BUFFERS TO DISK; CALLS WRITE-A-BYTE S~R; WRITES 5 BYTES AUTSYNC~
                                   STARTING DATA MARKS ($D5~$AA~$AD)~ 342 BYTES DATA~ ONE BYTE
                                   CHECKSUM~ AND CLOSING DATA MARKS ($DE~$AA~$EB). USES WRITE
                                   TRANSLATE TABLE ($BA29). ON ENTRY X-REG CONTAINS SLOT#*16. ON EXIT
                                   X-REG UNCHANGED;Y-REG $00; CARRY CLEAR. USES $0026~ $0027~ $678
$B86A~$B8FC (-18326~-18180) [WRITE] \SB\DOS 3.1~3.2~3.2.1 (SEE $382A FOR DOS 3.3 'WRITE') RWTS (READ-WRITE
                                   TRACK-SECTOR) WRITE MODULE. WRITES A BUFFER OF 410 ($19A) 5-BIT RIGHT-JUSTIFIED
                                   NIBBLES ONTO THE DISK SURFACE AS A SECTOR CONVERTING THEM TO A 8-BIT 'DISK
                                   BYTE' FORMAT FIRST
$B8B8~$B8C1 (-18248~-18239)        DOS 3.3 WRITE-A-BYTE S/R.  THIS IS TIMING-CRITCAL CODE USED TO WRITE BYTES AT 32
                                   CYCLE INTERVALS. EXITS TO CALLER
```

```
$B8C2~$B8DB (-18238~-18213) [POSTNB16] \SB\DOS 3.3 POSTNIBBLE ROUTINE. CONVERTS 342 6-BIT NIBBLES OF FORM 00XXXXXX TO
                              256 8-BIT BYTES. NIBLES STORED AT PRIMARY ($BB00-$BBFF) AND SECONDARY
                              ($BC00~$BC55) BUFFERS. POINTER TO DATA PARGE STORED AT 'BUFPTR'
                              ($003E~$003F). ON ENTRY X-REG= SLOT*16; CSW ($0036~$0037) POINTS TO USER
                              DATA; $0026= BYTE COUNT IN SECONDARY BUFFER. ON EXIT CARRY SET 'BUFPTR'
                              Y-REG CONTAINS BYTE COUNT IN SECONDARY BUFFER
$B8C2 (-18238) [POSTNIBL (DOS 3.3)] \SB\DOS 3.3 'POSTNIBL'
$B8DC~$B943 (-18212~-18109) [READ16] \SB\DOS 3.3 'READ' IN RWTS (READ-WRITE TRACK-SECTOR). READS A SECTOR OFF THE DISK
                              INTO SECONDARY BUFFER ($BC00-$BC55) HIGH TO LOW THEN INTO PRIMARY
                              ($BB00-$BBFF) LOW TO HIGH EN ROUTE TO OVERALL PROCESS OF  FORMING $153
                              RIGHT-JUSTIFIED 6-BIT NIBBLES
$B8FD~$B964 (-18179~-18C76) [READ] \SB\DOS 3.1~3.2~3.2.1 (SEE $B8DC FOR DOS 3.3 'READ') RWTS (READ-WRITE TRACK-SECTOR
                              READ MODULE. READS A SECTOR OFF THE DISK FORMING 410 ($19A) 5-BIT
                              RIGHT-JUSTIFIED NIBBLES
$B944~$B99F (-18108~-18017) [READADR-RDADR16 (DOS 3.3)] \SB\DOS 3.3 READADR. FUNCTION SAME AS READADR-RDADR16 (DOS 3.2)
$B944 (-18108) [.RDADR16]     DOS 3.3 SYNONYM FOR READADR
$B965~$B9C0 (-18075~-17984) [READADR (DOS 3.2)] \SB\DOS 3.1~3.2~3.2.1 (SEE $B944 FOR DOS 3.3 'READADR (DOS 3.2)') RWTS
                              (READ-WRITE TRACK SECTOR) READ ADDRESS MODULE. READS ADDRESSES ON
                              THE SECTORS OF CURRENT TRACK UNTIL IT FINDS A SECTOR. THEN IT
                              RETURNS PUTTING CHECKSUM INTO $002C;SECTOR INTO $002D;TRACK INTO
                              $002E; AND VOLUME INTO $002F. CARRY IS SET ON ERROR
$B9A0~$B9FC (-18016~-17924) [SEEKABS (DOS 3.3)] \SB\DOS 3.3 - MOVES DISK AREM TO DESIRED TRACK. CALLS ARM MOVE DELAY
                              SUBROUTINE ($B9FD). ON ENTRY $0478 CONTAINS CURRENT TRACK; X-REG
                              CONTAINS SLOT*16; A-REG DESIRED TRACK. ON EXIT X-REG UNCHANGED;
                              A-REG Y-REG CLOBBERED; $0478 &$002A: FINAL TRACK;$27 PRIOR TRACK
                              (IF SEEK NEEDED). USES $0026;$0027;$002A;$002B. EXITS TO CALLER
$B9C1~BA1D[POSTNIBL (DOS 3.2)] \SB\   DOS 3.1~3.2~3.2.1 (SEE $B8C2 FOR DOS 3.3) RWTS (READ-WRITE TRACK SECTOR) POSTNIBL
                              (DOS 3.2) MODULE. CONVERTS A BUFFER OF 410 ($19A) LEFT-JUSTIFIED 5-BIT NIBBLES TO
                              256 ($100) REAL BYTES. $003E~$003F POINTS TO BUFFER TO PUT THEM INTO
$B9A0 (-18016) [SEEKABS (DOS 3.2)] \SB\DOS 3.2 'SEEKABS'
$B9EC (-17940)                DOS 3.2 CODE TO IMPLEMENT INITIALIZATION WITH VOLUNME NUMBER TO BE INITIALIZED IN
                              $002F
$B9FD~$BA10 (-17923~-17904) \SB\   DOS 3.3 ARM MOVE DELAY SUBROUTINE. DELAYS SPECIFIED NUMBER OF 100 MICROSEC
                              INTERVALS. ON ENTRY A-REG CONTAINS NUMBER OF INTERVALS; 'MONTIME' ($0046) SHOULD
                              CONTAIN MOTOR-ON TIME ($EF~$D8) FROM DCT;$0478 CONTAIN CURRENT TRACK; ON EXIT
                              A-REG CURRENT X-REG CONTAIN $00; Y-REG UNCHANGED CARRY SET. EXIT TO CALLER
$BA00 (-17920) [MSWAIT] \SB\  DOS 3.3 RWTS OPERATION TIMER ROUTINE
$BA11 (-17903) \SB\           DOS 3.3 RWTS OPERATION TIMER  TABLE1
$BA1E~$BA8F (-17890~-17777) [SEEKABS] \SB\DOS 3.1~3.2~3.2.1 (SEE $B9A0 FOR DOS 3.3) RWTS (READ-WRITE TRACK SECTOR)
                              SEEKABS MODULE. MOVES HEAD TO TRACK SPECIFIED BY A-REG. $0478 IS CURRENT.
                              RWTS DOES PHASE OFF FOR ALL FOUR BEFORE CALL
$BA29 (-17879)                DOS 3.3 (48K) ROUTINE TO ENCODE NIBBLES( 6 DATA BITS PER NIBBLE INSTEAD OF 5 AS
                              IN DOS 3.1~3.2)
$BA11~BA28\SB\                DOS 3.3 ARM MOVE DELAY TABLE. CONTAINS VALUES OF 100 MICROSEC INTERVALUS USED
                              DURING PHASE-ON AND PHASE-OFF OF STEPPER MOTOR
$BA29~$BA68 (-17879~-17816)   DOS 3.3 WRITE TRANSLATE TABLE. CONTAINS 6-BIT NIBBLES USED TO CONVERT 8-BIT
                              BYTES. VALUES RANGE FROM $96 TO $FF AND CODES WITH MORE THAN ONE PAIR OF ADJACENT
                              ZEROS OR NO ADJACENT ONES ARE EXCLUDED
$BA69 (-17815)                DOS 3.3 - UNUSED
$BA96~$BAFF (-17770~-17665)   DOS 3.3 READ TRANSLATE TABLE. CONTAINS 8 BIT BYTES USED TO CONVERT 6-BIT NIBBLES.
                              VALUES RANGE FROM $96 TO $FF. CODES WITH MORE THAN ONE PAIR OF ADJACENT ZEROS OR
                              WITH NO ADJACENT ONES ARE EXCLUDED.
```

```
$BCC4~$BCDE (-17212~-17186) \SB\        DOS 3.3 WRITE DOUBLE BYTE SUBROUTINE. THIS IS TIMING CRITICAL CODE THAT ENCODES
                                        ADDRESS INFO INTO EVEN AND ODD BITS AND WRITES IT AT 32 CYCLE INTERVALS. EXIT TO
                                        CALLER
$BCDF~$BCFF (-17185~-17153)             DOS 3.2 UNUSED
$BD00~$BD18 (-17152~-17128)             DOS 3.3 MAIN ENTRY TO RWTS (READ-WRITE TRACK-SECTOR). UPON ENTRY STORE Y-REG AND
                                        A-REG AT $0048 AND $0049 AS POINTERS TO IOB. INITIALIZE NUMBER OF RECALS AT 1 AND
                                        SEEKS AT 4. IF SLOT # HAS NOT CHANGED BRANCH TO 'SAMESLOT' ($BD34)
$BD19~$BD33 (-17127~-17101)             DOS 3.3 - UPDATE SLOT NUMBER IN IOB AND WAIT FOR OLD DRIVE TO TURN OFF
$BEAE (-16722)                          DOS 3.2 START OF CODE TO INITIALIZE A SINGLE TRACK
$BFA2 (-16478)                          DOS 3.2 - TESTS TO SEE IF ALL $22 TRACKS HAVE BEEN INITIALIZED YET; IF SO EXITS
                                        RWTS AT $BFB8
$BA7B (-17797) [(TIMER DOS 3.2.1)] \SB\DOS 3.2.1 RWTS OPERATION TIMER ROUTINE
$BA7F (-17793) [(TIMER DOS 3.1~3.2)] \SB\DOS 3.1~3.2 RWTS OPERATION TIMER ROUTINE
$BA8C (-17780) [(TABLE1 DOS 3.2.1)] \SB\DOS 3.2.1 RWTS OPERATION TIMER ROUTINE TABLE1
$BA90~$BA93 (-17776~-17765) \SB\        DOS 3.1~3.2  RWTS (READ-WRITE TRACK-SECTOR) TABLE OF PHASE-ON TIMES TO WAIT
                                        (LOCATED AT $BA8C IN DOS 3.2.1 & AT $BA11 IN DOS 3.3)
$BA96~$BAFF (-17770~-17665)             DOS 3.3 NIBBLE ENCODE/DECODE TABLE
$BA9C~$BAA7 (-17764~-17753) \SB\        DOS 3.1~3.2 RWTS (READ-WRITE TRACK-SECTOR) TABLE OF PHASE-OFF TIMES TO WAIT
                                        (LOCATED AT $BA98 IN DOS 3.2.1 & AT $BA1D IN DOS 3.3)
$BAA8~$BAFF (-17752~-17665) \SB\        DOS 3.2 RWTS (READ-WRITE TRACK-SECTOR) TABLE OF NIBBLES IN POSITION OF
                                        CORRESPONDING DISK BYTE OFFSET FROM $BA00 USED FOR CONVERSION DISK BYTES->NIBBLES
$BB00~$BC99 (-17664~-17255) \BB\        BUFFER TO HOLD 410 5-BYTE NIBBLES CREATED FROM A PAGE OF 256 BYTES BY PRENIBL
                                        ROUTINE IN DOS 3.2 RWTS (READ-WRITE TRACK-SECTOR)
$BB00~$BBFF (-17664~-17409)             DOS 3.3 RWTS PRIMARY BUFFER
$BC00~$BC55 (-17408~-17323)             DOS 3.3 RWTS SECONDARY BUFFER
$BC56~$BCC3 (-17322~-17213)             DOS 3.3 WRITE ADDRESS FIELD DURING INITIALIZATION. CALLS WRITE DOUBLE BYE
                                        SUBROUTINE. WRITES # OF BYTES CONTAINED IN Y-REG; STARTING ADDRESS MARKS
                                        ($D5/$AA/$96); ADDRESS INFO (VOL/TRACK/SECTOR/CHECKSUM);CLOSING ADDRESS MARKS
                                        ($DE~$AA~$EB). ON ENTRY X-REG CONTAINS SLOT*16;Y-REGCONTAINS NUMBER OF AUTOSYNC
                                        TO WRITE;$3E:$AA;$3F:SECTOR#;$41:VOL#;$44:TRACK#. ON EXIT: A-REG ?;X-REG
                                        UNCHANGED;Y-REG $00;CARRY SET. EXIT TO CALLER
$BC9A~BCB9\PB\                          CONVERSION TABLE TO CONVERT 5-BIT NIBBLES TO 8-BIT 'DISK BYTES' USED BY DOS 3.2
                                        RWTS (READ-WRITE TRACK-SECTOR) PACKAGE WRITE SUBROUTINE
$BCD0~BCDC                              DOS 3.2 (48K) - 13 BYTES CONTAINING PERMUTATIONS OF 5 MOD 13 USED IN NYBBLE
                                        CONVERSION.  NO SUCH TABLE IN DOS 3.3
$BD00~$BFFF (-17152~-16385)             DOS 3.2 (48K) - MAINLINE READ-WRITE TRACK-SECTOR (RWTS) CODE
$BD00 (-17152) \SE\                     DOS 3.2 (48K) - ROUTINE WHICH READS IN DIRECTORY OFF DISK
$BD34~$BD53 (-17100~-17069) [SAMESLOT] \SB\ENTER READ MODE AND READ WITH DELAYS TO SEE IF DISK IS SPINNING. SAVE
                                        RESULTS OF TEST AND TURN ON MOTOR ANYHOW
$BD44 (-17084)                          ADDRESS OF DEVICE CHARACTERISTICS TABLE (DCT) AND BUFFER ARE MOVED FROM THE IOB
                                        INTO LOCNS $003C~$003D & $003E~$003F
$BD54~$BD73 (-17068~-17037) \SB\        DOS 3.3 - MOVE POINTER IN IOB TO ZERO PAGE. {SET DEVCTBL ($003C~$003D) AND BUFPTR
                                        ($003E~$003F) AND $0047 WITH $00D8 FROM DCT}. CHECK IF DRIVE # HAS CHANGED. IF
                                        NOT BRANCH TO $BD74
$BD74~$BD8F (-17036~-17009) \SB\        DOS 3.3 - SELECT APPROPRIATE DRIVE AND SAVE DRIVE BEING USED AS HIGH BIT OF
                                        'DRIVENO' ($0035). 1=DRIVE 1;0=DRIVE 2. IF DRIVE WAS ON BRANCH TO $BD90. IF NOT
                                        CALL 'MSWAIT' AT $BA00
$BD90~$BDAA (-17008~-16982) \SB\        DOS 3.3 - GET DESTINATION TRACK AND GO TO II USING 'MYSEEK'($BE5A)
$BD90~$BDAA (-17008~-16982) \SB\        DOS 3.3 - GET DESTINATION TRACK AND GO TO IT VIA 'MYSEEK'($BE5A). CHECK TEST
                                        RESULT AGAIN AND IF DRIVE ON BRANCH TO 'TRYTRK' ($BDAB)
```

```
$BDAB~$BDB3 (-16981~-16965) [TRYTRK] \SB\DOS 3.3 - GET COMMAND CODE.  IF NULL EXIT VIA 'ALLDONE' ($BE46) TURNING OFF
                                      DRIVE & RETURNING TO CALLER. IF COMMAND CODE=4 BRANCH TO 'FORMDSK' ($BE0D);
                                      OTHERWISE MOVE LOW BIT INTO CARRY (SET=READ;CLEAR=WRITE) AND SAVE VALUE ON
                                      STATUS REG. IF WRITE OPN DATA IS PRENIBBILIZED VIA 'PRENIB16' ($B800)
$BDBC~$BDEC (-16964~-16916) [RDRIGHT] \SB\DOS 3.3 - INITIALIZE MAX RETRIES AT 48. READ ADDRESS FIELD VIA 'RDADR16'
                                      ($B944). IF GOOD READ BRANCH TO 'RDRIGHT' ($BDED). IF BAD TRY AGAIN
                                      DECREMENTING RETRIES. IF NONE LEFT PREPARE TO RECALIBRATE. DECREMENT RECAL
                                      COUNT. IF NO MORE THEN 'DRVERR' ($BE04). OTHERWISE RESET RESEEKS AT 4 AND
                                      RECALIBRATE ARM. TRY AGAIN
$BDED~$BE03 (-16915~-16893) [RDRIGHT] \SE\DOS 3.3 - VERIFY TRACK. IF CORRECT BRANCH TO 'RTTRK' ($BE10) OTHERWISE GOTO
                                      'SETTRK' ($BE95) AND DECREMENT RESEEK COUNT. IF ZERO RECAL OTHERWISE RESEEK TRACK
$BE04~$BE0A (-16892~-16886) [DRVERR] \SE\DOS 3.3 - CLEAN UP STACK & STATUS REG; LOAD A-REG WITH $40 (DRIVE ERROR) AND
                                      GOTO 'HNDLERR' ($BE48)
$BE0B~$BE0C (-16885~-16884)           DOS 3.3 - BRANCH TO 'ALLDONE' ($BE46)
$BE0D~$BF0F (-16883~-16625) [FORMDSK] DOS 3.3 - JUMP TO 'DSKFORM' ($BEAF)
$BE10~$BE25 (-16880~-16859) [RTTRK]   DOS 3.3 -CHECK VOL# FOUND VS VOL# WANTED. IF NO VOL SPECIFIED NO ERROR OTHERWISE
                                      IF MISMATCH LOAD A-REG WITH $20 (VOLUME MISMATCH ERROR) AND EXIT VIA 'HNDLERR'
                                      ($BE48)
$BE26~$BE45 (-16858~-16827) [CRCTVOL] DOS 3.3 - CHECK TO SEE IF SECTOR CORRECT. USE 'ILEAV' TABLE ($BFB8) FOR SOFTWARE
                                      SECTOR INTERLEAVING. IF WRONG SECTOR TRY AGAIN AT 'TRYADR ($BDC1). IF WRITE
                                      BRANCH TO 'WRIT' ($BE51). OTHERWISE GOTO 'READ16' ($B8DC). IF GOOD READ CALL
                                      'POSTNB16' ($B8C2) AND RETURN TO CALLER WITH NO ERROR
$BE46~$BE47 (-16826~-16825) [ALLDONE] DOS 3.3 - SKIP OVER SET CARRY INSTRUCTION IN 'HNDLERR'
$BE48~$BE50 (-16824~-16816) [HNDLERR] DOS 3.3 - SET CARRY; STORE A-REG IN IOB AS RETURN CODE. TURN OFF MOTOR. RETURN TO
                                      CALLER
$BE51~$BE59 (-16815~-16807) [WRIT]    DOS 3.3 - WRITE A SECTOR USING 'WRITE16' ($B82A); IF GOOD WRITE EXIT VIA
                                      'ALLDONE' ($BE46) OTHERWISE LOAD A-REG WITH $10 (WRITE PROTECT ERROR) AND EXIT
                                      VIA 'HNDLERR' ($BE48)
$BE5A~$BE8D (-16806~-16755) [MYSEEK]  DOS 3.3 - HOUSEKEEPING BEFORE 'SEEKABS'. DETERMINES NUMBER OF PHASES PER TRACK &
                                      STORES TRACK INFO IN APPROPRIATE SLOT-DEPENDENT LOCN
$BE8E~$BE94 (-16754~-16748) [XTOY]    DOS 3.3 - X-REG/16 =>Y-REG. USED TO PUT SLOT INTO Y-REG
$BE95~$BEAE (-16747~-16722) [SETTRK]  DOS 3.3 - SET TRACK #
$BEAF~$BF0C (-16721~-16628) [DSKFORM] \SB\DOS 3.3 - INIT COMMAND HANDLER
$BF0D~$BF61 (-16627~-16543) \SB\      DOS 3.3 - TRACK WRITE ROUTINE
$BF62~$BF87 (-16542~-16505) \SB\      DOS 3.3 - VERIFY TRACK ROUTINE
$BF88~$BFA7 (-16504~-16473) \SB\      DOS 3.3 - SECTOR MAP ROUTINE - MARKS SECTOR INITIALIZATION MAP AS EACH SECTOR
                                      VERIFIED
$BFA8~BFB7                            DOS 3.3 - SECTOR INITIALIZATION MAP. CONTAINS $30 PRIOR TO INITIALIZATION OF
                                      TRACK. VALUE CHANGED TO $FF AS EACH SECTOR COMPLETED
$BFB8~$BFC7 (-16456~-16441) [ILEAV]   DOS 3.3 - SECTOR TRANSLATE TABLE. SECTOR INTERLEAVING DONE WITH SOFTWARE
$BFC8~$BFFF (-16440~-16385)           DOS 3.3 PATCH AREA
$BFC8~$BFD8 (-16440~-16424)           DOS 3.3 PATCH TO ZERO LANGUAGE CARD DURING BOOT
$BFD9~$BFDB (-16423~-16421)           DOS 3.3 - UNUSED
$BFDC~$BFE5 (-16420~-16411)           DOS 3.3 PATCH CALLED FROM $A032 TO SET ADDITIONAL DEFAULTS
$BFE6~$BFEC (-16410~-16404)           DOS 3.3 PATCH CALLED FROM ERROR HANDLER AT $A6D5. CALLS $A75B TO RESET STATE 0
                                      AND SET WARMSTART FLAG. MARK RUN NOT INTERRUPTED. RETURN TO CALLER
$BFED~$BFFF (-16403~-16385)           DOS 3.3 PATCH CALLED FROM DISK FULL ERROR EXIT ($B377). CALLS $AE7E TO SAVE FILE
                                      MANAGER WORK AREA; RESTORES STACK; CLOSES ALL OPEN FILES; SAVES STACK AGAIN;
                                      EXITS THRU $B385 ("DISK FULL ERROR")
$BFFF (-16385) \H\                    HIGHEST RAM MEMORY ADDRESS (FULL 48K APPLE) - NOTE: WITH LANGUAGE CARD SPECIAL
                                      RAM EXISTS HIGHER
```

```
$BFFF (-16385)                            DEFAULT INTEGER BASIC HIMEM (W/O DOS 3.2~ 48K MACHINE)
$C000~$CFFF (-16384~-12289) \HB\          ENTRY ADDRESSES DEDICATED TO I/O FUNCTIONS
$C000~$C00F (-16384~-16369) [M] \H1\      EQUIVALENT ADDRESSES - ALL FOR KEYBOARD INPUT BYTE. WHEN KEY PRESSED ASCII VALUE
                                          GOES THERE AND HIGH BIT SET
$C000~[KBD ~ IOADR] \H1\                  MONITOR I/O - PEEK TO READ KEYBOARD. IF VAL>127 KEY HAS BEEN PRESSED SINCE LAST
                                          STROBED AT $C010.
$C010~$C01F (-16368~-16353) \H1\          EQUIVALENT ADDRESSES - ALL CLEAR KEYBOARD STROBE  I.E. SET FLAG (HIGH) BET OF
                                          $C000 TO 0 (VAL<128) AND REACTIVATE KEYBOARD
$C010 (-16368) [KBDSTB] \H1\              KEYBOARD STROBE- REACTIVATES KEYBOARD SO THAT VALUE OF PRESSED KEY GOES TO $C000.
                                          SETS HIGH BITTO ZERO..-4
$C020~$C02F (-16352~-16337) [TAPEOUT] \H1\CASSETTE OUTPUT TOGGLE FLIP FLOP. READ ONLY DO NOT WRITE TO THESE ADDRESSES
                                          WHICH ARE DECODED AS SAME SINGLE BIT LOCN
$C020 (-16352) [TAPEOUT] \H1\             PEEK TO TOGGLE CASSETTE OUTPUT (CREATE A 'CLICK' ON RECORDING)
$C030~$C03F (-16336~-16321) [SPKR] \H1\SPEAKER TOGGLE FLIP FLOP. READ ONLY - DO NOT WRITE TO THES ADDRESSES WHICH ARE
                                          DECODED AS SAME SINGLE BIT LOCN
$C030 (-16336) [SPKR] \H1\                PEEK TO TOGGLE SPEAKER (PRODUCES A 'CLICK')
$C040~$C04F (-16320~-16305) \H1\          UTILITY STROBE. IF READ PIN 5 ON GAME I/O CONNECTOR DROPS FROM 5 V TO 0 V FOR 1
                                          MICROSECOND
$C040~$C04F (-16320~-16305) \H1\          ANY ONE OF THESE 16 LOCATIONS HAS SAME EFFECT IF POKED. IT OUTPUTS STROBE TO GAME
                                          I/O CONNECTOR
$C050 (-16304) [TXTCLR] \H1\              POKE TO 0 TO SET FROM TEXT TO GRAPHICS MODE W/O CLEARING SCREEN
$C051 (-16303) [TXTSET] \H1\              POKE TO 0 TO SET FROM GRAPHICS TO TEXT MODE W/O RESETTING SCROLLING WINDOW
$C052 (-16302) [MIXCLR] \H1\              POKE TO 0 TO RESET FROM MIXED GRAPHICS (W/4 LINES TEXT) TO FULL-SCREEN GRAPHICS
$C053 (-16301) [MIXSET] \H1\              POKE=0 TO SET TEXT/GRAPHICS MIX (BOTTOM 4 LINES TEXT)
$C054 (-16300) [LOWSCR] \H1\              POKE TO 0 TO DISPLAY PAGE 1 (DOES NOT CLEAR SCREEN)
$C055 (-16299) [HISCR] \H1\               POKE TO 0 TO DISPLAY PAGE 2  (DOES NOT CLEAR SCREEN)
$C056 (-16298) [LO-RES] \H1\              POKE TO 0 TO SET FROM HI-RES TO SAME PAGE # OF LO-RES OR TEXT
$C057 (-16297) [HI-RES] \H1\              POKE TO 0 TO SET TO HI-RES GRAPHICS FROM LO-RES OR TEXT (SAME PAGE)
$C058 (-16296) [SETAN0] \FF\              VALUE<>0 WHEN GAME AN0 IS SET. POKE 0 TO CLEAR GAME I/O OUTPUT AN0 (3.5V AT PIN
                                          15)
$C059 (-16295) [CLRAN0] \FF\              VALUE <>0 WHEN GAME AN0 IS RESET (CLEARED). POKE 0 TO SET GAME I/O OUTPUT AN0
                                          (0.3V AT PIN 15)
$C05A (-16294) [SETAN1] \FF\              POKE 0 TO CLEAR GAME I/O OUTPUT AN1 (3.5V AT PIN 14)
$C05B (-16293) [CLRAN1] \FF\              POKE 0 TO SET GAME I/O OUTPUT AN1 (0.3V AT PIN 14)
$C05C (-16292) [SETAN2] \FF\              POKE 0 TO CLEAR GAME I/O OUTPUT AN2 (3.5V AT PIN 13)
$C05D (-16291) [CLRAN2] \FF\              POKE 0 TO SET GAME I/O OUTPUT AN2 (0.3V AT PIN 13)
$C05E (-16290) [SETAN3] \FF\              POKE 0 TO CLEAR GAME I/O OUTPUT AN3 (3.5V AT PIN 12)
$C05F (-16289) [CLRAN3] \FF\              POKE 0 TO SET GAME I/O OUTPUT AN3 0.3V AT PIN 12)
$C060 (-16288) [TAPEIN]                   MONITOR MEMORY LOCATION 'TAPEIN'
$C060/8 (-16288) [TAPEIN] \H1\            STATE OF 'CASSETE DATA IN' APPEARS IN BIT 7
$C061 (-16287) \H1\                       PEEK TO READ PDL(0) PUSH BUTTON SWITCH. IF >127 SWITCH ON
$C062 (-16286) \H1\                       PEEK TO READ PDL(1) PUSH BUTTON SWITCH. IF >127 SWITCH ON
$C063 (-16285) \H1\                       PEEK TO READ PDL(2) PUSH BUTTON SWITCH. IF >127 SWITCH ON
$C064 (-16284) [PADDL0] \H1\              MONITOR MEMORY LOCATION PADDL0; HARDWARE INDISTINGUISHABLE FROM $C06C; STATE OF
                                          TIMER OUTPUT FOR PADDLE 0 APPEARS IN BIT 7 (NEGATIVE UNTIL TIMER EXPIRES)
$C065 (-16283) [PADDL1] \H1\              MONITOR MEMORY LOCATION PADDL1; HARDWARE INDISTINGUISHABLE FROM $C06D; STATE OF
                                          TIMER OUTPUT FOR PADDLE 1 APPEARS IN BIT 7 (NEGATIVE UNTIL TIMER EXPIRES)
$C066 (-16282) [PADDL2] \H1\              MONITOR MEMORY LOCATION PADDL2; HARDWARE INDISTINGUISHABLE FROM $C06E; STATE OF
                                          TIMER OUTPUT FOR PADDLE 2 APPEARS IN BIT 7 (NEGATIVE UNTIL TIMER EXPIRES)
$C067 (-16281) [PADDL3] \H1\              MONITOR MEMORY LOCATION PADDL3; HARDWARE INDISTINGUISHABLE FROM $C06F; STATE OF
                                          TIMER OUTPUT FOR PADDLE 3 APPEARS IN BIT 7 (NEGATIVE UNTIL TIMER EXPIRES)
```

```
$C06C (-16276) [PADDL0] \H1\          MONITOR MEMORY LOCATION PADDL0; HARDWARE INDISTINGUISHABLE FROM $C064; STATE OF
                                      TIMER OUTPUT FOR PADDLE 0 APPEARS IN BIT 7 (NEGATIVE UNTIL TIMER EXPIRES)
$C06D (-16275) [PADDL1] \H1\          MONITOR MEMORY LOCATION PADDL1; HARDWARE INDISTINGUISHABLE FROM $C065; STATE OF
                                      TIMER OUTPUT FOR PADDLE 1 APPEARS IN BIT 7 (NEGATIVE UNTIL TIMER EXPIRES)
$C06E (-16274) [PADDL2] \H1\          MONITOR MEMORY LOCATION PADDL2; HARDWARE INDISTINGUISHABLE FROM $C066; STATE OF
                                      TIMER OUTPUT FOR PADDLE 2 APPEARS IN BIT 7 (NEGATIVE UNTIL TIMER EXPIRES)
$C06F (-16273) [PADDL3] \H1\          MONITOR MEMORY LOCATION PADDL3; HARDWARE INDISTINGUISHABLE FROM $C067; STATE OF
                                      TIMER OUTPUT FOR PADDLE 3 APPEARS IN BIT 7 (NEGATIVE UNTIL TIMER EXPIRES)
$C070~$C07F (-16272~-16257) [PTRIG] \H1\GAME CONTROLLER STROBE. WHEN READ CAUSES FALG INPUTS OF GAME CONTROLLERS TO GO
                                      OFF & TIMING LOOPS RESTARTED
$C070~$C07F (-16272~-16257) [PTRIG] \H1\ALL 16 ADDRESSES DECODE TO SINGLE SWITCH WHICH TRIGGERS PADDLE TIMERS DURING
                                      PHI-2
$C080~$C08F (-16256~-16241) [(DEV SELECT 0)] 16 MEMORY LOCNS ALLOCATED TO USE OF PERIPHERAL DEVICE IN SLOT #0. WHEN
                                      ADDRESSED PIN 41 TELLS DEVICE IT IS SELECTED. SINCE SLOT #0 IS COMMON AREA
                                      USED IN COMMON FOR PARAMETERS OF INTEREST TO ALL SLOTS
$C080 (-16256) \H1\                   SELECT 2ND BANK OF$D000~$DFFF RAM IN LANGUAGE CARD. WRITE PROTECT RAM ($C084
                                      DECODES TO SAME ADDRESS & EFFECT)
$C080~$C081 (-16256~-16255) [PHSOFF~PHSON] \P4\DOS 3.2 READ\WRITE TRACK\SECTOR PACKAGE PARAMETER STATEMACHINE CONTROLS
                                      TABLE: LO LO=READ;HI LO=SENSE WRITE PROTECT;LO HI=WRITE;HI HI=WRITE LOAD
$C081 (-16255) \H1\                   READ-DESELECT 2ND BANK OF $D000~$DFFF RAM IN LANG. CARD (ENABLE ROM). TWO
                                      SUCCESSIVE READS WRITE-ENABLES RAM
$C081 (-16255) [PHASON] \P1\          DOS 3.2 READ\WRITE TRACK~SECTOR (RWTS) PACKAGE PARAMETER 'PHASON'
$C082 (-16254) \H1\                   READ-DESELECT 2ND BANK OF $D000~$DFFF RAM IN LANGUAGE CARD (ENABLE ROM). WRITE
                                      PROTECT RAM
$C082 (-16254) [PHSOFF] \P1\          DOS 3.2 READ\WRITE TRACK~SECTOR (RWTS) PACKAGE PARAMETER 'PHSOFF'
$C083 (-16253) \H1\                   SELECT 2ND BANK OF $D000~$DFFF RAM IN LANG. CARD. TWO SUCCESSIVE READS TO THIS
                                      ADDR WRITE-ENABLES RAM
$C084 (-16252) \H1\                   SELECT 2ND BANK OF$D000~$DFFF RAM IN LANGUAGE CARD. WRITE PROTECT RAM ($C080
                                      DECODES TO SAME ADDRESS & EFFECT)
$C085 (-16251) \H1\                   READ-DESELECT 2ND BANK OF $D000~$DFFF RAM IN LANG. CARD (ENABLE ROM). TWO
                                      SUCCESSIVE READS WRITE-ENABLES RAM
$C086 (-16250) \H1\                   READ-DESELECT 2ND BANK OF $D000~$DFFF RAM IN LANGUAGE CARD (ENABLE ROM). WRITE
                                      PROTECT RAM
$C087 (-16249) \H1\                   SELECT 2ND BANK OF $D000~$DFFF RAM IN LANG. CARD. TWO SUCCESSIVE READS TO THIS
                                      ADDR WRITE-ENABLES RAM
$C088 (-16248) \H1\                   SELECT 1ST BANK OF$D000~$DFFF RAM IN LANGUAGE CARD. WRITE PROTECT RAM
$C088 (-16248) [MOTOROFF] \P1\        DOS 3.2 READ\WRITE TRACK~SECTOR (RWTS) PACKAGE PARAMETER 'MOTOROFF'
$C089 (-16247) \H1\                   READ-DESELECT 1ST BANK OF $D000~$DFFF RAM IN LANG. CARD (ENABLE ROM). TWO
                                      SUCCESSIVE READS WRITE-ENABLES RAM
$C089 (-16247) [MOTORON] \P1\         DOS 3.2 READ\WRITE TRACK~SECTOR (RWTS) PACKAGE PARAMETER 'MOTORON'
$C08A (-16246) \H1\                   READ-DESELECT 1ST BANK OF $D000~$DFFF RAM IN LANGUAGE CARD (ENABLE ROM). WRITE
                                      PROTECT RAM
$C08A (-16246) [DRV0EN] \P1\          DOS 3.2 READ\WRITE TRACK~SECTOR (RWTS) PACKAGE PARAMETER 'DRV0EN' (DRIVE 0 ENABLE)
$C08B (-16245) \H1\                   SELECT 1ST BANK OF $D000~$DFFF RAM IN LANGUAGE CARD. TWO SUCCESSIVE READS TO THIS
                                      ADD WRITE-ENABLES RAM
$C08B (-16245) [DRV1EN] \P1\          DOS 3.2 READ\WRITE TRACK~SECTOR (RWTS) PACKAGE PARAMETER 'DRV1EN' (DRIVE 1 ENABLE)
$C08C~$C08D (-16244~-16243) [Q6L\Q6H] \P2\DOS 3.2 READ~WRITE TRACK\SECTOR PACKAGE PARAMETER 'Q6L~Q6H' (Q6 LOW CAUSES
                                      DOS 3.2 TO READ A BYTE)
$C08C (-16244) \H1\                   SELECT 1ST BANK OF$D000~$DFFF RAM IN LANGUAGE CARD. WRITE PROTECT RAM
$C08D (-16243) \H1\                   READ-DESELECT 1ST BANK OF $D000~$DFFF RAM IN LANG. CARD (ENABLE ROM). TWO
                                      SUCCESSIVE READS WRITE-ENABLES RAM
```

```
HEX LOCN (DEC LOCN) [NAME]  \USE-TYPE\ - DESCRIPTION
------------------------------------------------------------------------------------------------

$C08E~$C08F (-16242~-16241) [Q7L\Q7H] \P2\DOS 3.2 READ~WRITE TRACK\SECTOR PACKAGE PARAMETER 'Q7L~Q7H' (Q7 LOW SETS DOS
                                      3.2 FOR READ MODE)
$C08E (-16242) \H1\                   READ-DESELECT 1ST BANK OF $D000~$DFFF RAM IN LANGUAGE CARD (ENABLE ROM). WRITE
                                      PROTECT RAM
$C08F (-16241) \H1\                   SELECT 1ST BANK OF $D000~$DFFF RAM IN LANGUAGE CARD. TWO SUCCESSIVE READS TO THIS
                                      ADD WRITE-ENABLES RAM
$C090~$C09F (-16240~-16225) [(DEV SELECT 1)] 16 MEMORY LOCATIONS ALLOCATED TO USE OF PERIPHERAL DEVICE IN SLOT #1. WHEN
                                      ADDRESSED PIN 41 TELLS DEVICE IT IS SELECTED
$C0A0~$C0AF (-16224~-16209) [(DEV SELECT 2)] 16 MEMORY LOCATIONS ALLOCATED TO USE OF PERIPHERAL DEVICE IN SLOT #2. WHEN
                                      ADDRESS PIN 41 TELLS DEVICE IT IS SELECTED
$C0B0~$C0BF (-16208~-16193) [(DEV SELECT 3)] 16 MEMORY LOCATIONS ALLOCATED TO USE OF PERIPHERAL DEVICE IN SLOT #3. WHEN
                                      ADDRESSED PIN 41 TELLS DEVICE IT IS SELECTED
$C0C0~$C0CF (-16192~-16177) [(DEV SELECT 4)] 16 MEMORY LOCATIONS ALLOCATED TO USE OF PERIPHERAL DEVICE IN SLOT #4. WHEN
                                      ADDRESSED PIN 41 TELLS DEVICE IT IS SELECTED
$C0D0~$C0DF (-16176~-16161) [(DEV SELECT 5)] 16 MEMORY LOCATIONS ALLOCATED TO USE OF PERIPHERAL DEVICE IN SLOT #5. WHEN
                                      ADDRESSED PIN 41 TELLS DEVICE IT IS SELECTED
$C0E0~$C0EF (-16160~-16145) [(DEV SELECT 6)] 16 MEMORY LOCATIONS ALLOCATED TO USE OF PERIPHERAL DEVICE IN SLOT #6. WHEN
                                      ADDRESSED PIN 41 TELLS DEVICE IT IS SELECTED
$C0E0~C0E7                            EXAMPLE:DISK CONTROLLER IN SLOT 6 - ADDRESSES USED TO PULSE THE HEAD STEPPING
                                      MOTOR. (SEE PGS 145-146 IN DOS MANUAL FOR INFO ABOUT 4 CONTROL LINES TO STEPPING
                                      MOTOR) THESE ADDRESSES APPEAR IN 4 PAIRS WITH ODD ADDRESSES APPLYING VOLTAGE TO A
                                      LINE AND EVEN TURNING IT OFF AGAIN. IF REFERENCED IN DESCENDING ORDER HEAD STEPS
                                      TO A LOWER TRACK AND VICE-VERSA
$C0E8 (-16152)                        EXAMPLE: DISK CONTROLLER IN SLOT 6 - ENTRY ADDRESS TO POWER DOWN DISK
$C0E9 (-16151)                        EXAMPLE: DISK. NOTE: BASIC PROGRAMS CAN POKE TO THIS ADDRESS TO START THE MOTOR
                                      BEFORE ISSUING A DOS COMMAND AND GAIN A SLIGHT DECREASE IN ACCESS TIME CONTROLLER
                                      IN SLOT 6 - ENTRY ADDRESS TO POWER UP DISK. NOTE: BASIC PROGRAMS CAN POKE TO THIS
                                      ADDRESS TO START THE MOTOR BEFORE ISSUING A DOS COMMAND AND GAIN A SLIGHT
                                      DECREASE IN ACCESS TIME
$C0EA (-16150)                        EXAMPLE: DISK CONTROLLER IN SLOT 6 - SELECT DISK DRIVE #1
$C0EB (-16149)                        EXAMPLE: DISK CONTROLLER IN SLOT 6 - SELECT DISK DRIVE #2
$C0EC~$C0EF (-16148~-16145)           EXAMPLE: DISK CONTROLLER IN SLOT 6 - 4 BYTES TO DETERMINE WHETHER DISK CONTROLLER
                                      IS TO READ~ WRITE OR RETURN THE STATUS OF THE WRITE PROTECT MICROSWITCH.  ALSO
                                      USED FOR PASSING READ/WRITE DATA IN GROUPS OF 4-BIT NIBBLES
$C0F0~$C0FF (-16144~-16129) [(DEV SELECT 7)] 16 MEMORY LOCATIONS ALLOCATED TO USE OF PERIPHERAL DEVICE IN SLOT #7. WHEN
                                      ADDRESSED PIN 41 TELLS DEVICE IT IS SELECTED
$CS00~$CSFF                           256 BYTE PAGE OF MEMORY (USUALLY ROM) ALLOCATED TO PERIPHERAL DEVICE IN SLOT #S.
                                      PIN 1 DROPS WHEN ADDRESS SELECTED
$CS00\SE\                             EXAMPLE: CALL -16384+256*S TO TRANSMIT ASCII CHAR IN ACCUMULATOR OUT VIA APPLE
                                      SERIAL INTERFACE IN SLOT S
$C100~$C1FF (-16128~-15873)           256 BYTE PAGE OF MEMORY (USUALLY ROM) ALLOCATED TO PERIPHERAL DEVICE #1. PIN 1
                                      DROPS WHEN ADDRESS SELECTED
$C100 (-16128) \SE\                   STANDARD CHARACTER I/O SUBROUTINE ENTRY POINT FOR SLOT #1
$C100 (-16128) \SE\                   EXAMPLE: JSR $C100 OR CALL -16128 IS EQUIVALENT TO PR#1 FOR INITIALIZING APPLE
                                      SERIAL INTERFACE IN SLOT #1
$C200~$C2FF (-15872~-15617)           256 BYTE PAGE OF MEMORY (USUALLY ROM) ALLOCATED TO PERIPHERAL DEVICE #2. PIN 1
                                      DROPS WHEN ADDRESS SELECTED
$C200 (-15872) \SE\                   STANDARD CHARACTER I/O SUBROUTINE ENTRY POINT FOR SLOT #2
$C300~$C3FF (-15616~-15361)           256 BYTE PAGE OF MEMORY (USUALLY ROM) ALLOCATED TO PERIPHERAL DEVICE #3. PIN 1
                                      DROPS WHEN ADDRESS SELECTED
$C300 (-15616) \SE\                   STANDARD CHARACTER I/O SUBROUTINE ENTRY POINT FOR SLOT #3
------------------------------------------------------------------------------------------------
```

$C400~$C4FF (-15360~-15105)	256 BYTE PAGE OF MEMORY (USUALLY ROM) ALLOCATED TO PERIPHERAL DEVICE #4. PIN 1 DROPS WHEN ADDRESS SELECTED
$C400 (-15360) \SE\	STANDARD CHARACTER I/O SUBROUTINE ENTRY POINT FOR SLOT #4
$C500~$C5FF (-15104~-14849)	256 BYTE PAGE OF MEMORY (USUALLY ROM) ALLOCATED TO PERIPHERAL DEVICE #5. PIN 1 DROPS WHEN ADDRESS SELECTED
$C500 (-15104) \SE\	STANDARD CHARACTER I/O SUBROUTINE ENTRY POINT FOR SLOT #5
$C600~$C6FF (-14848~-14593)	256 BYTE PAGE OF MEMORY (USUALLY ROM) ALLOCATED TO PERIPHERAL DEVICE #6. PIN 1 DROPS WHEN ADDRESS SELECTED
$C600~$C6FF (-14848~-14593)	256 BYTE PAGE OF MEMORY USED BY DOS 3.2/3.3 IF DISK CONTROLLING IN STANDARD SLOT #6 (MEMORY PHYSICALLY ON CONTROLLER BOARD). PART OF THIS INFO IS TRANSFERED TO PAGE 3 ($300) ON BOOTING
$C600~$C65B (-14848~-14757)	DOS 3.2/3.3 - THIS CODE FROM DISK II CONTROLLER ROM IS FIRST CODE EXECUTED WHEN A DISK IS TO BE BOOTED. DYNAMICALLY BUILDS A TRANSLATE TABLE FOR CONVERTING DISK CODES TO 6 BIT HEX AT $0356~$03FF AND DOES INITIAL HOUSEKEEPING AND SETS UP TO READ SECTOR ZERO TRACK ZERO TO $0800 THEN FALLS THRU TO GENERAL SECTOR READ SR AT $C65C
$C600 (-14848) \SE\	STANDARD CHARACTER I/O SUBROUTINE ENTRY POINT FOR SLOT #6
$C65C~$C6FA (-14756~-14598)	DOS 3.3 GENERAL SECTOR READ ROUTINE. USES SECTOR # AT $3D ON THE TRACK INDICATED BY $0041. READS TO ADDRESS SPECIFIED AT $0026~$0027. IF D5/AA/AD FOUND ON SECTOR ADDRESS HEADER & SECTOR DATA WANTED GOTO $C6A6
$C683 (-14717)	DOS 3.3 S/R TO HANDLE SECTOR ADDRESS BLOCK. READS 3 DOUBLE BYTES AND COMBINE TO FORM VOLUME~ TRACK & SECTOR. STORE TRACK AT $0040. IF DESIRED SECTOR FOUND GOTO $C65D TO GET SECTOR DATA; OTHERWISE RETURN TO $C65C
$C6A6 (-14682)	DOS 3.3 SECTOR DATA HANDLING BLOCK. READS 85 BYTES OF SECONDARY DATA TO $0300-$0355 AND READS 256 BYTES OF PRIMARY DATA TO ADDRESS SPECIFIED BY $0026~$0027 & 'NIBBLIZE'. INCREMENT $0027 & $003D AND CHECK AGAINST $0800 TO SEE IF ADDITIONAL SECTORS TO BE READ
$C700~$C7FF (-14592~-14337)	256 BYTE PAGE OF MEMORY (USUALLY ROM) ALLOCATED TO PERIPHERAL DEVICE #7. PIN 1 DROPS WHEN ADDRESS SELECTED
$C700 (-14592) \SE\	STANDARD CHARACTER I/O SUBROUTINE ENTRY POINT FOR SLOT #7
$C800~$CFFF (-14336~-12289)	EXPANSION ROM MEMORY SPACE. RESERVED FOR 2K ROMS ON PERIPHERAL CARDS. ROM IS ACTIVE (ADRESSABLE) ONLY WHEN SLOT IS ACTIVE
$C800~$CFFF (-14336~-12289)	PIN 20 ON ALL PERIPH CONCTRS GOES LOW DURING PHIO ON READ OR WRITE TO THIS GP
$C93D (-14019) \SE\	SERIAL INTERFACE BATCH INPUT ROUTINE. A1&A2 SPECIFY MEMORY RANGE
$C941 (-14015) \SE\	SERIAL INTERFACE BATCH OUTPUT ROUTINE - A1 & A2 SPECIFY MEMORY RANGE
$CFFF (-12289) [CLRROM] \H1\	SPECIAL LOCATION RECOGNIZED BY PERIPHERAL CARDS AS SIGNAL TO TURN OFF FLIP FLOPS WHICH DISABLE EXPANSION ROM
$D000~$DFFF (-12288~-8193) \HB\	LANGUAGE CARD CONTAINS TWO SWITCHABLE BANKS OF RAM MEMORY WHICH SHARE THIS ADDRESS SPACE
$D000~$D7FF (-12288~-10241) \HB\	ROM SOCKET D0
$D000~$D3FF (-12288~-11265) \HB\	PROGRAMMERS AID #1 (HI-RES GRAPHICS ROM)
$D000 (-12288) [SETHRL] \SE\	HI-RES GRAPHICS INIT S/R CALL (ROM VERSION)
$D00E (-12274) [HCLR] \SE\	HI-RES GRAPHICS CLEAR S/R CALL
$D010 (-12272) [BKGND0]	HI-RES GRAPHICS 'BKGND0 (HCOLOR1 SET FOR BLACK BKGND)
$D012 (-12270) [BKGND] \P1\	HI-RES GRAPHICS MEMORY LOCATION 'BKGND' (ROM)
$D1FC (-11780) [HFIND] \SE\	HI-RES GRAPHICS FIND S/R CALL: PARAM=SHAPE~ROT~SCALE
$D2F9 (-11527) [BPOSN] \SE\	HI-RES GRAPHICS POSN S/R CALL PARAM= X0~Y0~COLR
$D30E (-11506) [BPLOT] \SE\	HI-RES GRAPHICS PLOT S/R CALL PARAM= X0~Y0~COLR
$D314 (-11500) [BLIN1] \SE\	HI-RES GRAPHICS LINE S/R CALL PARAM= X0~Y0~COLR
$D331 (-11471) [BGND] \SE\	HI-RES GRAPHICS BKGND S/R CALL PARAM= COLR
$D337 (-11465) [BDRAW1] \SE\	HI-RES GRAPHICS LINE S/R CALL: PARAM=X0~Y0~COLR

```
$D33A (-11462) [BDRAW] \SE\          HI-RES GRAPHICS  DRAW1 S/R CALL: PARAM= XO~YO~COLR~SHAPE~ROT~SCALE
$D393 (-11373) [BLTU] \SE\           APPLESOFT BLOCK TRANSFER UTILITY. MAKES ROOM BY MOVING EVERYTHING FORWARD.
                                     Y-REG(MSB)&A-REG(LSB) AND HIGHDS=DEST OF HIGH ADR;LOWTR=LOWEST ADDR TO BE
                                     MOVED;HIGHTR=HIGHEST ADDR TO BE MOVED+1
$D3E3 (-11293) [REASON] \SE\         CHECKS FOR ENOUGH ROOM IN MEMORY; CHECKS THAT ADDR Y-REG(MSB)&A-REG(LSB) LESS
                                     THAN FRETOP. MAY CAUSE GARBAGE COLLECTION. CAUSE OMERR IF NO ROOM
$D3B9 (-11335) [SHLOAD] \SE\         HI-RES GRAPHICS SHLOAD S/R CALL
$D410 (-11248) [(OUT OF MEM PRT)]    APPLESOFT - PRINT "OUT OF MEMORY" THEN HALT AT APPLESOFT (]) LEVEL
$D412 (-11246) [ERROR] \SE\          APPLESOFT ERROR PROCESSING - CHECKS ERRFLG AND JUMPS TO HNDLERR IF ONERR IS
                                     ACTIVE OTHERWISE PRINTS ERROR MSG BASED ON CODE IN X-REG
$D43C (-11204) \SE\                  APPLESOFT LOCATION TO WHICH DOS 3.2 JUMPS TO MAKE A SOFT ENTRY TO ROM (OR
                                     LANGUAGE PACK) APPLESOFT
$D4BC (-11076)                       INTEGER BASIC PA#1 APPEND PROGRAM ENTRY
$D4F2 (-11022) \SE\                  APPLESOFT - SET (OR RESET) POINTERS & LINKAGES FOR FIRMWARE APPLESOFT (ROM) (OR
                                     LANGUAGE PACK LOCATED IN TOP 16K OF 64K MEMORY)
$D4F2 (-11022) \SE\                  APPLESOFT - TO CONVERT  FROM RAM APPLESOFT STORED AT $0800-$3003 TO FIRMWARE
                                     APPLESOFT IN ROM OR TOP 16K RAM- ~CALL -11022~LIST~SAVE
$D52C (-10964) [INLIN] \SE\          APPLESOFT - INPUT LINE OF TEXT FROM CURRENT INPUT DEVICE INTO INPUT BUFFER (BUF)
                                     & FALL INTO GDBUFS. NO PROMPT!
$D52E (-10962) [INLIN+2] \SE\        APPLESOFT - INPUT LINE OF TEXT FROM CURRENT INPUT DEVICE INTO INPUT BUFFER (BUF)
                                     & FALL INTO GDBUFS. CHAR IN X-REG USED AS PROMPT
$D535 (-10955)                       INTEGER BASIC PA#1 TAPE VERIFY PROG ENTRY
$D539 (-10951) [GDBUFS] \SE\         APPLESOFT - PUT ZERO AT END OF INPUT BUFFER (BUF) AND MASK OFF MOST SIGNIFICANT
                                     BIT ON ALL BYTES. ON ENTRY X-REG=END OF INPUT LINE {A- X- Y-REGS ALTERED}
$D553 (-10925) [INCHR] \SE\          APPLESOFT - GET ONE CHAR FROM CURRENT INPUT DEVICE IN A-REG & MASK OF MSB. USES
                                     MAIN APPLE INPUT ROUTINES & SUPPORTS HANDSHAKING
$D566 (-10906) [RUN] \SE\            APPLESOFT - RUN THE PROGRAM IN MEMORY. THIS ROUTINE DOES NOT RETURN
$D61A (-10726) [FNDLIN] \SE\         APPLESOFT - SEARCHES PROGRAM FOR LINE WHOSE NUMBER IS IN LINNUM. ON EXIT IF CARRY
                                     SET LOWTR POINTS TO LINK FIELD OF DESIRED LINE; IF NOT LOWTR TO NEXT HIGHER LINE
$D64B (-10677) [SCRTCH] \SE\         APPLESOFT INITIALIZATION - THE 'NEW' COMMAND. CLEARS PROGRAM VARIABLES & STACK
$D66C (-10644) [CLEARC] \SE\         APPLESOFT INITIALIZATION - THE 'CLEAR' COMMAND. CLEARS VARIABLES & STACK
$D683 (-10621) [STKINI] \SE\         APPLESOFT STACK INITIALIZATION - CLEARS THE STACK
$D697 (-10601) [STXTPT] \SE\         APPLESOFT INITIALIZATION - SET TXTPTR TO BEGINNING OF PROGRAM
$D6DD (-10531) \SE\                  INTEGER BASIC PA#1 RENUMBER PROG ENTRY (WHOLE PROG)
$D6E7 (-10521) \SE\                  INTEGER BASIC PA#1 RENUMBER PROG ENTRY (PART PROG)
$D717 (-10473) \SE\                  INTEGER BASIC PA#1 MUSIC PROG ENTRY
$D7D2 (-10286) [NEWSTT] \SE\         APPLESOFT - EXECUTE A NEW STATEMENT. ON ENTRY TXTPTR POINTS TO THE':' PRECEDING
                                     THE STMT OR ZERO AT END OF PREVIOUS LIN. USE NEWSTT TO RESTART THE PROGRAM WITH
                                     CONT. THIS ROUTINE DOES NOT RETURN
$D800~$DFFF (-10240~-8193) \HB\      ROM SOCKET D8
$D849 (-10167) [RESTOR] \SE\         APPLESOFT RESTORE FUNCTION - SET DATA POINTER (DATPTR) TO BEGINNING OF THE PROGRAM
$D858 (-10152) [ISCNTC] \SE\         APPLESOFT - CHECK KEYBOARD FOR CONTROL-C ($83). EXECUTES BREAK ROUTINE IF THESE IS
$D865 (-10139) \SE\                  APPLESOFT - POINT TO WHICH DOS 3.2 JUMPS INTO ROM APPLESOFT WHEN PROCESSING ERRORS
$D898 (-10088) [CONT] \SE\           APPLESOFT - MOVES OLDTXT & OLDLIN INTO TXTPTR & CURLIN
$D8B0 (-10064) [SAVE] \SE\           APPLESOFT CASSETTE - SAVE THE PROGRAM IN MEMORY TO CASSETTE TAPE
$D8C9 (-10039) [LOAD] \SE\           APPLESOFT CASSETTE - LOAD A PROGRAM FROM CASSETTE TAPE
$D8F0 (-10000) [VARTIO] \SE\         APPLESOFT CASSETTE - SET UP A1 & A2 TO SAVE 3 BYTES ($0050~$0052) FOR LENGTH
$D901 (-9983) [PROGIO] \SE\          APPLESOFT CASSETTE - SET UP A1 & A2 TO SAVE PROGRAM TEXT ON CASSETTE
$D93E (-9922) [GOTO] \SE\            APPLESOFT - USES LINGET & FNDLIN TO UPDATE TXTPTR. GOTO ASSUMES 6502 REGS HAVE
                                     BEEN SET UP BY CHRGET THAT FETCHED 1ST DIGIT
$D979 (-9863) [(RET W/O GOSUB)]      APPLESOFT - PRINT "RETURN WITHOUT GOSUB" THEN HALT AT APPLESOFT (]) LEVEL
```

```
$D97C (-9860) [(UNDEF'D STMT PRT)]   APPLESOFT - PRINT "UNDEF'D STATEMENT" THEN HALT AT APPLESOFT (]) LEVEL
$D995 (-9835) [DATA] \SE\            APPLESOFT - MOVE TXTPTR TO END OF STATEMENT; LOOKS FOR ':' OR EOL(0).
$D9A3 (-9821) [DATAN] \SE\           APPLESOFT - CALCULATE OFFSET IN Y-REG FROM TXTPTR TO NEXT ':' OR EOL(0)
$D9A6 (-9818) [REMN] \SE\            APPLESOFT - CALCULATE OFFSET IN Y-REG FROM TXTPTR TO NEXT COL(0)
$D998 (-9832) [ADDON] \SE\           APPLESOFT - ADD Y-REG TO TXTPTR
$DA0C (-9716) [LINGET] \SE\          READ 16BIT INTEGER LINE # FROM TXTPTR INTO LINNUM. SEE APPLE ORCHARD V1#1P13 FOR
                                     DETAILS
$DA46 (-9658) [LET] \SE\             APPLESOFT LET - USES CHRGET TO GET ADDRESS OF '=';EVALUATES FORMULA & STORES IT.
                                     ON ENTRY TXTPTR POINTS TO FIRST CHAR OF VARIABLE NAME
$DA65 (-9627) \SE\                   APPLESOFT - PACK EXTENSION BYTE IN FAC AND CONVERT FAC (WHERE |FAC|<2^15) TO
                                     2-BYTE INTEGER. STORE INTEGER IN FORPNT ($0085^$0086) {Y-REG=>1}
$DAFB (-9477) [CRDO] \SE\            APPLESOFT - PRINT A CARRIAGE RETURN
$DAB7 (-9545) [COPY] \SE\            APPLESOFT - FREE STRING POINTED TO BY Y-REG (MSB) & A-REG (LSB) & MOVE IT TO MEM
                                     LOC POINTED TO BY FORPNT
$DB3A (-9414) [STROUT] \SE\          APPLESOFT - PRINT STRING POINTED TO BY Y-REG (MSB) & A-REG (LSB). STRING MUST END
                                     WITH A ZERO OR QUOTE
$DB3D (-9411) [STRPRT] \SE\          APPLESOFT - PRINT A STRING WHOSE DESCRIPTOR IS POINTED TO BY FACMO^FACLO
$DB5C (-9380) [OUTDO] \SE\           APPLESOFT - PRINT THE CHARACTER IN A-REG. INVERSE^FLASH^NORMAL OPTIONS IN EFFECT
$DB57 (-9385) [OUTSPC] \SE\          APPLESOFT - PRINT A SPACE
$DB5A (-9382) [OUTQST] \SE\          APPLESOFT - PRINT A QUESTION MARK
$DD0B (-8949) [(NEXT W/O FOR PRT)] \SE\APPLESOFT - PRINT ERROR MESSAGE "NEXT WITHOUT FOR" THEN HALT AT APPLESOFT (])
                                     LEVEL
$DD67 (-8857) [FRMNUM] \SE\          APPLESOFT - EVALUATE EXPRESSION POINTED TOBY TXTPTR ($00B8^$00B9) (POINTS TO 1ST
                                     CHAR OF FORMULA). PUT RESULT INTO FAC & MAKE SURE IT IS A NUMBER
$DD6A (-8854) [CHKNUM] \SE\          APPLESOFT - MAKE SURE FAC IS NUMERIC (SEE CHKVAL)
$DD6C (-8852) [CHKSTR] \SE\          APPLESOFT - MAKE SURE FAC IS STRING (SEE CHKVAL)
$DD6D (-8851) [CHKVAL] \SE\          APPLESOFT - IF C SET CHECK FOR STRINGS;C CLEAR CHECK FOR NUMRIC VBL. TYPE MISMATCH
                                     ERROR OCCURS IF C AND FAC DON'T AGREE
$DD76 (-8842) \SE\                   APPLESOFT - PRINT "TYPE MISMATCH" THEN HALT AT APPLESOFT (]) LEVEL
$DD7B (-8837) [FRMEVL] \SE\          APPLESOFT - EVAL FORMULA AT TXTPTR USING CHRGET & LEAVE RESULT IN FAC. ON ENTRY
                                     TXTPTR POINTS TO 1ST CHAR OF FORMULA
$DD7B (-8837) [FRMEVL] \SE\          APPLESOFT - EVAL FORMULA AT TXTPTR USING CHRGET. IF FORMULA IS STRING LITERAL
                                     FRMEVL GOBBLES OPENING QUOTE AND EXECUTES STRLIT & ST2TXT
$DE10 (-8688) \SE\                   APPLESOFT - PACK EXTENSION BYTE OF FAC INTO FAC & PUSH FAC ONTO STACK (6 BYTES).
                                     MODIFIES INDEX
$DE47 (-8633) \SE\                   APPLESOFT - PULL ARG AND PUT EXCLUSIVE OR OF SIGNS OF FAC & ARG INTO (XORFPSGN)
                                     $00AB. MUST BE EXECUTED BY JMP INSTRUCTION
$DE81 (-8575) [STRTXT] \SE\          APPLESOFT - SET Y-REG (MSB) & X-REG(LSB) TO TXTPTR + CARRY BIT AND FALL INTO STRLIT
$DE98 (-8552) [(NOTFAC)] \SE\        APPLESOFT - LET FAC = NOT(FAC); I.E. RETURNS FAC=1 IF FAC=0 OR FAC=0 IF FAC<>0
$DEB2 (-8526) [PARCHK] \SE\          APPLESOFT PARENTHESIS CHECK - CHECK FOR '(';EVALUATE FORMULA;CHECK FOR ')'. USES
                                     CHKOPN & FRMEVL THEN FALLS INTO CHKCLS
$DEB8 (-8520) [CHKCLS] \SE\          APPLESOFT CLOSE PARENTHESIS CHECK - CHECKS TXTPTR FOR ')'. USES SYNCHR.
$DEBB (-8517) [CHKOPN] \SE\          APPLESOFT OPEN PARENTHESIS CHECK - CHECKS TXTPTR FOR '('. USES SYNCHR.
$DEBE (-8514) [CHKCOM] \SE\          APPLESOFT COMMA CHECK - CHECKS TXTPTR FOR COMMA. USES SYNCHR.
$DEC0 (-8512) [SYNCHR] \SE\          APPLESOFT SYNTAX CHARACTER CHECK - CHECKS TO VERIFY TXTPTR POINTS TO SAME
                                     CHARACTER AS THAT IN A-REG. NORMAL EXIT THRU CHGET TO GET NEX CHAR FROM INPUT
                                     BUFFER OTHEWISE SYNTAX ERROR. TXTPTR NOT MODIFIED. {Y-REG RESET TO ZERO}
$DEC9 (-8503) \SE\                   SNERR S/R. PRINTS "SYNTAX ERROR" AND HALTS PROG
$DEE9 (-8471) [(INT=>FP)] \SE\       APPLESOFT - PULL INTEGER (%) VARIABLE POINTED TO BY FACMO^FACLO ($00A0^$00A1) INTO
                                     A-REG & Y-REG AND CONVERT TO FP IN FAC. RESETS VALTYP {RESETS Y-REG TO 0}
$DF4F (-8369) [(FAC/ARG OR)] \SE\    APPLESOFT - LET FAC = FAC 'OR' ARG; I.E. FAC=1 IF EITHER FAC OR ARG OR BOTH <>0;
                                     FAC=0 ONLY IF BOTH FAC & ARG = 0
```

```
$DF55 (-8363) [(FAC/ARG AND)] \SE\APPLESOFT - LET FAC = FAC 'AND' ARG; I.E. FAC=1 ONLY IF BOTH FAC & ARG <>0; IF EITHER
                  FAC OR ARG OR BOTH =0 THEN FAC=0
$DF6A (-8342) [(FAC/ARG COMPARE)] \SE\APPLESOFT - COMPARERS FAC WITH ARG. TYPE OF COMPARISON CONTROLLED BY $0016. IF
                  CONDITION MET FAC SET TO ONE; ELSE FAC RESET TO ZERO
$DFE3 (-8221) [PTRGET] \SE\APPLESOFT - READ VAR NAME FROM CHRGET AND FIND IT IN MEMORY (OR CREATE APPROPRIATE SIMPLE
                  VARIABLE OR ARRAY). DOES MUCH HOUSEKEEPING
$E000~$E7FF (-8192~-6145) \HB\      ROM SOCKET E0 (APPLE II (NOT II+) = INTEGER BASIC)
$E000 (-8192) [BASIC]               INTEGER BASIC - 'HARD' OR 'COLD' OR 'CONTROL-B' ENTRY POINT  (COMPLETE
                                    REINITIALIZATION. START WITH A TOTALLY FRESH SLATE)
$E000 (-8192) [BASIC]               APPLESOFT - 'HARD' OR 'COLD' OR 'CONTROL-B' ENTRY POINT (COMPLETE REINITIALIZATION.
                                    START WITH A TOTALLY FRESH SLATE.)
$E003 (-8189) [BASIC2] \SE\         INTEGER BASIC - 'SOFT' OR 'WARM' OR 'CONTROL-C' OR 'ENTRY2' ENTRY POINT (REENTRY
                                    WITHOUT REINITIALIZATION OF SYMBOL-TABLE~ VARIABLES OR DATA)
$E006 (-8186) [~SETPRMPT~] \SE\     INTEGER BASIC ENTRY POINT TO SET UP '>' PROMPT
$E02A (-8150) [~NXTBYTE~] \SE\      INTEGER BASIC ENTRY POINT TO GET NEXT BYTE 16-BIT POINTER
$E04B (-8117) \SE\                  INTEGER BASIC 'LIST' ROUTINE (LIST ALL THE PROGRAM)
$E05D (-8099) \SE\                  INTEGER BASIC ENTRY POINT TO LIST X~Y (LIST A RANGE OF THE PROGRAM
$E06D (-8083) [~UNPACK~] \SE\       INTEGER BASIC ENTRY POINT TO UNPACK TOKENED CODE TO MNEMONICS
$E07D (-8067) [ISLETC (CHARCHEK)] \SE\APPLESOFT - CHECKS A-REG FOR ASCII LETTER OTHERWISE CLEAR IT TO ZERO ('A' TO
                                    'Z'). SET C (CARRY FLAG) TO 1 IF A IS A LETTER OTHERWISE CLEAR IT TO ZERO (A- X-
                                    Y-REGS NOT ALTERED)
$E0FE~$E104 (-7938~-7932) [(-32K)] \P5\APPLESOFT FIVE-BYTE FLOATING POINT CONSTANT -32768 (-2~16)
$E105 (-7931) [(EVAL EXPR =>INT)] \SE\APPLESOFT - EVALUATE EXPRESSION POINTED TO BY TXTPTR ($00B8~$00B9) AND CONVERT
                                    RESULT (WHICH MUST BE NON-NEGATIVE) TOA TWO-BYTE INTEGER IN FACMO~FACLO
                                    ($00A0~$00A1)
$E108 (-7928) [(AYPOSINT +FP=>INT)] \SE\APPLESOFT - SAME AS AYINT ($E10C) EXCEPT FAC MUST BE POSITIVE
$E10C (-7924) [AYINT (FF=>INT)] \SE\APPLESOFT - IF FAC SUITABLE FOR CONVERSION TO INTEGER (FAC<32767 & FAC>-32768) THEN
                                    PERFORM QINT (RESET Y-REG=0)
$E130 (-7888) [~DIMSTR~] \SE\       INTEGER BASIC ENTRY POINT TO DIMENSION A STRING FOR MEMORY
$E171 (-7823) [~INPUTSTR~] \SE\     INTEGER BASIC ENTRY POINT TO 'INPUT A STRING' ROUTINE
$E196 (-7786) [(BAD SUBSCRPRT)] \SE\APPLESOFT - PRINT "BAD SUBSCRIPT" AND HALT AT APPLESOFT LEVEL (])
$E199 (-7783) [(ILLEGAL QTY PRT)] \SE\APPLESOFT - PRINT "ILLEGAL QUANTITY" AND HALT AT APPLESOFT LEVEL (])
$E222 (-7646) [~MULT~] \SE\         INTEGER BASIC ENTRY POINT TO MULTIPLY ROUTINE
$E27A (-7558) [~MOD~] \SE\          INTEGER BASIC ENTRY POINT TO MODULO FUNCTION
$E28A (-7542) [~SCRN~] \SE\         INTEGER BASIC ENTRY POINT TO SCREEN X~ Y~ COLOR VALUE FUNCTION
$E2B3 (-7501) [~MAINLINE~] \SE\     INTEGER BASIC ENTRY POINT TO MAIN LINE OF COMPILE/EXECUTE CODE
$E2F2 (-7438) [GIVAYF (INT=>FP)] \SE\APPLESOFT - FLOAT THE SIGNED INTEGER W/ LSB IN A-REG MSB IN Y-REG INTO FAC. RESETS
                                    VALTYP. (RESETS Y-REG=0)
$E301 (-7423) [SNGFLT] \SE\         APPLESOFT - FLOAT THE UNSIGNED INTEGER IN Y-REG INTO FAC. RESETS VALTYP. (RESET
                                    Y-REG=0)
$E306 (-7418) [ERRDIR] \SE\         APPLESOFT - CAUSES ILLEGAL DIRECT ERROR IF PROGRAM NOT RUNNING (X-REG ALTERED)
$E30B (-7413) [(ILLDIRPRT)] \SE\    PRINT "ILLEGAL DIRECT" THEN HALT AT APPLESOFT (]) LEVEL
$E30E (-7410) \SE\                  APPLESOFT - PRINT "UNDEFINED FUNCTION" THEN HALT AT APPLESOFT (]) LEVEL
$E36B (-7317) [MEMFUL] \SE\         INTEGER BASIC MEMORY FULL ERROR
$E36F (-7313) [~DELETE~] \SE\       INTEGER BASIC ENTRY POINT TO DELETE LINES OF TEXT X~Y
$E3C0 (-7232) [~ERRORMESS*~] \SE\   INTEGER BASIC ENTRY POINT - INPUT ERROR MESSAGE
$E3CE (-7218) [~GETCMD~] \SE\       INTEGER BASIC ENTRY POINT TO GET A COMMAND FROM THE KEYBOARD
$E3D5 (-7211) [STRINI] \SE\         APPLESOFT - GET SPACE FOR CREATION OF A STRING & CREATE DISCRIPTOR FOR IT IN
                                    DSCTMP. ON ENTRY A-REG = LEN OF STRING.
$E3DD (-7203) [STRSPA] \SE\         APPLESOFT - JSR TO GETSPA. STORE THE POINTER & LENGTH IN DSCTMP.
$E3E0 (-7200) [~ERRORMESS~] \SE\    INTEGER BASIC ENTRY POINT TO PRINT ERROR MESSAGE AND GOTO MAINLINE
```

$E3E3 (-7197) \SE\	INTEGER BASIC ENTRY POINT TO WHICH DOS 3.2 CHAINS WHEN PROCESSING ERRORS
$E3E7 (-7193) [STRLIT] \SE\	APPLESOFT - STORE A QUOTE IN ENDCHR AND CHARAC SO THAT STRLT2 WILL STOP ON IT
$E3ED (-7187) [STRLT2] \SE\	APPLESOFT - BUILD DESCRIPTOR FOR STRING LITERAL WHOSE 1ST CHAR POINTED TO BY Y-REG (MSB) & X-REG (LSB). PUT INTO TEMPORARY & POINTER TO IT IN FACMO~FACLO.
$E42A (-7126) [PUTNEW] \SE\	APPLESOFT - STRING FUNCTION RETURNING WITH RESULT INDSCTMP. MOVE DSCTMP TO TEMP DESCRIPTOR & PUT POINTER TO DESCRIPTOR IN FACMO~FACLO & FLAG RESULT AS STRING
$E430 (-7120) [(TOOCOMPLEX)] \SE\	APPLESOFT - PRINT "FORMULA TOO COMPLEX" THEN HALT AT APPLESOFT (]) LEVEL
$E452 (-7086) [GETSPA] \SE\	APPLESOFT - GET SPACE FOR CHARACTER STRING. MOVES FRESPC & FRETOP DOWN. A-REG = # OF CHARS. POINTER TO SPC IN Y-REG(MSB) & X-REG(LSB)
$E484 (-7036) [GARBAG] \SE\	APPLESOFT GARBAGE COLLECTOR - MOVES ALL CURRENTLY USED STRINGS UP IN MEMORY AS FAR AS POSSIBLE
$E51B (-6885) [~HEX/DEC~] \SE\	INTEGER BASIC - DECIMAL LPRINT (LINE NUMBER PRINT) S/R; CONVERTS 2-BYTE (16-BIT) BINARY/HEX TO UNSIGNED DECIMAL (0-65535)
$E597 (-6761) [CAT] \SE\	APPLESOFT - CONCATENATE TWO STRINGS. FACMO (MSB) & FACLO (LSB) POINT TO FIRST STRING'S DESCRIPTOR & TXTPTR POINTS TO '+'
$E5AD (-6739) [~NEW~] \SE\	INTEGER BASIC ENTRY POINT TO CLEAR OUT OLD PROGRAM AND RESET POINTERS FOR A NEW PROGRAM
$E5B7 (-6729) [~CLR~] \SE\	INTEGER BASIC ENTRY POINT TO CLEAR OUT VARIABLE WORK SPACE
$E5D4 (-6700) [MOVINS] \SE\	APPLESOFT - MOVE STRING WHOSE DESCRIPTOR IS POINTED TO BY STRNG1 TO MEM LOC POINTED TO BY FORPNT
$E5E2 (-6686) [MOVSTR] \SE\	APPLESOFT - MOVE STRING POINTED TO BY Y-REG (MSB) & X-REG (LSB) WITH LENGH IN A-REG TO MEMORY POINTED TO BY FRESPA
$E5FD (-6659) [FRESTR] \SE\	APPLESOFT - MAKE SURE THAT LAST FAC RESULT WAS A STRING & FALL INTO FREFAC
$E604 (-6652) [FRETMP] \SE\	APPLESOFT - FREE A TEMPORARY STRING. ON ENTRY POINTER TO DESCRIPTOR IS IN Y-REG (MSB) & X-REG (LSB)
$E635 (-6603) [FRETMS] \SE\	APPLESOFT - FREE TEMPORARY DESCRIPTOR W/O FREEING UP THE STRING. Y-REG (MSB) & X-REG(LSB) POINT TO DESCRIPTOR TO BE FREED. ON EXIT Z SET IF ANYTHING FREED
$E6EC (-6420) [~BRANCH~] \SE\	INTEGER BASIC ENTRY POINT TO BRANCH (GET LO/HI THEN JSR)
$E6F5 (-6411) [GTBYTC] \SE\	APPLESOFT - JSR TO CHRGET TO GOBBLE A CHARACTER AND FALL INTO GETBYT
$E6F8 (-6408) [GETBYT] \SE\	GETBYT S/R. EVALS EXPRESSION (FORMULA) POINTED TO BY TXTPTR ($00B8~$00B9) & CONVTS TO 1-BYT VAL IN X-REG & FACLO($00A1). A-REG GETS EXPRESSION TERMINAL SIGN {RESETS Y-REG=0}
$E6F8 (-6408) [GETBYT] \SE\	APPLESOFT - EVAL FORMULA AT TXTPTR. LEAVE RESULT IN FAC AND FALL INTO CONINT. AT ENTRY TXTPTR POINTS TO FIRST CHAR IN FORMULA FOR FIRST NUMBER PLOTFNS PUTS FIRST NUMBER IN FIRST AND SECOND NUMBER IN H2 AND V2
$E6FB (-6405) [CONINT] \SE\	APPLESOFT FP - CONVERT FAC INTO SINGLE BYTE IN X-REG & FACLO.NORMAL EXIT THRU CHRGET. IF FAC<0 OR FAC>255 ILLEGAL QUANT ERROR
$E6FF (-6401) [~GETVERB~] \SE\	INTEGER BASIC ENTRY TO GET NEXT VERB TO USE
$E715 (-6379) [~GET16BIT~] \SE\	INTEGER BASIC ENTRY TO GET A 16-BIT VALUE
$E736 (-6346) [~NOT~] \SE\	INTEGER BASIC ENTRY TO 'NOT' (NOT A VALUE FUNCTION)
$E746 (-6330) [GETNUM] \SE\	APPLESOFT FP - READ 2-BYTE NUM INTO LINNUM FROM TXTPTR. CHECK FOR COMMA. GET SINGLE BYTE NUMB IN X-REG.
$E74A (-6326) [~ABS~] \SE\	INTEGER BASIC ENTRY TO GET ABSOLUTE VALUE OF A NUMBER
$E74C (-6324) [COMBYTE] \SE\	APPLESOFT - CHECK FOR COMMA & GET A BYTE IN X-REG. USES CHKCOM& BETBYT. ON ENTRY TXTPTR POINTS TO COMMA
$E752 (-6318) [GETADR] \SE\	APPLESOFT FP - CONVERT FAC (-65535 TO 65535) INTO 2-BYTE INTEGER (0-65535) IN LINNUM. 'WRAPAROUND' OCCURS IF VALUE IN FAC TOO BIG {A- Y-REGS ALTERED}
$E75C (-6308) [~SGN~] \SE\	INTEGER BASIC ENTRY POINT TO GET SIGN OF A NUMBER
$E782 (-6270) [~SUBTRACTION~] \SE\	INTEGER BASIC ENTRY POINT TO SUBTRACTION FUNCTION
$E785 (-6267) [~ADDITION~] \SE\	INTEGER BASIC ENTRY POINT TO ADDITION FUNCTION
$E7A0 (-6240) [FADDH] \SE\	APPLESOFT FP - ADD 1/2 TO FAC (1/2 IN $EE64)

```
$E7A4 (-6236) [~TAB~] \SE\INTEGER BASIC ENTRY POINT TO HORIZONTAL TAB FUNCTION
$E7A7 (-6233) [FSUB (FPSUB)] \SE\APPLESOFT - MOVE FP NUMBER IN MEMORY POINTED TO BY Y-REG &A-REG INTO ARG AND FALL INTO
                     FSUB (FPSUB)T
$E7AA (-6230) [FSUBT] \SE\APPLESOFT - FP SUBTRACT FAC FROM ARG. ON ENTRY A-REG & 6502 ZERO FLAG REFLECT FACEXP. RESULT
                     TO FAC
$E7BE (-6210) [FADD (FPADD)] \SE\APPLESOFT FP - MOVE THE FP NUMBER IN MEMORY POINTED TO BY Y-REG & A-REG INTO ARG AND
                     FALL INTO FADDT (FPADD). MODIFIES INDEX & XORFPSGN
$E7C1 (-6207) [~COMMA~] \SE\INTEGER BASIC ENTRY POINT TO COMMA FUNCTION
$E7C1 (-6207) [FADDT] \SE\APPLESOFT FP - ADD FAC AND ARG. ON ENTRY A-REG AND ZERO FLAG REFLECT FACEXP. RESULT TO FAC
$E800~$EFFF (-6144~-4097) \HB\       ROM SOCKET E8 (INTEGER BASIC)
$E7E2 (-6174) [~AUTO~] \SE\          INTEGER BASIC ENTRY TO AUTO LINE NUMBERING FUNCTION
$E828 (-6104) [~IF/THEN~] \SE\       INTEGER BASIC ENTRY TO IF/THEN ROUTINE
$E836 (-6090) \SE\                   INTEGER BASIC 'RUN' - LOCATION INTO WHICH DOS CHAINS TO RUN AN INTEGER BASIC PROGRAM
$E83C (-6084) [~GOSUB~] \SE\         INTEGER BASIC ENTRY TO GOSUB HANDLER
$E84E (-6066) [(RESET)] \SE\         RESET FACEXP($009D) AND $00A2 (FACSIGN) & A-REG TO ZERO {A-REG=>0;X- Y-REG NOT
                                     ALTERED}
$E85B (-6053) [~GOTO~] \SE\          INTEGER BASIC ENTRY TO 'GOTO' HANDLER
$E875 (-6027) [~GETNEXT~] \SE\       INTEGER BASIC ENTRY TO 'GETNEXT' (FETCH NEXT STATEMENT FROM TEXT SOURCE)
$E8A5 (-5979) [~RETURN~] \SE\        INTEGER BASIC ENTRY TO ROUTINE FOR RETURN FROM GOSUB
$E8C3 (-5949) [~STOPPED AT~] \SE\    INTEGER BASIC ENTRY TO ROUTINE TO PRINT 'STOPED AT LINE #'
$E8D5 (-5931) [(OVERFLOWPRT)] \SE\   PRINT "OVERFLOW" THEN HALT AT THE APPLESOFT (]) LEVEL
$E8D6 (-5930) [~NEXT~] \SE\          INTEGER BASIC ENTRY TO ROUTINE TO HANDLE 'NEXT' LOOP END
$E913~$E917 (-5869~-5865) [(ONE)] \P5\APPLESOFT FP CONSTANT ONE =1.
$E92D~$E931 (-5843~-5839) [(SQR(.5))] \P5\APPLESOFT FP CONSTANT SQR(.5) = .707..
$E932~$E936 (-5838~-5834) [(SQR(2))] \P5\APPLESOFT FP CONSTANT SQR(2) = 1.414...
$E937~$E94B (-5833~-5813) [(MINUS.ONE.HALF)] \P5\APPLESOFT FP CONSTANT MINUS ONE HALF (-1/2)
$E93A (-5830) [~FOR~] \SE\           INTEGER BASIC ENTRY TO ROUTINE TO HANDLE 'FOR' LOOP INITIALIZATION
$E93C~$E940 (-5828~-5824) [(LN(2))] \P5\APPLESOFT FP CONSTANT (LN(2) = .30103...
$E950 (-5808) [~TO/FOR~] \SE\        INTEGER BASIC ENTRY POINT TO ROUTINE TO HANDLE LOOP COUNTER # TO # STEP #
$E97F (-5761) [FMULT (FPMULT)] \SE\ APPLESOFT FP - MOVE THE FP NUMBER IN MEMORY POINTED TO BY Y-REG & A -REG INTO ARG
                                     AND FALL INTO FMULTT (FPMULT). ALTERS INDEX XORFPSGN
$E982 (-5758) [FMULTT] \SE\          APPLESOFT FP - MULTIPLY FAC AND ARG. ON ENTRY A-REG & ZERO FLAG REFLECT FACEXP.
                                     RESULT TO FAC. XORFPSGN MUST BE COMPUTED BEFORE CALL
$E9E3 (-5661) [CONUPK] \SE\          APPLESOFT FP - LOAD ARG FROM MEMORY POINTED TO BY Y-REG & A-REG. ON EXIT A & Z
                                     REFLECT FACEXP. MODIFIES INDEX & XORFPSGN. {RESET Y-REG=0}
$E9E7 (-5657) \SE\                   APPLESOFT FP - SAME AS $E9E3 EXCEPT USE MEMORY LOCATION POINTED TO BY INDEX
                                     ($005E~$005F)
$EA10~$EA87 (-5616~-5497) [~VERBADL~] \PB\INTEGER BASIC VERB DISPATCH TABLE LOW BYTE
$EA39 (-5575) [MUL10] \SE\           APPLESOFT FP - MULTIPLY FAC BY 10. WORKS FOR BOTH POSITIVE & NEGATIVE NUMBERS
$EA55 (-5547) [DIV10] \SE\           APPLESOFT FP - DIVIDE FAC BY 10. RETURNS POSITIVE NUMBERS ONLY
$EA66 (-5530) [FDIV (FPDIV)] \SE\    APPLESOFT FP - MOVE THE FP NUMBER IN MEMORY POINTED TO BY R-REG & A-REG INTO ARG
                                     AND FALL INTO FDIVT. ALTERS INDEX & XORFPSGN
$EA69 (-5527) [FDIVT (FPDIV2)] \SE\ APPLESOFT FP - DIVIDE ARG BY FAC. ON ENTRY A-REG AND Z REFLECT FACEXP. RESULT IN
                                     FAC. XORFPSGN SHOULD BE COMPUTED BEFORE CALL
$EA88 (-5496) [~VERBADRH~] \PB\      INTEGER BASIC VERB DISPATCH TABLE HI BYTE
$EAE1 (-5407) [(DIVZEROPRT)] \SE\    APPLESOFT - PRINT "DIVISION BY ZERO" THEN HALT AT APPLESOFT (]) LEVEL
$EAF9 (-5383) [MOVFM (FPLOAD)] \SE\ APPLESOFT FP MOVE MEMORY POINTED TO BY Y-REG & A-REG INTO FAC. ON EXIT A-REG & ZERO
                                     FLAG REFLECT FACEXP. RESET EXTENSION BYTE=0 {RESET Y-REG=0}
$EAFD (-5379) \SE\                   APPLESOFT FP - PULL MEMORY POINTED TO BY INDEX ($005E~$005F) INTO FAC & RESET
                                     EXTENSION BYTE = 0 {RESET Y-REG=0}
$EB00~$EB99 (-5376~-5223) \PB\       INTEGER BASIC ERROR TABLE OF CANNED ERROR MESSAGES
```

```
$EB1E (-5346) [MOV2F] \SE\            APPLESOFT FP - PACK FAC AND MOVE IT INTO TEMP2 ($0098~$009C). USES MOVMF. ON EXIT
                                      A-REG & Z FLAG REFLECT FACEXP {RESET Y-REG=0}
$EB21 (-5343) [MOV1F] \SE\            APPLESOFT FP - PACK FAC AND MOVE IT INTO TEMP1 ($0093~$0097). USES MOVMF. ON EXIT
                                      A-REG & Z FLAG REFLECT FACEXP. MODIFIES INDEX ($005E~$005F) {RESET Y-REG=0}
$EB23 (-5341) [MOVML] \SE\            APPLESOFT FP - PACK FAC AND MOVE IT INTO ZERO PAGE AREA POINTED TO BY X-REG. USES
                                      MOVMF. ON EXIT A-REG & Z FLAG REFLECT FACEXP
$EB27 (-5337) \SE\                    APPLESOFT FP - PAC FAC AND STORE IT INTO MEMORY POINTED TO BY FORPNT ($0085~$0086).
                                       MODIFIES INDEX ($005E~$005F) {RESET Y-REG=0}
$EB2B (-5333) [MOVMF (FPSTR)] \SE\    APPLESOFT FP - PACK FAC AND MOVE IT INTO MEMORY POINTED TO BY Y-REG (MSB) & X-REG
                                      (LSB). ON EXIT A-REG & ZERO FLAG REFLECT FACEXP. MODIFIES INDEX ($005E~$005F)
$EB36 (-5322) \SE\                    INTEGER BASIC CONTINUE RUN ROUTINE (W/O DELETING VARIABLES)
$EB53 (-5293) [MOVFA (TR2=>1)] \SE\   APPLESOFT FP - MOVE ARG INTO FAC. ON EXIT A-REG = FACEXP AND ZERO FLAG IS SET
$EB63 (-5277) [MOVAF (TR1=>2)] \SE\   APPLESOFT FP - PACK EXTENSION BYTE INTO FAC & MOVE FAC INTO ARG. ON EXIT A-REG =
                                      FACEXP AND ZERO FLAG IS SET. RESET EXTENSION BYTE = 0 {RESET X-REG=0}
$EB66 (-5274) \SE\                    APPLESOFT FP - SAME AS $EB63 BUT EXTENSION BYTE NOT ALTERED
$EB82 (-5246) [SIGN] \SE\             APPLESOFT FP - SETS A-REG ACCORDING TO VALUE OF FAC. ON EXIT A-REG=1 IF FAC
                                      +;A-REG=0 IF FAC=0;A-REG=$FF IF FAC - {X- Y-REGS NOT ALTERED}
$EB90 (-5232) [SGN (FPSGN)] \SE\      APPLESOFT FP - CALLS SIGN AND FLOATS THE RESULT IN THE FAC. FAC=+1 IF FAC WAS +;=0
                                      IF FAC WAS 0;=-1 IF FAC WAS -
$EB93 (-5229) [FLOAT] \SE\            APLESOFT FP - FLOAT THE SIGNED INTEGER IN A-REG INTO FAC
$EBAA (-5206) [~INPUT~] \SE\          INTEGER BASIC ENTRY TO INPUT ROUTINE
$EBAF (-5201) [ABS (FPABS)] \SE\      APPLESOFT FP - TAKES ABS OLUTE VALUE OF NUMBER IN FAC & LEAVES RESULT IN FAC
$EBB2 (-5198) [FCOMP] \SE\            APPLESOFT FP - COMPARE FAC AND PACKED NUMBER IN MEMORY POINTED TO BY Y-REG & A-REG.
                                      ON EXIT A=1 IF MEM<FAC;A=0 IF MEM=FAC;A=$FF IF MEM>FAC
$EBF2 (-5134) [QINT] \SE\             APPLESOFT QUICK GREATEST INTEGER FUNCTION. LEAVE INT(FAC)IN FAC MANTISSA (HO~MO~LO
                                      SIGNED). ASUMES FAC<2~23 {RESET Y-REG=0}
$EC00~$EDFF (-5120~-4609) [~SYNTABL~] \PB\INTEGER BASIC SYNTAX TABLE
$EC23 (-5085) [INT (FPINT)] \SE\      APPLESOFT FP - COMPUTES GREATES INT (FPINT)EGER VALUE OF FAC. MODIFIES CHARAC
                                      ($000D). USES QINT (FPINT). RESULT TO FAC. MODIFIES CHARAC ($000D)
$EC40 (-5056) [(INITFACMANT)] \SE\    APPLESOFT FP - INITIALIZED MANTISSA OF FAC (EXCEPT EXTENSION BYTE) TO VALUE IN
                                      A-REGISTER
$EC4A (-5046) [FIN] \SE\              APPLESOFT - INPUT FP NUMB INTO FAC FROM CHRGET. ASSUMES 6502 REGS HAVE BEEN SET UP
                                      BY CHRGET THAT FETCHED 1ST DIGIT
$ED14~$$ED18[(ONE.BILLION)] \P5\      APPLESOFT 5-BYTE FLOATING POINT CONSTANT 1000000000 (1E9)
$ED19 (-4839) [INPRT] \SE\            APPLESOFT - PRINT 'IN' & CURRENT LINE # FROM CURLIN. USES LPRINT
$ED24 (-4828) [LINPRT] \SE\           APPLESOFT - PRINTS 2-BYTE UNSIGNED NUMBER IN X-REG (MSB) & A-REG (LSB)
$ED2E (-4818) [PRNTFAC] \SE\          APPLESOFT - PRINTS & DESTROYS CURRENT VALUE OF FAC. USES FOUT & STROUT
$ED34 (-4812) [FOUT] \SE\             CREATES A STRING IN FBUFFR EQUIVALENT IN VALUE TO FAC. ON EXITY-REG &A-REG POINT TO
                                      THE STRING. FAC SCRAMBLED
$EE03 (-4605) [~PRNTSTR~] \SE\        INTEGER BASIC ENTRY TO FUNCTION WHICH PRINTS A STRING
$EE22 (-4574) [~LEN~] \SE\            INTEGER BASIC ENTRY TO FUNCTION TO OBTAIN LENGTH OF A STRING
$EE34 (-4556) [~GETVAL~] \SE\         INTEGER BASIC ENTRY TO ROUTINE TO GET A VALUE WHICH WILL FIT INTO A SINGLE BYTE
                                      (VAL<=255)
$EE3F (-4545) [~PLOT~] \SE\           INTEGER BASIC ENTRY TO ROUTINE TO DO A LO~RES PLOT (I.E. PLOT A COLORED SQUARE ON
                                      LO-RES SCREEN)
$EE4E (-4530) [~COLOR~] \SE\          INTEGER BASIC ENTRY TO ROUTINE TO SET COLOR VALUE FOR LO-RES
$EE54 (-4524) [~MAN~] \SE\            INTEGER BASIC ENTRY TO MANUAL LINE NUMBER FUNCTION
$EE57 (-4521) [~VTAB~] \SE\           INTEGER BASIC ENTRY TO VERTICAL TAB FUNCTION
$EE64~$EE68 (-4508~-4504) [(ONE.HALF)] \P5\APPLESOFT 5-BYTE FP CONSTANT ONE HALF (1/2)
$EE68 (-4504) [RNGERR] \P1\           INTEGER BASIC RANGE ERROR
$EE8D (-4457) [SQR (FPSQR)] \SE\      APPLESOFT FP - TAKE SQUARE ROOT OF FAC. RESULT TO FAC. MODIFIES CHARAC INDEX AND
                                      MANY OTHER FP LOCNS
```

```
$EE97 (-4457) [FPWRT (FPEXP)] \SE\  APPLESOFT FP EXPONENTATION (ARG TO FAC POWER) ON ENTRY A-REG & ZERO FLAG SHOULD
                                    REFLECT VALUE OF FACEXP. RESULT TO FAC. MODIFIES MANY FP LOCNS
$EEA0 (-4448) [~CALL~] \SE\         INTEGER BASIC ENTRY POINT TO CALL A SUB/ROT FUNCTION
$EEB0 (-4432) [~HLIN~] \SE\         INTEGER BASIC ENTRY POINT TO DRAW A LO-RES HORIZONTAL LINE
$EEC6 (-4410) [~VLIN~] \SE\         INTEGER BASIC ENTRY POINT TO DRAW A LO-RES VERTICAL LINE
$EED0 (-4400) [NEGOP] \SE\          APPLESOFT FP - LET FAC = -FAC (X- Y-REGS NOT ALTERED)
$EED3 (-4397) [~PRINT~] \SE\        INTEGER BASIC ENTRY POINT TO PRINT ERROR MESSAGE/BELL
$EEDB~$EEDF (-4389~-4385) [(LOG(E)2)] \P5\APPLESOFT FP CONSTANT LOG(E)2
$EEF6 (-4362) [~PEEK~] \SE\         INTEGER BASIC ENTRY TO ROUTINE TO 'PEEK' AT THE CONTENTS OF A MEMORY LOCATION
$EF00 (-4352) [~GETVAL255~] \SE\    INTEGER BASIC ENTRY TO ROUTINE TO GET A ONE-BYTE VALUE
$EF09 (-4343) [EXP] \SE\            APPLESOFT FP - RAISE E TO THE FAC POWER. RESULT TO FAC. MODIFIES INDEX CHARAC
                                    COMPRTYP XORFPSGN AND MANY OTHER FP LOCNS
$EF10 (-4336) [~DIVIDE~] \SE\       INTEGER BASIC ENTRY TO DIVIDE FUNCTION
$EF1E (-4322) [~DIMVARB~] \SE\      INTEGER BASIC ENTRY TO ROUTINE TO DIMENSION A VARIABLE
$EF4E (-4274) [~RND~] \SE\          INTEGER BASIC ENTRY TO RANDOM NUMBER GENERATOR
$EFAE (-4178) [RND] \SE\            APPLESOFT FP - FORM A 'RANDOM' NUMBER IN FAC USING ORIGINAL VALUE IN FAC AS
                                    PARAMETER 'KEY' OR 'SEED'. MODIFIES MANY FP LOCNS
$EFEA (-4118) [COS] \SE\            APPLESOFT FP - COMPUTE THE COSINE OF THE NUMBER IN FAC. RESULT TO FAC. MODIFIES
                                    INDEX CHARAC COMPRTYP XORFPSGN AND MANY OTHER FP LOCNS
$EFEC (-4116) [~RUN~] \SE\          APPLE INTEGER BASIC RUN ROUTINE (RUN FROM BEGINNING)
$EFF2 (-4110) [~RUN #N~] \SE\       INTEGER BASIC ENTRY TO ROUTINE TO RUN FROM LINE #N
$EFF1 (-4111) [SIN] \SE\            APPLESOFT FP - COMPUTE THE SINE OF THE NUMBER IN FAC. RESULT TO FAC. MODIFIES INDEX
                                    CHARAC COMPTRTYP XORFPSGN & MANY OTHER FP LOCNS
$F000~$F7FF (-4096~-2049) \HB\      ROM SOCKET F0 (1K INTEGER BASIC~ 1 K MONITOR IN APPLE II (NOT II+))
$F000 (-4096) [~SCRATCH~] \SE\      INTEGER BASIC ENTRY TO SCRATCH EVERYTHING ROUTINE
$F03A (-4038) [TAN] \SE\            APPLESOFT FP - COMPUTE THE TANGENT OF THE NUMBER IN FAC. RESULT TO FAC. MODIFIES
                                    CHARAC INDEX XORFPSGN AND MANY OTHER FP LOCNS
$F04D (-4019) [~HIMEM~] \SE\        INTEGER BASIC ENTRY TO THE HIMEM FUNCTION
$F063~$F067 (-3997~-3993) [(PI/2)] \P5\APPLESOFT 5-BYTE FLOATING POINT CONSTANT PI/2 = 1.508..
$F06B~$F06F (-3989~-3985) [(TWO PI)] \P5\APPLESOFT 5-BYTE FLOATING POINT CONSTANT 2*PI = 6.2832...
$F070~$F075 (-3984~-3979) [(ONE-QUARTER)] \P5\APPLESOFT5-BYTE FLOATING POINT CONSTANT 1/4 (0.25)
$F078 (-3976)                       INTEGER BASIC 'LOAD' (CASSETTE TAPE)
$F09E (-3938) [ATN] \SE\            APPLESOFT FP COMPUTE THE ARCTANGENT OF NUMBER IN FAC. RESULT TO FAC. MODIFIES INDEX
                                    XORFPSGN AND MANY OTHER FP LOCNS
$F0C9 (-3895) [~LOMEM~] \SE\        INTEGER BASIC ENTRY TO LOMEM ROUTINE
$F0DF (-3873) [~LOAD~]              INTEGER BASIC ENTRY TO LOAD SUBROUTINE (LOAD A PROGRAM FROM CASSETTE TAPE)
$F11E (-3810) [~SETHDR~] \SE\       INTEGER BASIC ENTRY TO SET UP HEADER FOR SAVE/LOAD PARAMETERS
$F11E (-3810) [ACADR]               HI-RES GRAPHICS 2-BYTE TAPE READ SETUP
$F12C (-3796) [~SETBUF~] \SE\       INTEGER BASIC ENTRY TO ROUTINE TO SET UP PROGRAM SAVE/LOAD PARAMETERS
$F140 (-3776) [~SAVE~] \SE\         INTEGER BASIC ENTRY TO ROUTINE TO SAVE A PROGRAM TO CASSETTE TAPE
$F161 (-3743) [~PRTERR~] \SE\       INTEGER BASIC ENTRY TO ROUTINE TO PRINT AN ERROR MESSAGE
$F167 (-3737) [~POP~] \SE\          INTEGER BASIC ENTRY TO ROUTINE TO POP THE RETURN STACK FOR GOSUB
$F171 (-3727) [~TRACE~] \SE\        INTEGER BASIC ENTRY TO ROUTINE TO SET TRACE MODE FOR EXECUTION
$F176 (-3722) [~NOTRACE~] \SE\      INTEGER BASIC ENTRY TO ROUTINE TO TURN OFF TRACE MODE
$F17D (-3715) [~TRACEIT~] \SE\      INTEGER BASIC ENTRY TO ROUTINE TO EXECUTE THE TRACE FUNCTION
$F1EC (-3604) [PLOTFNS] \SE\        APPLESOFT - GET 2 LO-RES PLOTTING COORDS SEPARATED BY COMMA FM TXTPTR. PUT FIRST #
                                    IN FIRST AND SECOND # IN H2 & V2
$F279 (-3463) [~STEP~] \SE\         INTEGER BASIC ENTRY TO ROUTINE TO HANDLE STEP FUNCTION FOR FOR/NEXT LOOP
$F2E0 (-3360) [~NODSP~] \SE\        INTEGER BASIC ENTRY TO ROUTINE TO TURN OFF DISPLAY FUNCTION
$F2E9 (-3351) [HANDLERR] \SE\       APPLESOFT ERROR PROC - SAVE CURLIN IN ERRLIN;TXTPTR IN ERRPOS;X-REG IN ERRNUM;
                                    REMSTK IN ERRSTK
```

```
$F304 (-3324) ["DSP"] \SE\        INTEGER BASIC ENTRY TO ROUTINE TO DISPLAY A VARIABLE SET
$F30A (-3318) ["CON"] \SE\        INTEGER BASIC ENTRY TO ROUTINE TO CONTINUE EXECUTION
$F317 (-3305) [RESUME] \SE\       APPLESOFT ERROR PROC - RESTORE CURLIN FROM ERRLIN & TXTPTR FROM ERRPOS. TRANSFER
                                  ERRSTK INTO 6502 STACK POINTER
$F31D (-3299) ["ASC"] \SE\        INTEGER BASIC ENTRY TO ROUTINE TO PERFORM THE ASC (ASCII) FUNCTION
$F33B (-3269) ["PDL"] \SE\        INTEGER BASIC ENTRY TO ROUTINE TO READ A PADDLE
$F351 (-3247) ["RDKEY"] \SE\      INTEGER BASIC ENTRY TO ROUTINE TO READ AN INPUT FOR BASIC FROM KEYBOARD
$F371 (-3215) ["EXP"] \SE\        INTEGER BASIC ENTRY TO ROUTINE TO EXPONENTIATE (RAISE TO A POWER)
$F3C9 (-3127) ["PR#S"] \SE\       INTEGER BASIC ENTRY TO ROUTINE TO SET OUTPUT PORT
$F3D4 (-3116) [HGR2] \SE\         APPLESOFT HI-RES - INITIALIZE & CLEAR PAGE 2 HI-RES REGARDLESS OF SCREEN BEING
                                  DISPLAYED
$F3DE (-3106) [HGR] \SE\          APPLESOFT HI-RES - INITIALIZE & CLEAR PAGE 1 HI-RES REGARDLESS OF SCREEN BEING
                                  DISPLAYED
$F3EE (-3090) [HCLR] \SE\         APPLESOFT HI-RES - CLEAR HI-RES SCREEN TO BLACK
$F3F2 (-3086) [BKGND] \SE\        APPLESOFT HI-RES - CLEAR HI-RES SCREEN TO LAST PLOTTED COLOR
$F40D (-3059) [HPOSN] \SE\        APPLESOFT HI-RES - POSN HI-RES CURSOR W/O PLOTTING. HPAG DETERMINES WHICH PAGE;
                                  HORIZ = Y-REG(MSB)&X-REG(LSB);VERT= A-REG
$F41A (-3046) ["IN#S"] \SE\       INTEGER BASIC ENTRY TO ROUTINE TO SET INPUT PORT
$F425"$F65D (-3035"-2467)         APPLE II FLOATING POINT PACKAGE (NOT USED IN APPLESOFT)
$F453 (-2989) [HPLOT] \SE\        APPLESOFT HI-RES - CALL HPOSN THEN PLOT DOT THERE. NO DOT MAY BE PLOTTED IS
                                  PLOTTING NON-WHITE AT COMPLEMENTARY COLOR X COORD
$F425 (-3035) [ADD] \SE\          ADD 3-BYTE M1 TO 3-BYTE M2 AND LEAVE RESULT IN M1 (NOT FP ADD BUT USED IN FP PKG)
                                  {A- X-REGS ALTERED}
$F437 (-3017) [ABSWAP] \SE\       TAKE ABSOLUTE VALUE OF FP1; THEN SWAP FP1 WITH FP2 (FP1=$00F8;$FP2=$00F4) {A-
                                  X-REGS ALTERED}
$F451 (-2991) [FLOAT] \SE\        CONVERT INTEGER (HIGH BYTE IN M1;LOW BYTE IN M1+1;M1+2 CLEARED) TO NORMALIZED FL
                                  POINT EQUIV IN FP1 {A-REG ALTERED}
$F463 (-2973) [NORM] \SE\         NORMALIZE FLOATING POINT NUMBER IN FP1 {A-REG ALTERED}
$F4A4 (-2908) [FCOMPL] \SE\       VALUE OF FLOATING POINT NUMBER IN FP1 IS NEGATED THEN NORMALIZED {A- X-REGS ALTERED}
$F468 (-2968) [FSUB] \SE\         FLOATING POINT SUBTRACTION MINUEND IN FP1;SUBTRAHEND IN FP2;NORMALIZED DIFFERENCE
                                  TO FP1 {A- X-REGS ALTERED}
$F46E (-2962) [FADD] \SE\         FLOATING POINT NUMBER IN FP1 ADDED TO THAT IN FP2. NORMALIZED RESULT LEFT IN FP1
                                  {A- X-REGS ALTERED}
$F47D (-2947) [RTAR] \SE\         DENORMALIZE FP1 BY SHIFTING M1(&E) RIGHT 1 BIT POSN & INCREMENTING X1 {A- X-REGS
                                  ALTERED}
$F48C (-2932) [FMUL] \SE\         FLOATING POINT MULTIPLY S/R: MUTIPLICAND IN FP1; MULTIPLIER IN FP2; SIGNED
                                  NORMALIZED PRODUCT IN FP1 {A- X- Y-REGS ALTERED}
$F4B2 (-2894) [FMUL] \SE\         FL PT DIVIDE S/R: NORM DIVIDEND IN FP2;NORM DIVIDER IN FP1;SIGNED NORM FP QUOTIENT
                                  TO FP1 {A- X- Y-REGS ALTERED}
$F500"$F666 (-2816"-2458)         APPLE II MINIASSEMBLER SOFTWARE PACKAGE
$F500 (-2816) [REL]               MINIASSEMBLER MEMORY LOCATION 'REL'
$F50C (-2804) [REL2]              MINIASSEMBLER MEMORY LOCATION 'REL2'
$F516 (-2794) [REL3]              MINIASSEMBLER MEMORY LOCATION 'REL3'
$F519 (-2791) [ERR3]              MINIASSEMBLER MEMORY LOCATION 'ERR3'
$F51B (-2789) [FINDOP]            MINIASSEMBLER MEMORY LOCATION 'FINDOP'
$F51D (-2787) [FNDOP2]            MINIASSEMBLER MEMORY LOCATION 'FNDOP2'
$F530 (-2768) [HLIN] \SE\         APPLESOFT HI-RES HORIZ LINE DRAWING FROM LAST POINT PLOTTED TOX-COORD =
                                  X-REG(MSB)&A-REG(LSB);Y-COORD=Y-REG
$F538 (-2760) [FAKEMON3]          MINIASSEMBER MEMORY LOCATION 'FAKEMON3'
$F53D (-2755) [FAKEMON]           MINIASSEMBLER MEMORY LOCATION 'FAKEMON'
$F544 (-2748) [FAKEMON2]          MINIASSEMBLER MEMORY LOCATION 'FAKEMON2'
```

```
$F55C (-2724) [TRYNEXT]           MINIASSEMBLER MEMORY LOCATION 'TRYNEXT'
$F578 (-2696) [NREL]              MINIASSEMBLER MEMORY LOCATION 'NREL'
$F57C (-2692) [NEXTOP]            MINIASSEMBLER MEMORY LOCATION 'NEXTOP'
$F586 (-2682) [ERR]               MINIASSEMBLER MEMORY LOCATION 'ERR'
$F588 (-2680) [ERR2]              MINIASSEMBLER MEMORY LOCATION 'ERR2'
$F592 (-2670) [RESETZ]            MINIASSEMBLER MEMORY LOCATION 'RESETZ'
$F595 (-2667) [NXTLINE]           MINIASSEMBER MEMORY LOCATION 'NXTLINE'
$F5B1 (-2639) [ERR4]              MINIASSEMBLER MEMORY LOCATION 'ERR4'
$F5B9 (-2631) [SPACE]             MINIASSEMBLER MEMORY LOCATION 'SPACE'
$F5BD (-2627) [NXTMN]             MINIASSEMBLER MEMORY LOCATION 'NXTMN'
$F5C0 (-2624) [NXTM]              MINIASSEMBLER MEMORY LOCATION 'NXTM'
$F5CB (-2613) [HFIND] \SE\        APPLESOFT HI-RES HFIND. CONVERT HI-RES CURSOR POSN TO X-Y COORDS. ON EXIT
                                  $00E0=HORIZ LSB;$00E1=HORIZ MSB;$00E2=VERT
$F5CB (-2613) [NXTM2]             MINIASSEMBLER MEMORY LOCATION 'NXTM2'
$F5D9 (-2599) [FORM1]             MINIASSEMBLER MEMORY LOCATION 'FORM1'
$F5DB (-2597) [FORM2]             MINIASSEMBLER MEMORY LOCATION 'FORM2'
$F5F8 (-2568) [FORM3]             MINIASSEMBLER MEMORY LOCATION 'FORM3'
$F5F9 (-2567) [FORM4]             MINIASSEMBLER MEMORY LOCATION 'FORM4'
$F5FA (-2566) [FORM5]             MINIASSEMBLER MEMORY LOCATION 'FORM5'
$F601 (-2559) [DRAW] \SE\         APPLESOFT HI-RES - DRAW SHAPE POINTED TO BY Y-REG(MSB)&X-REG(LSB) BY INVERTING
                                  EXISTING COLOR OF DOTS THE SHAPE DRAWS OVER. A-REG=ROTATION FACTOR
$F608 (-2552) [FORM6]             MINIASSEMBLER MEMORY LOCATION 'FORM6'
$F60D (-2547) [FORM7]             MINIASSEMBLER MEMORY LOCATION 'FORM7'
$F622 (-2526) [FORM8]             MINIASSEMBLER MEMORY LOCATION 'FORM8'
$F631 (-2511) [FORM9]             MINIASSEMBLER MEMORY LOCATION 'FORM9'
$F634 (-2508) [GETNSP]            MINIASSEMBLER MEMORY LOCATION 'GETNSP'
$F640 (-2496) [FIX] \SE\          FROMFLOATING POINT NUMBER IN FP1 EXTRACT INTEGER. PUT HIGH-ORDER BYTE IN
                                  M1;LOW-ORDER IN M1+1 {A- X-REGS ALTERED}
$F65D (-2467) [XDRAW] \SE\        APPLESOFT HI-RES - DRAW SHAPE POINTED TO BY Y-REG(MSB)&X-REG(LSB) BY INVERTING
                                  EXISTING COLOR OF DOTS SHAPE DRAWS OVER. A-REG = ROT FACTOR
$F666 (-2458) [MINASM]            TURN ON MINIASSEMBLER (KEYBOARD INPUT WILL BE INTERPRETED AS A SEMBLY-LANGUAGE
                                  INSTRUCTION)
$F689~$F7FA (-2423~-2054) \SB\    'SWEET-16' 16-BIT PSEUDO-MACHINE INTERPRETER
$F689 (-2423) \SE\                SWEET-16 INTERPRETER ENTRY
$F6B9 (-2375) [HFNS] \SE\         APPLESOFT - GET HI-RES PLOTTING COORDINATE FROM TXTPTR SETS UP 6502 REGISTERS FOR
                                  HPOSN: A-REG=VERT COORD;X-REG LSB OF HORIZ;Y-REG MSB OF HORIZ {A- X- Y-REGS ALTERED}
$F6EC (-2324) [SETHCOL] \SE\      APPLESOFT HI-RES - SET COLOR TO CONTENTS OF X-REG (MUST BE LESS THAN 8)
$F775 (-2187) [SHLOAD] \SE\       APPLESOFT HI-RES. LOADS SHAPE TABLE INTO MEMORY FROM TAPE ABOVE MEMSIZ (HIMEM) AND
                                  SETS POINTER AT $00E8
$F7D9 (-2087) [GETARYPT] \SE\     APPLESOFT - READ VAR NAME FROM CHRGET & FIND IT IN MEMORY.ON EXIT VAL OF VAR IN
                                  VARPNT AND Y-REG(MSB)&A-REG(LSB)
$F800~$FFFF (-2048~-1) \HB\       ROM SOCKET F8 (MONITOR) NOTE: WHEN LANGUAGE CARD RAM DESELECTED MONITOR ON CARD
                                  ACTIVE
$F800~$FFFF (-2048~-1) \SB\       APPLE II SYSTEM MONITOR (MAIN BODY)
$F800~$FFFF (-2048~-1) \HB\       APPLE LANGUAGE CARD ADDITIONAL ROM/RAM
$F800 (-2048) [PLOT] \SE\         LO-RES PLOT POINT AT X-COORD=(Y-REG) Y-COORD=(A-REG) LEAVING GBASL~H AND MASK SET
                                  (SEE CALL-APPLE DEC 78) {A-REG ALTERED}
$F80C (-2036) [RTMASK]            MONITOR MEMORY LOCATION 'RTMASK'
$F80E (-2034) [PLOT1] \SE\        LO-RES PLOT A POINT X-COORD=(Y-REG) Y-COORD PER GBASL~H & MASK {A-REG ALTERED}
$F819 (-2023) \SE\                HLINE S/R (SEE CALL-APPLE NOV/DEC 78 PG4)
$F819 (-2023) [HLINE] \SE\        LO-RES S/R TO DRAW HORIZONTAL LINE AT Y-COORD = (A-REG) WITH X-COORDS FROM (A-REG)
                                  THRU (H2)($002C) {A- Y-REGS ALTERED}
```

```
$F81C (-2020) [HLINE1] \SE\      LO-RES S/R. DRAW HORZ LINE AT Y-COORD ESTAB BY GBASL~H & MASK. X-CORDS FROM (Y-REG)
                                 THRU ($002C) {A- Y-REGS ALTERED}
$F826 (-2010) [VLINEZ] \SE\      LO-RES PLOT VERTICAL LINE AT X-COORD = (Y-REG) AND Y-COORD FROM (A-REG)+1+CARRY
                                 THRU ($002D) {A-REG ALTERED}
$F828 (-2008) [VLINE] \SE\       LO-RES PLOT VERT LINE AT X-COORD = (Y-REG) AND Y-COORD FROM (A-REG) THRU ($002D)
                                 {A-REG ALTERED}
$F831 (-1999) [RTS1]             MONITOR MEMORY LOCATION 'RTS1'
$F832 (-1998) [CLRSCR] \SE\      MONITOR S/R TO CLEAR SCREEN - GRAPHICS MODE FULL SCREEN) {A- Y-REGS ALTERED}
$F832 (-1998) [CLRSCR] \SE\      CLEAR LO-RES GRAPHICS SCREEN1 TO BLACK (INVERSE @ IN TEXT MODE) MIXED GRAPHICS AREA
                                 ONLY {A- Y-REGS ALTERED}
$F836 (-1994) [CLRTOP] \SE\      CLEAR TOP 20 LINES PAGE1 TO INVERSE @ IN TEXT; BLACK IN LO-RES GRAPHICS (40 LO-RES
                                 GRAPHIC 'LINES') {A- Y-REGS ALTERED}
$F838 (-1992) [CLRSC2] \SE\      CLEAR LINES 0 THRU (Y-REG) 40 COLUMNS WIDE TO BLACK IN LO-RES GRAPHICS OR INVERSE @
                                 IN TEXT PAGE 1 {A- Y-REGS ALTERED}
$F83C (-1988) [CLRSC3] \SE\      CLEAR LO-RES GRAPHICS PARTIAL TOP LEFT: X-COORD 0 THRU (Y-REG); Y-COORD 0 THRU
                                 ($002D) {A- Y-REGS ALTERED}
$F847 (-1977) [GBASCALC] \SE\    COMPUTE GRAPHICS BASE MEMORY ADDRESS FOR LINE IN A-REG (NOTE: 2 LO-RES GRAPHICS
                                 LINES PER TEXT LINE SO (A)= LINE/2); SET GBASL~H {A-REG ALTERED}
$F856 (-1962) [GBCALC]           MONITOR MEMORY LOCATION 'GBCALC'
$F85F (-1953) [NXTCOL] \SE\      MONITOR LO-RES S/R. CHANGE COLOR TO (COLOR)+3 {A-REG ALTERED}
$F864 (-1948) [SETCOL] \SE\      SET LO-RES COLOR TO COLOR CODE SPECIFIED BY A-REG FOR FUTURE PLOTTING {A-REG
                                 ALTERED}
$F871 (-1935) [SCRN] \SE\        GET (LOAD TO A-REG) LO-RES GRAPHICS COLOR OF POINT Y-COORD = (A-REG); X-COORD =
                                 (X-REG)  {A-REG ALTERED}
$F879 (-1927) [SCRN2]            MONITOR MEMORY LOCATION 'SCRN2'
$F87F (-1921) [RTMSKZ]           MONITOR MEMORY LOCATION 'RTMSKZ'
$F882 (-1918) [INSDS1]           MONITOR MEMORY LOCATION 'INSDS1'
$F88E (-1906) [INSDS2]           MONITOR S/R - DISASSEMBLER ENTRY
$F89B (-1893) [IEVEN]            MONITOR MEMORY LOCATION 'IEVEN'
$F8A5 (-1883) [ERR]              MONITOR MEMORY LOCATION 'ERR'
$F8A9 (-1879) [GETFMT]           MONITOR MEMORY LOCATION GETFMT
$F8BE (-1858) [MNNDX1]           MONITOR MEMORY LOCATION 'MNNDX1'
$F8C2 (-1854) [MNNDX2]           MONITOR MEMORY LOCATION 'MNNDX2'
$F8C9 (-1847) [MNNDX3]           MONITOR MEMORY LOCATION 'MNNDX3'
$F8D0 (-1840) [INSTDSP]          MONITOR & MINIASSEMBLER MEMORY LOCATION 'INSTDSP' (INSTRUCTION DISPLAY)
$F8D4 (-1836) [PRNTOP]           MONITOR MEMORY LOCATION 'PRNTOP' (PRINT OPERATION CODE)
$F8DB (-1829) [PRNTBL]           MONITOR MEMORY LOCATION 'PRNTBL'
$F8F5 (-1803) [PRMN1]            MONITOR MEMORY LOCATION 'PRMN1' (PRINT MNEMONIC)
$F8F5 (-1803) [NXTCOL]           AUTOSTART MONITOR MEMORY LOCATION 'NXTCOL'
$F8F9 (-1799) [PRMN2]            MONITOR MEMORY LOCATION 'PRMN2'
$F910 (-1776) [PRADR1]           MONITOR MEMORY LOCATION 'PRADR1' (PRINT ADDRESS)
$F914 (-1772) [PRADR2]           MONITOR MEMORY LOCATION 'PRADR2'
$F926 (-1754) [PRADR3]           MONITOR MEMORY LOCATION 'PRADR3'
$F92A (-1750) [PRADR4]           MONITOR MEMORY LOCATION 'PRADR4'
$F930 (-1744) [PRADR5]           MONITOR MEMORY LOCATION 'PRADR5'
$F938 (-1736) [RELADR]           MONITOR MEMORY LOCATION 'RELADR' (RELATIVE ADDRESS)
$F940 (-1728) [PRNTYX] \SE\      MONITOR S/R- PRINT CONTENTS OF Y AND X AS 4 HEX DIGITS {A- X-REGS ALTERED}
$F941 (-1727) [PRNTAX] \SE\      MONITOR S/R-PRINT CONTENTS OF A-REG & X-REG AS HEX DIGITS {A- X-REGS ALTERED}
$F944 (-1724) [PRNTX] \SE\       PRINT CONTENTS OF X-REG AS HEX DIGITS {A- X-REGS ALTERED}
$F948 (-1720) [PRBLNK] \SE\      PRINT THREE BLANKS THROUGH COUT {A- X-REGS ALTERED}
$F94C (-1716) [PRBL2] \SE\       MONITOR S/R- PRINT BLANKS: X REG CONTAINS NUMBER TO PRINT. CLOBBERS AC~X {A- X-REGS
                                 ALTERED}
```

```
$F94C (-1716) [PRBL3] \SE\PRINT A-REG FOLLOWED BY (X-REG)-1 BLANKS {A- X-REGS ALTERED}
$F953 (-1709) [PCADJ]   MINIASSEMBLER MEMORY LOCATION 'PCADJ' (PROGRAM COUNTER ADJUST: 0=1 BYTE; 1=2 BYTES; 2=3 BYTES)
$F954 (-1708) [PCADJ2]  MONITOR & MINIASSEMBLER MEMORY LOCATION 'PCADJ2'
$F956 (-1706) [PCADJ3]  MONITOR MEMORY LOCATION 'PCADJ3'
$F95C (-1700) [PCADJ4]  MONITOR MEMORY LOCATION 'PCADJ4'
$F961 (-1695) [RTS2]    MONITOR MEMORY LOCATION 'RTS2'
$F962 (-1694) [FMT1]    MONITOR MEMORY LOCATION 'FMT1'
$F9A6 (-1626) [FMT2]    MONITOR MEMORY LOCATION 'FMT2'
$F9B4 (-1612) [CHAR1]   MONITOR & MINIASSEMBER MEMORY LOCATION 'CHAR1'
$F9BA (-1606) [CHAR2]   MONITOR & MINIASSEMBLER MEMORY LOCATION 'CHAR2'
$F9C0 (-1600) [MNEML]   MONITOR & MINIASSEMBLER MEMORY LOCATION 'MNEML'
$FA00 (-1536) [MNEMR]   MONITOR & MINIASSEMBER MEMORY LOCATION 'MNEMR'
$FA40~$FA85 (-1472~-1403)          SINGLE-STEP SIMULATOR SUBROUTINE (NOT IN AUTOSTART ROM)
$FA40 (-1472) [IRQ] \SE\           AUTOSTART ROM MONITOR S/R - IRQ HANDLER
$FA43 (-1469) [STEP]               MONITOR S/R- PERFORM A SINGLE STEP (NOT AVAILABLE WITH AUTOSTART ROM). EXECUTES ONE
                                   INSTRUCTION AT (PCL~H) WITH REGISTER RESTORE BEFORE; REGISTER SAVE AFTER; UPDATE OF
                                   PCL~H; DISPLAY OF INSTRUCTION & DISPLAY OF RESULT REGISTERS
$FA4E (-1458) [XQINIT]             MONITOR MEMORY LOCATION 'XQINIT'
$FA59 (-1447) [OLDBRK]             AUTOSTART MONITOR MEMORY LOCATION 'OLDBRK'
$FA62 (-1438) [RESET]              AUTOSTART MONITOR MEMORY LOCATION 'RESET'
$FA6F (-1425) [INITAN]             AUTOSTART MONITOR MEMORY LOCATION 'INITAN'
$FA78 (-1416) [XQ1]                MONITOR MEMORY LOCATION 'XQ1'
$FA7A (-1414) [XQ2]                MONITOR MEMORY LOCATION 'XQ2'
$FA81 (-1407) [NEWMON]             AUTOSTART MONITOR MEMORY LOCATION 'NEWMON'
$FA86 (-1402) [IRQ] \SE\           MONITOR S/R- IRQ HANDLER. NOTE: MOVED TO $FA40 IN AUTOSTART ROM
$FA92 (-1390) [BREAK] \SE\         MONITOR S/R - BREAK HANDLER
$FA9B (-1381)                      AUTOSTART MONITOR MEMORY LOCATION 'FIXSEV'
$FA9C (-1380) [XBRK]               MONITOR MEMORY LOCATION 'XBRK'
$FAA5~$FAD6 (-1371~-1322)          BLOCK OF CODE ASSOCIATED WITH SINGLE-STEP SIMULATOR IN NORMAL MONITOR REMOVED FROM
                                   AUTOSTART ROM
$FAA5 (-1371) [XRTI]               MONITOR MEMORY LOCATION 'XRTI'
$FAA6 (-1370) [PWRUP]              AUTOSTART MONITOR MEMORY LOCATION 'PWRUP'
$FAA9 (-1367) [SETPG3]             AUTOSTART MONITOR MEMORY LOCATION 'SETPG3'
$FAA9 (-1367) [XRTS]               MONITOR MEMORY LOCATION 'XRTS'
$FAAD (-1363) [PCINC2]             MONITOR MEMORY LOCATION 'PCINC2'
$FAAF (-1361) [PCINC3]             MONITOR MEMORY LOCATION 'PCINC3'
$FAB9 (-1351) [XJSR]               MONITOR MEMORY LOCATION 'XJSR'
$FAB9 (-1351) [SLOOP]              AUTOSTART MONITOR MEMORY LOCATION 'SLOOP'
$FAC4 (-1340) [XJMP]               MONITOR MEMORY LOCATION 'XJMP'
$FAC5 (-1339) [XJMPAT]             MONITOR MEMORY LOCATION 'XJMPAT'
$FAC7 (-1337) [NXTBYT]             AUTOSTART MONITOR MEMORY LOCATION 'NXTBYT'
$FACD (-1331) [NEWPCL]             MONITOR MEMORY LOCATION 'NEWPCL'
$FAD1 (-1327) [RTNJMP]             MONITOR MEMORY LOCATION 'RTNJMP'
$FAD7 (-1321) [REGDSP] \SE\        DISPLAY SAVED REGISTER CONTENTS FROM MEMORY LOCNS $0045~$0049 WITH PRECEDING
                                   CARRIAGE RETURN (SEE 'SAVE' ROUTINE AT $FF4A) {A- X-REGS ALTERED}
$FADA (-1318) [RGDSP1] \SE\        DISPLAY SAVED REGISTER CONTENTS FROM MEMORY LOCNS $0045~$0049 WITHOUT PRECEDING
                                   CARRIAGE RETURN (SEE 'SAVE' ROUTINE AT $FF4A) {A- X-REGS ALTERED}
$FAE4 (-1308) [RDSP1]              MONITOR MEMORY LOCATION 'RDSP1'
$FAFD~$FB18 (-1283~-1256)          BLOCK OF CODE ASSOCIATED WITH SINGLE-STEP SIMULATOR IN NORMAL MONITOR REMOVED FROM
                                   AUTOSTART ROM
$FAFD (-1283) [BRANCH]             MONITOR MEMORY LOCATION 'BRANCH'
```

HEX LOCN (DEC LOCN) [NAME] \USE-TYPE\	- DESCRIPTION
$FAFD (-1283) [PWRCON]	AUTOSTART MONITOR MEMORY LOCATION 'PWRCON'
$FB05 (-1275) [DISKID]	AUTOSTART MONITOR MEMORY LOCATION 'DISKID'
$FB09 (-1271) [TITLE]	AUTOSTART MONITOR MEMORY LOCATION 'TITLE'
$FB0B (-1269) [NBRNCH]	MONITOR MEMORY LOCATION 'NBRNCH'
$FB11 (-1263) [INITBL]	MONITOR MEMORY LOCATION 'INITBL'
$FB11 (-1263)	AUTOSTART MONITOR MEMORY LOCATION 'XLTBL'
$FB19 (-1255) [RTBL]	MONITOR MEMORY LOCATION 'RTBL'
$FB1E (-1250) [PREAD] \SE\	MONITOR S/R TO READ PADDLE. X-REG CONTAINS PADDLE NUMBER (0-3) OF PADDLE TO BE READ. PADDLE VALUE TO Y-REG {A- Y-REGS ALTERED}
$FB25 (-1243) [PREAD2]	MONITOR MEMORY LOCATION 'PREAD2'
$FB2E (-1234) [RTS2D]	MONITOR MEMORY LOCATION 'RTS2D'
$FB2F (-1233) [INIT] \SE\	MONITOR S/R- SCREEN INITIALIZATION (RESET TEXT MODE)
$FB39 (-1223) [SETTXT] \SE\	MONITOR S/R- SET SCREEN TO TEXT MODE. CLOBBERS ACCUMULATOR {A-REG ALTERED}
$FB40 (-1216) [SETGR] \SE\	MONITOR S/R- SET GRAPHIC MODE (GR). THIS INCLUDES SETTING TO MIXED MODE;CLEARING GRAPHICS PART OF SCREEN; AND RESETTING WNDTOP~WNDLFT~WNDWDTH~WNDBTM & TABV {A-REG ALTERED}
$FB43 (-1213) \SE\	MONITOR S/R - ALL OF SETGR EXCEPT SETTING COLOR GRAPHICS DISPLAY MODE
$FB46 (-1210) \SE\	MONITOR S/R - ALL OF SETGR EXCEPT SETTING COLOR GRAPHICS DISPLAY MODE & CLEARING GRAPHICS PART OF SCREEN; I.E. WINDOW & TAB SETTING ONLY
$FB4B (-1205) [SETWND] \SE\	MONITOR S/R- SET NORMAL LOW-RESOLUTION GRAPHICS WINDOW
$FB5B (-1189) [TABV] \SE\	PLACE CURSOR AT LINE (A-REG) COLUMN (CH) SETTING CV AND BASL~H FROM A-REG {A-REG ALTERED}
$FB60~$FB80 (-1184~-1152) [MULPM] \SB\	MONITOR 16-BIT MULTIPLY S/R (NOT IN AUTOSTART ROM). MULTIPLIER IN AUXL~AUXH ($0054~$0055); MULTIPLICAND IN ACL~ACH ($0050~$0051);XTNDL~XTNDH ($0052~$0053) CLEARED TO ZEROS; RESULT GOES TO EXTENDED AC ($0050~$0053). ALSO SEE 'SIGN' AT $002F. {A- X-REGSY-REG ALTERED}
$FB60 (-1184) [MULPM] \SE\	MONITOR - SIGNED 16-BIT MULTIPLY LEAVING SIGN IN LSB OF 'SIGN' {A- X- Y-REGS ALTERED}
$FB60 (-1184) [APPLEII] \SE\	CLEAR SCREEN AND POKE 'APPLE II' INTO FIRST LINE OF TEXT BUFFER (AUTOSTART ROM ONLY) {A- Y-REGS ALTERED}
$FB63 (-1181) [MUL] \SE\	MONITOR - UNSIGNED 16-BIT MULTIPLY S/R (NOT AVAILABLE WITH AUTOSTART ROM). SAME AS MULPM ($FB60) EXCEPT UNSIGNED. SEE 'SIGN' AT $002F {A- X- Y-REGS ALTERED}
$FB65 (-1179) [MUL2]	MONITOR MEMORY LOCATION 'MUL2'
$FB65 (-1179) [STITLE]	AUTOSTART MONITOR MEMORY LOCATION 'STITLE'
$FB6D (-1171) [MUL3]	MONITOR MEMORY LOCATION 'MUL3'
$FB6F (-1169) [SETPWRC] \SE\	SET POWER CONDITION (AUTOSTART ROM ONLY)
$FB76 (-1162) [MUL4]	MONITOR MEMORY LOCATION 'MUL4'
$FB78 (-1160) [MUL5]	MONITOR MEMORY LOCATION 'MUL5'
$FB78 (-1160) [VIDWAIT]	AUTOSTART MONITOR MEMORY LOCATION 'VIDWAIT'
$FB81~$FBC0 (-1151~-1088)	MONITOR 16-BIT DIVIDE ROUTINE (NOT IN AUTOSTART ROM)
$FB81 (-1151) [DIVPM]	MONITOR SIGNED DIVISION - DIVIDES NUMBER IN EXTENDED AC ($0050~$0053) BY NUMBER IN AUXL~AUXH ($0054~$0055) LEAVING QUOTIENT IN ACL~ACH ($0050~$0051) AND REMAINDER IN $0053. BE CAREFUL OF SIGNS SCALING & OVERFLOW. IF (XTNDL~XTNDH ($0052~$0053))>(AUXL~AUXH ($0054~$0055)) OVERFLOW WILL RESULT
$FB84 (-1148) [DIV] \SE\	MONITOR S/R- UNSIGNED DIVIDE ROUTINE - SAME AS $FB81 (DIVPM) EXCEPT NO SIGNS USED.
$FB86 (-1146) [DIV2]	MONITOR MEMORY LOCATION 'DIV2'
$FB88 (-1144)	AUTOSTART MONITOR MEMORY LOCATION 'KBDWAIT'
$FBA0 (-1120) [DIV3]	MONITOR MEMORY LOCATION 'DIV3'
$FBA4 (-1116) [MD1]	MONITOR 16-BIT MULITIPLY/DIVIDE SIGN-PROCESSOR. SETS ABSOLUTE VALUES OF ACL~H MEMORY LOCATION 'MD1' AUXL~H LEAVING RESULTING SIGN IN LSB OF SIGN ($002F)
$FBAF (-1105) [MD2]	MONITOR MEMORY LOCATION 'MD2'

HEX LOCN (DEC LOCN) [NAME] \USE-TYPE\	- DESCRIPTION
$FBB4 (-1100) [MD3]	MONITOR MEMORY LOCATION 'MD3'
$FBC0 (-1088) [MDRTS]	MONITOR MEMORY LOCATION 'MDRTS'
$FBC1 (-1087) [BASCALC] \SE\	MONITOR S/R- CALCULATE TEXT BASE ADDRESS. SET BASL~H TO LEFT END OF SCREEN LINE (NOT WINDOW LINE) IN A-REG {A-REG ALTERED}
$FBD0 (-1072) [BSCLC2]	MONITOR MEMORY LOCATION 'BSCLC2'
$FBD9 (-1063) [BELL1]	MONITOR MEMORY LOCATION 'BELL1'
$FBDD (-1059)	SOUNDS BELL IN APPLE REGARDLESS OF OUTPUT DEVICE IN USE {A- Y-REGS ALTERED}
$FBE4 (-1052) [BELL2] \SE\	MONITOR S/R- SOUND BELL (BEEPER)
$FBEF (-1041) [RTS2B]	MONITOR MEMORY LOCATION 'RTS2B'
$FBF0 (-1040) [STOADV] \SE\	MONITOR - LOAD Y FROM CH; STORE A-REG TO SCREEN AT (BASL)~Y; AND GOTO ADVANCE ($FBF4) {A- Y-REG ALTERED}
$FBF4 (-1036) [ADVANCE] \SE\	MONITOR S/R- MOVE CURSOR RIGHT; I.E. INCREMENT (CH); COMPARE (CH) WITH (WNDWDTH) GO TO CR IF CH NOT LESS ELSE RETURN (RTS) {A-REG ALTERED}
$FBF6 (-1034) \SE\	COMPARE (CH) WITH (WNDWDTH) GO TO CR IF CH NOT LESS ELSE RETURN (RTS) {A-REG ALTERED}
$FBFC (-1028) [RTS3]	MONITOR MEMORY LOCATION 'RTS3'
$FBFD (-1027) [VIDOUT] \SE\	MONITOR S/R- OUTPUT A-REGISTER AS ASCII ON TEXT SCREEN OR PROCESS CONTROL CHARACTER. IF (A)<$80 GOTO STOADV; =$87 SOUND BELL; =$88 GOTO BS; =$8A GOTO LF; =$8D GOTO CR; >$9F GOTO STOADV; OTHERWISE IGNORE ENTRY SCREEN RTS 1
$FC10 (-1008) [BS] \SE\	MONITOR S/R TO MOVE CURSOR LEFT (BACKSPACE); IF AT START OF LINE MOVE UP TO RIGHT END OF LINE ABOVE IF POSSIBLE {A-REG ALTERED}
$FC1A (-998) [UP ~ CURSUP] \SE\	MONITOR S/R TO MOVE CURSOR UPWARD (IF POSSIBLE) {A-REG ALTERED}
$FC22 (-990) [VTAB] \SE\	PERFORM A VERTICAL TAB TO ROW SPECIFIED IN A-REG ($0~$17). SET BASL~H FROM CV (AND WNDLFT) {A-REG ALTERED}
$FC24 (-988) [VTABZ] \SE\	SET BASL~H FROM (A-REG) AND WNDLFT WITHOUT REGARD TO CV {A-REG ALTERED}
$FC2B (-981) [RTS4]	MONITOR MEMORY LOCATION 'RTS4'
$FC2C (-980) [ESC1] \SE\	ROUTINE (IF A=@ GO TO HOME; =A GO TO ADVANCE; =B GO TO BS (BACKSPACE); =C GO TO LF (LINEFEED); =D GO TO UP (INVERSE LINEFEED); =E GOTO CLREOL; =F GOTO CLREOP; =ANYTHING ELSE RTS & IGNORE ENTRY) CALLED BY 'RDCHAR' IF ESCAPE KEY IS INPUTTED. CALLS APPROPRIATE SCROLL WINDOW SERVICE ROUTINE (IF A=@ GO TO HOME; =A GO TO ADVANCE; =B GO TO BS (BACKSPACE); =C GO TO LF (LINEFEED); =D GO TO UP (INVERSE LINEFEED); =E GOTO CLREOL; =F GOTO CLREOP; =ANYTHING ELSE RTS & IGNORE ENTRY) {USES A-REG}
$FC42 (-958) [CLREOP] \SE\	MONITOR S/R TO CLEAR FROM CURSOR TO END OF PAGE. {A- Y-REGS ALTERED}
$FC46 (-954) [CLEOP1]	MONITOR MEMORY LOCATION 'CLEOP1'
$FC58 (-936) [HOME] \SE\	CLEAR SCROLL WINDOW TO BLANKS. SET CURSOR TO TOP LEFT CORNER {A- Y-REGS ALTERED}
$FC5A (-934) \SE\	SET CV (CURSOR VERTICAL POSN) FROM A-REG. CLEAR WINDOW TO END OF WINDOW; SET CH=0 {A- Y-REGS ALTERED}
$FC62 (-926) [CR] \SE\	MONITOR S/R TO PERFORM A CARRIAGE RETURN; I.E. LOAD ZERO TO A-REG & CH {A-REG ALTERED}
$FC66 (-922) [LF] \SE\	MONITOR S/R TO TO PERFORM A LINE FEED; I.E. INCREMENT CV; COMPARE CV TO WNDBTM IF CV<WNDBTM GOTO VTABZ TO SET BASL~H AND RETURN ELSE DECREMENT CV AND DO SCROLL {A-REG ALTERED}
$FC70 (-912) [SCROLL] \SE\	MONITOR S/R TO SCROLL UP 1 LINE. {A- Y-REGS ALTERED}
$FC76 (-906) [SCRL1]	MONITOR MEMORY LOCATION 'SCRL1'
$FC8C (-884) [SCRL2]	MONITOR MEMORY LOCATION 'SCRL2'
$FC95 (-875) [SCRL3]	MONITOR - CLEAR LINE (BASL~H) {WHOLE LINE} THEN SET NEW BASL~H FROM CV & WNDLFT
$FC9C (-868) [CLREOL] \SE\	MONITOR S/R TO CLEAR TO END OF LINE {A- Y-REGS ALTERED}
$FC9E (-866) [CLEOLZ]	MONITOR MEMORY LOCATION 'CLEOLZ'
$FCA0 (-864) [CLEOL2]	MONITOR MEMORY LOCATION 'CLEOL2'
$FCA8 (-856) [WAIT] \SE\	CALL FOR WAIT LOOP. WAIT ESTIMATED AT 2.5A^2+13.5A+13 WAIT CYCLES OF 1.02 MICROSECONDS WHERE A IS CONTENTS OF A-REG WHEN S/R CALLED

```
$FCA9 (-855) [WAIT2]     MONITOR MEMORY LOCATION 'WAIT2'
$FCAA (-854) [WAIT3]     MONITOR MEMORY LOCATION 'WAIT3'
$FCB4 (-844) [NXTA4] \SE\MONITOR S/R TO INCREMENT A4 (16 BITS) THEN DO NXTA1 {A-REG ALTERED}
$FCBA (-838) [NXTA1] \SE\MONITOR S/R TO INCREMENT A1 (16 BITS). SET CARRY IF RESULT >=A2. {A-REG ALTERED}
$FCC8 (-824) [RTS4B]     MONITOR MEMORY LOCATION 'RTS4B'
$FCC9 (-823) [HEADR]     MONITOR - WRITES SYNCHRONIZATION MONOTONE WHICH IS FIRST PART OF EVERY CASSETTE TAPE RECORD
$FCD6 (-810) [WRBIT]     MONITOR - WRITES A BIT TO CASSETTE TAPE (CALLED BY WRBYTE AND HEADR)
$FCDB (-805) [ZERDLY]    MONITOR MEMORY LOCATION 'ZERDLY'
$FCE2 (-798) [ONEDLY]    MONITOR MEMORY LOCATION 'ONEDLY'
$FCE5 (-795) [WRTAPE]    MONITOR MEMORY LOCATION 'WRTAPE'
$FCEC (-788) [RDBYTE]    MONITOR - READS BITS FROM CASSETTE TAPE UNTIL BYTE ACCUMULATED (CALLED BY MONITOR READ MEMORY
                         LOCATION 'RDBYTE' SHAPE TABLE LOAD)
$FCEE (-786) [RDBYT2]    MONITOR MEMORY LOCATION 'RDBYT2'
$FCFA (-774) [RD2BIT]    MONITOR TWO-EDGE TAPE SENSE; I.E. LOOPS DECREMENTING Y-REG UNTIL HARDWARE HAS INDICATED TWO
                         TRANSITIONS OF TAPE INPUT REGISTER.  CONTENTS OF Y-REG ON RETURN COMPARED WITH CONTENTS ON
                         ENTRY MEASURE TIME REQUIRED FOR TRANSITIONS. CALLS RDBIT
$FCFD (-771) [RDBIT]     MONITOR - LOOPS DECREMENTING Y-REG UNTIL CASSETTE TAPE INPUT REGISTER CHANGES (EITHER 0=>1 OR
                         1=>0). BIT VALUE RETURNED IS DETERMINED FROM RESIDUAL COUNT OF Y-REG.  CALLED BY RD2BIT AND READ
$FD0C (-756) [RDKEY] \SE\SAME AS RDCHAR EXCEPT BYPASSES ESCAPE KEY MONITOR SUPPORT; PICKS UP AND SAVE THE CHARACTER IN
                         THE SCREEN AREA AT BASL~H CH (LEAVING Y-REG CONTAINING CONTENTS OF CH) IT THEN CHANGES THAT
                         CHARACTER TO BLINKING TO INDICATE CURRENT CURSOR POSN; ASKS FOR NEXT INPUT CHAR TO BE PLACED
                         IN A-REG BY DOING AN INDIRECT JUMP VIA KSWL~H WHICH IS NORMALLY POINTING AT KEYIN. RETURN IS
                         THEREFORE TO THE CALLER OF RDKEY - NOT TO RDKEY ROUTINE ITSELF. SET-UP: A- X- Y-REGS NOT
                         SIGNIFICANT; CV AND BASL~H SHOULD BE COMPATABLE POINTING IN THE SCROLL WINDOW; CH INDICATES
                         HORIZONTAL POSITION WHERE CURSOR WILL BLINK. RESULTS: A-REG CONTAINS THE INPUT CHARACTER
                         (WHICH MAY BE ANY CHARACTER INCLUDING ANY CONTROL KEY OR ESCAPE KEY);X-REG IS UNCHANGED; Y-REG
                         CONTAINS CONTENTS OF CH; CV CH BASL~H REMAIN UNCHANGED {A- X- Y-REGS ALTERED}
$FD1B (-741) [KEYIN] \SE\GETS NEXT KEY INPUT FROM KEYBOARD HARDWARE. REQUIRES LOOP TO TEST THAT KEY HAS INDEED BEEN
                         READ; BY PRESENCE OF $80 BIT. ALSO REQUIRES KEYBOARD STROBE TO BE HIT BEFORE NEXT KEYBOARD
                         INPUT. AUXILLIARY ACTIONS TAKEN BY KEYIN INCLUDE RESTORING TO THE SCREEN AREA THE CHARACTER
                         MODIFIED  BY RDKEY TO REMOVE BLINK INSERTED BY RDKEY AND COUNTING UP THE RANDOM NUMBER FIELD~
                         IGNORING OVERFLOW. SET-UP: X-REG NOT SIGNIFICANT & NOT AFFECTED; A-REG INPUT TO THIS ROUTINE
                         STORED AT (BASL)~Y WHEN A KEY IS PRESSED BEFORE THE A-REG IS FILLED FROM THE KEYBOARD
                         REGISTER; Y-REG USED FOR STORING A-REG IN SCREEN AREA TO (BASL)~Y; CH AND CV NOT
                         REFEENCED;BASL~H ARE USED AS INDICATED IN RDKEY. RESULT: A-REG CONTAINS INPUT FROM KEYBOARD
                         REGISTER; IT IS ONLY ITEM CHANGED {A-REG ALTERED}
$FD21 (-735) [KEYIN2]    MONITOR MEMORY LOCATION KEYIN2
$FD2F (-721) [ESC]       MONITOR MEMORY LOCATION 'ESC'
$FD35 (-715) [RDCHAR] \SE\CALLS RDKEY TO GET NEXT CHAR PLACED INTO A-REG. IF ESCAPE KEY PRESSED CALLS 'ESC1' FOR ESCAPE
                         KEY PROCESSING; AFTER ESCAPE KEY AND KEY FOLLOWING HAVE BEEN READ & PROCESSED CONTROL RETURNS
                         TO RDCHAR ROUTINE AS IF IT WERE JUST BEING ENTERED {A- X- Y-REGS ALTERED}
$FD3D (-707) [NOTCR]     MONITOR MEMORY LOCATION 'NOTCR'
$FD5F (-673) [NOTCR1]    MONITOR MEMORY LOCATION 'NOTCR1'
$FD62 (-670) [CANCEL] \SE\MONITOR S/R TO PERFORM A LINE CANCEL (\)
$FD67 (-665) [GETLNZ] \SE\OUTPUT A C/R (THROUGH COUT). GO TO GETLN TO WRITE PROMPT & GET A LINE OF DATA (USUALLY FROM
                         KEYBOARD); ON SET-UP A- X- Y-REGS CH AND BASL~H NOT SIGNIFICANT. CV SHOULD POINT TO A LINE IN
                         SCROLL WINDOW; ON OUTPUT KEYED IN INFO IS IN $200 THRU $200~X WHERE $200~X CONTAINS A
                         CARRIAGE RETURN;A-REG CONTAINS CARRIAGE RETURN;X-REG CONTAINS NUMBER OF CHARACTERS READ
                         EXCLUDING TERMINATING CARRIAGE RETURN;Y-REG CONTAINS CONTENTS OF WNDWDTH; CH CONTAINS ZERO;CV
                         CONTAINS LINE POINTER (CURRENT VALUE);BASL~H CONTAINS MEMORY ADDRESS CORRESPONDING TO CV AND
                         WNDLFT; SCREEN LINE IS BLANKS TO THE RIGHT OF THE END OF ECHOED INPUT {A- X- Y-REGS ALTERED}
```

```
$FD6A (-662) [GETLN] \SE\PROMPT & GET LINE OF TEXT. ON CALLING A- X- Y-REGS NOT SIGNIFICANT. CV AND BASL~H SHOULD BE
                     COMPATIBLE POINTING IN THE SCROLL WINDOW. CH INDICATES WHERE ON LINE THE PROMPT CHARACTER IS
                     TO BE PLACED TO BE FOLLOWED BY ECHOED KEYBOARD INPUT; OUTPUT AS FOR GETLNZ {X-REG GETS #CHARS
                     READ. DATA TO $200~$200~X (MAX $2FF) $200~X & Y-REG GET C/R (USES NXTCHAR)} {A- X- Y-REGS
                     ALTERED}
$FD6F (-657) \SE\    MONITOR S/R TO GET LINE OF TEXT FM KEYBD (SAME AS GETLN EXCEPT NO PROMPT!) {A- X- Y-REGS ALTERED}
$FD71 (-655) [BCKSPC] MONITOR MEMORY LOCATION 'BCKSPC'
$FD75 (-651) [NXTCHAR] \SE\TOP POINT IN CHAR INPUT LOOP. SAME EFFECT AS GETLN EXCEPT BYPASS PRINT OF PROMPT CHARACTER;
                     ON SET-UP X-REG SHOULD BE SET TO ZERO TO BEGIN STORING OF INPUT AT $200; A- Y-REGS NOT
                     SIGNIFICANT;CV AND BASL~H SHOULD BE COMPATIBLE POINTING IN THE SCROLL WINDOW; CH INDICATES
                     WHERE ECHOING OF KEYBOARD INPUT IS TO START & SHOULD BE LESS THAN WNDWDTH; RESULTS SAME AS
                     FOR GETLNZ {A- X- Y-REGS ALTERED}
$FD7E (-642) [CAPTST] MONITOR MEMORY LOCATION 'CAPTST'
$FD80 (-640) [INSTDSP] MONITOR S/R TO DISASSEMBLE INSTRUCTION AT PCH/PCL {A- X- Y-REGS ALTERED}
$FD84 (-636) [ADDINP] MONITOR MEMORY LOCATION 'ADDINP'
$FD8E (-626) [CROUT] \SE\MONITOR S/R TO PRINT A CARRIAGE RETURN THROUGH COUT {A- Y-REGS ALTERED}
$FD92 (-622) [PRA1] \SE\PRINT CARRIAGE RET; THEN HEX OF A1H~A1L; THEN MINUS SIGN {A- X- Y-REGS ALTERED}
$FD96 (-618) [PRYX2] \SE\MONITOR S/R TO PRINT CAR RET THEN HEX OF Y-REG & X-REG THEN A DASH {A-REG ALTERED}
$FD99 (-615) \SE\    PRINT HEX OF Y-REG & X-REG THEN MINUS SIGN {A-REG ALTERED}
$FDA3 (-605) [XAM8] \SE\MONITOR S/R TO EXAMINE 8 MEM LOCNS. PRINTS HEX OF MEMORY FROM XXXX TO XXX7 WHERE XXXX IS
                     CONTENTS OF A1L~A1H; Y-REG MUST =0 ON ENTRY {A-REG ALTERED }
$FDAD (-595) [MOD8CHK] MONITOR MEMORY LOCATION 'MOD8CHK'
$FDB3 (-589) [XAM] \SE\MONITOR S/R TO EXAMINE CONTENTS OF MEMORY FROM (A1L~A1H) TO(A2L~A2H). Y-REG=0 BEFORE CALL {A-REG
                     ALTERED}
$FDB6 (-586) [DATAOUT] MONITOR MEMORY LOCATION 'DATAOUT'
$FDC5 (-571) [RTS4C]  MONITOR MEMORY LOCATION 'RTS4C'
$FDC6 (-570) [XAMPM]  MONITOR MEMORY LOCATION 'XAMPM'
$FDD1 (-559) [ADD]    MONITOR MEMORY LOCATION 'ADD'
$FDDA (-550) [PRBYTE] \SE\MONITOR S/R TO PRINT CONTENTS OF A-REG AS 2 HEX DIGITS {A-REG ALTERED}
$FDE3 (-541) [PRHEX] \SE\MONITOR S/R TO PRINT RIGHT NIBBLE OF A-REG AS A SINGLE HEX DIGIT {A-REG ALTERED}
$FDE5 (-539) [PRHEXZ] MONITOR MEMORY LOCATION 'PRHEXZ'
$FDED (-531) [COUT] \SE\PRINT BYTE IN A-REG TO OUTPUT DEVICE SPECIFIED BY 'CSWL' (NORMALLY 'COUT1') {A-REG ALTERED}
$FDF0 (-528) [COUT1] \SE\WRITE BYTE IN A-REG TO SCREEN AT CURSOR POSN (CV)~(CH) USING 'INVFLG' & SUPPORTING CURSOR MOVE
$FDF6 (-522) [COUTZ] \SE\WRITE BYTE FROM A-REG TO SCREEN AT (CV)~(CH) WITH CURSOR MOVE BUT NOT 'INVFLG' {NONE ALTERED}
$FE00 (-512) [BL1]    MONITOR & MINIASSEMBLER MEMORY LOCATION 'BL1'
$FE04 (-508) [BLANK]  MONITOR MEMORY LOCATION 'BLANK'
$FE0B (-501) [STOR]   MONITOR MEMORY LOCATION 'STOR'
$FE17 (-489) [RTS5]   MONITOR MEMORY LOCATION 'RTS5'
$FE18 (-488) [SETMODE] MONITOR MEMORY LOCATION 'SETMODE'
$FE1D (-483) [SETMDZ] MONITOR MEMORY LOCATION 'SETMDZ'
$FE20 (-480) [LT]     MONITOR MEMORY LOCATION 'LT'
$FE22 (-478) [LT2]    MONITOR MEMORY LOCATION 'LT2'
$FE2C (-468) [MOVE] \SE\MONITOR S/R TO PERFORM A MEMORY MOVE (A1-A2 TO A4)(Y-REG MUST =0 AT CALL) (A-REG ALTERED)
$FE36 (-458) [VFY] \SE\MONITOR S/R TO PERFORM A MEMORY VERIFY (A1-A2 TO A4)
$FE58 (-424) [VFYOK]  MONITOR MEMORY LOCATION 'VFYOK'
$FE5E (-418) [LIST] \SE\CALL TO DISASSEMBLE 20 INSTRUCTIONS
$FE63 (-413) [LIST2]  MONITOR MEMORY LOCATION 'LIST2'
$FE78 (-392) [A1PCLP] MONITOR & MINIASSEMBLER MEMORY LOCATION 'A1PCLP'
$FE7F (-385) [A1PCRTS] MONITOR MEMORY LOCATION 'A1PCRTS'
$FE80 (-384) [SETINV] \SE\MONITOR S/R TO SET VIDEO OUTPUT TO INVERSE
$FE84 (-380) [SETNORM] \SE\MONITOR S/R TO SET VIDEO OUTPUT TO NORMAL (NOT INVERSE)
```

```
$FE86 (-378) [SETIFLG] MONITOR MEMORY LOCATION 'SETIFLG'
$FE89 (-375) [SETKBD]  MONITOR MEMORY LOCATION 'SETKBD'
$FE8B (-373) [INPORT]  MONITOR MEMORY LOCATION  'INPORT'
$FE8D (-371) [INPRT]   MONITOR MEMORY LOCATION 'INPRT'
$FE93 (-365) [SETVID]  MONITOR MEMORY LOCATION'SETVID'
$FE95 (-363) [OUTPORT] MONITOR MEMORY LOCATION 'OUTPORT'
$FE97 (-361) [OUTPRT]  MONITOR MEMORY LOCATION 'OUTPRT'
$FE9B (-357) [IOPRT]   MONITOR MEMORY LOCATION 'IOPRT'
$FEA7 (-345) [IOPRT1]  MONITOR MEMORY LOCATION 'IOPRT1'
$FEA9 (-343) [IOPRT2]  MONITOR MEMORY LOCATION 'IOPRT2'
$FEB0 (-336) [XBASIC] \SE\MONITOR S/R TO JUMP TO BASIC
$FEB3 (-333) [BASCONT] \SE\MONITOR S/R TO CONTINUE BASIC
$FEB6 (-330) [GO] \SE\ MONITOR MEMORY LOCATION 'GO'
$FEB9 (-327) \SE\      RESTORE REGISTERS (CALL RESTORE) THEN JMP (PCL) TO CONTINUE EXECUTION {A- X- Y- P-REGS ALTERED}
$FEBF (-321) [REGZ] \SE\MONITOR S/R TO DISPLAY REGISTERS
$FEC2 (-318) [TRACE] \SE\CALL TO PERFORM MONITOR TRACE
$FEC4 (-316) [STEPZ]   MONITOR MEMORY LOCATION 'STEPZ'
$FECA (-310) [USR]     MONITOR MEMORY LOCATION 'USR'
$FECD (-307) [WRITE] \SE\MONITOR S/R TO WRITE DATA FROM MEMORY TO CASSETTE TAPE - FIRST MEMORY LOCATION POINTED TO BY
                       A1L~H ($003C~$003D); LAST BY A2L~H ($003E~$003F).  CASSETTE TAPE GETS 10 SECONDS OF TONE
                       HEADER THEN THE DESIGNATED DATA BITS AND ONE CHECKSUM BYTE
$FED4 (-300) [WR1]     MONITOR MEMORY LOCATION 'WR1'
$FEED (-275) [WRBYTE]  MONITOR - USES WRBIT TO WRITE 10 BITS  TO CASSETTE TAPE
$FEEF (-273) [WRBYT2]  MONITOR MEMORY LOCATION 'WRBYT2'
$FEF6 (-266) [CRMON]   MONITOR MEMORY LOCATION 'CRMON'
$FEFD (-259) [READ] \SE\READS DATA FROM CASSETTE TAPE PUTTING FIRST DATA READ INTO LOCATION POINTED TO BY A1L~H
                       ($003C~$003D) AND CONTINUING TO READ UNTIL DATA GOES TO LOCATION POINTED TO BY A2L~H
                       ($003E~$003F). ALSO COMPUTES A RUNNING EXCLUSIVE OR CHECKSUM IN 'CHECKSUM' ($002E)
$FF02 (-254) [READX1]  HI-RES GRAPHICS - READ WITHOUT HEADER
$FF0A (-246) [RD2]     MONITOR MEMORY LOCATION 'RD2'
$FF16 (-234) [RD3]     MONITOR MEMORY LOCATION 'RD3'
$FF2D (-211) [PRERR] \SE\MONITOR S/R TO PRINT "ERR" AND SOUND BELL. {A- Y-REGS(?) ALTERED}
$FF3A (-198) [BELL] \SE\MONITOR S/R TO SOUND BELL IN CURRENT OUTPUT DEVICE (WHETHER IT IS APPLE OR EXTERNAL PRINTER)
                       {A--REG ALTERED}
$FF3F (-193) [RESTORE] \SE\RESTORE 6502 REGISTERS:  ($0045)=>A-Reg; ($0046)=>X-Reg; ($0047)=>Y-Reg; ($0048)=>P-Reg;
                       {A- X- Y- P-REGS ALTERED}
$FF44 (-188) [RESTR1]  MONITOR MEMORY LOCATION 'RESTR1'
$FF4A (-182) [SAVE] \SE\MONITOR S/R TO SAVE 6502 REGISTERS: (A-REG)=>$0045; (X-REG)=>$0046; (Y-REG)=>$0047;
                       (P-REG)=>$0048; (S-REG)=>$0049 {NONE}
$FF4C (-180) [SAV1]    MONITOR MEMORY LOCATION 'SAV1'
$FF58 (-168) [IORTS]   JSR HERE TO FIND OUT WHERE ONE IS. SETS OVERFLOW FLAG
$FF59 (-167) [RESET] \SE\CALL HERE HAS SAME EFFECT AS PUSHING RESET BUTTON
$FF65 (-155) [MON] \SE\MONITOR S/R- NORMAL ENTRY TO 'TOP' OF MONITOR WHEN RUNNING (BEEPS!)
$FF69 (-151) [MONZ] \SE\MONITOR S/R TO RESET AND ENTER MONITOR (NO BEEP)
$FF70 (-144) \SE\      MONITOR S/R TO SCAN INPUT BUFFER
$FF73 (-141) [NXTITM]  MONITOR MEMORY LOCATION 'NXTITM'
$FF7A (-134) [CHRSRCH] MONITOR MEMORY LOCATION 'CHRSRCH'
$FF7C (-132) [ZMODE]   MONITOR & MINIASSEMBLER MEMORY LOCATION 'ZMODE'
$FF8A (-118) [DIG]     MONITOR MEMORY LOCATION 'DIG'
$FF90 (-112) [NXTBIT]  MONITOR MEMORY LOCATION 'NXTBIT'
$FF98 (-104) [NXTBAS]  MONITOR MEMORY LOCATION 'NXTBAS'
```

```
$FFA2 (-94) [NXTBS2]   MONITOR MEMORY LOCATION 'NXTBS2'
$FFA7 (-89) [GETNUM]   MONITOR & MINIASSEMBLER MEMORY LOCATION 'GETNUM'
$FFAD (-83) [NXTCHR]   MONITOR - TOP POINT IN GETLN CHARACTER INPUT LOOP;RDCHAR CALLED TO GET CHAR INTO A-REG; ON
                       RETURN A-REG TESTED FOR PRESENCE OF CTRL-U (RIGHT ARROW); IF SO A-REG LOADED FROM SC/REEN MEMORY
                       ASSUMING Y-REG CONTAINS SAME VALUE AS CH; IF A-REG VAL >$DF LOWER-CASE LETTER CONVERTED TO UPPER
                       CASE; IF CHAR IS A C/R IT IS PRINTED THROUGH COUT AND RTS EXIT OF COUT WILL GIVE CONTROL BACK TO
                       CALLING PROGRAM W/ X-REG INDICATING INPUT CHAR COUNT +1; THAT IS INPUT IS IN LOCNS $200 THRU
                       $200~X WHERE $200~X CONTAINS A C/R; ON SET-UP A- X- Y-REGS NOT SIGNIFICANT; CV & BASL~H SHOULD
                       BE COMPATIBLE (POINTING IN THE SCROLL WINDOW);CH INDICATES HORIZ POSN IN SCROLL WINDOW WHERE
                       CURSOR WILL BE INDICATED BY BLINKING. ON RETURN CALLER A-REG WILL CONTAIN KEY VALUE;Y-REG WILL
                       CONTAIN CONTENTS OF CH;X-REG WILL CONTAIN SAME VALUE AS INPUT; CV CH & BASL~H WILL HAVE CHANGE
                       ONLY IF AN ESCAPE KEY SEQUENCE HAS BEEN PERFORMED
$FFBE (-66) [TOSUB]    MONITOR & MINIASSEMBER MEMORY LOCATION 'TOSUB'
$FFC7 (-57) [ZMODE]    MONITOR MEMORY LOCATION 'ZMODE'
$FFCC (-52) [CHRTBL]   MONITOR & MINIASSEMBLER MEMORY LOCATION 'CHRTBL' (TABLE USED TO DECODE MONITOR KEYBOARD INPUT)
$FFE3~$FFE9 (-29~-23) [SUBTBL] \PB\TABLE OF SUBROUTINE ADDRESSES -1 (INDEX PC WITH TBL ITEM FOR S/R ENTRY): (ADDRESS
                                   MSB = $FE; LSB = TABLE ENTRY +1)
$FFE3 (-29) [SUBTBL]               'SUBTBL' L.S.B. ADDRESS-1 OF BASCONT SUBROUTINE
$FFE4 (-28) \P1\                   'SUBTBL' L.S.B. ADDRESS-1 OF USR SUBROUTINE (M.S.B.=$FE)
$FFE5 (-27) \P1\                   'SUBTBL' L.S.B. ADDRESS-1 OF REGZ SUBROUTINE (M.S.B.=$FE)
$FFE6 (-26) \P1\                   'SUBTBL' L.S.B. ADDRESS-1 OF TRACE SUBROUTINE (M.S.B.=$FE)
$FFE7 (-25) \P1\                   'SUBTBL' L.S.B. ADDRESS-1 OF VFY SUBROUTINE (M.S.B.=$FE)
$FFE8 (-24) \P1\                   'SUBTBL' L.S.B. ADDRESS-1 OF INPRT SUBROUTINE (M.S.B.=$FE)
$FFE9 (-23) \P1\                   'SUBTBL' L.S.B. ADDRESS-1 OF STEPZ SUBROUTINE (M.S.B.=$FE)
$FFEA (-22) \P1\                   'SUBTBL' L.S.B. ADDRESS-1 OF OUTPRT SUBROUTINE (M.S.B.=$FE)
$FFEB (-21) \P1\                   'SUBTBL' L.S.B. ADDRESS-1 OF XBASIC SUBROUTINE (M.S.B.=$FE)
$FFEC (-20) \P1\                   'SUBTBL' L.S.B. ADDRESS-1 OF SETMODE SUBROUTINE (M.S.B.=$FE)
$FFED (-19) \P1\                   'SUBTBL' L.S.B. ADDRESS-1 OF SETMODE SUBROUTINE (M.S.B.=$FE)
$FFEE (-18) \P1\                   'SUBTBL' L.S.B. ADDRESS-1 OF MOVE SUBROUTINE (M.S.B.=$FE)
$FFEF (-17) \P1\                   'SUBTBL' L.S.B. ADDRESS-1 OF LT SUBROUTINE (M.S.B.=$FE)
$FFF0 (-16) \P1\                   'SUBTBL' L.S.B. ADDRESS-1 OF SETNORM SUBROUTINE (M.S.B.=$FE)
$FFF1 (-15) \P1\                   'SUBTBL' L.S.B. ADDRESS-1 OF SETINV SUBROUTINE (M.S.B.=$FE)
$FFF2 (-14) \P1\                   'SUBTBL' L.S.B. ADDRESS-1 OF LIST SUBROUTINE (M.S.B.=$FE)
$FFF3 (-13) \P1\                   'SUBTBL' L.S.B. ADDRESS-1 OF WRITE SUBROUTINE (M.S.B.=$FE)
$FFF5 (-11) \P1\                   'SUBTBL' L.S.B. ADDRESS-1 OF READ SUBROUTINE (M.S.B.=$FE)
$FFF6 (-10) \P1\                   'SUBTBL' L.S.B. ADDRESS-1 OF SETMODE SUBROUTINE (M.S.B.=$FE)
$FFF7 (-9) \P1\                    'SUBTBL' L.S.B. ADDRESS-1 OF SETMODE SUBROUTINE (M.S.B.=$FE)
$FFF8 (-8) \P1\                    'SUBTBL' L.S.B. ADDRESS-1 OF CRMON SUBROUTINE (M.S.B.=$FE)
$FFFA~$FFFB (-6~-5) \P2\           FULL (16-BIT) ADDRESS OF NMI (NON-MASKABLE INTERRUPT) VECTOR
$FFFC~$FFFD (-4~-3) \P2\           FULL (16-BIT) ADDRESS OF RESET VECTOR
$FFFE~$FFFF (-2~-1) \P2\           FULL (16-BIT) ADDRESS OF IRQ (INTERUPT REQUEST) VECTOR
```

GAZETTEER

```
(-32K)   (-7938~-7932) [$E0FE~$E104] \P5\APPLESOFT FIVE-BYTE FLOATING POINT CONSTANT -32768 (-2~16)
1002   (1002) [$03EA] \SE\        DOS 3.2 ENTRY POINT FOR ROUTINE THAT UPDATES I/O HOOK TABLES IN $0036~$0039. (JMP
                                  $A851 - SAVES ADDRESSES OF CHARACTER INPUT & OUTPUT ROUTINES CURRENTLY IN USE AND
                                  RECONNECTS DOS I/O)
(3D0G)   (976) [$03D0] \SE\       DOS 3.2 SOFT-ENTRY POINT; I.E. RE-ENTRY POINT (3D0G) FOR RE-INITIALIZATION SAVING ALL
                                  VARIABLES & DATA OF CURRENT BASIC PROGRAM (JMP $9DBF)
995    (995) [$03E3] \SE\         DOS 3.1~3.2 ENTRY POINT TO LOAD Y~A WITH ADDRESS OF IOBLK
A   (74) [$004A] \P1\             DOS DISK SYSTEM FORMATTER DUMMY LOCATION FOR TIMING PURPOSES AND SCRATCH. DOS WILL
                                  REPAIR IN INIT COMMAND; USER MUST REPAIR IF RWTS FORMATTER CALLED DIRECTLY
(A/S POINTERS)   (80~97) [$0050~$0061] \PB\GENERAL PURPOSE POINTERS FOR APPLESOFT (PB)
(A/S RESVD)   (10~22) [$000A~$0016] \PB\APPLESOFT RESERVED BLOCK IN PAGE ZERO
A1L-A1H   (60~61) [$003C~$003D] \P2\MONITOR GENERAL USAGE SUBROUTINE PARAMETER A1. MANY USES INCLUDE SOURCE POINTER
                                    DURING MONITOR MOVE
A1PCLP   (-392) [$FE78]             MONITOR & MINIASSEMBLER MEMORY LOCATION 'A1PCLP'
A1PCRTS   (-385) [$FE7F]            MONITOR MEMORY LOCATION 'A1PCRTS'
A2L-A2H   (62~63) [$003E~$003F] \P2\MONITOR GENERAL USAGE SUBROUTINE PARAMETER A2. USED IN CALLING LIST OF MANY MONITOR
                                    SUBROUTINES SUCH AS MOVE & CASSETTE ROUTINES
A3L-A3H   (64~65) [$0040~$0041] \P1\MONITOR GENERAL USAGE SUBROUTINE PARAMETER A3. USED IN CALLING LIST OF MOST MONITOR
                                    SUBROUTINES
A4L-A4H   (66~67) [$0042~$0043] \P2\MONITOR GENERAL USAGE SUBROUTINE PARAMETER A4.  USED IN CALLING LIST OF SOME
                                    MONITOR SUBROUTINES
A5L-A5H   (68~69) [$0044~$0045] \P2\MONITOR GENERAL USAGE SUBROUTINE PARAMETER A5. USED MOSTLY BY SINGLE-CYLCLE & TRACE
ABS (FPABS)   (-5201) [$EBAF] \SE\ APPLESOFT FP - TAKES ABSOLUTE VALUE OF NUMBER IN FAC & LEAVES RESULT IN FAC
ABSWAP   (-3017) [$F437] \SE\       TAKE ABSOLUTE VALUE OF FP1; THEN SWAP FP1 WITH FP2 (FP1=$00F8;$FP2=$00F4) {A- X-REGS
                                    ALTERED}
~ABS~   (-6326) [$E74A] \SE\        INTEGER BASIC ENTRY TO GET ABSOLUTE VALUE OF A NUMBER
AC   (80~83) [$0050~$0053] \P4\     32-BIT EXTENDED ACCUMULATOR USED IN MONITOR 16-BIT MULT & DIVIDE
ACADR   (-3810) [$F11E]             HI-RES GRAPHICS 2-BYTE TAPE READ SETUP
ACC   (69) [$0045] \P1\             USER A-REG SAVED HERE ON BRK TO MONITOR & DURING TRACE
ACL~ACH   (80~81) [$0050~$0051] \P2\OLD MONITOR (NOT AUTOSTART). USED BY 16 BIT MULT & DIVIDE ROUTINES AS
                                    PSEUDO-ACCUMULATOR
ACL~ACH   (206~207) [$00CE~$00CF] \P2\INTEGER BASIC MAIN ACCUMULATOR
ADD   (-3035) [$F425] \SE\          ADD 3-BYTE M1 TO 3-BYTE M2 AND LEAVE RESULT IN M1 (NOT FP ADD BUT USED IN FP PKG)
                                    {A- X-REGS ALTERED}
ADD   (-559) [$FDD1]                MONITOR MEMORY LOCATION 'ADD'
ADDINP   (-636) [$FD84]             MONITOR MEMORY LOCATION 'ADDINP'
~ADDITION~   (-6267) [$E785] \SE\   INTEGER BASIC ENTRY POINT TO ADDITION FUNCTION
ADDON   (-9832) [$D998] \SE\        APPLESOFT - ADD Y-REG TO TXTPTR
ADVANCE   (-1036) [$FBF4] \SE\      MONITOR S/R- MOVE CURSOR RIGHT; I.E. INCREMENT (CH); COMPARE (CH) WITH (WNDWDTH) GO
                                    TO CR IF CH NOT LESS ELSE RETURN (RTS) {A-REG ALTERED}
ALLDONE   (15911) [$3E27] \SL\      DOS 3.2 RWTS (READ-WRITE TRACK-SECTOR) INTERIOR LABEL 'ALLDONE'
ALLDONE   (-16826~-16825) [$BE46~$BE47] DOS 3.3 - SKIP OVER SET CARRY INSTRUCTION IN 'HNDLERR'
AMPERV   (1013~1015) [$03F5~$03F7]  APPLESOFT - HOLDS JMP (JUMP) INSTRUCTION TO S/R WHICH HANDLES & COMMANDS.  DEFAULT
                                    $4C $58 $FF (JUMP TO $FF58)
APPLEII   (-1184) [$FB60] \SE\      CLEAR SCREEN AND POKE 'APPLE II' INTO FIRST LINE OF TEXT BUFFER (AUTOSTART ROM
                                    ONLY) {A- Y-REGS ALTERED}
ARG   (165~170) [$00A5~$00AA] \PB\  APPLESOFT SECONDARY FLOATING POINT ACCUMULATOR (USES 6-BYTE UNPACKED MATH PACKAGE
                                    FORMAT DESCRIBED BELOW)
ARGEXP   (165) [$00A5] \P1\         EXPONENT PART OF ARG. SINGLE BYTE SIGNED NUMBER IN EXCESS $80 FORM (SIGNED VALUE
                                    HAS $80 ADDED TO IT)
ARYTAB   (107~108) [$006B~$006C] \P2\APPLESOFT ARRAY TABLE POINTER (POINTS TO BEGINNING OF ARRAY SPACE)
```

```
~ASC~    (-3299) [$F31D] \SE\        INTEGER BASIC ENTRY TO ROUTINE TO PERFORM THE ASC (ASCII) FUNCTION
ATN    (-3938) [$F09E] \SE\          APPLESOFT FP COMPUTE THE ARCTANGENT OF NUMBER IN FAC. RESULT TO FAC. MODIFIES INDEX
                                     XORFPSGN AND MANY OTHER FP LOCNS
AUTOINCL~AUTOINCH   (244~245) [$00F4~$00F5] \P2\INTEGER BASIC MEMORY LOCATIONS 'AUTOINCL~AUTOINCH' (CURRENT AUTO LINE
                                          NUMBER VALUE)
AUTOLNL~AUTOLNH   (246~247) [$00F6~$00F7] \P2\INTEGER BASIC MEMORY LOCATIONS 'AUTOLNL~AUTOLNH'
AUTOMODE   (248) [$00F8] \P1\             INTEGER BASIC MEMORY LOCATION 'AUTOMODE' (THE AUTOMODE FLAG)
(AUTOSTART RESVD)   (32~79) [$0020~$004F] \PB\AUTOSTART MONITOR RESERVED LOCATIONS
~AUTO~   (-6174) [$E7E2] \SE\             INTEGER BASIC ENTRY TO AUTO LINE NUMBERING FUNCTION
AUXL~AUXH   (84~85) [$0054~$0055] \P2\   OLD MONITOR (NOT AUTOSTART) - USED FOR 16-BIT MULT & DIVIDE AS AUXILLIARY
                                          REGISTER
AUXL~AUXH   (218~219) [$00DA~$00DB] \P2\INTEGER BASIC MEMORY LOCATIONS 'AUXL~AUXH' (AULILIARY COUNTER)
AYINT (FP=>INT)   (-7924) [$E10C] \SE\   APPLESOFT - IF FAC SUITABLE FOR CONVERSION TO INTEGER (FAC<32767 & FAC>-32768)
                                          THEN PERFORM QINT {RESET Y-REG=0}
(AYPOSINT +FP=>INT)   (-7928) [$E108] \SE\APPLESOFT - SAME AS AYINT ($E10C) EXCEPT FAC MUST BE POSITIVE
(BAD SUBSCRPRT)   (-7786) [$E196] \SE\   APPLESOFT - PRINT "BAD SUBSCRIPT" AND HALT AT APPLESOFT LEVEL (])
BAS2L~BAS2H   (42~43) [$002A~$002B] \P2\USED DURING SCROLLING AS DESTINATION LINE POINTER AS EACH LINE IS MOVED TO
                                          POSITION ABOVE CURRENT
BASCALC   (-1087) [$FBC1] \SE\            MONITOR S/R- CALCULATE TEXT BASE ADDRESS. SET BASL~H TO LEFT END OF SCREEN LINE
                                          (NOT WINDOW LINE) IN A-REG {A-REG ALTERED}
BASCONT   (-333) [$FEB3] \SE\             MONITOR S/R TO CONTINUE BASIC
BASIC   (-8192) [$E000]                   APPLESOFT - 'HARD' OR 'COLD' OR 'CONTROL-B' ENTRY POINT (COMPLETE
                                          REINITIALIZATION. START WITH A TOTALLY FRESH SLATE.)
BASIC   (-8192) [$E000]                   INTEGER BASIC - 'HARD' OR 'COLD' OR 'CONTROL-B' ENTRY POINT  (COMPLETE
                                          REINITIALIZATION. START WITH A TOTALLY FRESH SLATE)
BASIC2   (-8189) [$E003] \SE\             INTEGER BASIC - 'SOFT' OR 'WARM' OR 'CONTROL-C' OR 'ENTRY2' ENTRY POINT
                                          (REENTRY WITHOUT REINITIALIZATION OF SYMBOL-TABLE~ VARIABLES OR DATA)
BASL~BASH   (40~41) [$0028~$0029] \P2\   MEMORY ADDRESS FOR LEFT END CHARACTER POS'N OF CURRENT TEXT LINE
BCKSPC   (-655) [$FD71]                   MONITOR MEMORY LOCATION 'BCKSPC'
BDRAW   (-11462) [$D33A] \SE\             HI-RES GRAPHICS  DRAW1 S/R CALL: PARAM= XO~YO~COLR~SHAPE~ROT~SCALE
BDRAW1   (-11465) [$D337] \SE\            HI-RES GRAPHICS LINE S/R CALL: PARAM=XO~YO~COLR
BELL   (-198) [$FF3A] \SE\                MONITOR S/R TO SOUND BELL IN CURRENT OUTPUT DEVICE (WHETHER IT IS APPLE OR
                                          EXTERNAL PRINTER) {A--REG ALTERED}
BELL1   (-1063) [$FBD9]                   MONITOR MEMORY LOCATION 'BELL1'
BELL2   (-1052) [$FBE4] \SE\              MONITOR S/R- SOUND BELL (BEEPER)
BGND   (-11471) [$D331] \SE\              HI-RES GRAPHICS BKGND S/R CALL  PARAM= COLR
BKGND   (-12270) [$D012] \P1\             HI-RES GRAPHICS MEMORY LOCATION 'BKGND' (ROM)
BKGND   (-3086) [$F3F2] \SE\              APPLESOFT HI-RES - CLEAR HI-RES SCREEN TO LAST PLOTTED COLOR
BKGNDO   (-12272) [$D010]                 HI-RES GRAPHICS 'BKGNDO (HCOLOR1 SET FOR BLACK BKGND)
BL1   (-512) [$FE00]                      MONITOR & MINIASSEMBLER MEMORY LOCATION 'BL1'
BLANK   (-508) [$FE04]                    MONITOR MEMORY LOCATION 'BLANK'
BLIN1   (-11500) [$D314] \SE\             HI-RES GRAPHICS LINE S/R CALL PARAM= XO~YO~COLR
BLTU   (-11373) [$D393] \SE\              APPLESOFT BLOCK TRANSFER UTILITY. MAKES ROOM BY MOVING EVERYTHING FORWARD.
                                          Y-REG(MSB)&A-REG(LSB) AND HIGHDS=DEST OF HIGH ADR;LOWTR=LOWEST ADDR TO BE
                                          MOVED;HIGHTR=HIGHEST ADDR TO BE MOVED+1
(BOOT DISK #)   (1528) [$05F8] \P1\       CONTAINS SLOT # OF DISK CONTROLLER CARD FROM WHICH ANY ACTIVE DOS 3.2 WAS BOOTED
BPLOT   (-11506) [$D30E] \SE\             HI-RES GRAPHICS PLOT S/R CALL PARAM= XO~YO~COLR
BPOSN   (-11527) [$D2F9] \SE\             HI-RES GRAPHICS POSN S/R CALL PARAM= XO~YO~COLR
BRANCH   (-1283) [$FAFD]                  MONITOR MEMORY LOCATION 'BRANCH'
~BRANCH~   (-6420) [$E6EC] \SE\           INTEGER BASIC ENTRY POINT TO BRANCH (GET LO/HI THEN JSR)
BRATE   (1144+S) [$0478+S] \P1\           EXAMPLE: SERIAL INTERFACE BAUD QUANTUM RATE. $1= 19200 BAUD;$40=300 BAUD
```

```
NAME  (DEC LOCN)  [HEX LOCN] \USE-TYPE\ - DESCRIPTION
--------------------------------------------------------------------------------------------------------

BREAK   (-1390) [$FA92] \SE\                MONITOR S/R - BREAK HANDLER
BRKV   (1008~1009) [$03F0~$03F1] \P2\       AUTOSTART ROM BREAK VECTOR - DEFAULT VALUE $FA59
BS   (-1008) [$FC10] \SE\                   MONITOR S/R TO MOVE CURSOR LEFT (BACKSPACE); IF AT START OF LINE MOVE UP TO
                                            RIGHT END OF LINE ABOVE IF POSSIBLE (A-REG ALTERED)
BSCLC2   (-1072) [$FBD0]                    MONITOR MEMORY LOCATION 'BSCLC2'
BUF INBUFF   (512~767) [$0200~$02FF] \HB\KEYIN (CHARACTER INPUT) BUFFER (MONITOR~INTEGER BASIC~APPLESOFT BASIC)
BUFPTR   (62~63) [$003E~$003F] \P2\         DOS RWTS (READ-WRITE TRACK-SECTOR) PARAMETER 'BUFPTR' (POINTS TO DATA BUFFER IN
                                            RWTS)
BXSAV   (803) [$0323]                       HI-RES GRAPHICS 'BXSAV'
BYTE   (1656+S) [$0678+S]                   EXAMPLE: APPLE SERIAL INTERFACE IN SLOT #S INPUT OUTPUT BUFFER
~CALL~   (-4448) [$EEA0] \SE\               INTEGER BASIC ENTRY POINT TO CALL A SUB/ROT FUNCTION
CANCEL   (-670) [$FD62] \SE\                MONITOR S/R TO PERFORM A LINE CANCEL (\)
CAPTST   (-642) [$FD7E]                     MONITOR MEMORY LOCATION 'CAPTST'
CAT   (-6761) [$E597] \SE\                  APPLESOFT - CONCATENATE TWO STRINGS. FACMO (MSB) & FACLO (LSB) POINT TO FIRST
                                            STRING'S DESCRIPTOR & TXTPTR POINTS TO '+'
CH   (36) [$0024] \P1\                      CURSOR HORIZONTAL DISPLACEMENT FROM WNDLFT: RANGE 0 TO (WNDWDTH)-1
CHAR   (249) [$00F9] \P1\                   INTEGER BASIC MEMORY LOCATION 'CHAR' (CURRENT CHARACTER)
CHAR1   (-1612) [$F9B4]                     MONITOR & MINIASSEMBER MEMORY LOCATION 'CHAR1'
CHAR2   (-1606) [$F9BA]                     MONITOR & MINIASSEMBLER MEMORY LOCATION 'CHAR2'
CHARAC   (13) [$000D]                       APPLESOFT - USED BY STRLT2 STRING UTILITY
CHGIT   (16326) [$3FC6] \SL\                DOS 3.2 DISK FORMATTER INTERIOR LABEL 'CHGIT'
CHKCLS   (-8520) [$DEB8] \SE\               APPLESOFT CLOSE PARENTHESIS CHECK - CHECKS TXTPTR FOR ')'. USES SYNCHR.
CHKCOM   (-8514) [$DEBE] \SE\               APPLESOFT COMMA CHECK - CHECKS TXTPTR FOR COMMA. USES SYNCHR.
CHKNUM   (-8854) [$DD6A] \SE\               APPLESOFT - MAKE SURE FAC IS NUMERIC (SEE CHKVAL)
CHKOPN   (-8517) [$DEBB] \SE\               APPLESOFT OPEN PARENTHESIS CHECK - CHECKS TXTPTR FOR '('. USES SYNCHR.
CHKSTR   (-8852) [$DD6C] \SE\               APPLESOFT - MAKE SURE FAC IS STRING (SEE CHKVAL)
CHKSUM   (46) [$002E] \P1\                  LOCN WHERE CHECKSUM IS ACCUMULATED DURING CASSETTE TAPE READ
CHKVAL   (-8851) [$DD6D] \SE\               APPLESOFT - IF C SET CHECK FOR STRINGS;C CLEAR CHECK FOR NUMRIC VBL. TYPE
                                            MISMATCH ERROR OCCURS IF C AND FAC DON'T AGREE
CHRGET   (177) [$00B1] \SE\                 APPLESOFT CHRGET S/R CALL - GETS NEXT SEQUENTIAL CHR OR TOKEN - LOADS A-REG
                                            FROM LOCN SPECIFIED BY TXTPTR($00B8~$00B9 & INCREMENTS TXTPTR. CARRY IS RESET
                                            TO ZERO IF CHARACTER IS A DIGIT OTHERWISE IT IS SET; ZERO FLAT SET IF CHAR =0
                                            (END OF LINE SIGN) OR $3A (END OF STATEMENT SIGN ':') OTHERWISE RESET (X-
                                            Y-REGS NOT ALTERED)
CHRGET   (177~200) [$00B1~$00C8] \SB\       APPLESOFT CHRGET ROUTINE. CALLED WHEN WANTS ANOTHER CHARACTER (X- Y-REGS NOT
                                            ALTERED)
CHRGOT   (183) [$00B7] \SE\                 APPLESOFT CHRGOT S/R CALL. CHRGET INCREMENTS TXTPTR. CHRGOT DOES NOT
CHRSRCH   (-134) [$FF7A]                    MONITOR MEMORY LOCATION 'CHRSRCH'
CHRTBL   (-52) [$FFCC]                      MONITOR & MINIASSEMBLER MEMORY LOCATION 'CHRTBL' (TABLE USED TO DECODE MONITOR
                                            KEYBOARD INPUT)
CIN   (-22120~-22119) [$A998~$A999] \P2\DOS 3.1  INTERNAL HOOK ENTRY ADDRESS TO INPUT A CHARACTER
CLEARC   (-10644) [$D66C] \SE\              APPLESOFT INITIALIZATION - THE 'CLEAR' COMMAND. CLEARS VARIABLES & STACK
CLEOL2   (-864) [$FCA0]                     MONITOR MEMORY LOCATION 'CLEOL2'
CLEOLZ   (-866) [$FC9E]                     MONITOR MEMORY LOCATION 'CLEOLZ'
CLEOP1   (-954) [$FC46]                     MONITOR MEMORY LOCATION 'CLEOP1'
CLRAN0   (-16295) [$C059] \FF\              VALUE <>0 WHEN GAME AN0 IS RESET (CLEARED). POKE 0 TO SET GAME I/O OUTPUT AN0
                                            (0.3V AT PIN 15)
CLRAN1   (-16293) [$C05B] \FF\              POKE 0 TO SET GAME I/O OUTPUT AN1 (0.3V AT PIN 14)
CLRAN2   (-16291) [$C05D] \FF\              POKE 0 TO SET GAME I/O OUTPUT AN2 (0.3V AT PIN 13)
CLRAN3   (-16289) [$C05F] \FF\              POKE 0 TO SET GAME I/O OUTPUT AN3 0.3V AT PIN 12)
CLREOL   (-868) [$FC9C] \SE\                MONITOR S/R TO CLEAR TO END OF LINE (A- Y-REGS ALTERED)
--------------------------------------------------------------------------------------------------------
```

```
NAME  (DEC LOCN)  [HEX LOCN] \USE-TYPE\ - DESCRIPTION
-------------------------------------------------------------------------------------------

CLREOP   (-958) [$FC42] \SE\      MONITOR S/R TO CLEAR FROM CURSOR TO END OF PAGE. {A- Y-REGS ALTERED}
CLRROM   (-12289) [$CFFF] \H1\    SPECIAL LOCATION RECOGNIZED BY PERIPHERAL CARDS AS SIGNAL TO TURN OFF FLIP FLOPS WHICH
                                  DISABLE EXPANSION ROM
CLRSC2   (-1992) [$F838] \SE\     CLEAR LINES 0 THRU (Y-REG) 40 COLUMNS WIDE TO BLACK IN LO-RES GRAPHICS OR INVERSE @ IN
                                  TEXT PAGE 1 {A- Y-REGS ALTERED}
CLRSC3   (-1988) [$F83C] \SE\     CLEAR LO-RES GRAPHICS PARTIAL TOP LEFT: X-COORD 0 THRU (Y-REG); Y-COORD 0 THRU ($002D)
                                  {A- Y-REGS ALTERED}
CLRSCR   (-1998) [$F832] \SE\     CLEAR LO-RES GRAPHICS SCREEN1 TO BLACK (INVERSE @ IN TEXT MODE) MIXED GRAPHICS AREA
                                  ONLY {A- Y-REGS ALTERED}
CLRSCR   (-1998) [$F832] \SE\     MONITOR S/R TO CLEAR SCREEN - GRAPHICS MODE FULL SCREEN) {A- Y-REGS ALTERED}
CLRTOP   (-1994) [$F836] \SE\     CLEAR TOP 20 LINES PAGE1 TO INVERSE @ IN TEXT; BLACK IN LO-RES GRAPHICS (40 LO-RES
                                  GRAPHIC 'LINES') {A- Y-REGS ALTERED}
"CLR"   (-6729) [$E5B7] \SE\      INTEGER BASIC ENTRY POINT TO CLEAR OUT VARIABLE WORK SPACE
CNUM   (68"69) [$0044"$0045]      DOS - POINTS TO AVAILABLE BUFFER IN OPEN. ALSO USED AS ARITHMETIC REGISTER BY DOS
                                  FIRST & SECOND LEVEL ROUTINES
COLLSN   (810) [$032A] \P1\       COLLISION COUNT FROM DRAW"DRAW1
COLOR   (48) [$0C30] \P1\         LOW-RES COLOR GRAPHICS COLOR CODE (FOR PLOT/HLIN/VLIN FUNCTIONS) - CONTAINS SELECTED
                                  COLOR VALUES FOR TWO LOW-RES GRAPHICS 'LINES' ONE IN EACH NIBBLE OF BYTE
"COLOR"   (-4530) [$EE4E] \SE\    INTEGER BASIC ENTRY TO ROUTINE TO SET COLOR VALUE FOR LO-RES
COMBYTE   (-6324) [$E74C] \SE\    APPLESOFT - CHECK FOR COMMA & GET A BYTE IN X-REG. USES CHKCOM& GETBYT. ON ENTRY
                                  TXTPTR POINTS TO COMMA
(COMMAND TBL)   (26756) [$6884] \PB\DOS 3.2 COMMAND TABLE (32K APPLE ONLY!)
"COMMA"   (-6207) [$E7C1] \SE\     INTEGER BASIC ENTRY POINT TO COMMA FUNCTION
(COMPRTYP)   (22) [$0016] \P1\     APPLESOFT - PARAMETER TO CONTROL TYPE OF COMPARISON MADE BY FLOATING POINT COMPARISON
                                   ROUTINE AT $DF6A (1:> ;2:= ;3:>= ;4:< ;5:<> ;6:<=)
CONINT   (-6405) [$E6FB] \SE\      APPLESOFT FP - CONVERT FAC INTO SINGLE BYTE IN X-REG & FACLO.NORMAL EXIT THRU CHRGET.
                                   IF FAC<0 OR FAC>255 ILLEGAL QUANT ERROR
CONL"CONH   (242"243) [$00F2"$00F3] \P2\INTEGER BASIC MEMORY LOCATIONS 'CONL"CONH' (CONTINUE POINTER)
CONSYNC   (16074) [$3ECA] \SL\     DOS 3.2 DISK FORMATTER - LABEL AT POINT WHERE CONSTRUCTION OF SYNC BEGINS
CONT   (-10088) [$D898] \SE\       APPLESOFT - MOVES OLDTXT & OLDLIN INTO TXTPTR & CURLIN
CONUPK   (-5661) [$E9E3] \SE\      APPLESOFT FP - LOAD ARG FROM MEMORY POINTED TO BY Y-REG & A-REG. ON EXIT A & Z
                                   REFLECT FACEXP. MODIFIES INDEX & XORFPSGN. {RESET Y-REG=0}
CONWAIT   (15743) [$3D7F] \SL\     DOS 3.2 RWTS (READ-WRITE TRACK-SECTOR INTERIOR LABEL - STARTS CONSTANT WAIT DELAY
                                   LOOP RETURN POINT
"CON"   (-3318) [$F30A] \SE\       INTEGER BASIC ENTRY TO ROUTINE TO CONTINUE EXECUTION
COPY   (-9545) [$DAB7] \SE\        APPLESOFT - FREE STRING POINTED TO BY Y-REG (MSB) & A-REG (LSB) & MOVE IT TO MEM LOC
                                   POINTED TO BY FORPNT
CORRECTSECT   (15895) [$3E17] \SL\DOS 3.2 RWTS (READ-WRITE TRACK-SECTOR) INTERIOR LABEL AT START OF CODE WHICH ASSUME
                                   SECTOR CORRECTLY CHOSEN AND JUMPS TO APPROPRIATE SUBROUTINE TO READ OR WRITE
CORRECTVOL   (15878) [$3E06] \SL\ DOS 3.2 RWTS (READ-WRITE TRACK-SECTOR) INTERIOR LABEL WHICH ASSUMES CORRECT VOLUME
                                   HAS BEEN DETECTED AND CHECKS FOR SECTOR SELECTION
COS   (-4118) [$EFEA] \SE\         APPLESOFT FP - COMPUTE THE COSINE OF THE NUMBER IN FAC. RESULT TO FAC. MODIFIES INDEX
                                   CHARAC COMPRTYP XORFPSGN AND MANY OTHER FP LOCNS
COUNT - CSUM   (44) [$002C] \P1\  DOS RWTS (READ-WRITE TRACK-SECTOR) PARAMETER (RETURNS CHECKSUM)
COUNT   (249) [$00F9] \P1\         INTEGER BASIC MEMORY LOCATION 'COUNT'
COUNTH   (29) [$001D] \P1\         HI-RES GRAPHICS HIGH-ORDER BYTE OF STEP COUNT FOR LINE
COUT   (-22122"-22121) [$A996"$A997] \P2\DOS 3.1 INTERNAL HOOK ENTRY ADDRESS TO OUTPUT A CHARACTER
COUT   (-531) [$FDED] \SE\         PRINT BYTE IN A-REG TO OUTPUT DEVICE SPECIFIED BY 'CSWL' (NORMALLY 'COUT1') (A-REG
                                   ALTERED)
COUT1   (-528) [$FDF0] \SE\        WRITE BYTE IN A-REG TO SCREEN AT CURSOR POSN (CV)"(CH) USING 'INVFLG' & SUPPORTING
                                   CURSOR MOVE
-------------------------------------------------------------------------------------------
```

```
COUTZ   (-522) [$FDF6] \SE\        WRITE BYTE FROM A-REG TO SCREEN AT (CV)~(CH) WITH CURSOR MOVE BUT NOT 'INVFLG' (NONE
                                   ALTERED)
CR   (-926) [$FC62] \SE\           MONITOR S/R TO PERFORM A CARRIAGE RETURN; I.E. LOAD ZERO TO A-REG & CH (A-REG ALTERED)
CRCTVOL   (-16858~-16827) [$BE26~$BE45] DOS 3.3 - CHECK TO SEE IF SECTOR CORRECT. USE 'ILEAV' TABLE ($BFB8) FOR
                                     SOFTWARE SECTOR INTERLEAVING. IF WRONG SECTOR TRY AGAIN AT 'TRYADR ($BDC1). IF
                                     WRITE BRANCH TO 'WRIT' ($BE51). OTHERWISE GOTO 'READ16' ($B8DC). IF GOOD READ
                                     CALL 'POSTNB16' ($B8C2) AND RETURN TO CALLER WITH NO ERROR
CRDO   (-9477) [$DAFB] \SE\          APPLESOFT - PRINT A CARRIAGE RETURN
CRFLAG   (213) [$0CD5] \P1\          INTEGER BASIC MEMORY LOCATION 'CRFLAG' (CARRIAGE RETURN FLAG)
CRMON   (-266) [$FEF6]               MONITOR MEMORY LOCATION 'CRMON'
CROUT   (-626) [$FD8E] \SE\          MONITOR S/R TO PRINT A CARRIAGE RETURN THROUGH COUT (A- Y-REGS ALTERED)
CSWL~CSWH   (54~55) [$0C36~$0037] \P2\MONITOR OUTPUT REG & OUTPUT HOOK TO DOS; I.E. ADDRESS OF ROUTINE WHICH IS TO
                                     RECEIVE AND DISPOSE OF OUTPUT CHARACTERS. RESET 0 CTRL-P & PR#0 SET THIS LOCN TO
                                     $FDF0 (MONITOR OUTPUT TO SCREEN); S CTRL-P & PR#S SET THIS LOCN TO $CS00 (SLOT S
                                     ROM)
CURLIN   (117~118) [$0075~$0076] \P2\APPLESOFT - LINE # OF LINE CURRENTLY BEING EXECUTED NOTE: HI BYTE OF CURLIN TESTED
                                     BY DOS FOR DIRECT-DEFERRED MODE USAGE - BYTE SET TO $FF IN DIRECT. IF CONTENTS OF
                                     $AAB6<>0 AND IF PROMPT=']' OR IF THIS LOCN CONTAINS $FF DOS ASSUMES DIRECT MODE
                                     AND WILL NOT DO OPEN OR OTHER DIRECT MODE COMMANDS
CURTRK   (1144) [$0478] \P1\         DOS 3.2 RWTS (READ-WRITE TRACK-SECTOR) PARAMETER CURRENT TRACK (LAST TRACK
                                     'SEEK'-ED)
CV   (37) [$0025] \P1\               CURSOR VERTICAL POSITION RELATIVE TO TOP OF SCREEN: RANGE 0-23 ($0~$17)
DATA   (-9835) [$D995] \SE\          APPLESOFT - MOVE TXTPTR TO END OF STATEMENT; LOOKS FOR ':' OR EOL(0).
DATAN   (-9821) [$D9A3] \SE\         APPLESOFT - CALCULATE OFFSET IN Y-REG FROM TXTPTR TO NEXT ':' OR EOL(0)
DATAOUT   (-586) [$FDB6]             MONITOR MEMORY LOCATION 'DATAOUT'
DATLIN   (123~124) [$007B~$007C] \P2\APPLESOFT CURRENT LINE # FROM WHICH DATA IS BEING READ
DATPTR   (125~126) [$007D~$007E] \P2\POINTS TO ABS LOC IN MEM FROM WHICH DATA IS BEING READ BY APPLESOFT
~DELETE~   (-7313) [$E36F] \SE\      INTEGER BASIC ENTRY POINT TO DELETE LINES OF TEXT X~Y
DELL~DELH   (226~227) [$00E2~$00E3] \P2\INTEGER BASIC MEMORY LOCATIONS 'DELL~DELH' (DELETE LINE POINTER)
(DEV SELECT 0)   (-16256~-16241) [$C080~$C08F] 16 MEMORY LOCNS ALLOCATED TO USE OF PERIPHERAL DEVICE IN SLOT #0. WHEN
                                        ADDRESSED PIN 41 TELLS DEVICE IT IS SELECTED. SINCE SLOT #0 IS COMMON
                                        AREA USED IN COMMON FOR PARAMETERS OF INTEREST TO ALL SLOTS
(DEV SELECT 1)   (-16240~-16225) [$C090~$C09F] 16 MEMORY LOCATIONS ALLOCATED TO USE OF PERIPHERAL DEVICE IN SLOT #1.
                                        WHEN ADDRESSED PIN 41 TELLS DEVICE IT IS SELECTED
(DEV SELECT 2)   (-16224~-16209) [$C0A0~$C0AF] 16 MEMORY LOCATIONS ALLOCATED TO USE OF PERIPHERAL DEVICE IN SLOT #2.
                                        WHEN ADDRESS PIN 41 TELLS DEVICE IT IS SELECTED
(DEV SELECT 3)   (-16208~-16193) [$C0B0~$C0BF] 16 MEMORY LOCATIONS ALLOCATED TO USE OF PERIPHERAL DEVICE IN SLOT #3.
                                        WHEN ADDRESSED PIN 41 TELLS DEVICE IT IS SELECTED
(DEV SELECT 4)   (-16192~-16177) [$C0C0~$C0CF] 16 MEMORY LOCATIONS ALLOCATED TO USE OF PERIPHERAL DEVICE IN SLOT #4.
                                        WHEN ADDRESSED PIN 41 TELLS DEVICE IT IS SELECTED
(DEV SELECT 5)   (-16176~-16161) [$C0D0~$C0DF] 16 MEMORY LOCATIONS ALLOCATED TO USE OF PERIPHERAL DEVICE IN SLOT #5.
                                        WHEN ADDRESSED PIN 41 TELLS DEVICE IT IS SELECTED
(DEV SELECT 6)   (-16160~-16145) [$C0E0~$C0EF] 16 MEMORY LOCATIONS ALLOCATED TO USE OF PERIPHERAL DEVICE IN SLOT #6.
                                        WHEN ADDRESSED PIN 41 TELLS DEVICE IT IS SELECTED
(DEV SELECT 7)   (-16144~-16129) [$C0F0~$C0FF] 16 MEMORY LOCATIONS ALLOCATED TO USE OF PERIPHERAL DEVICE IN SLOT #7.
                                        WHEN ADDRESSED PIN 41 TELLS DEVICE IT IS SELECTED
DEVCTBL   (60~61) [$003C~$003D] \P2\    DOS RWTS  DEVICE IN READ-WRITE TRACK-SECTOR PARAMETER POINTING TO DEVICE
                                        TABLE. PRESET TO 'PTRSDEST' = POINTER TO DESTINATION  DEVICE IN DEVICE
                                        TABLE. NOT A SYNONYM FOR BUFPTR
DEVCTBL   (60~61) [$003C~$003D]         DOS RWTS (READ-WRITE TRACK-SECTOR) DEVICE TABLE ~ SYNONYM FOR BUFPTR
DIG   (-118) [$FF8A]                    MONITOR MEMORY LOCATION 'DIG'
```

```
~DIMSTR~   (-7888) [$E130] \SE\            INTEGER BASIC ENTRY POINT TO DIMENSION A STRING FOR MEMORY
~DIMVARB~   (-4322) [$EF1E] \SE\           INTEGER BASIC ENTRY TO ROUTINE TO DIMENSION A VARIABLE
DISKID   (-1275) [$FB05]                   AUTOSTART MONITOR MEMORY LOCATION 'DISKID'
DIV   (-1148) [$FB84] \SE\                 MONITOR S/R- UNSIGNED DIVIDE ROUTINE - SAME AS $FB81 (DIVPM) EXCEPT NO SIGNS
                                           USED.
DIV10   (-5547) [$EA55] \SE\               APPLESOFT FP - DIVIDE FAC BY 10. RETURNS POSITIVE NUMBERS ONLY
DIV2   (-1146) [$FB86]                     MONITOR MEMORY LOCATION 'DIV2'
DIV3   (-1120) [$FBA0]                     MONITOR MEMORY LOCATION 'DIV3'
~DIVIDE~   (-4336) [$EF10] \SE\            INTEGER BASIC ENTRY TO DIVIDE FUNCTION
DIVPM   (-1151) [$FB81]                    MONITOR SIGNED DIVISION - DIVIDES NUMBER IN EXTENDED AC ($0050~$0053) BY
                                           NUMBER IN AUXL~AUXH ($0054~$0055) LEAVING QUOTIENT IN ACL~ACH ($0050~$0051)
                                           AND REMAINDER IN $0053. BE CAREFUL OF SIGNS SCALING & OVERFLOW. IF
                                           (XTNDL~XTNDH ($0052~$0053))>(AUXL~AUXH ($0054~$0055)) OVERFLOW WILL RESULT
(DIVZEROPRT)   (-5407) [$EAE1] \SE\        APPLESOFT - PRINT "DIVISION BY ZERO" THEN HALT AT APPLESOFT (]) LEVEL
DONEDSK   (16312) [$3FB8] \SL\             DOS 3.2 DISK FORMATTER INTERIOR LABEL AT POINT WHERE DISK IS COMPLETED AND
                                           NO ERRORS HAVE BEEN DETECTED
(DOS 3.1 COMMAND TBL)   (-22560~-22429) [$A7E0~$A863] \PB\DOS 3.1 COMMAND TABLE (DOS 3.1 - 48K APPLE ONLY!)
(DOS 3.1 ERROR MSGS)   (-22323~-22144) [$A8CD~$A980] \PB\DOS 3.1 ERROR MSG TABLE (DOS 3.1 - 48K APPLE ONLY!)
(DOS 3.2 ERR MSGS)   (26996) [$6974] \PB\          DOS 3.2 ERROR MESSAGES (32K APPLE ONLY!)
(DOS 3.2/3.3 COMMAND TBL)  [L)$A884~$A908] \PB\    DOS 3.2 (48K) COMMAND NAME TABLE OF DOS COMMAND DECODER (TABLE-DRIVEN
                                                   COMMAND PARSER). CONTAINS NAMES OF DOS COMMANDS WITH LAST BYTE OF
                                                   EACH VAME HAVING HIGH (7TH) BIT SET; OTHER BYTES HAVE IT CLEAR. THIS
                                                   PERMITS CLOSE PACKING FOR SEQUENTIAL SEARCH. EOT IS $00 BYTE
(DOS 3.2/3.3 ERROR MSGS)  [)$A971~$AA3E] \PB\      DOS 3.2/3.3 ERROR MESSAGES (DOS 3.2/3.3 - 48K APPLE ONLY!)
DRAW   (-2559) [$F601] \SE\                        APPLESOFT HI-RES - DRAW SHAPE POINTED TO BY Y-REG(MSB)&X-REG(LSB) BY
                                                   INVERTING EXISTING COLOR OF DOTS THE SHAPE DRAWS OVER. A-REG=ROTATION
                                                   FACTOR
DRIVENO   (53) [$0035] \P1\                        DOS DISK DRIVE NO
DRIVERR   (16307) [$3FB3] \SL\                     DOS 3.2 DISK FORMATTER INTERIOR LABEL AT BEGINNING OF CLEANUP IF
                                                   DRIVE ERROR IS DETECTED
DRV0EN   (-16246) [$C08A] \P1\                     DOS 3.2 READ\WRITE TRACK~SECTOR (RWTS) PACKAGE PARAMETER 'DRV0EN'
                                                   (DRIVE 0 ENABLE)
DRV1EN   (-16245) [$C08B] \P1\                     DOS 3.2 READ\WRITE TRACK~SECTOR (RWTS) PACKAGE PARAMETER 'DRV1EN'
                                                   (DRIVE 1 ENABLE)
DRV1TRK   (1272+S) [$04F8+S] \P1\                  EXAMPLE: 'DRV1TRK' = DISK DRIVE 1 CURRENT TRACK (VALUE = 2*TRACK#);
                                                   DOS 3.2 PARAMETER FOR DISK IN SLOT #S
DRVERR   (15838) [$3DDE] \SL\                      DOS 3.2 RWTS (READ-WRITE TRACK-SECTOR) INTERIOR LABEL - STARTS CODE
                                                   FOR CLEANUP WHEN DRIVE ERROR DETECTED
DRVERR   (-16892~-16886) [$BE04~$BE0A] \SE\        DOS 3.3 - CLEAN UP STACK & STATUS REG; LOAD A-REG WITH $40 (DRIVE
                                                   ERROR) AND GOTO 'HNDLERR' ($BE48)
DRVSEL   (15719) [$3D67] \SL\                      DOS 3.2 RWTS (READ-WRITE TRACK-SECTOR) INTERIOR LABEL
DSCTMP   (157~159) [$009D~$009F] \P3\              APPLESOFT TEMPORARY STRING DESCRIPTOR (SEE VALTYP & TEMPPT)
DSKF2   (16043) [$3EAB] \SL\                       DOS 3.2 DISK FORMATTER LABEL AT POINT WHERE MOTOR IS RUNNING AND ON
                                                   TRACK 0. BEGINS CODE WHICH FORMATS THIS TRACK
DSKFORM   (16028) [$3E9C] \SE\                     DOS 3.2 DISK FORMATTER ENTRY POINT - TURN MOTOR ON & FILL TRACK WITH
                                                   SYNC
DSKFORM   (16028~16089) [$3E9C~$3ED9] \SB\         DOS 3.2 DISK FORMATTER MODULE TO FILL TRACK WITH SYNC
DSKFORM   (16028~16340) [$3E9C~$3FD4] \SB\         DOS 3.2 DISK FORMATTER PACKAGE
DSKFORM   (-16721~-16628) [$BEAF~$BF0C] \SB\       DOS 3.3 - INIT COMMAND HANDLER
~DSP~   (-3324) [$F304] \SE\                       INTEGER BASIC ENTRY TO ROUTINE TO DISPLAY A VARIABLE SET
DV0TRK   (1144+S) [$0478+S] \P1\                   EXAMPLE:'DRV0TRAK'= DISK DRIVE 0 CURRENT TRACK (VALUE = 2*TRACK#);
                                                   DOS 3.2 PARAMETER FOR DISK IN SLOT #S
```

DXL~DXH (80~81) [$0050~$0051] \P2\	HI-RES GRAPHICS DELTA-X FOR HLIN SHAPE
DY (82) [$0052] \P1\	HI-RES GRAPHICS DELTA-Y FOR HLIN SHAPE
E (252~254) [$00FC~$00FE] \P3\	MONITOR & FLOATING POINT ROUTINES MEMORY LOC 'E' (3 BYTE MANTISSA EXTENTION OF FP ACCUMULATOR 1)
EL~EH (84~85) [$0054~$0055] \P2\	HI-RES GRAPHICS ERROR FOR HLIN
ENDCHR (14) [$000E]	APPLESOFT - USED BY STRLT2 STRING UTILITY
ERR (-2682) [$F586]	MINIASSEMBLER MEMORY LOCATION 'ERR'
ERR (-1883) [$F8A5]	MONITOR MEMORY LOCATION 'ERR'
ERR2 (-2680) [$F588]	MINIASSEMBLER MEMORY LOCATION 'ERR2'
ERR3 (-2791) [$F519]	MINIASSEMBLER MEMORY LOCATION 'ERR3'
ERR4 (-2639) [$F5B1]	MINIASSEMBLER MEMORY LOCATION 'ERR4'
ERRDIR (-7418) [$E306] \SE\	APPLESOFT - CAUSES ILLEGAL DIRECT ERROR IF PROGRAM NOT RUNNING {X-REG ALTERED}
ERRFLG (208) [$00D0] \P1\	ERROR FLAG. ON IF BIT 7 SET (PEEK(216)>127). POKE 0 TO CLEAR.
ERRFLG (216) [$00D8] \P1\	APPLESOFT ERROR FLAG: $80 IF ONERR ACTIVE. SET TO 0 TO DISABLE 'ONERR GOTO'
ERRLIN (218~219) [$00DA~$00DB] \P2\	APPLESOFT LINE # WHERE ERROR OCCURED
ERRNUM (222) [$00DE] \P1\	APPLESOFT - WHEN ERROR OCCURS~ TYPE-OF-ERROR CODE APPEARS HERE - SEE MANUAL FOR CODE NUMBER MEANINGS
ERROR (-11246) [$D412] \SE\	APPLESOFT ERROR PROCESSING - CHECKS ERRFLG AND JUMPS TO HNDLERR IF ONERR IS ACTIVE OTHERWISE PRINTS ERROR MSG BASED ON CODE IN X-REG
~ERRORMESS*~ (-7232) [$E3C0] \SE\	INTEGER BASIC ENTRY POINT - INPUT ERROR MESSAGE
~ERRORMESS~ (-7200) [$E3E0] \SE\	INTEGER BASIC ENTRY POINT TO PRINT ERROR MESSAGE AND GOTO MAINLINE
ERRPOS (220~221) [$00DC~$00DD] \P2\	APPLESOFT TEXPTR SAVE FOR HNDLERR SUBROUTINE
ERRSTK (223) [$00DF] \P1\	APPLESOFT STACK POINTER VALUE BEFORE ERROR OCCURED
ESC (-721) [$FD2F]	MONITOR MEMORY LOCATION 'ESC'
ESC1 (-980) [$FC2C] \SE\	ROUTINE (IF A=@ GO TO HOME; =A GO TO ADVANCE; =B GO TO BS (BACKSPACE); =C GO TO LF (LINEFEED); =D GO TO UP (INVERSE LINEFEED); =E GOTO CLREOL; =F GOTO CLREOP; =ANYTHING ELSE RTS & IGNORE ENTRY) CALLED BY 'RDCHAR' IF ESCAPE KEY IS INPUTTED. CALLS APPROPRIATE SCROLL WINDOW SERVICE ROUTINE (IF A=@ GO TO HOME; =A GO TO ADVANCE; =B GO TO BS (BACKSPACE); =C GO TO LF (LINEFEED); =D GO TO UP (INVERSE LINEFEED); =E GOTO CLREOL; =F GOTO CLREOP; =ANYTHING ELSE RTS & IGNORE ENTRY) {USES A-REG}
ESDFO (15975) [$3E67] \SL\	DOS 3.2 RWTS (READ-WRITE TRACK-SECTOR INTERIOR LABEL 'WASDO'
(EVAL EXPR =>INT) (-7931) [$E105] \SE\	APPLESOFT - EVALUATE EXPRESSION POINTED TO BY TXTPTR ($00B8~$00B9) AND CONVERT RESULT (WHICH MUST BE NON-NEGATIVE) TOA TWO-BYTE INTEGER IN FACMO~FACLO ($00A0~$00A1)
EXCNT (70) [$0046] \P1\	DOS DISK SYSTEM FORMATTER GENERAL COUNTER
EXP (-4343) [$EF09] \SE\	APPLESOFT FP - RAISE E TO THE FAC POWER. RESULT TO FAC. MODIFIES INDEX CHARAC COMPRTYP XORFPSGN AND MANY OTHER FP LOCNS
~EXP~ (-3215) [$F371] \SE\	INTEGER BASIC ENTRY TO ROUTINE TO EXPONENTIATE (RAISE TO A POWER)
FAC (157~163) [$009D~$00A3] \P6\	APPLESOFT MAIN FLOATING-POINT ACCUMULATOR (USES 6-BYTE UNPACKED MATH PACKAGE FORMAT DESCRIBED BELOW)
(FAC/ARG AND) (-8363) [$DF55] \SE\	APPLESOFT - LET FAC = FAC 'AND' ARG; I.E. FAC=1 ONLY IF BOTH FAC & ARG <>0; IF EITHER FAC OR ARG OR BOTH =0 THEN FAC=0
(FAC/ARG COMPARE) (-8342) [$DF6A] \SE\	APPLESOFT - COMPARERS FAC WITH ARG. TYPE OF COMPARISON CONTROLLED BY $0016. IF CONDITION MET FAC SET TO ONE; ELSE FAC RESET TO ZERO
(FAC/ARG OR) (-8369) [$DF4F] \SE\	APPLESOFT - LET FAC = FAC 'OR' ARG; I.E. FAC=1 IF EITHER FAC OR ARG OR BOTH <>0; FAC=0 ONLY IF BOTH FAC & ARG = 0
FACEXP (157) [$009D] \P1\	EXPONENT BYTE OF FAC. SIGNED NUMBER IN EXCESS $80 FORM (SIGNED VALUE HAS $80 ADDED)

```
FACHO    (158) [$009E] \P1\              HIGH ORDER BYTE OF MANTISSA OF FAC
FACLO    (161) [$00A1] \P1\              LOW ORDER BYTE OF MANTISSA OF FAC
FACMO    (160) [$00A0] \P1\              MIDDLE ORDER BYTE OF MANTISSA OF FAC
FACMOH    (159) [$009F] \P1\             MIDDLE ORDER HIGH BYTE OF MANTISSA OF FAC
FACMO~FACLO    (160~161) [$00A0~$00A1] \P2\POINTER TO STRING DESCRIPTOR USED IN STRING UTILITIES
(FACSIGN)    (162) [$00A2] \P1\          SINGLE BYTE SIGN OF FAC. WHILE IN MATH PKG SIGN IS KEPT IN SGN WHERE ONLY BIT 7
                                         IS SIGNIFICANT
FADD (FPADD)    (-6210) [$E7BE] \SE\     APPLESOFT FP - MOVE THE FP NUMBER IN MEMORY POINTED TO BY Y-REG & A-REG INTO ARG
                                         AND FALL INTO FADDT (FPADD). MODIFIES INDEX & XORFPSGN
FADD    (-2962) [$F46E] \SE\             FLOATING POINT NUMBER IN FP1 ADDED TO THAT IN FP2. NORMALIZED RESULT LEFT IN FP1
                                         {A- X-REGS ALTERED}
FADDH    (-6240) [$E7A0] \SE\            APPLESOFT FP - ADD 1/2 TO FAC (1/2 IN $EE64)
FADDT    (-6207) [$E7C1] \SE\            APPLESOFT FP - ADD FAC AND ARG. ON ENTRY A-REG AND ZERO FLAG REFLECT FACEXP.
                                         RESULT TO FAC
FAKEMON    (-2755) [$F53D]               MINIASSEMBLER MEMORY LOCATION 'FAKEMON'
FAKEMON2    (-2748) [$F544]              MINIASSEMBLER MEMORY LOCATION 'FAKEMON2'
FAKEMON3    (-2760) [$F538]              MINIASSEMBER MEMORY LOCATION 'FAKEMON3'
FAKESCT    (16192) [$3F40] \SL\          DOS 3.2 DISK FORMATTER INTERIOR LABEL 'FAKESCT' AT BEGINNING OF CODE TO WRITE
                                         FAKE SECTOR
FCBFOP ZPGWRK V NPE    (64~65) [$0040~$0041] DOS - USED AS GENERAL POINTER BY 1ST LEVEL (COMMAND DECODE) ROUTINES IN DOS
FCOMP    (-5198) [$EBB2] \SE\               APPLESOFT FP - COMPARE FAC AND PACKED NUMBER IN MEMORY POINTED TO BY Y-REG &
                                            A-REG. ON EXIT A=1 IF MEM<FAC;A=0 IF MEM=FAC;A=$FF IF MEM>FAC
FCOMPL    (-2908) [$F4A4] \SE\              VALUE OF FLOATING POINT NUMBER IN FP1 IS NEGATED THEN NORMALIZED {A- X-REGS
                                            ALTERED}
FDIV (FPDIV)    (-5530) [$EA66] \SE\        APPLESOFT FP - MOVE THE FP NUMBER IN MEMORY POINTED TO BY R-REG & A-REG INTO
                                            ARG AND FALL INTO FDIVT. ALTERS INDEX & XORFPSGN
FDIVT (FPDIV2)    (-5527) [$EA69] \SE\      APPLESOFT FP - DIVIDE ARG BY FAC. ON ENTRY A-REG AND Z REFLECT FACEXP. RESULT
                                            IN FAC. XORFPSGN SHOULD BE COMPUTED BEFORE CALL
FILLCNT - SCTR    (75) [$004B] \P1\         DOS DISK SYSTEM FORMATTER GENERAL COUNTER & SECTOR NUMBER
FIN    (-5046) [$EC4A] \SE\                 APPLESOFT - INPUT FP NUMB INTO FAC FROM CHRGET. ASSUMES 6502 REGS HAVE BEEN SET
                                            UP BY CHRGET THAT FETCHED 1ST DIGIT
FINDOP    (-2789) [$F51B]                   MINIASSEMBLER MEMORY LOCATION 'FINDOP'
FIRST    (240) [$00F0] \P1\                 APPLESOFT - USED BY UTILITY PLOTFNS FOR DESTINATION OF FIRST NUMBER OF LO-RES
                                            PLOT COORDINATES
FIX    (-2496) [$F640] \SE\                 FROMFLOATING POINT NUMBER IN FP1 EXTRACT INTEGER. PUT HIGH-ORDER BYTE IN
                                            M1;LOW-ORDER IN M1+1 {A- X-REGS ALTERED}
FLAG    (228) [$00E4]                       INTEGER BASIC MEMORY LOCATION 'FLAG' (GENERAL FLAG BYTE)
FLAGS    (2040+S) [$07F8+S] \P1\            EXAMPLE: APPLE SERIAL INTERFACE IN SLOT #S OPERATION MODE
FLOAT    (-5229) [$EB93] \SE\               APLESOFT FP - FLOAT THE SIGNED INTEGER IN A-REG INTO FAC
FLOAT    (-2991) [$F451] \SE\               CONVERT INTEGER (HIGH BYTE IN M1;LOW BYTE IN M1+1;M1+2 CLEARED) TO NORMALIZED
                                            FL POINT EQUIV IN FP1 {A-REG ALTERED}
FMT    (68) [$0044] \P1\                    MINIASSEMBLER MEMORY LOCATION 'FMT'
FMT1    (-1694) [$F962]                     MONITOR MEMORY LOCATION 'FMT1'
FMT2    (-1626) [$F9A6]                     MONITOR MEMORY LOCATION 'FMT2'
FMUL    (-2932) [$F48C] \SE\                FLOATING POINT MULTIPLY S/R: MUTIPLICAND IN FP1; MULTIPLIER IN FP2; SIGNED
                                            NORMALIZED PRODUCT IN FP1 {A- X- Y-REGS ALTERED}
FMUL    (-2894) [$F4B2] \SE\                FL PT DIVIDE S/R: NORM DIVIDEND IN FP2;NORM DIVIDER IN FP1;SIGNED NORM FP
                                            QUOTIENT TO FP1 {A- X- Y-REGS ALTERED}
FMULT (FPMULT)    (-5761) [$E97F] \SE\      APPLESOFT FP - MOVE THE FP NUMBER IN MEMORY POINTED TO BY Y-REG & A -REG INTO
                                            ARG AND FALL INTO FMULTT (FPMULT). ALTERS INDEX XORFPSGN
FMULTT    (-5758) [$E982] \SE\              APPLESOFT FP - MULTIPLY FAC AND ARG. ON ENTRY A-REG & ZERO FLAG REFLECT FACEXP.
                                            RESULT TO FAC. XORFPSGN MUST BE COMPUTED BEFORE CALL
```

NAME (DEC LOCN) [HEX LOCN] \USE-TYPE\	- DESCRIPTION
FNDLIN (-10726) [$D61A] \SE\	APPLESOFT - SEARCHES PROGRAM FOR LINE WHOSE NUMBER IS IN LINNUM. ON EXIT IF CARRY SET LOWTR POINTS TO LINK FIELD OF DESIRED LINE; IF NOT LOWTR TO NEXT HIGHER LINE
FNDOP2 (-2787) [$F51D]	MINIASSEMBLER MEMORY LOCATION 'FNDOP2'
FORM1 (-2599) [$F5D9]	MINIASSEMBLER MEMORY LOCATION 'FORM1'
FORM2 (-2597) [$F5DB]	MINIASSEMBLER MEMORY LOCATION 'FORM2'
FORM3 (-2568) [$F5F8]	MINIASSEMBLER MEMORY LOCATION 'FORM3'
FORM4 (-2567) [$F5F9]	MINIASSEMBLER MEMORY LOCATION 'FORM4'
FORM5 (-2566) [$F5FA]	MINIASSEMBLER MEMORY LOCATION 'FORM5'
FORM6 (-2552) [$F608]	MINIASSEMBLER MEMORY LOCATION 'FORM6'
FORM7 (-2547) [$F60D]	MINIASSEMBLER MEMORY LOCATION 'FORM7'
FORM8 (-2526) [$F622]	MINIASSEMBLER MEMORY LOCATION 'FORM8'
FORM9 (-2511) [$F631]	MINIASSEMBLER MEMORY LOCATION 'FORM9'
FORMAT (46) [$002E] \P1\	USED BY MINIASSEMBLER & DISASSEMBLER TO SPECIFY FORMAT OF INSTRUCTION FOR DISPLAY PURPOSES
FORMDSK (-16883~-16625) [$BE0D~$BF0F]	DOS 3.3 - JUMP TO 'DSKFORM' ($BEAF)
FORNDX (251) [$00FB] \P1\	INTEGER BASIC MEMORY LOCATION 'FORNDX' (FOR-NEXT LOOP INDEX)
FORPNT (133~134) [$0085~$0086] \P2\	APPLESOFT GENERAL POINTER. SEE COPY SUBROUTINE FOR EXAMPLE
~FOR~ (-5830) [$E93A] \SE\	INTEGER BASIC ENTRY TO ROUTINE TO HANDLE 'FOR' LOOP INITIALIZATION
FOUT (256~272) [$0100~$0110] \PB\	FOUT BUFFER
FOUT (-4812) [$ED34] \SE\	CREATES A STRING IN FBUFFR EQUIVALENT IN VALUE TO FAC. ON EXITY-REG &A-REG POINT TO THE STRING. FAC SCRAMBLED
FP1 (244~247) [$00F4~$00F7] \P4\	MONITOR & FLOATING POINT ROUTINES FLOATING POINT ACCUMULATOR 2 (CONTAINS X2 & M2)
FP1 (248~254) [$00F8~$00FE] \P6\	OLD (NON-APPLESOFT) FLOATING POINT ROUTINES FLOATING POINT ACCUMULATOR FP1 (CONTAINS X1 M1 AND E (EXTENSION))
FPWRT (FPEXP) (-4457) [$EE97] \SE\	APPLESOFT FP EXPONENTATION (ARG TO FAC POWER) ON ENTRY A-REG & ZERO FLAG SHOULD REFLECT VALUE OF FACEXP. RESULT TO FAC. MODIFIES MANY FP LOCNS
FRESPC (113~114) [$0071~$0072] \P2\	APPLESOFT TEMPORARY POINTER FOR STRING-STORAGE ROUTINES
FRESTR (-6659) [$E5FD] \SE\	APPLESOFT - MAKE SURE THAT LAST FAC RESULT WAS A STRING & FALL INTO FREFAC
FRETMP (-6652) [$E604] \SE\	APPLESOFT - FREE A TEMPORARY STRING. ON ENTRY POINTER TO DESCRIPTOR IS IN Y-REG (MSB) & X-REG (LSB)
FRETMS (-6603) [$E635] \SE\	APPLESOFT - FREE TEMPORARY DESCRIPTOR W/O FREEING UP THE STRING. Y-REG (MSB) & X-REG(LSB) POINT TO DESCRIPTOR TO BE FREED. ON EXIT Z SET IF ANYTHING FREED
FRETOP (111~112) [$006F~$0070] \P2\	APPLESOFT POINTER TO END OF STRING STORAGE OR TOP OF USER-AVAILABLE FREE SPACE. DEFAULTS TO HIMEM - USUALLY $BFFF FOR 48K APPLE)
FRMEVL (-8837) [$DD7B] \SE\	APPLESOFT - EVAL FORMULA AT TXTPTR USING CHRGET & LEAVE RESULT IN FAC. ON ENTRY TXTPTR POINTS TO 1ST CHAR OF FORMULA
FRMEVL (-8837) [$DD7B] \SE\	APPLESOFT - EVAL FORMULA AT TXTPTR USING CHRGET. IF FORMULA IS STRING LITERAL FRMEVL GOBBLES OPENING QUOTE AND EXECUTES STRLIT & ST2TXT
FRMNUM (-8857) [$DD67] \SE\	APPLESOFT - EVALUATE EXPRESSION POINTED TOBY TXTPTR ($00B8~$00B9) (POINTS TO 1ST CHAR OF FORMULA). PUT RESULT INTO FAC & MAKE SURE IT IS A NUMBER
FRMWSYNC (16096) [$3EE0] \SL\	DOS 3.2 DISK FORMATTER INTERIOR LABEL 'FRMWSYNC'
FSUB (FPSUB) (-6233) [$E7A7] \SE\	APPLESOFT - MOVE FP NUMBER IN MEMORY POINTED TO BY Y-REG &A-REG INTO ARG AND FALL INTO FSUB (FPSUB)T
FSUB (-2968) [$F468] \SE\	FLOATING POINT SUBTRACTION MINUEND IN FP1;SUBTRAHEND IN FP2;NORMALIZED DIFFERENCE TO FP1 (A- X-REGS ALTERED)
FSUBT (-6230) [$E7AA] \SE\	APPLESOFT - FP SUBTRACT FAC FROM ARG. ON ENTRY A-REG & 6502 ZERO FLAG REFLECT FACEXP. RESULT TO FAC
GARBAG (-7036) [$E484] \SE\	APPLESOFT GARBAGE COLLECTOR - MOVES ALL CURRENTLY USED STRINGS UP IN MEMORY AS FAR AS POSSIBLE

```
NAME  (DEC LOCN)  [HEX LOCN] \USE-TYPE\ - DESCRIPTION
--------------------------------------------------------------------------------------------------------------

GBASCALC   (-1977) [$F847] \SE\        COMPUTE GRAPHICS BASE MEMORY ADDRESS FOR LINE IN A-REG (NOTE: 2 LO-RES GRAPHICS
                                       LINES PER TEXT LINE SO (A)= LINE/2); SET GBASL~H {A-REG ALTERED}
GBASL~GBASH    (38~39) [$0026~$0027] \P2\MEMORY ADDRESS OF LEFT END POINT OF DESIRED LINE FOR LO-RES PLOT (SET BY
                                       GBASCALC)
GBCALC   (-1962) [$F856]               MONITOR MEMORY LOCATION 'GBCALC'
GDBUFS   (-10951) [$D539] \SE\         APPLESOFT - PUT ZERO AT END OF INPUT BUFFER (BUF) AND MASK OFF MOST SIGNIFICANT BIT
                                       ON ALL BYTES. ON ENTRY X-REG=END OF INPUT LINE {A- X- Y-REGS ALTERED}
~GET16BIT~    (-6379) [$E715] \SE\     INTEGER BASIC ENTRY TO GET A 16-BIT VALUE
GETADR   (-6318) [$E752] \SE\          APPLESOFT FP - CONVERT FAC (-65535 TO 65535) INTO 2-BYTE INTEGER (0-65535) IN
                                       LINNUM. 'WRAPAROUND' OCCURS IF VALUE IN FAC TOO BIG {A- Y-REGS ALTERED}
GETARYPT   (-2087) [$F7D9] \SE\        APPLESOFT - READ VAR NAME FROM CHRGET & FIND IT IN MEMORY.ON EXIT VAL OF VAR IN
                                       VARPNT AND Y-REG(MSB)&A-REG(LSB)
GETBYT   (-6408) [$E6F8] \SE\          APPLESOFT - EVAL FORMULA AT TXTPTR. LEAVE RESULT IN FAC AND FALL INTO CONINT. AT
                                       ENTRY TXTPTR POINTS TO FIRST CHAR IN FORMULA FOR FIRST NUMBER PLOTFNS PUTS FIRST
                                       NUMBER IN FIRST AND SECOND NUMBER IN H2 AND V2
GETBYT   (-6408) [$E6F8] \SE\          GETBYT S/R. EVALS EXPRESSION (FORMULA) POINTED TO BY TXTPTR ($00B8~$00B9) & CONVTS
                                       TO 1-BYT VAL IN X-REG & FACLO($00A1). A-REG GETS EXPRESSION TERMINAL SIGN {RESETS
                                       Y-REG=0}
~GETCMD~    (-7218) [$E3CE] \SE\       INTEGER BASIC ENTRY POINT TO GET A COMMAND FROM THE KEYBOARD
GETFMT   (-1879) [$F8A9]               MONITOR MEMORY LOCATION GETFMT
GETLN   (-662) [$FD6A] \SE\            PROMPT & GET LINE OF TEXT. ON CALLING A- X- Y-REGS NOT SIGNIFICANT. CV AND BASL~H
                                       SHOULD BE COMPATIBLE POINTING IN THE SCROLL WINDOW. CH INDICATES WHERE ON LINE THE
                                       PROMPT CHARACTER IS TO BE PLACED TO BE FOLLOWED BY ECHOED KEYBOARD INPUT; OUTPUT AS
                                       FOR GETLNZ {X-REG GETS #CHARS READ. DATA TO $200~$200~X (MAX $2FF) $200~X & Y-REG
                                       GET C/R (USES NXTCHAR)} {A- X- Y-REGS ALTERED}
GETLNZ   (-665) [$FD67] \SE\           OUTPUT A C/R (THROUGH COUT). GO TO GETLN TO WRITE PROMPT & GET A LINE OF DATA
                                       (USUALLY FROM KEYBOARD); ON SET-UP A- X- Y-REGS CH AND BASL~H NOT SIGNIFICANT. CV
                                       SHOULD POINT TO A LINE IN SCROLL WINDOW; ON OUTPUT KEYED IN INFO IS IN $200 THRU
                                       $200~X WHERE $200~X CONTAINS A CARRIAGE RETURN;A-REG CONTAINS CARRIAGE RETURN;X-REG
                                       CONTAINS NUMBER OF CHARACTERS READ EXCLUDING TERMINATING CARRIAGE RETURN;Y-REG
                                       CONTAINS CONTENTS OF WNDWDTH; CH CONTAINS ZERO;CV CONTAINS LINE POINTER (CURRENT
                                       VALUE);BASL~H CONTAINS MEMORY ADDRESS CORRESPONDING TO CV AND WNDLFT; SCREEN LINE
                                       IS BLANKS TO THE RIGHT OF THE END OF ECHOED INPUT {A- X- Y-REGS ALTERED}
~GETNEXT~    (-6027) [$E875] \SE\      INTEGER BASIC ENTRY TO 'GETNEXT' (FETCH NEXT STATEMENT FROM TEXT SOURCE)
GETNSP   (-2508) [$F634]               MINIASSEMBLER MEMORY LOCATION 'GETNSP'
GETNUM   (-6330) [$E746] \SE\          APPLESOFT FP - READ 2-BYTE NUM INTO LINNUM FROM TXTPTR. CHECK FOR COMMA. GET SINGLE
                                       BYTE NUMB IN X-REG.
GETNUM   (-89) [$FFA7]                 MONITOR & MINIASSEMBLER MEMORY LOCATION 'GETNUM'
GETSPA   (-7086) [$E452] \SE\          APPLESOFT - GET SPACE FOR CHARACTER STRING. MOVES FRESPC & FRETOP DOWN. A-REG = #
                                       OF CHARS. POINTER TO SPC IN Y-REG(MSB) & X-REG(LSB)
~GETVAL255~    (-4352) [$EF00] \SE\    INTEGER BASIC ENTRY TO ROUTINE TO GET A ONE-BYTE VALUE
~GETVAL~    (-4556) [$EE34] \SE\       INTEGER BASIC ENTRY TO ROUTINE TO GET A VALUE WHICH WILL FIT INTO A SINGLE BYTE
                                       (VAL<=255)
~GETVERB~    (-6401) [$E6FF] \SE\      INTEGER BASIC ENTRY TO GET NEXT VERB TO USE
GIVAYF (INT=>FP)    (-7438) [$E2F2] \SE\APPLESOFT - FLOAT THE SIGNED INTEGER W/ LSB IN A-REG MSB IN Y-REG INTO FAC.
                                       RESETS VALTYP. {RESETS Y-REG=0}
GO   (-330) [$FEB6] \SE\               MONITOR MEMORY LOCATION 'GO'
GOCAL   (15809) [$3DC1] \SL\           DOS 3.2 RWTS (READ-WRITE TRACK-SECTOR) INTERIOR LABEL - GO CALCULATE CORRECT TRACK
GOSEEK   (15992) [$3E78] \DL\          DOS 3.2 RWTS (READ-WRITE TRACK-SECTOR) INTERIOR LABEL 'GOSEEK'
GOSUBNDX    (252) [$00FC] \P1\         INTEGER BASIC MEMORY LOCATION 'GOSUBNDX' (GOSUB INDEX)
~GOSUB~    (-6084) [$E83C] \SE\        INTEGER BASIC ENTRY TO GOSUB HANDLER
--------------------------------------------------------------------------------------------------------------
```

```
GOTO    (-9922) [$D93E] \SE\           APPLESOFT - USES LINGET & FNDLIN TO UPDATE TXTPTR. GOTO ASSUMES 6502 REGS HAVE
                                       BEEN SET UP BY CHRGET THAT FETCHED 1ST DIGIT
"GOTO"   (-6053) [$E85B] \SE\          INTEGER BASIC ENTRY TO 'GOTO' HANDLER
GTBYTC   (-6411) [$E6F5] \SE\          APPLESOFT - JSR TO CHRGET TO GOBBLE A CHARACTER AND FALL INTO GETBYT
H2   (44) [$002C] \P1\                 RIGHT END POINT OF A HORIZONTAL LINE BEING DRAWN BY HLINE: RANGE 0-39 ($0"$27)
HANDLERR   (-3351) [$F2E9] \SE\        APPLESOFT ERROR PROC - SAVE CURLIN IN ERRLIN;TXTPTR IN ERRPOS;X-REG IN ERRNUM;
                                       REMSTK IN ERRSTK
HBASL"HBASH   (38"39) [$0026"$0027] \P2\HI-RES GRAPHICS ON-THE-FLY BASE ADDRESS (LEFT END POINT OF DESIRED LINE FOR
                                       HI-RES PLOT)
HCLR   (-12274) [$D00E] \SE\           HI-RES GRAPHICS CLEAR S/R CALL
HCLR   (-3090) [$F3EE] \SE\            APPLESOFT HI-RES - CLEAR HI-RES SCREEN TO BLACK
HCOLOR   (804) [$0324] \P1\            HI-RES GRAPHICS COLOR FOR HPLOT" HPOSN
HCOLOR1   (28) [$001C] \P1\            HI-RES RUNNING COLOR MASK (ON-THE-FLY COLOR BYTE)
HEADR   (-823) [$FCC9]                 MONITOR - WRITES SYNCHRONIZATION MONOTONE WHICH IS FIRST PART OF EVERY CASSETTE
                                       TAPE RECORD
"HEX/DEC"   (-6885) [$E51B] \SE\       INTEGER BASIC - DECIMAL LPRINT (LINE NUMBER PRINT) S/R; CONVERTS 2-BYTE (16-BIT)
                                       BINARY/HEX TO UNSIGNED DECIMAL (0-65535)
HFIND   (-11780) [$D1FC] \SE\          HI-RES GRAPHICS FIND S/R CALL: PARAM=SHAPE"ROT"SCALE
HFIND   (-2613) [$F5CB] \SE\           APPLESOFT HI-RES HFIND. CONVERT HI-RES CURSOR POSN TO X-Y COORDS. ON EXIT
                                       $00E0=HORIZ LSB;$00E1=HORIZ MSB;$00E2=VERT
HFNS   (-2375) [$F6B9] \SE\            APPLESOFT - GET HI-RES PLOTTING COORDINATE FROM TXTPTR SETS UP 6502 REGISTERS FOR
                                       HPOSN: A-REG=VERT COORD;X-REG LSB OF HORIZ;Y-REG MSB OF HORIZ (A- X- Y-REGS
                                       ALTERED)
HGR   (-3106) [$F3DE] \SE\             APPLESOFT HI-RES - INITIALIZE & CLEAR PAGE 1 HI-RES REGARDLESS OF SCREEN BEING
                                       DISPLAYED
HGR2   (-3116) [$F3D4] \SE\            APPLESOFT HI-RES - INITIALIZE & CLEAR PAGE 2 HI-RES REGARDLESS  OF SCREEN BEING
                                       DISPLAYED
(HI-RES P1)   (8192"16383) [$2000"$3FFF] \HB\HI-RES GRAPHICS PAGE 1
(HI-RES PAGE 2)   (16384"24575) [$4000"$5FFF] \HB\HI-RES GRAPHICS PAGE 2
HI-RES   (-16297) [$C057] \H1\               POKE TO 0 TO SET TO HI-RES GRAPHICS FROM LO-RES OR TEXT (SAME PAGE)
HIGHDS   (148"149) [$0094"$0095] \P2\        USED BY BLOCK TRANSFER UTILITY (BLTU) AS HIGH DESTINATION
HIGHTR   (150"151) [$0096"$0097] \P2\        APPLESOFT - USED BY BLOCK TRANSFER UTILITY (BLTU) AS HIGH END OF BLOCK TO BE
                                             TRANSFERRED
HIMEML"HIMEMH   (76"77) [$004C"$004D] \P2\ADDRESS POINTER TO HIMEM (INTEGER BASIC - END OF BASIC PROGRAM)(APPLESOFT -
                                             START OF STRING DATA)
"HIMEM"   (-4019) [$F04D] \SE\               INTEGER BASIC ENTRY TO THE HIMEM FUNCTION
(HIRES P1L000)   (8192"8231) [$2000"$2027] \HB\HI-RES GRAPHICS: PAGE 1 - LINE #000
(HIRES P1L001)   (9216"9255) [$2400"$2427] \HB\HI-RES GRAPHICS: PAGE 1 - LINE #001
(HIRES P1L002)   (10240"10279) [$2800"$2827] \HB\HI-RES GRAPHICS: PAGE 1 - LINE #002
(HIRES P1L003)   (11264"11303) [$2C00"$2C27] \HB\HI-RES GRAPHICS: PAGE 1 - LINE #003
(HIRES P1L004)   (12288"12327) [$3000"$3027] \HB\HI-RES GRAPHICS: PAGE 1 - LINE #004
(HIRES P1L005)   (13312"13351) [$3400"$3427] \HB\HI-RES GRAPHICS: PAGE 1 - LINE #005
(HIRES P1L006)   (14336"14375) [$3800"$3827] \HB\HI-RES GRAPHICS: PAGE 1 - LINE #006
(HIRES P1L007)   (15360"15399) [$3C00"$3C27] \HB\HI-RES GRAPHICS: PAGE 1 - LINE #007
(HIRES P1L008)   (8320"8359) [$2080"$20A7] \HB\HI-RES GRAPHICS: PAGE 1 - LINE #008
(HIRES P1L009)   (9344"9383) [$2480"$24A7] \HB\HI-RES GRAPHICS: PAGE 1 - LINE #009
(HIRES P1L010)   (10368"10407) [$2880"$28A7] \HB\HI-RES GRAPHICS: PAGE 1 - LINE #010
(HIRES P1L011)   (11392"11431) [$2C80"$2CA7] \HB\HI-RES GRAPHICS: PAGE 1 - LINE #011
(HIRES P1L012)   (12416"12455) [$3080"$30A7] \HB\HI-RES GRAPHICS: PAGE 1 - LINE #012
(HIRES P1L013)   (13440"13479) [$3480"$34A7] \HB\HI-RES GRAPHICS: PAGE 1 - LINE #013
(HIRES P1L014)   (14464"14503) [$3880"$38A7] \HB\HI-RES GRAPHICS: PAGE 1 - LINE #014
```

```
NAME  (DEC LOCN)  [HEX LOCN] \USE-TYPE\ - DESCRIPTION
------------------------------------------------------------------------------------------

(HIRES P1L015)   (15488~15527) [$3C80~$3CA7] \HB\HI-RES GRAPHICS: PAGE 1 - LINE #015
(HIRES P1L016)   (8448~8487) [$2100~$2127] \HB\HI-RES GRAPHICS: PAGE 1 - LINE #016
(HIRES P1L017)   (9472~9511) [$2500~$2527] \HB\HI-RES GRAPHICS: PAGE 1 - LINE #017
(HIRES P1L018)   (10496~10535) [$2900~$2927] \HB\HI-RES GRAPHICS: PAGE 1 - LINE #018
(HIRES P1L019)   (11520~11559) [$2D00~$2D27] \HB\HI-RES GRAPHICS: PAGE 1 - LINE #019
(HIRES P1L020)   (12544~12583) [$3100~$3127] \HB\HI-RES GRAPHICS: PAGE 1 - LINE #020
(HIRES P1L021)   (13568~13607) [$3500~$3527] \HB\HI-RES GRAPHICS: PAGE 1 - LINE #021
(HIRES P1L022   (14592~14631) [$3900~$3927] \HB\HI-RES GRAPHICS: PAGE 1 - LINE #022
(HIRES P1L023)   (15616~15655) [$3D00~$3D27] \HB\HI-RES GRAPHICS: PAGE 1 - LINE #023
(HIRES P1L024)   (8576~8615) [$2180~$21A7] \HB\HI-RES GRAPHICS: PAGE 1 - LINE #024
(HIRES P1L025)   (9600~9639) [$2580~$25A7] \HB\HI-RES GRAPHICS: PAGE 1 - LINE #025
(HIRES P1L026)   (10624~10663) [$2980~$29A7] \HB\HI-RES GRAPHICS: PAGE 1 - LINE #026
(HIRES P1L027)   (11648~11687) [$2D80~$2DA7] \HB\HI-RES GRAPHICS: PAGE 1 - LINE #027
(HIRES P1L028)   (12672~12711) [$3180~$31A7] \HB\HI-RES GRAPHICS: PAGE 1 - LINE #028
(HIRES P1L029)   (13696~13735) [$3580~$35A7] \HB\HI-RES GRAPHICS: PAGE 1 - LINE #029
(HIRES P1L030)   (14720~14759) [$3980~$39A7] \HB\HI-RES GRAPHICS: PAGE 1 - LINE #030
(HIRES P1L031)   (15744~15783) [$3D80~$3DA7] \HB\HI-RES GRAPHICS: PAGE 1 - LINE #031
(HIRES P1L032)   (8704~8743) [$2200~$2227] \HB\HI-RES GRAPHICS: PAGE 1 - LINE #032
(HIRES P1L033)   (9728~9767) [$2600~$2627] \HB\HI-RES GRAPHICS: PAGE 1 - LINE #033
(HIRES P1L034)   (10752~10791) [$2A00~$2A27] \HB\HI-RES GRAPHICS: PAGE 1 - LINE #034
(HIRES P1L035)   (11776~11815) [$2E00~$2E27] \HB\HI-RES GRAPHICS: PAGE 1 - LINE #035
(HIRES P1L036)   (12800~12839) [$3200~$3227] \HB\HI-RES GRAPHICS: PAGE 1 - LINE #036
(HIRES P1L037)   (13824~13863) [$3600~$3627] \HB\HI-RES GRAPHICS: PAGE 1 - LINE #037
(HIRES P1L038)   (14848~14887) [$3A00~$3A27] \HB\HI-RES GRAPHICS: PAGE 1 - LINE #038
(HIRES P1L039)   (15872~15911) [$3E00~$3E27] \HB\HI-RES GRAPHICS: PAGE 1 - LINE #039
(HIRES P1L040)   (8832~8871) [$2280~$22A7] \HB\HI-RES GRAPHICS: PAGE 1 - LINE #040
(HIRES P1L041)   (9856~9895) [$2680~$26A7] \HB\HI-RES GRAPHICS: PAGE 1 - LINE #041
(HIRES P1L042)   (10880~10919) [$2A80~$2AA7] \HB\HI-RES GRAPHICS: PAGE 1 - LINE #042
(HIRES P1L043)   (11904~11943) [$2E80~$2EA7] \HB\HI-RES GRAPHICS: PAGE 1 - LINE #043
(HIRES P1L044)   (12928~12967) [$3280~$32A7] \HB\HI-RES GRAPHICS: PAGE 1 - LINE #044
(HIRES P1L045)   (13056~13095) [$3300~$3327] \HB\HI-RES GRAPHICS: PAGE 1 - LINE #045
(HIRES P1L045)   (13952~13991) [$3680~$36A7] \HB\HI-RES GRAPHICS: PAGE 1 - LINE #045
(HIRES P1L046)   (14976~15015) [$3A80~$3AA7] \HB\HI-RES GRAPHICS: PAGE 1 - LINE #046
(HIRES P1L047)   (16000~16039) [$3E80~$3EA7] \HB\HI-RES GRAPHICS: PAGE 1 - LINE #047
(HIRES P1L048)   (8960~8999) [$2300~$2327] \HB\HI-RES GRAPHICS: PAGE 1 - LINE #048
(HIRES P1L049)   (9984~10023) [$2700~$2727] \HB\HI-RES GRAPHICS: PAGE 1 - LINE #049
(HIRES P1L050)   (11008~11047) [$2B00~$2B27] \HB\HI-RES GRAPHICS: PAGE 1 - LINE #050
(HIRES P1L051)   (12032~12071) [$2F00~$2F27] \HB\HI-RES GRAPHICS: PAGE 1 - LINE #051
(HIRES P1L053)   (14080~14119) [$3700~$3727] \HB\HI-RES GRAPHICS: PAGE 1 - LINE #053
(HIRES P1L054)   (15104~15143) [$3B00~$3B27] \HB\HI-RES GRAPHICS: PAGE 1 - LINE #054
(HIRES P1L055)   (16128~16167) [$3F00~$3F27] \HB\HI-RES GRAPHICS: PAGE 1 - LINE #055
(HIRES P1L056)   (9088~9127) [$2380~$23A7] \HB\HI-RES GRAPHICS: PAGE 1 - LINE #056
(HIRES P1L057)   (10112~10151) [$2780~$27A7] \HB\HI-RES GRAPHICS: PAGE 1 - LINE #057
(HIRES P1L058)   (11136~11175) [$2B80~$2BA7] \HB\HI-RES GRAPHICS: PAGE 1 - LINE #058
(HIRES P1L059)   (12160~12199) [$2F80~$2FA7] \HB\HI-RES GRAPHICS: PAGE 1 - LINE #059
(HIRES P1L060)   (13184~13223) [$3380~$33A7] \HB\HI-RES GRAPHICS: PAGE 1 - LINE #060
(HIRES P1L061)   (14208~14247) [$3780~$37A7] \HB\HI-RES GRAPHICS: PAGE 1 - LINE #061
(HIRES P1L062)   (15232~15271) [$3B80~$3BA7] \HB\HI-RES GRAPHICS: PAGE 1 - LINE #062
(HIRES P1L063)   (16256~16295) [$3F80~$3FA7] \HB\HI-RES GRAPHICS: PAGE 1 - LINE #063
(HIRES P1L064)   (8232~8271) [$2028~$204F] \HB\HI-RES GRAPHICS: PAGE 1 - LINE #064
(HIRES P1L065)   (9256~9295) [$2428~$244F] \HB\HI-RES GRAPHICS: PAGE 1 - LINE #065
------------------------------------------------------------------------------------------
```

```
(HIRES P1L066)   (10280~10319) [$2828~$284F] \HB\HI-RES GRAPHICS: PAGE 1 - LINE #066
(HIRES P1L067)   (11304~11343) [$2C28~$2C4F] \HB\HI-RES GRAPHICS: PAGE 1 - LINE #067
(HIRES P1L068)   (12328~12367) [$3028~$304F] \HB\HI-RES GRAPHICS: PAGE 1 - LINE #068
(HIRES P1L069)   (13352~13391) [$3428~$344F] \HB\HI-RES GRAPHICS: PAGE 1 - LINE #069
(HIRES P1L070)   (14376~14415) [$3828~$384F] \HB\HI-RES GRAPHICS: PAGE 1 - LINE #070
(HIRES P1L071)   (15400~15439) [$3C28~$3C4F] \HB\HI-RES GRAPHICS: PAGE 1 - LINE #071
(HIRES P1L072)   (8360~8399) [$20A8~$20CF] \HB\HI-RES GRAPHICS: PAGE 1 - LINE #072
(HIRES P1L073)   (9384~9423) [$24A8~$24CF] \HB\HI-RES GRAPHICS: PAGE 1 - LINE #073
(HIRES P1L074)   (10408~10447) [$28A8~$28CF] \HB\HI-RES GRAPHICS: PAGE 1 - LINE #074
(HIRES P1L075)   (11432~11471) [$2CA8~$2CCF] \HB\HI-RES GRAPHICS: PAGE 1 - LINE #075
(HIRES P1L076)   (12456~12495) [$30A8~$30CF] \HB\HI-RES GRAPHICS: PAGE 1 - LINE #076
(HIRES P1L077)   (13480~13519) [$34A8~$34CF] \HB\HI-RES GRAPHICS: PAGE 1 - LINE #077
(HIRES P1L078)   (14504~14543) [$38A8~$38CF] \HB\HI-RES GRAPHICS: PAGE 1 - LINE #078
(HIRES P1L079)   (15528~15567) [$3CA8~$3CCF] \HB\HI-RES GRAPHICS: PAGE 1 - LINE #079
(HIRES P1L081)   (9512~9551) [$2528~$254F] \HB\HI-RES GRAPHICS: PAGE 1 - LINE #081
(HIRES P1L082)   (10536~10575) [$2928~$294F] \HB\HI-RES GRAPHICS: PAGE 1 - LINE #082
(HIRES P1L083)   (11560~11599) [$2D28~$2D4F] \HB\HI-RES GRAPHICS: PAGE 1 - LINE #083
(HIRES P1L084)   (12584~12623) [$3128~$314F] \HB\HI-RES GRAPHICS: PAGE 1 - LINE #084
(HIRES P1L085)   (13608~13647) [$3528~$354F] \HB\HI-RES GRAPHICS: PAGE 1 - LINE #085
(HIRES P1L086)   (14632~14671) [$3928~$394F] \HB\HI-RES GRAPHICS: PAGE 1 - LINE #086
(HIRES P1L087)   (15656~15695) [$3D28~$3D4F] \HB\HI-RES GRAPHICS: PAGE 1 - LINE #087
(HIRES P1L088)   (8616~8655) [$21A8~$21CF] \HB\HI-RES GRAPHICS: PAGE 1 - LINE #088
(HIRES P1L089)   (9640~9679) [$25A8~$25CF] \HB\HI-RES GRAPHICS: PAGE 1 - LINE #089
(HIRES P1L090)   (10664~10703) [$29A8~$29CF] \HB\HI-RES GRAPHICS: PAGE 1 - LINE #090
(HIRES P1L091)   (11688~11727) [$2DA8~$2DCF] \HB\HI-RES GRAPHICS: PAGE 1 - LINE #091
(HIRES P1L092)   (12712~12751) [$31A8~$31CF] \HB\HI-RES GRAPHICS: PAGE 1 - LINE #092
(HIRES P1L093)   (13736~13775) [$35A8~$35CF] \HB\HI-RES GRAPHICS: PAGE 1 - LINE #093
(HIRES P1L094)   (14760~14799) [$39A8~$39CF] \HB\HI-RES GRAPHICS: PAGE 1 - LINE #094
(HIRES P1L095)   (15784~15823) [$3DA8~$3DCF] \HB\HI-RES GRAPHICS: PAGE 1 - LINE #095
(HIRES P1L096)   (8744~8783) [$2228~$224F] \HB\HI-RES GRAPHICS: PAGE 1 - LINE #096
(HIRES P1L097)   (9768~9807) [$2628~$264F] \HB\HI-RES GRAPHICS: PAGE 1 - LINE #097
(HIRES P1L098)   (10792~10831) [$2A28~$2A4F] \HB\HI-RES GRAPHICS: PAGE 1 - LINE #098
(HIRES P1L099)   (11816~11855) [$2E28~$2E4F] \HB\HI-RES GRAPHICS: PAGE 1 - LINE #099
(HIRES P1L100)   (12840~12879) [$3228~$324F] \HB\HI-RES GRAPHICS: PAGE 1 - LINE #100
(HIRES P1L101)   (13864~13903) [$3628~$364F] \HB\HI-RES GRAPHICS: PAGE 1 - LINE #101
(HIRES P1L102)   (14888~14927) [$3A28~$3A4F] \HB\HI-RES GRAPHICS: PAGE 1 - LINE #102
(HIRES P1L103)   (15912~15951) [$3E28~$3E4F] \HB\HI-RES GRAPHICS: PAGE 1 - LINE #103
(HIRES P1L104)   (8872~8911) [$22A8~$22CF] \HB\HI-RES GRAPHICS: PAGE 1 - LINE #104
(HIRES P1L105)   (9896~9935) [$26A8~$26CF] \HB\HI-RES GRAPHICS: PAGE 1 - LINE #105
(HIRES P1L106)   (10920~10959) [$2AA8~$2ACF] \HB\HI-RES GRAPHICS: PAGE 1 - LINE #106
(HIRES P1L107)   (11944~11983) [$2EA8~$2ECF] \HB\HI-RES GRAPHICS: PAGE 1 - LINE #107
(HIRES P1L108)   (12968~13007) [$32A8~$32CF] \HB\HI-RES GRAPHICS: PAGE 1 - LINE #108
(HIRES P1L109)   (13992~14031) [$36A8~$36CF] \HB\HI-RES GRAPHICS: PAGE 1 - LINE #109
(HIRES P1L110)   (15016~15055) [$3AA8~$3ACF] \HB\HI-RES GRAPHICS: PAGE 1 - LINE #110
(HIRES P1L111)   (16040~16079) [$3EA8~$3ECF] \HB\HI-RES GRAPHICS: PAGE 1 - LINE #111
(HIRES P1L112)   (9000~9039) [$2328~$234F] \HB\HI-RES GRAPHICS: PAGE 1 - LINE #112
(HIRES P1L113)   (10024~10063) [$2728~$274F] \HB\HI-RES GRAPHICS: PAGE 1 - LINE #113
(HIRES P1L114)   (11048~13871) [$2B28~$362F] \HB\HI-RES GRAPHICS: PAGE 1 - LINE #114
(HIRES P1L115)   (12072~12111) [$2F28~$2F4F] \HB\HI-RES GRAPHICS: PAGE 1 - LINE #115
(HIRES P1L116)   (13096~13135) [$3328~$334F] \HB\HI-RES GRAPHICS: PAGE 1 - LINE #116
(HIRES P1L117)   (14120~14159) [$3728~$374F] \HB\HI-RES GRAPHICS: PAGE 1 - LINE #117
```

```
NAME  (DEC LOCN)  [HEX LOCN] \USE-TYPE\ - DESCRIPTION
-----------------------------------------------------------------------------------------------------

(HIRES P1L118)   (15144~13871) [$3B28~$362F] \HB\HI-RES GRAPHICS: PAGE 1 - LINE #118
(HIRES P1L119)   (16168~16207) [$3F28~$3F4F] \HB\HI-RES GRAPHICS: PAGE 1 - LINE #119
(HIRES P1L120)   (9128~9167) [$23A8~$23CF] \HB\HI-RES GRAPHICS: PAGE 1 - LINE #120
(HIRES P1L121)   (10152~10191) [$27A8~$27CF] \HB\HI-RES GRAPHICS: PAGE 1 - LINE #121
(HIRES P1L122)   (11176~11215) [$2BA8~$2BCF] \HB\HI-RES GRAPHICS: PAGE 1 - LINE #122
(HIRES P1L123)   (12200~12239) [$2FA8~$2FCF] \HB\HI-RES GRAPHICS: PAGE 1 - LINE #123
(HIRES P1L124)   (13224~13263) [$33A8~$33CF] \HB\HI-RES GRAPHICS: PAGE 1 - LINE #124
(HIRES P1L125)   (14248~14287) [$37A8~$37CF] \HB\HI-RES GRAPHICS: PAGE 1 - LINE #125
(HIRES P1L126)   (15272~15311) [$3BA8~$3BCF] \HB\HI-RES GRAPHICS: PAGE 1 - LINE #126
(HIRES P1L127)   (16296~16335) [$3FA8~$3FCF] \HB\HI-RES GRAPHICS: PAGE 1 - LINE #127
(HIRES P1L128)   (8272~8311) [$2050~$2077] \HB\HI-RES GRAPHICS: PAGE 1 - LINE #128
(HIRES P1L129)   (9296~9335) [$2450~$2477] \HB\HI-RES GRAPHICS: PAGE 1 - LINE #129
(HIRES P1L130)   (10320~10359) [$2850~$2877] \HB\HI-RES GRAPHICS: PAGE 1 - LINE #130
(HIRES P1L131)   (11344~11383) [$2C50~$2C77] \HB\HI-RES GRAPHICS: PAGE 1 - LINE #131
(HIRES P1L132)   (12368~12407) [$3050~$3077] \HB\HI-RES GRAPHICS: PAGE 1 - LINE #132
(HIRES P1L133)   (13392~13431) [$3450~$3477] \HB\HI-RES GRAPHICS: PAGE 1 - LINE #133
(HIRES P1L134)   (14416~14455) [$3850~$3877] \HB\HI-RES GRAPHICS: PAGE 1 - LINE #134
(HIRES P1L135)   (15440~15479) [$3C50~$3C77] \HB\HI-RES GRAPHICS: PAGE 1 - LINE #135
(HIRES P1L136)   (8400~8423) [$20D0~$20E7] \HB\HI-RES GRAPHICS: PAGE 1 - LINE #136
(HIRES P1L137)   (9424~9447) [$24D0~$24E7] \HB\HI-RES GRAPHICS: PAGE 1 - LINE #137
(HIRES P1L138)   (10448~10471) [$28D0~$28E7] \HB\HI-RES GRAPHICS: PAGE 1 - LINE #138
(HIRES P1L139)   (11472~11495) [$2CD0~$2CE7] \HB\HI-RES GRAPHICS: PAGE 1 - LINE #139
(HIRES P1L140)   (12496~12519) [$30D0~$30E7] \HB\HI-RES GRAPHICS: PAGE 1 - LINE #140
(HIRES P1L141)   (13520~13543) [$34D0~$34E7] \HB\HI-RES GRAPHICS: PAGE 1 - LINE #141
(HIRES P1L142)   (14544~14567) [$38D0~$38E7] \HB\HI-RES GRAPHICS: PAGE 1 - LINE #142
(HIRES P1L143)   (15568~15591) [$3CD0~$3CE7] \HB\HI-RES GRAPHICS: PAGE 1 - LINE #143
(HIRES P1L144)   (8528~8575) [$2150~$217F] \HB\HI-RES GRAPHICS: PAGE 1 - LINE #144
(HIRES P1L145)   (9552~9599) [$2550~$257F] \HB\HI-RES GRAPHICS: PAGE 1 - LINE #145
(HIRES P1L146)   (10576~10623) [$2950~$297F] \HB\HI-RES GRAPHICS: PAGE 1 - LINE #146
(HIRES P1L147)   (11600~11647) [$2D50~$2D7F] \HB\HI-RES GRAPHICS: PAGE 1 - LINE #147
(HIRES P1L148)   (12624~12671) [$3150~$317F] \HB\HI-RES GRAPHICS: PAGE 1 - LINE #148
(HIRES P1L149)   (13648~13695) [$3550~$357F] \HB\HI-RES GRAPHICS: PAGE 1 - LINE #149
(HIRES P1L150)   (14672~14719) [$3950~$397F] \HB\HI-RES GRAPHICS: PAGE 1 - LINE #150
(HIRES P1L151)   (15696~15743) [$3D50~$3D7F] \HB\HI-RES GRAPHICS: PAGE 1 - LINE #151
(HIRES P1L152)   (8656~8695) [$21D0~$21F7] \HB\HI-RES GRAPHICS: PAGE 1 - LINE #152
(HIRES P1L153)   (9680~9719) [$25D0~$25F7] \HB\HI-RES GRAPHICS: PAGE 1 - LINE #153
(HIRES P1L154)   (10704~10743) [$29D0~$29F7] \HB\HI-RES GRAPHICS: PAGE 1 - LINE #154
(HIRES P1L155)   (11728~11767) [$2DD0~$2DF7] \HB\HI-RES GRAPHICS: PAGE 1 - LINE #155
(HIRES P1L156)   (12752~12791) [$31D0~$31F7] \HB\HI-RES GRAPHICS: PAGE 1 - LINE #156
(HIRES P1L157)   (13776~13815) [$35D0~$35F7] \HB\HI-RES GRAPHICS: PAGE 1 - LINE #157
(HIRES P1L158)   (14800~14839) [$39D0~$39F7] \HB\HI-RES GRAPHICS: PAGE 1 - LINE #158
(HIRES P1L159)   (15824~15863) [$3DD0~$3DF7] \HB\HI-RES GRAPHICS: PAGE 1 - LINE #159
(HIRES P1L160)   (8784~8823) [$2250~$2277] \HB\HI-RES GRAPHICS: PAGE 1 - LINE #160
(HIRES P1L161)   (9808~9847) [$2650~$2677] \HB\HI-RES GRAPHICS: PAGE 1 - LINE #161
(HIRES P1L162)   (10832~10871) [$2A50~$2A77] \HB\HI-RES GRAPHICS: PAGE 1 - LINE #162
(HIRES P1L163)   (11856~11895) [$2E50~$2E77] \HB\HI-RES GRAPHICS: PAGE 1 - LINE #163
(HIRES P1L164)   (12880~12919) [$3250~$3277] \HB\HI-RES GRAPHICS: PAGE 1 - LINE #164
(HIRES P1L165)   (13904~13943) [$3650~$3677] \HB\HI-RES GRAPHICS: PAGE 1 - LINE #165
(HIRES P1L166)   (14928~14967) [$3A50~$3A77] \HB\HI-RES GRAPHICS: PAGE 1 - LINE #166
(HIRES P1L167)   (15952~15991) [$3E50~$3E77] \HB\HI-RES GRAPHICS: PAGE 1 - LINE #167
(HIRES P1L168)   (8912~8951) [$22D0~$22F7] \HB\HI-RES GRAPHICS: PAGE 1 - LINE #168
-----------------------------------------------------------------------------------------------------
```

```
NAME  (DEC LOCN)  [HEX LOCN] \USE-TYPE\ - DESCRIPTION
------------------------------------------------------------------------------------------------------------

(HIRES P1L169)   (9936~9975) [$26D0~$26F7] \HB\HI-RES GRAPHICS: PAGE 1 - LINE #169
(HIRES P1L170)   (10960~10999) [$2AD0~$2AF7] \HB\HI-RES GRAPHICS: PAGE 1 - LINE #170
(HIRES P1L171)   (11984~12023) [$2ED0~$2EF7] \HB\HI-RES GRAPHICS: PAGE 1 - LINE #171
(HIRES P1L172)   (13008~13047) [$32D0~$32F7] \HB\HI-RES GRAPHICS: PAGE 1 - LINE #172
(HIRES P1L173)   (14032~14071) [$36D0~$36F7] \HB\HI-RES GRAPHICS: PAGE 1 - LINE #173
(HIRES P1L174)   (15056~15095) [$3AD0~$3AF7] \HB\HI-RES GRAPHICS: PAGE 1 - LINE #174
(HIRES P1L175)   (16080~16119) [$3ED0~$3EF7] \HB\HI-RES GRAPHICS: PAGE 1 - LINE #175
(HIRES P1L176)   (9040~9087) [$2350~$237F] \HB\HI-RES GRAPHICS: PAGE 1 - LINE #176
(HIRES P1L177)   (10064~10111) [$2750~$277F] \HB\HI-RES GRAPHICS: PAGE 1 - LINE #177
(HIRES P1L178)   (11088~11135) [$2B50~$2B7F] \HB\HI-RES GRAPHICS: PAGE 1 - LINE #178
(HIRES P1L179)   (12112~12159) [$2F50~$2F7F] \HB\HI-RES GRAPHICS: PAGE 1 - LINE #179
(HIRES P1L180)   (13136~13183) [$3350~$337F] \HB\HI-RES GRAPHICS: PAGE 1 - LINE #180
(HIRES P1L181)   (14160~14207) [$3750~$377F] \HB\HI-RES GRAPHICS: PAGE 1 - LINE #181
(HIRES P1L182)   (15184~15231) [$3B50~$3B7F] \HB\HI-RES GRAPHICS: PAGE 1 - LINE #182
(HIRES P1L183)   (16208~16255) [$3F50~$3F7F] \HB\HI-RES GRAPHICS: PAGE 1 - LINE #183
(HIRES P1L184)   (9168~9207) [$23D0~$23F7] \HB\HI-RES GRAPHICS: PAGE 1 - LINE #184
(HIRES P1L185)   (10192~18423) [$27D0~$47F7] \HB\HI-RES GRAPHICS: PAGE 1 - LINE #185
(HIRES P1L186)   (11216~11255) [$2BD0~$2BF7] \HB\HI-RES GRAPHICS: PAGE 1 - LINE #186
(HIRES P1L187)   (12240~12279) [$2FD0~$2FF7] \HB\HI-RES GRAPHICS: PAGE 1 - LINE #187
(HIRES P1L188)   (13264~13303) [$33D0~$33F7] \HB\HI-RES GRAPHICS: PAGE 1 - LINE #188
(HIRES P1L189)   (14288~14327) [$37D0~$37F7] \HB\HI-RES GRAPHICS: PAGE 1 - LINE #189
(HIRES P1L190)   (15312~15351) [$3BD0~$3BF7] \HB\HI-RES GRAPHICS: PAGE 1 - LINE #190
(HIRES P1L191)   (16336~16375) [$3FD0~$3FF7] \HB\HI-RES GRAPHICS: PAGE 1 - LINE #191
(HIRES P1L80)   (8488~8527) [$2128~$214F] \HB\HI-RES GRAPHICS: PAGE 1 - LINE #80
(HIRES P2L000)   (16384~16423) [$4000~$4027] \HB\HI-RES GRAPHICS: PAGE 2 - LINE #000
(HIRES P2L001)   (17408~17447) [$4400~$4427] \HB\HI-RES GRAPHICS: PAGE 2 - LINE #001
(HIRES P2L002)   (18432~18471) [$4800~$4827] \HB\HI-RES GRAPHICS: PAGE 2 - LINE #002
(HIRES P2L003)   (19456~19495) [$4C00~$4C27] \HB\HI-RES GRAPHICS: PAGE 2 - LINE #003
(HIRES P2L004)   (20480~20519) [$5000~$5027] \HB\HI-RES GRAPHICS: PAGE 2 - LINE #004
(HIRES P2L005)   (21504~21543) [$5400~$5427] \HB\HI-RES GRAPHICS: PAGE 2 - LINE #005
(HIRES P2L006)   (22528~22567) [$5800~$5827] \HB\HI-RES GRAPHICS: PAGE 2 - LINE #006
(HIRES P2L007)   (23552~23591) [$5C00~$5C27] \HB\HI-RES GRAPHICS: PAGE 2 - LINE #007
(HIRES P2L008)   (16512~16551) [$4080~$40A7] \HB\HI-RES GRAPHICS: PAGE 2 - LINE #008
(HIRES P2L009)   (17536~17575) [$4480~$44A7] \HB\HI-RES GRAPHICS: PAGE 2 - LINE #009
(HIRES P2L010)   (18560~18599) [$4880~$48A7] \HB\HI-RES GRAPHICS: PAGE 2 - LINE #010
(HIRES P2L011)   (19584~19623) [$4C80~$4CA7] \HB\HI-RES GRAPHICS: PAGE 2 - LINE #011
(HIRES P2L012)   (20608~20647) [$5080~$50A7] \HB\HI-RES GRAPHICS: PAGE 2 - LINE #012
(HIRES P2L013)   (21632~21671) [$5480~$54A7] \HB\HI-RES GRAPHICS: PAGE 2 - LINE #013
(HIRES P2L014)   (22656~22695) [$5880~$58A7] \HB\HI-RES GRAPHICS: PAGE 2 - LINE #014
(HIRES P2L015)   (23680~23719) [$5C80~$5CA7] \HB\HI-RES GRAPHICS: PAGE 2 - LINE #015
(HIRES P2L016)   (16640~16679) [$4100~$4127] \HB\HI-RES GRAPHICS: PAGE 2 - LINE #016
(HIRES P2L017)   (17664~17703) [$4500~$4527] \HB\HI-RES GRAPHICS: PAGE 2 - LINE #017
(HIRES P2L018)   (18688~18727) [$4900~$4927] \HB\HI-RES GRAPHICS: PAGE 2 - LINE #018
(HIRES P2L019)   (19712~19751) [$4D00~$4D27] \HB\HI-RES GRAPHICS: PAGE 2 - LINE #019
(HIRES P2L020)   (20736~20775) [$5100~$5127] \HB\HI-RES GRAPHICS: PAGE 2 - LINE #020
(HIRES P2L021)   (21760~21799) [$5500~$5527] \HB\HI-RES GRAPHICS: PAGE 2 - LINE #021
(HIRES P2L022)   (22784~22823) [$5900~$5927] \HB\HI-RES GRAPHICS: PAGE 2 - LINE #022
(HIRES P2L023)   (23808~23847) [$5D00~$5D27] \HB\HI-RES GRAPHICS: PAGE 2 - LINE #023
(HIRES P2L024)   (16768~16807) [$4180~$41A7] \HB\HI-RES GRAPHICS: PAGE 2 - LINE #024
(HIRES P2L025)   (17792~17831) [$4580~$45A7] \HB\HI-RES GRAPHICS: PAGE 2 - LINE #025
(HIRES P2L026)   (18816~18855) [$4980~$49A7] \HB\HI-RES GRAPHICS: PAGE 2 - LINE #026
------------------------------------------------------------------------------------------------------------
```

```
(HIRES P2L027)   (19840~19879) [$4D80~$4DA7] \HB\HI-RES GRAPHICS: PAGE 2 - LINE #027
(HIRES P2L028)   (20864~20903) [$5180~$51A7] \HB\HI-RES GRAPHICS: PAGE 2 - LINE #028
(HIRES P2L029)   (21888~21927) [$5580~$55A7] \HB\HI-RES GRAPHICS: PAGE 2 - LINE #029
(HIRES P2L030)   (22912~22951) [$5980~$59A7] \HB\HI-RES GRAPHICS: PAGE 2 - LINE #030
(HIRES P2L031)   (23936~23975) [$5D80~$5DA7] \HB\HI-RES GRAPHICS: PAGE 2 - LINE #031
(HIRES P2L032)   (16896~16935) [$4200~$4227] \HB\HI-RES GRAPHICS: PAGE 2 - LINE #032
(HIRES P2L033)   (17920~17959) [$4600~$4627] \HB\HI-RES GRAPHICS: PAGE 2 - LINE #033
(HIRES P2L034)   (18944~18983) [$4A00~$4A27] \HB\HI-RES GRAPHICS: PAGE 2 - LINE #034
(HIRES P2L035)   (19968~20007) [$4E00~$4E27] \HB\HI-RES GRAPHICS: PAGE 2 - LINE #035
(HIRES P2L036)   (20992~21031) [$5200~$5227] \HB\HI-RES GRAPHICS: PAGE 2 - LINE #036
(HIRES P2L037)   (22016~22055) [$5600~$5627] \HB\HI-RES GRAPHICS: PAGE 2 - LINE #037
(HIRES P2L038)   (23040~23079) [$5A00~$5A27] \HB\HI-RES GRAPHICS: PAGE 2 - LINE #038
(HIRES P2L039)   (24064~24103) [$5E00~$5E27] \HB\HI-RES GRAPHICS: PAGE 2 - LINE #039
(HIRES P2L040)   (17024~17063) [$4280~$42A7] \HB\HI-RES GRAPHICS: PAGE 2 - LINE #040
(HIRES P2L041)   (18048~18087) [$4680~$46A7] \HB\HI-RES GRAPHICS: PAGE 2 - LINE #041
(HIRES P2L042)   (19072~19111) [$4A80~$4AA7] \HB\HI-RES GRAPHICS: PAGE 2 - LINE #042
(HIRES P2L043)   (20096~20135) [$4E80~$4EA7] \HB\HI-RES GRAPHICS: PAGE 2 - LINE #043
(HIRES P2L044)   (21120~21159) [$5280~$52A7] \HB\HI-RES GRAPHICS: PAGE 2 - LINE #044
(HIRES P2L045)   (21248~21287) [$5300~$5327] \HB\HI-RES GRAPHICS: PAGE 2 - LINE #045
(HIRES P2L045)   (22144~22183) [$5680~$56A7] \HB\HI-RES GRAPHICS: PAGE 2 - LINE #045
(HIRES P2L046)   (23168~23207) [$5A80~$5AA7] \HB\HI-RES GRAPHICS: PAGE 2 - LINE #046
(HIRES P2L047)   (24192~24231) [$5E80~$5EA7] \HB\HI-RES GRAPHICS: PAGE 2 - LINE #047
(HIRES P2L048)   (17152~17191) [$4300~$4327] \HB\HI-RES GRAPHICS: PAGE 2 - LINE #048
(HIRES P2L049)   (18176~18215) [$4700~$4727] \HB\HI-RES GRAPHICS: PAGE 2 - LINE #049
(HIRES P2L050)   (19200~19239) [$4B00~$4B27] \HB\HI-RES GRAPHICS: PAGE 2 - LINE #050
(HIRES P2L051)   (20224~20263) [$4F00~$4F27] \HB\HI-RES GRAPHICS: PAGE 2 - LINE #051
(HIRES P2L053)   (22272~22311) [$5700~$5727] \HB\HI-RES GRAPHICS: PAGE 2 - LINE #053
(HIRES P2L054)   (23296~23335) [$5B00~$5B27] \HB\HI-RES GRAPHICS: PAGE 2 - LINE #054
(HIRES P2L055)   (24320~24359) [$5F00~$5F27] \HB\HI-RES GRAPHICS: PAGE 2 - LINE #055
(HIRES P2L056)   (17280~17319) [$4380~$43A7] \HB\HI-RES GRAPHICS: PAGE 2 - LINE #056
(HIRES P2L057)   (18304~18343) [$4780~$47A7] \HB\HI-RES GRAPHICS: PAGE 2 - LINE #057
(HIRES P2L058)   (19328~19367) [$4B80~$4BA7] \HB\HI-RES GRAPHICS: PAGE 2 - LINE #058
(HIRES P2L059)   (20352~20391) [$4F80~$4FA7] \HB\HI-RES GRAPHICS: PAGE 2 - LINE #059
(HIRES P2L060)   (21376~21415) [$5380~$53A7] \HB\HI-RES GRAPHICS: PAGE 2 - LINE #060
(HIRES P2L061)   (22400~22439) [$5780~$57A7] \HB\HI-RES GRAPHICS: PAGE 2 - LINE #061
(HIRES P2L062)   (23424~23463) [$5B80~$5BA7] \HB\HI-RES GRAPHICS: PAGE 2 - LINE #062
(HIRES P2L063)   (24448~24487) [$5F80~$5FA7] \HB\HI-RES GRAPHICS: PAGE 2 - LINE #063
(HIRES P2L064)   (16424~16463) [$4028~$404F] \HB\HI-RES GRAPHICS: PAGE 2 - LINE #064
(HIRES P2L065)   (17448~17487) [$4428~$444F] \HB\HI-RES GRAPHICS: PAGE 2 - LINE #065
(HIRES P2L066)   (18472~18511) [$4828~$484F] \HB\HI-RES GRAPHICS: PAGE 2 - LINE #066
(HIRES P2L067)   (19496~19535) [$4C28~$4C4F] \HB\HI-RES GRAPHICS: PAGE 2 - LINE #067
(HIRES P2L068)   (20520~20559) [$5028~$504F] \HB\HI-RES GRAPHICS: PAGE 2 - LINE #068
(HIRES P2L069)   (21544~21583) [$5428~$544F] \HB\HI-RES GRAPHICS: PAGE 2 - LINE #069
(HIRES P2L070)   (22568~22607) [$5828~$584F] \HB\HI-RES GRAPHICS: PAGE 2 - LINE #070
(HIRES P2L071)   (23592~23631) [$5C28~$5C4F] \HB\HI-RES GRAPHICS: PAGE 2 - LINE #071
(HIRES P2L072)   (16552~16591) [$40A8~$40CF] \HB\HI-RES GRAPHICS: PAGE 2 - LINE #072
(HIRES P2L073)   (17576~17615) [$44A8~$44CF] \HB\HI-RES GRAPHICS: PAGE 2 - LINE #073
(HIRES P2L074)   (18600~18639) [$48A8~$48CF] \HB\HI-RES GRAPHICS: PAGE 2 - LINE #074
(HIRES P2L075)   (19624~19663) [$4CA8~$4CCF] \HB\HI-RES GRAPHICS: PAGE 2 - LINE #075
(HIRES P2L076)   (20648~20687) [$50A8~$50CF] \HB\HI-RES GRAPHICS: PAGE 2 - LINE #076
(HIRES P2L077)   (21672~21711) [$54A8~$54CF] \HB\HI-RES GRAPHICS: PAGE 2 - LINE #077
```

```
NAME  (DEC LOCN)  [HEX LOCN] \USE-TYPE\ - DESCRIPTION
---------------------------------------------------------------------------------------------

(HIRES P2L078)   (22696~22735) [$58A8~$58CF] \HB\HI-RES GRAPHICS: PAGE 2 - LINE #078
(HIRES P2L079)   (23720~23759) [$5CA8~$5CCF] \HB\HI-RES GRAPHICS: PAGE 2 - LINE #079
(HIRES P2L080)   (16680~16719) [$4128~$414F] \HB\HI-RES GRAPHICS: PAGE 2 - LINE #080
(HIRES P2L081)   (17704~17743) [$4528~$454F] \HB\HI-RES GRAPHICS: PAGE 2 - LINE #081
(HIRES P2L082)   (18728~18767) [$4928~$494F] \HB\HI-RES GRAPHICS: PAGE 2 - LINE #082
(HIRES P2L083)   (19752~19791) [$4D28~$4D4F] \HB\HI-RES GRAPHICS: PAGE 2 - LINE #083
(HIRES P2L084)   (20776~20815) [$5128~$514F] \HB\HI-RES GRAPHICS: PAGE 2 - LINE #084
(HIRES P2L085)   (21800~21839) [$5528~$554F] \HB\HI-RES GRAPHICS: PAGE 2 - LINE #085
(HIRES P2L086)   (22824~22863) [$5928~$594F] \HB\HI-RES GRAPHICS: PAGE 2 - LINE #086
(HIRES P2L087)   (23848~23887) [$5D28~$5D4F] \HB\HI-RES GRAPHICS: PAGE 2 - LINE #087
(HIRES P2L088)   (16808~16847) [$41A8~$41CF] \HB\HI-RES GRAPHICS: PAGE 2 - LINE #088
(HIRES P2L089)   (17832~17871) [$45A8~$45CF] \HB\HI-RES GRAPHICS: PAGE 2 - LINE #089
(HIRES P2L090)   (18856~18895) [$49A8~$49CF] \HB\HI-RES GRAPHICS: PAGE 2 - LINE #090
(HIRES P2L091)   (19880~19919) [$4DA8~$4DCF] \HB\HI-RES GRAPHICS: PAGE 2 - LINE #091
(HIRES P2L092)   (20904~20943) [$51A8~$51CF] \HB\HI-RES GRAPHICS: PAGE 2 - LINE #092
(HIRES P2L093)   (21928~21967) [$55A8~$55CF] \HB\HI-RES GRAPHICS: PAGE 2 - LINE #093
(HIRES P2L094)   (22952~22991) [$59A8~$59CF] \HB\HI-RES GRAPHICS: PAGE 2 - LINE #094
(HIRES P2L095)   (23976~24015) [$5DA8~$5DCF] \HB\HI-RES GRAPHICS: PAGE 2 - LINE #095
(HIRES P2L096)   (16936~16975) [$4228~$424F] \HB\HI-RES GRAPHICS: PAGE 2 - LINE #096
(HIRES P2L098)   (18984~19023) [$4A28~$4A4F] \HB\HI-RES GRAPHICS: PAGE 2 - LINE #098
(HIRES P2L099)   (20008~20047) [$4E28~$4E4F] \HB\HI-RES GRAPHICS: PAGE 2 - LINE #099
(HIRES P2L100)   (21032~21071) [$5228~$524F] \HB\HI-RES GRAPHICS: PAGE 2 - LINE #100
(HIRES P2L101)   (22056~22095) [$5628~$564F] \HB\HI-RES GRAPHICS: PAGE 2 - LINE #101
(HIRES P2L102)   (23080~23119) [$5A28~$5A4F] \HB\HI-RES GRAPHICS: PAGE 2 - LINE #102
(HIRES P2L103)   (24104~24143) [$5E28~$5E4F] \HB\HI-RES GRAPHICS: PAGE 2 - LINE #103
(HIRES P2L104)   (17064~17103) [$42A8~$42CF] \HB\HI-RES GRAPHICS: PAGE 2 - LINE #104
(HIRES P2L105)   (18088~18127) [$46A8~$46CF] \HB\HI-RES GRAPHICS: PAGE 2 - LINE #105
(HIRES P2L106)   (19112~19151) [$4AA8~$4ACF] \HB\HI-RES GRAPHICS: PAGE 2 - LINE #106
(HIRES P2L107)   (20136~20175) [$4EA8~$4ECF] \HB\HI-RES GRAPHICS: PAGE 2 - LINE #107
(HIRES P2L108)   (21160~21199) [$52A8~$52CF] \HB\HI-RES GRAPHICS: PAGE 2 - LINE #108
(HIRES P2L109)   (22184~22223) [$56A8~$56CF] \HB\HI-RES GRAPHICS: PAGE 2 - LINE #109
(HIRES P2L110)   (23208~23247) [$5AA8~$5ACF] \HB\HI-RES GRAPHICS: PAGE 2 - LINE #110
(HIRES P2L111)   (24232~24271) [$5EA8~$5ECF] \HB\HI-RES GRAPHICS: PAGE 2 - LINE #111
(HIRES P2L112)   (17192~17231) [$4328~$434F] \HB\HI-RES GRAPHICS: PAGE 2 - LINE #112
(HIRES P2L113)   (18216~18255) [$4728~$474F] \HB\HI-RES GRAPHICS: PAGE 2 - LINE #113
(HIRES P2L114)   (19240~22063) [$4B28~$562F] \HB\HI-RES GRAPHICS: PAGE 2 - LINE #114
(HIRES P2L115)   (20264~20303) [$4F28~$4F4F] \HB\HI-RES GRAPHICS: PAGE 2 - LINE #115
(HIRES P2L116)   (21288~21327) [$5328~$534F] \HB\HI-RES GRAPHICS: PAGE 2 - LINE #116
(HIRES P2L117)   (22312~22351) [$5728~$574F] \HB\HI-RES GRAPHICS: PAGE 2 - LINE #117
(HIRES P2L118)   (23336~22063) [$5B28~$562F] \HB\HI-RES GRAPHICS: PAGE 2 - LINE #118
(HIRES P2L119)   (24360~24399) [$5F28~$5F4F] \HB\HI-RES GRAPHICS: PAGE 2 - LINE #119
(HIRES P2L120)   (17320~17359) [$43A8~$43CF] \HB\HI-RES GRAPHICS: PAGE 2 - LINE #120
(HIRES P2L121)   (18344~18383) [$47A8~$47CF] \HB\HI-RES GRAPHICS: PAGE 2 - LINE #121
(HIRES P2L122)   (19368~19407) [$4BA8~$4BCF] \HB\HI-RES GRAPHICS: PAGE 2 - LINE #122
(HIRES P2L123)   (20392~20431) [$4FA8~$4FCF] \HB\HI-RES GRAPHICS: PAGE 2 - LINE #123
(HIRES P2L124)   (21416~21455) [$53A8~$53CF] \HB\HI-RES GRAPHICS: PAGE 2 - LINE #124
(HIRES P2L125)   (22440~22479) [$57A8~$57CF] \HB\HI-RES GRAPHICS: PAGE 2 - LINE #125
(HIRES P2L126)   (23464~23503) [$5BA8~$5BCF] \HB\HI-RES GRAPHICS: PAGE 2 - LINE #126
(HIRES P2L127)   (24488~24527) [$5FA8~$5FCF] \HB\HI-RES GRAPHICS: PAGE 2 - LINE #127
(HIRES P2L128)   (16464~16503) [$4050~$4077] \HB\HI-RES GRAPHICS: PAGE 2 - LINE #128
(HIRES P2L129)   (17488~17527) [$4450~$4477] \HB\HI-RES GRAPHICS: PAGE 2 - LINE #129
---------------------------------------------------------------------------------------------
```

```
(HIRES P2L130)   (18512¯18551) [$4850¯$4877] \HB\HI-RES GRAPHICS: PAGE 2 - LINE #130
(HIRES P2L131)   (19536¯19575) [$4C50¯$4C77] \HB\HI-RES GRAPHICS: PAGE 2 - LINE #131
(HIRES P2L132)   (20560¯20599) [$5050¯$5077] \HB\HI-RES GRAPHICS: PAGE 2 - LINE #132
(HIRES P2L133)   (21584¯21623) [$5450¯$5477] \HB\HI-RES GRAPHICS: PAGE 2 - LINE #133
(HIRES P2L134)   (22608¯22647) [$5850¯$5877] \HB\HI-RES GRAPHICS: PAGE 2 - LINE #134
(HIRES P2L135)   (23632¯23671) [$5C50¯$5C77] \HB\HI-RES GRAPHICS: PAGE 2 - LINE #135
(HIRES P2L136)   (16592¯16615) [$40D0¯$40E7] \HB\HI-RES GRAPHICS: PAGE 2 - LINE #136
(HIRES P2L137)   (17616¯17639) [$44D0¯$44E7] \HB\HI-RES GRAPHICS: PAGE 2 - LINE #137
(HIRES P2L138)   (18640¯18663) [$48D0¯$48E7] \HB\HI-RES GRAPHICS: PAGE 2 - LINE #138
(HIRES P2L139)   (19664¯19687) [$4CD0¯$4CE7] \HB\HI-RES GRAPHICS: PAGE 2 - LINE #139
(HIRES P2L140)   (20688¯20711) [$50D0¯$50E7] \HB\HI-RES GRAPHICS: PAGE 2 - LINE #140
(HIRES P2L141)   (21712¯21735) [$54D0¯$54E7] \HB\HI-RES GRAPHICS: PAGE 2 - LINE #141
(HIRES P2L142)   (22736¯22759) [$58D0¯$58E7] \HB\HI-RES GRAPHICS: PAGE 2 - LINE #142
(HIRES P2L143)   (23760¯23783) [$5CD0¯$5CE7] \HB\HI-RES GRAPHICS: PAGE 2 - LINE #143
(HIRES P2L144)   (16720¯16767) [$4150¯$417F] \HB\HI-RES GRAPHICS: PAGE 2 - LINE #144
(HIRES P2L145)   (17744¯17791) [$4550¯$457F] \HB\HI-RES GRAPHICS: PAGE 2 - LINE #145
(HIRES P2L146)   (18768¯18815) [$4950¯$497F] \HB\HI-RES GRAPHICS: PAGE 2 - LINE #146
(HIRES P2L147)   (19792¯19839) [$4D50¯$4D7F] \HB\HI-RES GRAPHICS: PAGE 2 - LINE #147
(HIRES P2L148)   (20816¯20863) [$5150¯$517F] \HB\HI-RES GRAPHICS: PAGE 2 - LINE #148
(HIRES P2L149)   (21840¯21887) [$5550¯$557F] \HB\HI-RES GRAPHICS: PAGE 2 - LINE #149
(HIRES P2L150)   (22864¯22911) [$5950¯$597F] \HB\HI-RES GRAPHICS: PAGE 2 - LINE #150
(HIRES P2L151)   (23888¯23935) [$5D50¯$5D7F] \HB\HI-RES GRAPHICS: PAGE 2 - LINE #151
(HIRES P2L152)   (16848¯16887) [$41D0¯$41F7] \HB\HI-RES GRAPHICS: PAGE 2 - LINE #152
(HIRES P2L153)   (17872¯17911) [$45D0¯$45F7] \HB\HI-RES GRAPHICS: PAGE 2 - LINE #153
(HIRES P2L154)   (18896¯18935) [$49D0¯$49F7] \HB\HI-RES GRAPHICS: PAGE 2 - LINE #154
(HIRES P2L155)   (19920¯19959) [$4DD0¯$4DF7] \HB\HI-RES GRAPHICS: PAGE 2 - LINE #155
(HIRES P2L156)   (20944¯20983) [$51D0¯$51F7] \HB\HI-RES GRAPHICS: PAGE 2 - LINE #156
(HIRES P2L157)   (21968¯22007) [$55D0¯$55F7] \HB\HI-RES GRAPHICS: PAGE 2 - LINE #157
(HIRES P2L158)   (22992¯23031) [$59D0¯$59F7] \HB\HI-RES GRAPHICS: PAGE 2 - LINE #158
(HIRES P2L159)   (24016¯24055) [$5DD0¯$5DF7] \HB\HI-RES GRAPHICS: PAGE 2 - LINE #159
(HIRES P2L160)   (16976¯17015) [$4250¯$4277] \HB\HI-RES GRAPHICS: PAGE 2 - LINE #160
(HIRES P2L161)   (18000¯18039) [$4650¯$4677] \HB\HI-RES GRAPHICS: PAGE 2 - LINE #161
(HIRES P2L162)   (19024¯19063) [$4A50¯$4A77] \HB\HI-RES GRAPHICS: PAGE 2 - LINE #162
(HIRES P2L163)   (20048¯20087) [$4E50¯$4E77] \HB\HI-RES GRAPHICS: PAGE 2 - LINE #163
(HIRES P2L164)   (21072¯21111) [$5250¯$5277] \HB\HI-RES GRAPHICS: PAGE 2 - LINE #164
(HIRES P2L165)   (22096¯22135) [$5650¯$5677] \HB\HI-RES GRAPHICS: PAGE 2 - LINE #165
(HIRES P2L166)   (23120¯23159) [$5A50¯$5A77] \HB\HI-RES GRAPHICS: PAGE 2 - LINE #166
(HIRES P2L167)   (24144¯24183) [$5E50¯$5E77] \HB\HI-RES GRAPHICS: PAGE 2 - LINE #167
(HIRES P2L168)   (17104¯17143) [$42D0¯$42F7] \HB\HI-RES GRAPHICS: PAGE 2 - LINE #168
(HIRES P2L169)   (18128¯18167) [$46D0¯$46F7] \HB\HI-RES GRAPHICS: PAGE 2 - LINE #169
(HIRES P2L170)   (19152¯19191) [$4AD0¯$4AF7] \HB\HI-RES GRAPHICS: PAGE 2 - LINE #170
(HIRES P2L171)   (20176¯20215) [$4ED0¯$4EF7] \HB\HI-RES GRAPHICS: PAGE 2 - LINE #171
(HIRES P2L172)   (21200¯21239) [$52D0¯$52F7] \HB\HI-RES GRAPHICS: PAGE 2 - LINE #172
(HIRES P2L173)   (22224¯22263) [$56D0¯$56F7] \HB\HI-RES GRAPHICS: PAGE 2 - LINE #173
(HIRES P2L174)   (23248¯23287) [$5AD0¯$5AF7] \HB\HI-RES GRAPHICS: PAGE 2 - LINE #174
(HIRES P2L175)   (24272¯24311) [$5ED0¯$5EF7] \HB\HI-RES GRAPHICS: PAGE 2 - LINE #175
(HIRES P2L176)   (17232¯17279) [$4350¯$437F] \HB\HI-RES GRAPHICS: PAGE 2 - LINE #176
(HIRES P2L177)   (18256¯18303) [$4750¯$477F] \HB\HI-RES GRAPHICS: PAGE 2 - LINE #177
(HIRES P2L178)   (19280¯19327) [$4B50¯$4B7F] \HB\HI-RES GRAPHICS: PAGE 2 - LINE #178
(HIRES P2L179)   (20304¯20351) [$4F50¯$4F7F] \HB\HI-RES GRAPHICS: PAGE 2 - LINE #179
(HIRES P2L180)   (21328¯21375) [$5350¯$537F] \HB\HI-RES GRAPHICS: PAGE 2 - LINE #180
```

```
(HIRES P2L181)   (22352~22399) [$5750~$577F] \HB\HI-RES GRAPHICS: PAGE 2 - LINE #181
(HIRES P2L182)   (23376~23423) [$5B50~$5B7F] \HB\HI-RES GRAPHICS: PAGE 2 - LINE #182
(HIRES P2L183)   (24400~24447) [$5F50~$5F7F] \HB\HI-RES GRAPHICS: PAGE 2 - LINE #183
(HIRES P2L184)   (17360~17399) [$43D0~$43F7] \HB\HI-RES GRAPHICS: PAGE 2 - LINE #184
(HIRES P2L185)   (18384~18423) [$47D0~$47F7] \HB\HI-RES GRAPHICS: PAGE 2 - LINE #185
(HIRES P2L186)   (19408~19447) [$4BD0~$4BF7] \HB\HI-RES GRAPHICS: PAGE 2 - LINE #186
(HIRES P2L187)   (20432~20471) [$4FD0~$4FF7] \HB\HI-RES GRAPHICS: PAGE 2 - LINE #187
(HIRES P2L188)   (21456~21495) [$53D0~$53F7] \HB\HI-RES GRAPHICS: PAGE 2 - LINE #188
(HIRES P2L189)   (22480~22519) [$57D0~$57F7] \HB\HI-RES GRAPHICS: PAGE 2 - LINE #189
(HIRES P2L190)   (23504~23543) [$5BD0~$5BF7] \HB\HI-RES GRAPHICS: PAGE 2 - LINE #190
(HIRES P2L191)   (24528~24567) [$5FD0~$5FF7] \HB\HI-RES GRAPHICS: PAGE 2 - LINE #191
(HIRES P2L97)   (17960~17999) [$4628~$464F] \HB\HI-RES GRAPHICS: PAGE 2 - LINE #97
HISCR   (-16299) [$C055] \H1\                    POKE TO 0 TO DISPLAY PAGE 2  (DOES NOT CLEAR SCREEN)
HLIN   (-2768) [$F530] \SE\                      APPLESOFT HI-RES HORIZ LINE DRAWING FROM LAST POINT PLOTTED TOX-COORD =
                                                 X-REG(MSB)&A-REG(LSB);Y-COORD=Y-REG
HLINE   (-2023) [$F819] \SE\                     LO-RES S/R TO DRAW HORIZONTAL LINE AT Y-COORD = (A-REG) WITH X-COORDS FROM
                                                 (A-REG) THRU (H2)($002C) {A- Y-REGS ALTERED}
HLINE1   (-2020) [$F81C] \SE\                    LO-RES S/R. DRAW HORZ LINE AT Y-COORD ESTAB BY GBASL~H & MASK. X-CORDS FROM
                                                 (Y-REG) THRU ($002C) {A- Y-REGS ALTERED}
~HLIN~   (-4432) [$EEB0] \SE\                    INTEGER BASIC ENTRY POINT TO DRAW A LO-RES HORIZONTAL LINE
HMASK   (48) [$0030] \P1\                        HI-RES GRAPHICS ON-THE-FLY BIT MASK
HNDLERR   (15913) [$3E29] \SL\                   DOS 3.2 RWTS (READ-WRITE TRACK-SECTOR) INTERIOR LABEL AT START OF ERROR
                                                 HANDLING MODULE
HNDLERR   (-16824~-16816) [$BE48~$BE50]          DOS 3.3 - SET CARRY; STORE A-REG IN IOB AS RETURN CODE. TURN OFF MOTOR. RETURN
                                                 TO CALLER
HNDX   (805) [$0325] \P1\                        HI-RES  ON-THE-FLY BYTE INDEX FROM BASE ADDRESS TO CURRENT PLOT BYTE (FUNCTION
                                                 OF CURRENT X-COORD)
HOME   (-936) [$FC58] \SE\                       CLEAR SCROLL WINDOW TO BLANKS. SET CURSOR TO TOP LEFT CORNER {A- Y-REGS
                                                 ALTERED}
HPAG   (230) [$00E6] \P1\                        HI-RES PAGE TO PLOT ON REGARDLESS OF WHICH PAGE BEING DISPLAYED - $20 FOR PG1;
                                                 $40 FOR PG2
HPAG   (806) [$0326] \P1\                        HI-ORDER BYTE OF START ADDR OF CURRENT HI-RES DISPLAY MEM PG (POKE 32 FOR
                                                 HI-RES PG1 ~ 64 FOR PG2)
HPAG   (806) [$0326] \P1\                        HI-RES GRAPHICS MEM PAGE FOR PLOTTING GRAPHICS $20 FOR PG1 ~$40 FOR PG2
HPLOT   (-2989) [$F453] \SE\                     APPLESOFT HI-RES - CALL HPOSN THEN PLOT DOT THERE. NO DOT MAY BE PLOTTED IS
                                                 PLOTTING NON-WHITE AT COMPLEMENTARY COLOR X COORD
HPOSN   (-3059) [$F40D] \SE\                     APPLESOFT HI-RES - POSN HI-RES CURSOR W/O PLOTTING. HPAG DETERMINES WHICH
                                                 PAGE; HORIZ = Y-REG(MSB)&X-REG(LSB);VERT= A-REG
(I/O HOOK TBLS)   (54~57) [$0036~$0039] \PB\MONITOR OUTPUT & INPUT HOOKS (VECTORS TO DOS OUTPUT & INPUT ROUTINES)
IEVEN   (-1893) [$F89B]                          MONITOR MEMORY LOCATION 'IEVEN'
~IF/THEN~   (-6104) [$E828] \SE\                 INTEGER BASIC ENTRY TO IF/THEN ROUTINE
IFSKIP   (212) [$00D4] \P1\                      INTEGER BASIC MEMORY LOCATION 'IFSKIP' (IF\THEN FAIL FLAG)
ILEAV   (-16456~-16441) [$BFB8~$BFC7]            DOS 3.3 - SECTOR TRANSLATE TABLE. SECTOR INTERLEAVING DONE WITH SOFTWARE
(ILLDIRPRT)   (-7413) [$E30B] \SE\               PRINT "ILLEGAL DIRECT" THEN HALT AT APPLESOFT (]) LEVEL
(ILLEGAL QTY PRT)   (-7783) [$E199] \SE\ APPLESOFT - PRINT "ILLEGAL QUANTITY" AND HALT AT APPLESOFT LEVEL (])
~IN#S~   (-3046) [$F41A] \SE\                    INTEGER BASIC ENTRY TO ROUTINE TO SET INPUT PORT
IN   (512) [$0200]                               MONITOR & MINIASSEMBLER MEMORY LOCATION 'IN'
INCHR   (-10925) [$D553] \SE\                    APPLESOFT - GET ONE CHAR FROM CURRENT INPUT DEVICE IN A-REG & MASK OF MSB.
                                                 USES MAIN APPLE INPUT ROUTINES & SUPPORTS HANDSHAKING
INDEX   (94~95) [$005E~$005F] \P2\               APPLESOFT TEMPORARY (STACK) POINTER FOR MOVING STRINGS
INIT   (-1233) [$FB2F] \SE\                      MONITOR S/R- SCREEN INITIALIZATION (RESET TEXT MODE)
```

```
NAME  (DEC LOCN)  [HEX LOCN] \USE-TYPE\ - DESCRIPTION
-----------------------------------------------------------------------------------------------

INITAN   (-1425) [$FA6F]                AUTOSTART MONITOR MEMORY LOCATION 'INITAN'
INITBL   (-1263) [$FB11]                MONITOR MEMORY LOCATION 'INITBL'
(INITFACMANT)   (-5056) [$EC40] \SE\    APPLESOFT FP - INITIALIZED MANTISSA OF FAC (EXCEPT EXTENSION BYTE) TO VALUE IN
                                        A-REGISTER
INLIN   (-10964) [$D52C] \SE\           APPLESOFT - INPUT LINE OF TEXT FROM CURRENT INPUT DEVICE INTO INPUT BUFFER
                                        (BUF) & FALL INTO GDBUFS. NO PROMPT!
INLIN+2   (-10962) [$D52E] \SE\         APPLESOFT - INPUT LINE OF TEXT FROM CURRENT INPUT DEVICE INTO INPUT BUFFER
                                        (BUF) & FALL INTO GDBUFS. CHAR IN X-REG USED AS PROMPT
(INP SOURCE PTR)   (127~128) [$007F~$0080] \P2\APPLESOFT - PTR TO CURRENT SOURCE OF INPUT. $201 DURING INPUT STATEMENT
                                        IF STANDARD BUFFER IN USE
INPORT   (-373) [$FE8B]                 MONITOR MEMORY LOCATION  'INPORT'
INPRT   (-4839) [$ED19] \SE\            APPLESOFT - PRINT 'IN' & CURRENT LINE # FROM CURLIV. USES LPRINT
INPRT   (-371) [$FE8D]                  MONITOR MEMORY LOCATION 'INPRT'
~INPUTSTR~   (-7823) [$E171] \SE\       INTEGER BASIC ENTRY POINT TO 'INPUT A STRING' ROUTINE
~INPUT~   (-5206) [$EBAA] \SE\          INTEGER BASIC ENTRY TO INPUT ROUTINE
INSDS1   (-1918) [$F882]                MONITOR MEMORY LOCATION 'INSDS1'
INSDS2   (-1906) [$F88E]                MONITOR S/R - DISASSEMBLER ENTRY
INSTDSP   (-1840) [$F8D0]               MONITOR & MINIASSEMBLER MEMORY LOCATION 'INSTDSP' (INSTRUCTION DISPLAY)
INSTDSP   (-640) [$FD80]                MONITOR S/R TO DISASSEMBLE INSTRUCTION AT PCH/PCL (A- X- Y-REGS ALTERED)
INT (FPINT)   (-5085) [$EC23] \SE\      APPLESOFT FP - COMPUTES GREATES INT (FPINT)EGER VALUE OF FAC. MODIFIES CHARAC
                                        ($000D). USES QINT (FPINT). RESULT TO FAC. MODIFIES CHARAC ($000D)
(INT=>FP)   (-8471) [$DEE9] \SE\        APPLESOFT - PULL INTEGER (%) VARIABLE POINTED TO BY FACMO~FACLO ($00A0~$00A1)
                                        INTO A-REG & Y-REG AND CONVERT TO FP IN FAC. RESETS VALTYP (RESETS Y-REG TO 0)
INTOIT   (16198) [$3F46] \SL\           DOS 3.2 DISK FORMATTER INTERIOR LABEL 'INTOIT'
INVFLG   (50) [$0032] \P1\              VIDEO FORMAT CONTROL: 255($FF)=NORMAL;127($7F)=FLASHING;63($3F)=INVERSE
IOBPL~H   (72~73) [$0048~$0049] \P2\    DOS READ-WRITE-TRACK-SECTOR (RWTS)  'IOBPL~H' (INPUT-OUTPUT CONTROL BLOCK
                                        POINTER)
IOPRT   (-357) [$FE9B]                  MONITOR MEMORY LOCATION 'IOPRT'
IOPRT1   (-345) [$FEA7]                 MONITOR MEMORY LOCATION 'IOPRT1'
IOPRT2   (-343) [$FEA9]                 MONITOR MEMORY LOCATION 'IOPRT2'
IORTS   (-168) [$FF58]                  JSR HERE TO FIND OUT WHERE ONE IS. SETS OVERFLOW FLAG
IRQ   (-1472) [$FA40] \SE\              AUTOSTART ROM MONITOR S/R - IRQ HANDLER
IRQ   (-1402) [$FA86] \SE\              MONITOR S/R- IRQ HANDLER. NOTE: MOVED TO $FA40 IN AUTOSTART ROM
IRQADR~IRQLOC   (1022~1023) [$03FE~$03FF] \P2\IRQ'S VECTORED BY POINTER HERE TO SUBROUTINE TO HANDLE INTERRUPT REQUESTS
ISCNTC   (-10152) [$D858] \SE\          APPLESOFT - CHECK KEYBOARD FOR CONTROL-C ($83). EXECUTES BREAK ROUTINE IF
                                        THESE IS
ISDRVO   (15989) [$3E75] \DL\           DOS 3.2 RWTS (READ-WRITE TRACK-SECTOR) INTERIOR LABEL 'ISDRVO'
ISLETC (CHARCHEK)   (-8067) [$E07D] \SE\ APPLESOFT - CHECKS A-REG FOR ASCII LETTER OTHERWISE CLEAR IT TO ZERO ('A' TO
                                        'Z'). SET C (CARRY FLAG) TO 1 IF A IS A LETTER OTHERWISE CLEAR IT TO ZERO (A-
                                        X- Y-REGS NOT ALTERED)
ITSGOOD   (16286) [$3F9E] \SL\          DOS 3.2 DISK FORMATTER INTERIOR LABEL AT BEGINNING OF CONTINUATION IF GOOD
                                        CONDITION DETECTED
JJTOER   (15893) [$3E15] \SL\           DOS 3.2 RWTS (READ-WRITE TRACK-SECTOR) INTERIOR LABEL 'JJTOER'
JMPTO1   (15841) [$3DE1] \SL\           DOS 3.2 RWTS (READ-WRITE TRACK-SECTOR) INTERIOR LABEL 'JMPTO1'
JMPTOERR   (15842) [$3DE2] \SL\         DOS 3.2 RWTS (READ-WRITE TRACK-SECTOR) INTERIOR LABEL 'JMPTOERR' (JUMP TO
                                        ERROR HANDING ROUTINE HNDLERR)
KBD ~ IOADR  [$C000~] \H1\              MONITOR I/O - PEEK TO READ KEYBOARD. IF VAL>127 KEY HAS BEEN PRESSED SINCE
                                        LAST STROBED AT $C010.
KBDSTB   (-16368) [$C010] \H1\          KEYBOARD STROBE- REACTIVATES KEYBOARD SO THAT VALUE OF PRESSED KEY GOES TO
                                        $C000. SETS HIGH BITTO ZERO..-4
-----------------------------------------------------------------------------------------------
```

```
KEYIN   (-741) [$FD1B] \SE\              GETS NEXT KEY INPUT FROM KEYBOARD HARDWARE. REQUIRES LOOP TO TEST THAT KEY HAS
                                         INDEED BEEN READ; BY PRESENCE OF $80 BIT. ALSO REQUIRES KEYBOARD STROBE TO BE
                                         HIT BEFORE NEXT KEYBOARD INPUT. AUXILLIARY ACTIONS TAKEN BY KEYIN INCLUDE
                                         RESTORING TO THE SCREEN AREA THE CHARACTER MODIFIED BY RDKEY TO REMOVE BLINK
                                         INSERTED BY RDKEY AND COUNTING UP THE RANDOM NUMBER FIELD~ IGNORING OVERFLOW.
                                         SET-UP: X-REG NOT SIGNIFICANT & NOT AFFECTED; A-REG INPUT TO THIS ROUTINE STJRED
                                         AT (BASL)~Y WHEN A KEY IS PRESSED BEFORE THE A-REG IS FILLED FROM THE KEYBOARD
                                         REGISTER; Y-REG USED FOR STORING A-REG IN SCREEN AREA TO (BASL)~Y; CH AND CV NOT
                                         REFEENCED;BASL~H ARE USED AS INDICATED IN RDKEY. RESJLT: A-REG CONTAINS INPUT
                                         FROM KEYBOARD REGISTER; IT IS ONLY ITEM CHANGED (A-REG ALTERED)
KEYIN2   (-735) [$FD21]                  MONITOR MEMORY LOCATION KEYIN2
KSWL~KSWH   (56~57) [$0038~$0039] \P2\ DOS INPUT HOOK; I.E. ADDRESS OF THE USER INPUT ROUTINE. CONTROLLED BY CURRIN
                                         PORT IN# & KEYIN. RESET ~ 0 CTRL-K & IN#0 SET THIS LJCN TO $FDIB (MONITOR
                                         KEYBOARD INPUT ROUTINE); S CTRL-K &IN#S SET THIS LOCN TO $CS00(SLOT S ROM)
                                         (MONITOR INPUT REG)
L   (53) [$0035] \P1\                    MINIASSEMBER MEMORY LOCATION 'L'
(LAST CHAR PTR)   (184~185) [$00B8~$00B9] \P2\APPLESOFT PTR TO LAST CHAR OBTAINED THRU CHRGET ROUTINE
(LAST VBL NAME)   (129~130) [$0081~$0082] \P2\APPLESOFT - HOLDS LAST-USED VARIABLE'S NAME
LASTIN   (47) [$002F] \P1\               USED IN CASSETTE INPUT BY RDBIT AS WORK AREA TO DETERMINE WHETHER INPUT HAS
                                         CHANGED
LASTPT   (83) [$0053] \P1\               APPLESOFT LAST USED TEMPORARY STRING POINTER
LEAD2R   (250) [$00FA] \P1\              INTEGER BASIC MEMORY LOCATION 'LEADZR' (LEADING ZEROS INDEX)
LEADBL   (201) [$00C9]                   INTEGER BASIC MEMORY LOCATION 'LEADBL' (LEADING BLANKS INDEX)
LENGTH   (47) [$002F] \P1\               USED BY DISASSEMBLER TO INDICATE LENGTH OF THE INSTRUCTION. ALSO BY TRACE
~LEN~   (-4574) [$EE22] \SE\             INTEGER BASIC ENTRY TO FUNCTION TO OBTAIN LENGTH OF A STRING
LET   (-9658) [$DA46] \SE\               APPLESOFT LET - USES CHRGET TO GET ADDRESS OF '=';EVALUATES FORMULA & STORES IT.
                                         ON ENTRY TXTPTR POINTS TO FIRST CHAR OF VARIABLE NAME
LF   (-922) [$FC66] \SE\                 MONITOR S/R TO TO PERFORM A LINE FEED; I.E. INCREMENT CV; COMPARE CV TO WNDBTM
                                         IF CV<WNDBTM GOTO VTABZ TO SET BASL~H AND RETURN ELSE DECREMENT CV AND DO SCROLL
                                         (A-REG ALTERED)
LINGET   (-9716) [$DA0C] \SE\            READ 16BIT INTEGER LINE # FROM TXTPTR INTO LINNUM. SEE APPLE ORCHARD V1#1P13 FOR
                                         DETAILS
LINNUM   (80~81) [$0050~$0051] \P2\      APPLESOFT GENERAL PURPOSE 16 BIT NUMBER LOCATION (USES INCLUED LOCATION FOR LINE
                                         NUMBER)
LINPRT   (-4828) [$ED24] \SE\            APPLESOFT - PRINTS 2-BYTE UNSIGNED NUMBER IN X-REG (MSB) & A-REG (LSB)
LIST   (-418) [$FE5E] \SE\               CALL TO DISASSEMBLE 20 INSTRUCTIONS
LIST2   (-413) [$FE63]                   MONITOR MEMORY LOCATION 'LIST2'
LMNEM~RMNEM   (44~45) [$002C~$002D] \P2\ADDRESS POINTER USED BY DISASSEMBLER FOR INDEX TO MNEMONICS TABLE
(LN(2))   (-5828~-5824) [$E93C~$E940] \P5\APPLESOFT FP CONSTANT (LN(2) = .30103...
LNAL~LNAH   (228~229) [$00E4~$00E5] \P2\INTEGER BASIC MEMORY LOCATIONS 'LNAL~LNAH' (LINE NUMBER ADDRESS)(NEXT LINE
                                         NUMBER)
(LO-RES PAGE 2)   (2048~3071) [$0800~$0BFF] \HB\SECONDARY SCREEN BUFFER (TEXT & LOW-RES GRAPHICS PAGE 2)
LO-RES   (-16298) [$C056] \H1\             POKE TO 0 TO SET FROM HI-RES TO SAME PAGE # OF LO-RES OR TEXT
(LO-RESLNS0/1)   [$C400-$0427] \BB\        VIDEO SCREEN BUFFER LO-RES LINES 0 AND 1
(LO-RESLNS10/11)   [$0680-$06A7] \BB\      VIDEO SCREEN BUFFER LO-RES LINES 10 AND 11
(LO-RESLNS12/13)   [$0700-$0727] \BB\      VIDEO SCREEN BUFFER LO-RES LINES 12 AND 13
(LO-RESLNS14/15)   [$0780-$07A7] \BB\      VIDEO SCREEN BUFFER LO-RES LINES 14 AND 15
(LO-RESLNS16/17)   [$0428-$044F] \BB\      VIDEO SCREEN BUFFER LO-RES LINES 16 AND 17
(LO-RESLNS18/19)   [$04A8-$04CF] \BB\      VIDEO SCREEN BUFFER LO-RES LINES 18 AND 19
(LO-RESLNS2/3)   [$0480-$04A7] \BB\        VIDEO SCREEN BUFFER LO-RES LINES 2 AND 3
(LO-RESLNS20/21)   [$0528-$054F] \BB\      VIDEO SCREEN BUFFER LO-RES LINES 20 AND 21
```

```
(LO-RESLNS22/23)   [$05A8-$05CF] \BB\    VIDEO SCREEN BUFFER LO-RES LINES 22 AND 23
(LO-RESLNS24/25)   [$0628-$064F] \BB\    VIDEO SCREEN BUFFER LO-RES LINES 24 AND 25
(LO-RESLNS26/27)   [$06A8-$06CF] \BB\    VIDEO SCREEN BUFFER LO-RES LINES 26 AND 27
(LO-RESLNS28/29)   [$0728-$074F] \BB\    VIDEO SCREEN BUFFER LO-RES LINES 28 AND 29
(LO-RESLNS30/31)   [$07A8-$07CF] \BB\    VIDEO SCREEN BUFFER LO-RES LINES 30 AND 31
(LO-RESLNS32/33)   [$0450-$0477] \BB\    VIDEO SCREEN BUFFER LO-RES LINES 32 AND 33
(LO-RESLNS34/35)   [$04D0-$04F7] \BB\    VIDEO SCREEN BUFFER LO-RES LINES 34 AND 35
(LO-RESLNS36/37)   [$0550-$0577] \BB\    VIDEO SCREEN BUFFER LO-RES LINES 36 AND 37
(LO-RESLNS38/39)   [$05D0-$05F7] \BB\    VIDEO SCREEN BUFFER LO-RES LINES 38 AND 39
(LO-RESLNS4/5)   [$0500-$0527] \BB\      VIDEO SCREEN BUFFER LO-RES LINES 4 AND 5
(LO-RESLNS40/41)   [$06=0-$0677] \BB\    VIDEO SCREEN BUFFER LO-RES LINES 40 AND 41
(LO-RESLNS42/43)   [$06D0-$06F7] \BB\    VIDEO SCREEN BUFFER LO-RES LINES 42 AND 43
(LO-RESLNS44/45)   [$0750-$0777] \BB\    VIDEO SCREEN BUFFER LO-RES LINES 44 AND 45
(LO-RESLNS46/47)   [$07D0-$07F7] \BB\    VIDEO SCREEN BUFFER LO-RES LINES 46 AND 47
(LO-RESLNS6/7)   [$0580-$05A7] \BB\      VIDEO SCREEN BUFFER LO-RES LINES 6 AND 7
(LO-RESLNS8/9)   [$0600-$0627] \BB\      VIDEO SCREEN BUFFER LO-RES LINES 8 AND 9
(LOAD DOS 3.2 REGS)   (1002) [$03EA] \SE\RECONNECT DOS 3.2 VIA APPLE MONITOR REGS. PREVIOUS CONTENTS OF MONITOR I/O
                                         REGS ($0036~$0039) TO DOS 3.2 INPUT & OUTPUT REGS (DOS 3.2 REGS ALTERED)
LOAD   (-10039) [$D8C9] \SE\             APPLESOFT CASSETTE - LOAD A PROGRAM FROM CASSETTE TAPE
~LOAD~   (-3873) [$F0DF]                 INTEGER BASIC ENTRY TO LOAD SUBROUTINE (LOAD A PROGRAM FROM CASSETTE TAPE)
LOC0   (0) [$0000] \P1\                  MONITOR MEMORY LOCATION 'LOC0'. PRESET TO $4C (JMP) - (JUMP ADDRESS IN
                                         $001~$002)
LOC1   (1~2) [$0001~$0002] \P2\          MONITOR MEMORY LOCATION 'LOC1' - POINTER PRESET TO ADDRESS OF APPLESOFT SOFT
                                         ENTRY
(LOG(E)2)   (-4389~-4385) [$EEDB~$EEDF]  \P5\APPLESOFT FP CONSTANT LOG(E)2
LOMEML~LOMEMH   (74~75) [$004A~$004B] \P2\POINTER TO LOMEM (CONTAINS 'START OF BASIC VARIABLES' FOR INTEGER BASIC -
                                         START OF PROGRAM FOR APPLESOFT BASIC)
~LOMEM~   (-3895) [$F0C9] \SE\           INTEGER BASIC ENTRY TO LOMEM ROUTINE
LOWSCR   (-16300) [$C054] \H1\           POKE TO 0 TO DISPLAY PAGE 1 (DOES NOT CLEAR SCREEN)
LOWTR   (155~156) [$009B~$009C] \P2\     APPLESOFT GENERAL PURPOSE REGISTER USED BY GETARYPT~FNDLN~BLTU (E.G. LOW END OF
                                         BLOCK TO BE TRANSFERRED IN BLTU)
LT   (-480) [$FE20]                      MONITOR MEMORY LOCATION 'LT'
LT2   (-478) [$FE22]                     MONITOR MEMORY LOCATION 'LT2'
M   (-16384~-16369) [$C000~$C00F] \H1\   EQUIVALENT ADDRESSES - ALL FOR KEYBOARD INPUT BYTE. WHEN KEY PRESSED ASCII
                                         VALUE GOES THERE AND HIGH BIT SET
M1   (249~251) [$00F9~$00FB] \P3\        FLOATING POINT ROUTINES FLOATING POINT ACCUMULATOR FP1 MEMORY LOC 'M1'
                                         (MANTISSA)
M2   (245~247) [$00F5~$00F7] \P3\        MONITOR & OLD (NON-APPLESOFT) FLOATING POINT ACCUMULATOR 2 MEMORY LOC 'M2'
                                         (MANTISSA - 3 BYTES)
(MACROLINE0)   (1024~1143) [$0400~$0477] \HB\TEXT VIDEO SCREEN DISPLAY PAGE 1 - MACROLINE ORSUBPAGE CONSISTING OF LINES
                                         0 ~ 8 & 16
(MACROLINE1)   (1152~1271) [$0480~$04F7] \HB\TEXT PAGE 1 - MACROLINE OR SUBPAGE CONSISTING OF 3 TEXT LINES OF 40 BYTES
                                         (CHARACTERS) EACH PLUS A BLOCK OF 8 I-O PERIPHERAL BYTES. SUBSEQUENT
                                         MACROLINES WILL BE OMITTED FROM DATABASE
~MAINLINE~   (-7501) [$E2B3] \SE\        INTEGER BASIC ENTRY POINT TO MAIN LINE OF COMPILE/EXECUTE CODE
~MAN~   (-4524) [$EE54] \SE\             INTEGER BASIC ENTRY TO MANUAL LINE NUMBER FUNCTION
MASK   (46) [$002E] \P1\                 LOW-RES COLOR GRAPHICS MASK. $0F OR $F0 TO SELECT HIGH OR LOW NIBBLE TO SPECIFY
                                         WHICH OF 2 PLOT LINES REP BY GBASL~H POINTER
MD1   (-1116) [$FBA4]                    MONITOR 16-BIT MULITIPLY/DIVIDE SIGN-PROCESSOR. SETS ABSOLUTE VALUES OF ACL~H
                                         MEMORY LOCATION 'MD1' AUXL~H LEAVING RESULTING SIGN IN LSB OF SIGN ($002F)
MD2   (-1105) [$FBAF]                    MONITOR MEMORY LOCATION 'MD2'
```

```
MD3    (-1100) [$FBB4]                    MONITOR MEMORY LOCATION 'MD3'
MDRTS   (-1088) [$FBC0]                   MONITOR MEMORY LOCATION 'MDRTS'
MEMFUL   (-7317) [$E36B] \SE\             INTEGER BASIC MEMORY FULL ERROR
MEMSIZE   (115-116) [$0073-$0074] \P2\ APPLESOFT HIMEM (HIGHEST LOC IN MEM AVAIL + 1). INIT TO HIGHEST RAM - $BFFF FOR
                                          48K APPLE IF DOS NOT ACTIVE BEGINNING OF DOS IF DOS ACTIVE
MINASM   (-2458) [$F666]                  TURN ON MINIASSEMBLER (KEYBOARD INPUT WILL BE INTERPRETED AS A SEMBLY-LANGUAGE
                                          INSTRUCTION)
(MINUS.ONE.HALF)   (-5833~-5813) [$E937~$E94B] \P5\APPLESOFT FP CONSTANT MINUS ONE HALF (-1/2)
MIXCLR   (-16302) [$C052] \H1\                 POKE TO 0 TO RESET FROM MIXED GRAPHICS (W/4 LINES TEXT) TO FULL-SCREEN
                                               GRAPHICS
MIXSET   (-16301) [$C053] \H1\                 POKE=0 TO SET TEXT/GRAPHICS MIX (BOTTOM 4 LINES TEXT)
MNEML   (-1600) [$F9C0]                        MONITOR & MINIASSEMBLER MEMORY LOCATION 'MNEML'
MNEMR   (-1536) [$FA00]                        MONITOR & MINIASSEMBER MEMORY LOCATION 'MNEMR'
MNNDX1   (-1858) [$F8BE]                       MONITOR MEMORY LOCATION 'MNNDX1'
MNNDX2   (-1854) [$F8C2]                       MONITOR MEMORY LOCATION 'MNNDX2'
MNNDX3   (-1847) [$F8C9]                       MONITOR MEMORY LOCATION 'MNNDX3'
MOD8CHK   (-595) [$FDAD]                       MONITOR MEMORY LOCATION 'MOD8CHK'
MODE   (49) [$0031] \P1\                       USED BY MONITOR COMMAND PROCESSING TO INDICATE DISPOSITION OF HEX INFO IN
                                               THE INPUT LINE
~MOD~   (-7558) [$E27A] \SE\                   INTEGER BASIC ENTRY POINT TO MODULO FUNCTION
MON   (-155) [$FF65] \SE\                      MONITOR S/R- NORMAL ENTRY TO 'TOP' OF MONITOR WHEN RUNNING (BEEPS!)
(MONITOR RESVD)   (32~85) [$0020~$0055] \PB\APPLE II SYSTEM MONITOR RESERVED LOCATIONS ($0050~$0055 USED ONLY BY
                                               MULTIPLY-DIVIDE ROUTINES AND THUS AVAILABLE IN MANY SITUATIONS)
MONTIME   (70) [$0046] \P1\                    DOS RWTS (READ-WRITE TRACK-SECTOR) PARAMETER 'MONTIME'
MONZ   (-151) [$FF69] \SE\                     MONITOR S/R TO RESET AND ENTER MONITOR (NO BEEP)
MOTOF   (15741) [$3D7D] \SL\                   DOS 3.2 RWTS (READ-WRITE TRACK-SECTOR INTERIOR LABEL - STARTSCODE TO DELAY
                                               UNTIL MOTOR UP TO SPEED
MOTOROFF   (-16248) [$C088] \P1\               DOS 3.2 READ\WRITE TRACK~SECTOR (RWTS) PACKAGE PARAMETER 'MOTOROFF'
MOTORON   (-16247) [$C089] \P1\                DOS 3.2 READ\WRITE TRACK~SECTOR (RWTS) PACKAGE PARAMETER 'MOTORON'
MOV1F   (-5343) [$EB21] \SE\                   APPLESOFT FP - PACK FAC AND MOVE IT INTO TEMP1 ($0093~$0097). USES MOVMF. ON
                                               EXIT A-REG & Z FLAG REFLECT FACEXP. MODIFIES INDEX ($005E~$005F) (RESET
                                               Y-REG=0)
MOV2F   (-5346) [$EB1E] \SE\                   APPLESOFT FP - PACK FAC AND MOVE IT INTO TEMP2 ($0098~$009C). USES MOVMF. ON
                                               EXIT A-REG & Z FLAG REFLECT FACEXP (RESET Y-REG=))
MOVAF (TR1=>2)   (-5277) [$EB63] \SE\          APPLESOFT FP - PACK EXTENSION BYTE INTO FAC & MOVE FAC INTO ARG. ON EXIT
                                               A-REG = FACEXP AND ZERO FLAG IS SET. RESET EXTENSION BYTE = 0 (RESET X-REG=0)
MOVE   (-468) [$FE2C] \SE\                     MONITOR S/R TO PERFORM A MEMORY MOVE (A1-A2 TO A4)(Y-REG MUST =0 AT CALL)
                                               (A-REG ALTERED)
MOVFA (TR2=>1)   (-5293) [$EB53] \SE\          APPLESOFT FP - MOVE ARG INTO FAC. ON EXIT A-REG = FACEXP AND ZERO FLAG IS SET
MOVFM (FPLOAD)   (-5383) [$EAF9] \SE\          APPLESOFT FP MOVE MEMORY POINTED TO BY Y-REG & A-REG INTO FAC. ON EXIT A-REG
                                               & ZERO FLAG REFLECT FACEXP. RESET EXTENSION BYTE=0 (RESET Y-REG=0)
MOVINS   (-6700) [$E5D4] \SE\                  APPLESOFT - MOVE STRING WHOSE DESCRIPTOR IS POINTED TO BY STRNG1 TO MEM LOC
                                               POINTED TO BY FORPNT
MOVMF (FPSTR)   (-5333) [$EB2B] \SE\           APPLESOFT FP - PACK FAC AND MOVE IT INTO MEMORY POINTED TO BY Y-REG (MSB) &
                                               X-REG (LSB). ON EXIT A-REG & ZERO FLAG REFLECT FACEXP. MODIFIES INDEX
                                               ($005E~$005F)
MOVML   (-5341) [$EB23] \SE\                   APPLESOFT FP - PACK FAC AND MOVE IT INTO ZERO PAGE AREA POINTED TO BY X-REG.
                                               USES MOVMF. ON EXIT A-REG & Z FLAG REFLECT FACEXP
MOVSTR   (-6686) [$E5E2] \SE\                  APPLESOFT - MOVE STRING POINTED TO BY Y-REG (MSB) & X-REG (LSB) WITH LENGH
                                               IN A-REG TO MEMORY POINTED TO BY FRESPA
MSWAIT   (-17920) [$BA00] \SB\                 DOS 3.3 RWTS OPERATION TIMER ROUTINE
```

NAME (DEC LOCN) [HEX LOCN] \USE-TYPE\	DESCRIPTION
MUL (-1181) [$FB63] \SE\	MONITOR - UNSIGNED 16-BIT MULTIPLY S/R (NOT AVAILABLE WITH AUTOSTART ROM). SAME AS MULPM ($FB60) EXCEPT UNSIGNED. SEE 'SIGN' AT $002F (A- X- Y-REGS ALTERED)
MUL10 (-5575) [$EA39] \SE\	APPLESOFT FP - MULTIPLY FAC BY 10. WORKS FOR BOTH POSITIVE & NEGATIVE NUMBERS
MUL2 (-1179) [$FB65]	MONITOR MEMORY LOCATION 'MUL2'
MUL3 (-1171) [$FB6D]	MONITOR MEMORY LOCATION 'MUL3'
MUL4 (-1162) [$FB76]	MONITOR MEMORY LOCATION 'MUL4'
MUL5 (-1160) [$FB78]	MONITOR MEMORY LOCATION 'MUL5'
MULPM (-1184) [$FB60] \SE\	MONITOR - SIGNED 16-BIT MULTIPLY LEAVING SIGN IN LSB OF 'SIGN' (A- X- Y-REGS ALTERED)
MULPM (-1184~-1152) [$FB60~$FB80] \SB\	MONITOR 16-BIT MULTIPLY S/R (NOT IN AUTOSTART ROM). MULTIPLIER IN AUXL~AUXH ($0054~$0055); MULTIPLICAND IN ACL~ACH ($0050~$0051);XTNDL~XTNDH ($0052~$0053) CLEARED TO ZEROS; RESULT GOES TO EXTENDED AC ($0050~$0053). ALSO SEE 'SIGN' AT $002F. (A- X-REGSY-REG ALTERED)
~MULT~ (-7646) [$E222] \SE\	INTEGER BASIC ENTRY POINT TO MULTIPLY ROUTINE
MYSEEK (15931) [$3E3B] \SE\	DOS 3.2 RWTS (READ-WRITE TRACK-SECTOR) INTERIOR LABEL AT START OF ROUTINE WHICH SEEKS TRACK 'N' IN SLOT #X/$10. (IF DRIVENO IS - THEN DRIVE 0;IF DRIVENO IS + THEN DRIVE 1
MYSEEK (-16806~-16755) [$BE5A~$BE8D]	DOS 3.3 - HOUSEKEEPING BEFORE 'SEEKABS'. DETERMINES NUMBER OF PHASES PER TRACK & STORES TRACK INFO IN APPROPRIATE SLOT-DEPENDENT LOCN
NBITS (1912+S) [$0778+S] \P1\	EXAMPLE: APPLE SERIAL INTERFACE IN SLOT #S NUMBER OF DATA BITS PLUS 1 FOR START BIT
NBRNCH (-1269) [$FB0B]	MONITOR MEMORY LOCATION 'NBRNCH'
NEGOP (-4400) [$EED0] \SE\	APPLESOFT FP - LET FAC = -FAC (X- Y-REGS NOT ALTERED)
NEWMON (-1407) [$FA81]	AUTOSTART MONITOR MEMORY LOCATION 'NEWMON'
NEWPCL (-1331) [$FACD]	MONITOR MEMORY LOCATION 'NEWPCL'
NEWSTT (-10286) [$D7D2] \SE\	APPLESOFT - EXECUTE A NEW STATEMENT. ON ENTRY TXTPTR POINTS TO THE':' PRECEDING THE STMT OR ZERO AT END OF PREVIOUS LIN. USE NEWSTT TO RESTART THE PROGRAM WITH CONT. THIS ROUTINE DOES NOT RETURN
~NEW~ (-6739) [$E5AD] \SE\	INTEGER BASIC ENTRY POINT TO CLEAR OUT OLD PROGRAM AND RESET POINTERS FOR A NEW PROGRAM
(NEXT W/O FOR PRT) (-8949) [$DD0B] \SE\	APPLESOFT - PRINT ERROR MESSAGE "NEXT WITHOUT FOR" THEN HALT AT APPLESOFT (]) LEVEL
NEXTOP (-2692) [$F57C]	MINIASSEMBLER MEMORY LOCATION 'NEXTOP'
~NEXT~ (-5930) [$E8D6] \SE\	INTEGER BASIC ENTRY TO ROUTINE TO HANDLE 'NEXT' LOOP END
NMI (1019) [$03FB]	NMI'S VECTORED TO THIS LOCATION
~NODSP~ (-3360) [$F2E0] \SE\	INTEGER BASIC ENTRY TO ROUTINE TO TURN OFF DISPLAY FUNCTION
NOGOOD (16276) [$3F94] \SL\	DOS 3.2 DISK FORMATTER INTERIOR LABEL AT BEGINNING OF CLEAN UP IF NOGOOD CONDITION DETECTED
NORM (-2973) [$F463] \SE\	NORMALIZE FLOATING POINT NUMBER IN FP1 (A-REG ALTERED)
NOTCR (-707) [$FD3D]	MONITOR MEMORY LOCATION 'NOTCR'
NOTCR1 (-673) [$FD5F]	MONITOR MEMORY LOCATION 'NOTCR1'
(NOTFAC) (-8552) [$DE98] \SE\	APPLESOFT - LET FAC = NOT(FAC); I.E. RETURNS FAC=1 IF FAC=0 OR FAC=0 IF FAC<>0
~NOTRACE~ (-3722) [$F176] \SE\	INTEGER BASIC ENTRY TO ROUTINE TO TURN OFF TRACE MODE
NOTSURE (15651) [$3D23] \SL\	DOS 3.2 RWTS (READ-WRITE TRACK-SECTOR) INTERIOR LABEL - AT THIS POINT PROGRAM NOT SURE WHETHER MOTOR IS RUNNING (STABLE LONG ENOUGH)
~NOT~ (-6346) [$E736] \SE\	INTEGER BASIC ENTRY TO 'NOT' (NOT A VALUE FUNCTION)
NOUNSTKC (160~191) [$00A0~$00BF]	INTEGER BASIC MEMORY LOCATION 'NOUNSTKC' (NOUN STACK COUNTER)
NOUNSTKH (120~151) [$0078~$0097]	INTEGER BASIC MEMORY LOCATION 'NOUNSTKH' (NOUN STACK HI BYTE)
NOUNSTKL (80~87) [$0050~$0057] \P8\	INTEGER BASIC MEMORY LOCATION 'NOUNSTKL'

```
NREL (-2696) [$F578]                      MINIASSEMBLER MEMORY LOCATION 'NREL'
NXTA1 (-838) [$FCBA] \SE\                 MONITOR S/R TO INCREMENT A1 (16 BITS). SET CARRY IF RESULT >=A2. {A-REG ALTERED}
NXTA4 (-844) [$FCB4] \SE\                 MONITOR S/R TO INCREMENT A4 (16 BITS) THEN DO NXTA1 {A-REG ALTERED}
NXTBAS (-104) [$FF98]                     MONITOR MEMORY LOCATION 'NXTBAS'
NXTBIT (-112) [$FF90]                     MONITOR MEMORY LOCATION 'NXTBIT'
NXTBS2 (-94) [$FFA2]                      MONITOR MEMORY LOCATION 'NXTBS2'
NXTBYT (-1337) [$FAC7]                    AUTOSTART MONITOR MEMORY LOCATION 'NXTBYT'
"NXTBYTE" (-8150) [$E02A] \SE\            INTEGER BASIC ENTRY POINT TO GET NEXT BYTE 16-BIT POINTER
NXTCHAR (-651) [$FD75] \SE\               TOP POINT IN CHAR INPUT LOOP. SAME EFFECT AS GETLN EXCEPT BYPASS PRINT OF PROMPT
                                          CHARACTER; ON SET-UP X-REG SHOULD BE SET TO ZERO TO BEGIN STORING OF INPUT AT
                                          $200; A- Y-REGS NOT SIGNIFICANT;CV AND BASL~H SHOULD BE COMPATIBLE POINTING IN
                                          THE SCROLL WINDOW; CH INDICATES WHERE ECHOING OF KEYBOARD INPUT IS TO START &
                                          SHOULD BE LESS THAN WNDWDTH; RESULTS SAME AS FOR GETLNZ {A- X- Y-REGS ALTERED}
NXTCHR (-83) [$FFAD]                      MONITOR - TOP POINT IN GETLN CHARACTER INPUT LOOP;RDCHAR CALLED TO GET CHAR INTO
                                          A-REG; ON RETURN A-REG TESTED FOR PRESENCE OF CTRL-U (RIGHT ARROW); IF SO A-REG
                                          LOADED FROM SC/REEN MEMORY ASSUMING Y-REG CONTAINS SAME VALUE AS CH; IF A-REG
                                          VAL >$DF LOWER-CASE LETTER CONVERTED TO UPPER CASE; IF CHAR IS A C/R IT IS
                                          PRINTED THROUGH COUT AND RTS EXIT OF COUT WILL GIVE CONTROL BACK TO CALLING
                                          PROGRAM W/ X-REG INDICATING INPUT CHAR COUNT +1; THAT IS INPUT IS IN LOCNS $200
                                          THRU $200~X WHERE $200~X CONTAINS A C/R; ON SET-UP A- X- Y-REGS NOT SIGNIFICANT;
                                          CV & BASL~H SHOULD BE COMPATIBLE (POINTING IN THE SCROLL WINDOW);CH INDICATES
                                          HORIZ POSN IN SCROLL WINDOW WHERE CURSOR WILL BE INDICATED BY BLINKING. ON
                                          RETURN CALLER A-REG WILL CONTAIN KEY VALUE;Y-REG WILL CONTAIN CONTENTS OF
                                          CH;X-REG WILL CONTAIN SAME VALUE AS INPUT; CV CH & BASL~H WILL HAVE CHANGE ONLY
                                          IF AN ESCAPE KEY SEQUENCE HAS BEEN PERFORMED
NXTCOL (-1953) [$F85F] \SE\               MONITOR LO-RES S/R. CHANGE COLOR TO (COLOR)+3 {A-REG ALTERED}
NXTCOL (-1803) [$F8F5]                    AUTOSTART MONITOR MEMORY LOCATION 'NXTCOL'
NXTITM (-141) [$FF73]                     MONITOR MEMORY LOCATION 'NXTITM'
NXTLINE (-2667) [$F595]                   MINIASSEMBER MEMORY LOCATION 'NXTLINE'
NXTL~NXTH (230~231) [$00E6~$00E7] \P2\INTEGER BASIC MEMORY LOCATIONS 'NXTL~NXTH' (NEXT POINTER)
NXTM (-2624) [$F5C0]                      MINIASSEMBLER MEMORY LOCATION 'NXTM'
NXTM2 (-2613) [$F5CB]                     MINIASSEMBLER MEMORY LOCATION 'NXTM2'
NXTMN (-2627) [$F5BD]                     MINIASSEMBLER MEMORY LOCATION 'NXTMN'
NXTPRT (16086) [$3ED6] \SL\               DOS 3.2 DISK FORMATTER - LABEL AT POINT WHERE CHECK IS MADE TO SEE IF TRACK DONE
NXTTRY (16208) [$3F50] \SL\               DOS 3.2 DISK FORMATTER INTERIOR LABEL 'NXTTRY'
OK (15710) [$3D5E] \SL\                   DOS 3.2 RWTS (READ-WRITE TRACK-SECTOR) INTERIOR LABEL - STARTS CODE THAT IT IS
                                          OKAY TO CONTINUE
(OLD TEXT PTR) (121~122) [$0079~$007A] \P2\APPLESOFT OLD TEXT PTR. PTS TO LOC IN MEM FOR NEXT STMT TO BE EXE
OLDBRK (-1447) [$FA59]                    AUTOSTART MONITOR MEMORY LOCATION 'OLDBRK'
OLDLIN (119~120) [$0077~$0078] \P2\       APPLESOFT - LAST LINE EXECUTED - LINE # AT WHICH EXECUTION INTERRUPED BY CTRL-C
                                          STOP ETC.
ONDRVO (16027) [$3E9B] \DL\               DOS 3.2 RWTS (READ-WRITE TRACK-SECTOR) INTERIOR LABEL 'ONDRVO'
(ONE) (-5869~-5865) [$E913~$E917] \P5\APPLESOFT FP CONSTANT ONE =1.
(ONE-QUARTER) (-3984~-3979) [$F070~$F075] \P5\APPLESOFT5-BYTE FLOATING POINT CONSTANT 1/4 (0.25)
(ONE.BILLION) [$ED14~$$ED18] \P5\            APPLESOFT 5-BYTE FLOATING POINT CONSTANT 1000000000 (1E9)
(ONE.HALF) (-4508~-4504) [$EE64~$EE68] \P5\APPLESOFT 5-BYTE FP CONSTANT ONE HALF (1/2)
ONEDLY (-798) [$FCE2]                        MONITOR MEMORY LOCATION 'ONEDLY'
ORMASK (243) [$00F3] \P1\                    MASK FOR OUTPUT CONTROL: NORMAL/FLASHING/INVERSE
(OUT OF MEM PRT) (-11248) [$D410]            APPLESOFT - PRINT "OUT OF MEMORY" THEN HALT AT APPLESOFT (]) LEVEL
OUTDO (-9380) [$DB5C] \SE\                   APPLESOFT - PRINT THE CHARACTER IN A-REG. INVERSE~FLASH~NORMAL OPTIONS IN EFFECT
OUTPORT (-363) [$FE95]                       MONITOR MEMORY LOCATION 'OUTPORT'
```

```
NAME  (DEC LOCN)  [HEX LOCN] \USE-TYPE\ - DESCRIPTION
--------------------------------------------------------------------------------------------------------

OUTPRT    (-361) [$FE97]                      MONITOR MEMORY LOCATION 'OUTPRT'
OUTQST    (-9382) [$DB5A] \SE\                APPLESOFT - PRINT A QUESTION MARK
OUTSPC    (-9385) [$DB57] \SE\                APPLESOFT - PRINT A SPACE
OUTVAL    (200) [$00C8]                       INTEGER BASIC MEMORY LOCATION 'OUTVAL' (OUTPUT VALUE TEMPORARY)
(OVERFLOWPRT)    (-5931) [$E8D5] \SE\         PRINT "OVERFLOW" THEN HALT AT THE APPLESOFT (]) LEVEL
P1L~P1H    (50~227) [$0032~$00E3] \P2\        INTEGER BASIC MEMORY LOCATIONS 'P1L~P1H' (AUXILIARY POINTER ONE)
P2L~P2H    (228~229) [$00E4~$00E5] \P2\       INTEGER BASIC MEMORY LOCATIONS 'P2L~P2H' (AUXILIARY POINTER TWO)
P3L~P3H    (230~231) [$0CE6~$00E7] \P2\       INTEGER BASIC MEMORY LOCATIONS 'P3L~P3H' (AUXILIARY POINTER THREE)
PADDL0    (-16284) [$C064] \H1\               MONITOR MEMORY LOCATION PADDL0; HARDWARE INDISTINGUISHABLE FROM $C06C; STATE OF
                                              TIMER OUTPUT FOR PADDLE 0 APPEARS IN BIT 7 (NEGATIVE UNTIL TIMER EXPIRES)
PADDL0    (-16276) [$C06C] \H1\               MONITOR MEMORY LOCATION PADDL0; HARDWARE INDISTINGUISHABLE FROM $C064; STATE OF
                                              TIMER OUTPUT FOR PADDLE 0 APPEARS IN BIT 7 (NEGATIVE UNTIL TIMER EXPIRES)
PADDL1    (-16283) [$C065] \H1\               MONITOR MEMORY LOCATION PADDL1; HARDWARE INDISTINGUISHABLE FROM $C06D; STATE OF
                                              TIMER OUTPUT FOR PADDLE 1 APPEARS IN BIT 7 (NEGATIVE UNTIL TIMER EXPIRES)
PADDL1    (-16275) [$C06D] \H1\               MONITOR MEMORY LOCATION PADDL1; HARDWARE INDISTINGUISHABLE FROM $C065; STATE OF
                                              TIMER OUTPUT FOR PADDLE 1 APPEARS IN BIT 7 (NEGATIVE UNTIL TIMER EXPIRES)
PADDL2    (-16282) [$C066] \H1\               MONITOR MEMORY LOCATION PADDL2; HARDWARE INDISTINGUISHABLE FROM $C06E; STATE OF
                                              TIMER OUTPUT FOR PADDLE 2 APPEARS IN BIT 7 (NEGATIVE UNTIL TIMER EXPIRES)
PADDL2    (-16274) [$C06E] \H1\               MONITOR MEMORY LOCATION PADDL2; HARDWARE INDISTINGUISHABLE FROM $C066; STATE OF
                                              TIMER OUTPUT FOR PADDLE 2 APPEARS IN BIT 7 (NEGATIVE UNTIL TIMER EXPIRES)
PADDL3    (-16281) [$C067] \H1\               MONITOR MEMORY LOCATION PADDL3; HARDWARE INDISTINGUISHABLE FROM $C06F; STATE OF
                                              TIMER OUTPUT FOR PADDLE 3 APPEARS IN BIT 7 (NEGATIVE UNTIL TIMER EXPIRES)
PADDL3    (-16273) [$C06F] \H1\               MONITOR MEMORY LOCATION PADDL3; HARDWARE INDISTINGUISHABLE FROM $C067; STATE OF
                                              TIMER OUTPUT FOR PADDLE 3 APPEARS IN BIT 7 (NEGATIVE UNTIL TIMER EXPIRES)
PARCHK    (-8526) [$DEB2] \SE\                APPLESOFT PARENTHESIS CHECK - CHECK FOR '(';EVALUATE FORMULA;CHECK FOR ')'.
                                              USES CHKOPN & FRMEVL THEN FALLS INTO CHKCLS
PCADJ    (-1709) [$F953]                      MINIASSEMBLER MEMORY LOCATION 'PCADJ' (PROGRAM COUNTER ADJUST: 0=1 BYTE; 1=2
                                              BYTES; 2=3 BYTES)
PCADJ2    (-1708) [$F954]                     MONITOR & MINIASSEMBLER MEMORY LOCATION 'PCADJ2'
PCADJ3    (-1706) [$F956]                     MONITOR MEMORY LOCATION 'PCADJ3'
PCADJ4    (-1700) [$F95C]                     MONITOR MEMORY LOCATION 'PCADJ4'
PCINC2    (-1363) [$FAAD]                     MONITOR MEMORY LOCATION 'PCINC2'
PCINC3    (-1361) [$FAAF]                     MONITOR MEMORY LOCATION 'PCINC3'
PCL~PCH    (58~59) [$003A~$003B] \P2\         SAVE AND CONTROL AREA FOR PROGRAM COUNTER. USED IN BREAK PROCESSING AND
                                              MINIASSEMBLER. SET BY MONITOR CMDS L G S &T (PC SAVED HERE BY MONITOR)
~PDL~    (-3269) [$F33B] \SE\                 INTEGER BASIC ENTRY TO ROUTINE TO READ A PADDLE
~PEEK~    (-4362) [$EEF6] \SE\                INTEGER BASIC ENTRY TO ROUTINE TO 'PEEK' AT THE CONTENTS OF A MEMORY LOCATION
PHASON    (-16255) [$C081] \P1\               DOS 3.2 READ\WRITE TRACK~SECTOR (RWTS) PACKAGE PARAMETER 'PHASON'
PHSOFF    (-16254) [$C082] \P1\               DOS 3.2 READ\WRITE TRACK~SECTOR (RWTS) PACKAGE PARAMETER 'PHSOFF'
PHSOFF~PHSON    (-16256~-16255) [$C080~$C081] \P4\DOS 3.2 READ\WRITE TRACK\SECTOR PACKAGE PARAMETER STATEMACHINE
                                               CONTROLS TABLE: LO LO=READ;HI LO=SENSE WRITE PROTECT;LO HI=WRITE;HI
                                               HI=WRITE LOAD
(PI/2)    (-3997~-3993) [$F063~$F067] \P5\APPLESOFT 5-BYTE FLOATING POINT CONSTANT PI/2 = 1.508..
PLOT    (-2048) [$F800] \SE\                   LO-RES PLOT POINT AT X-COORD=(Y-REG) Y-COORD=(A-REG) LEAVING GBASL~H AND MASK
                                               SET (SEE CALL-APPLE DEC 78) (A-REG ALTERED)
PLOT1    (-2034) [$F80E] \SE\                  LO-RES PLOT A POINT X-COORD=(Y-REG) Y-COORD PER GBASL~H & MASK (A-REG ALTERED)
PLOTFNS    (-3604) [$F1EC] \SE\                APPLESOFT - GET 2 LO-RES PLOTTING COORDS SEPARATED BY COMMA FM TXTPTR. PUT
                                               FIRST # IN FIRST AND SECOND # IN H2 & V2
~PLOT~    (-4545) [$EE3F] \SE\                 INTEGER BASIC ENTRY TO ROUTINE TO DO A LO~RES PLOT (I.E. PLOT A COLORED SQUARE
                                               ON LO-RES SCREEN)
PNL~PNH    (222~223) [$00DE~$00DF] \P2\        INTEGER BASIC MEMORY LOCATIONS 'PNL~PNH' (CURRENT NOUN POINTER)
--------------------------------------------------------------------------------------------------------
```

```
"POP"   (-3737) [$F167] \SE\              INTEGER BASIC ENTRY TO ROUTINE TO POP THE RETURN STACK FOR GOSUB
POSTNB16   (-18238"-18213) [$B8C2"$B8DB]  \SB\DOS 3.3 POSTNIBBLE ROUTINE. CONVERTS 342 6-BIT NIBBLES OF FORM 00XXXXXX TO
                                          256 8-BIT BYTES. NIBLES STORED AT PRIMARY ($BB00-$BBFF) AND SECONDARY
                                          ($BC00"$BC55) BUFFERS. POINTER TO DATA PARGE STORED AT 'BUFPTR'
                                          ($003E"$003F). ON ENTRY X-REG= SLOT*16; CSW ($0036"$0037) POINTS TO USER
                                          DATA; $0026= BYTE COUNT IN SECONDARY BUFFER. ON EXIT CARRY SET 'BUFPTR'
                                          Y-REG CONTAINS BYTE COUNT IN SECONDARY BUFFER
POSTNIBL (DOS 3.2)  [$B9C1"BA1D] \SB\     DOS 3.1"3.2"3.2.1 (SEE $B8C2 FOR DOS 3.3) RWTS (READ-WRITE TRACK SECTOR)
                                          POSTNIBL (DOS 3.2) MODULE. CONVERTS A BUFFER OF 410 ($19A) LEFT-JUSTIFIED
                                          5-BIT NIBBLES TO 256 ($100) REAL BYTES. $003E"$003F POINTS TO BUFFER TO PUT
                                          THEM INTO
POSTNIBL (DOS 3.3)   (-18238) [$B8C2] \SB\DOS 3.3 'POSTNIBL'
PPL"PPH   (202"203) [$00CA"$00CB] \P2\    INTEGER BASIC PROGRAM POINTER (START-OF-PROGRAM EQUAL TO HIMEM IF NO PROGRAM)
"PR#S"   (-3127) [$F3C9] \SE\             INTEGER BASIC ENTRY TO ROUTINE TO SET OUTPUT PORT
PRA1   (-622) [$FD92] \SE\                PRINT CARRIAGE RET; THEN HEX OF A1H"A1L; THEN MINUS SIGN {A- X- Y-REGS ALTERED}
PRADR1   (-1776) [$F910]                  MONITOR MEMORY LOCATION 'PRADR1' (PRINT ADDRESS)
PRADR2   (-1772) [$F914]                  MONITOR MEMORY LOCATION 'PRADR2'
PRADR3   (-1754) [$F926]                  MONITOR MEMORY LOCATION 'PRADR3'
PRADR4   (-1750) [$F92A]                  MONITOR MEMORY LOCATION 'PRADR4'
PRADR5   (-1744) [$F930]                  MONITOR MEMORY LOCATION 'PRADR5'
PRBL2   (-1716) [$F94C] \SE\              MONITOR S/R- PRINT BLANKS: X REG CONTAINS NUMBER TO PRINT. CLOBBERS AC"X {A-
                                          X-REGS ALTERED}
PRBL3   (-1716) [$F94C] \SE\              PRINT A-REG FOLLOWED BY (X-REG)-1 BLANKS {A- X-REGS ALTERED}
PRBLNK   (-1720) [$F948] \SE\             PRINT THREE BLANKS THROUGH COUT {A- X-REGS ALTERED}
PRBYTE   (-550) [$FDDA] \SE\              MONITOR S/R TO PRINT CONTENTS OF A-REG AS 2 HEX DIGITS {A-REG ALTERED}
PREAD   (-1250) [$FB1E] \SE\              MONITOR S/R TO READ PADDLE. X-REG CONTAINS PADDLE NUMBER (0-3) OF PADDLE TO BE
                                          READ. PADDLE VALUE TO Y-REG {A- Y-REGS ALTERED}
PREAD2   (-1243) [$FB25]                  MONITOR MEMORY LOCATION 'PREAD2'
PRENIBL-PRENIB16   (-18432"-18327) [$B800"$B869] \SB\DOS 3.1"3.2"3.3 RWTS (READ-WRITE TRACK-SECTOR) PRENIBL MODULE.
                                               CONVERTS A PAGE OF 256 OF REAL BYTES TO A SECTOR OF 410 ($19A)
                                               RIGHT JUSTIFIED 5 BIT NIBBLES (EXCEPT DOS 3.3 CONVERTS TO 342 6
                                               BIT NIBBLES OF THE FORM 00XXXXXX). POINTER TO PAGE TO CONVERT AT
                                               $003E"$003F; DATA STORED AT PRIMARY XXX) SECONDARY BUFFERS; ON
                                               EXIT X-REG XXX) Y-REG CONTAIN $FF & CARRY SET.
PRERR   (-211) [$FF2D] \SE\                    MONITOR S/R TO PRINT "ERR" AND SOUND BELL. {A- Y-REGS(?) ALTERED}
PRGEND   (175"176) [$00AF"$00B0] \P2\          APPLESOFT POINTER TO END OF PROGRAM. NOT CHANGED BY LOMEM:
PRHEX   (-541) [$FDE3] \SE\                    MONITOR S/R TO PRINT RIGHT NIBBLE OF A-REG AS A SINGLE HEX DIGIT {A-REG
                                               ALTERED}
PRHEXZ   (-539) [$FDE5]                        MONITOR MEMORY LOCATION 'PRHEXZ'
PRINOW   (215) [$00D7] \P1\                    INTEGER BASIC MEMORY LOCATION 'PRINOW' (PRINT IT NOW FLAG)
"PRINT"   (-4397) [$EED3] \SE\                 INTEGER BASIC ENTRY POINT TO PRINT ERROR MESSAGE/BELL
PRL"PRH   (220"221) [$00DC"$00DD] \P2\         INTEGER BASIC MEMORY LOCATIONS 'PRL"PRH' (CURRENT LINE VALUE)
PRMN1   (-1803) [$F8F5]                        MONITOR MEMORY LOCATION 'PRMN1' (PRINT MNEMONIC)
PRMN2   (-1799) [$F8F9]                        MONITOR MEMORY LOCATION 'PRMN2'
PRNTAX   (-1727) [$F941] \SE\                  MONITOR S/R-PRINT CONTENTS OF A-REG & X-REG AS HEX DIGITS {A- X-REGS
                                               ALTERED}
PRNTBL   (-1829) [$F8DB]                       MONITOR MEMORY LOCATION 'PRNTBL'
PRNTFAC   (-4818) [$ED2E] \SE\                 APPLESOFT - PRINTS & DESTROYS CURRENT VALUE OF FAC. USES FOUT & STROUT
PRNTOP   (-1836) [$F8D4]                       MONITOR MEMORY LOCATION 'PRNTOP' (PRINT OPERATION CODE)
"PRNTSTR"   (-4605) [$EE03] \SE\               INTEGER BASIC ENTRY TO FUNCTION WHICH PRINTS A STRING
PRNTX   (-1724) [$F944] \SE\                   PRINT CONTENTS OF X-REG AS HEX DIGITS {A- X-REGS ALTERED}
```

```
NAME   (DEC LOCN)   [HEX LOCN] \USE-TYPE\ - DESCRIPTION
----------------------------------------------------------------------------------------------------------------

PRNTYX   (-1728) [$F940] \SE\                    MONITOR S/R- PRINT CONTENTS OF Y AND X AS 4 HEX DIGITS (A- X-REGS ALTERED)
PROGIO   (-9983) [$D901] \SE\                    APPLESOFT CASSETTE - SET UP A1 & A2 TO SAVE PROGRAM TEXT ON CASSETTE
PROMPT   (51) [$0033] \P1\                       PROMPT CHARACTER WRITTEN TO SCREEN WHENEVER A LINE OF INPUT IS CALLED FOR
                                                 BY GETLN ROUTINE
~PRTERR~   (-3743) [$F161] \SE\                  INTEGER BASIC ENTRY TO ROUTINE TO PRINT AN ERROR MESSAGE
PRYX2   (-618) [$FD96] \SE\                      MONITOR S/R TO PRINT CAR RET THEN HEX OF Y-REG & X-REG THEN A DASH (A-REG
                                                 ALTERED)
PTRGET   (-8221) [$DFE3] \SE\                    APPLESOFT - READ VAR NAME FROM CHRGET AND FIND IT IN MEMORY (OR CREATE
                                                 APPROPRIATE SIMPLE VARIABLE OR ARRAY). DOES MUCH HOUSEKEEPING
PTRIG   (-16272~-16257) [$C070~$C07F] \H1\       ALL 16 ADDRESSES DECODE TO SINGLE SWITCH WHICH TRIGGERS PADDLE TIMERS
                                                 DURING PHI-2
PTRIG   (-16272~-16257) [$C070~$C07F] \H1\       GAME CONTROLLER STROBE. WHEN READ CAUSES FALG INPUTS OF GAME CONTROLLERS
                                                 TO GO OFF & TIMING LOOPS RESTARTED
PTRMOV   (15684) [$3D44] \SL\                    DOS 3.2 RWTS (READ-WRITE TRACK-SECTOR) INTERIOR LABEL - STARTS CODE TO
                                                 MOVE OUT ALL POINTERS FROM IOB (IN-OUT-BLOCK) TO ZERO PAGE
PUTNEW   (-7126) [$E42A] \SE\                    APPLESOFT -- STRING FUNCTION RETURNING WITH RESULT INDSCTMP. MOVE DSCTMP TO
                                                 TEMP DESCRIPTOR & PUT POINTER TO DESCRIPTOR IN FACMO~FACLO & FLAG RESULT
                                                 AS STRING
PVL~PVH   (204~205) [$00CC~$00CD] \P2\           INTEGER BASIC CURRENT VARIABLE POINTER (END OF CURRENT VARIABLE EQUAL TO
                                                 LOMEM IF NO ACTIVE CURRENT VARIABLE )
PWDTH   (1784+S) [$06F8+S] \P1\                  EXAMPLE:APPLE SERIAL INTERFACE CARD IN SLOT #S - PRINTER WIDTH ('PWDTH')
PWRCON   (-1283) [$FAFD]                         AUTOSTART MONITOR MEMORY LOCATION 'PWRCON'
PWREDUP   (1012) [$03F4] \P1\                    AUTOSTART ROM POWER UP MASK. SET BY SETPWRC TO EXCLUSIVE 'OR' OF $03F3 &
                                                 $00A5
PWRUP   (-1370) [$FAA6]                          AUTOSTART MONITOR MEMORY LOCATION 'PWRUP'
PXL~PXH   (224~225) [$0CE0~$00E1] \P2\           INTEGER BASIC MEMORY LOCATIONS 'PXL~PXH' (CURRENT VERB POINTER)
Q6L\Q6H   (-16244~-16243) [$C08C~$C08D] \P2\ DOS 3.2 READ~WRITE TRACK\SECTOR PACKAGE PARAMETER 'Q6L~Q6H' (Q6 LOW CAUSES
                                                 DOS 3.2 TO READ A BYTE)
Q7L\Q7H   (-16242~-16241) [$C08E~$C08F] \P2\ DOS 3.2 READ~WRITE TRACK\SECTOR PACKAGE PARAMETER 'Q7L~Q7H' (Q7 LOW SETS
                                                 DOS 3.2 FOR READ MODE)
QDRNT   (83) [$0053] \P1\                        HI-RES GRAPHICS QDRNT: 2 LSB'S ARE ROTATION QUADRANT FOR DRAW
QINT   (-5134) [$EBF2] \SE\                      APPLESOFT QUICK GREATEST INTEGER FUNCTION. LEAVE INT(FAC)IN FAC MANTISSA
                                                 (HO~MO~LO SIGNED). ASUMES FAC<2~23 (RESET Y-REG=0)
(R0-R15)   (0~31) [$0000~$001F] \PB\             'SWEET-16' REGISTERS R0 THRU R15 OF 'SWEET-16' (16-BIT INTERPRETER IN
                                                 MONITOR)
R0L~R0H   (0~1) [$0000~$0001] \P2\               'SWEET-16' REGISTER R0 (IN 16-BIT PSEUDOMACHINE IN APPLE SYSTEM MONITOR)
(R1)   (2~3) [$0002~$0003] \P2\                  'SWEET-16' REGISTER R1 (IN 16-BIT PSEUDOMACHINE IN APPLE SYSTEM MONITOR)
(R10)   (20~21) [$0014~$0015] \P2\               'SWEET-16' REGISTER R10 (IN 16-BIT PSEUDOMACHINE IN APPLE SYSTEM MONITOR)
(R11)   (22~23) [$0016~$0017] \P2\               'SWEET-16' REGISTER R11 (IN 16-BIT PSEUDOMACHINE IN APPLE SYSTEM MONITOR)
(R12)   (24~25) [$0018~$0019] \P2\               'SWEET-16' REGISTER R12 (IN 16-BIT PSEUDOMACHINE IN APPLE SYSTEM MONITOR)
(R13)   (26~27) [$001A~$001B] \P2\               'SWEET-16' REGISTER R13 (IN 16-BIT PSEUDOMACHINE IN APPLE SYSTEM MONITOR)
(R14)   (28~29) [$001C~$001D] \P2\               'SWEET-16' REGISTER R14 (IN 16-BIT PSEUDOMACHINE IN APPLE SYSTEM MONITOR)
R15L~R15H   (30~31) [$001E~$001F] \P2\           'SWEET-16' REGISTER R15 (USED AS PROGRAM COUNTER IN 16-BIT PSEUDOMACHINE
                                                 IN APPLE SYSTEM MONITOR) (REG-R15 )
(R2)   (4~5) [$0004~$0005] \P2\                  'SWEET-16' REGISTER R2 (IN 16-BIT PSEUDOMACHINE IN APPLE SYSTEM MONITOR)
(R3)   (6~7) [$0006~$0007] \P2\                  'SWEET-16' REGISTER R3 (IN 16-BIT PSEUDOMACHINE IN APPLE SYSTEM MONITOR)
(R4)   (8~9) [$0008~$0009] \P2\                  'SWEET-16' REGISTER R4 (IN 16-BIT PSEUDOMACHINE IN APPLE SYSTEM MONITOR)
(R5)   (10~11) [$000A~$000B] \P2\                'SWEET-16' REGISTER R5 (IN 16-BIT PSEUDOMACHINE IN APPLE SYSTEM MONITOR)
(R6)   (12~13) [$000C~$000D] \P2\                'SWEET-16' REGISTER R6 (IN 16-BIT PSEUDOMACHINE IN APPLE SYSTEM MONITOR)
(R7)   (14~15) [$000E~$000F] \P2\                'SWEET-16' REGISTER R7 (IN 16-BIT PSEUDOMACHINE IN APPLE SYSTEM MONITOR)
(R8)   (16~17) [$0010~$0011] \P2\                'SWEET-16' REGISTER R8 (IN 16-BIT PSEUDOMACHINE IN APPLE SYSTEM MONITOR)
----------------------------------------------------------------------------------------------------------------
```

```
(R9)    (18~19) [$0012~$0013] \P2\    'SWEET-16' REGISTER R9 (IN 16-BIT PSEUDOMACHINE IN APPLE SYSTEM MONITOR)
RD2    (-246) [$FF0A]                 MONITOR MEMORY LOCATION 'RD2'
RD2BIT    (-774) [$FCFA]              MONITOR TWO-EDGE TAPE SENSE; I.E. LOOPS DECREMENTING Y-REG UNTIL HARDWARE HAS
                                      INDICATED TWO TRANSITIONS OF TAPE INPUT REGISTER.  CONTENTS OF Y-REG ON RETURN
                                      COMPARED WITH CONTENTS ON ENTRY MEASURE TIME REQUIRED FOR TRANSITIONS. CALLS RDBIT
RD3    (-234) [$FF16]                 MONITOR MEMORY LOCATION 'RD3'
RDADR16   [B944]                      DOS 3.3 SYNONYM FOR READADR
RDBIT    (-771) [$FCFD]               MONITOR - LOOPS DECREMENTING Y-REG UNTIL CASSETTE TAPE INPUT REGISTER CHANGES
                                      (EITHER 0=>1 OR 1=>0). BIT VALUE RETURNED IS DETERMINED FROM RESIDUAL COUNT OF
                                      Y-REG.  CALLED BY RD2BIT AND READ
RDBYT2    (-786) [$FCEE]              MONITOR MEMORY LOCATION 'RDBYT2'
RDBYTE    (-788) [$FCEC]              MONITOR - READS BITS FROM CASSETTE TAPE UNTIL BYTE ACCUMULATED (CALLED BY MONITOR
                                      READ MEMORY LOCATION 'RDBYTE' SHAPE TABLE LOAD)
RDCHAR    (-715) [$FD35] \SE\         CALLS RDKEY TO GET NEXT CHAR PLACED INTO A-REG. IF ESCAPE KEY PRESSED CALLS 'ESC1'
                                      FOR ESCAPE KEY PROCESSING; AFTER ESCAPE KEY AND KEY FOLLOWING HAVE BEEN READ &
                                      PROCESSED CONTROL RETURNS TO RDCHAR ROUTINE AS IF IT WERE JUST BEING ENTERED (A- X-
                                      Y-REGS ALTERED)
RDKEY    (-756) [$FD0C] \SE\          SAME AS RDCHAR EXCEPT BYPASSES ESCAPE KEY MONITOR SUPPORT; PICKS UP AND SAVE THE
                                      CHARACTER IN THE SCREEN AREA AT BASL~H CH (LEAVING Y-REG CONTAINING CONTENTS OF CH)
                                      IT THEN CHANGES THAT CHARACTER TO BLINKING TO INDICATE CURRENT CURSOR POSN; ASKS
                                      FOR NEXT INPUT CHAR TO BE PLACED IN A-REG BY DOING AN INDIRECT JUMP VIA KSWL~H
                                      WHICH IS NORMALLY POINTING AT KEYIN. RETURN IS THEREFORE TO THE CALLER OF RDKEY -
                                      NOT TO RDKEY ROUTINE ITSELF. SET-UP: A- X- Y-REGS NOT SIGNIFICANT; CV AND BASL~H
                                      SHOULD BE COMPATABLE POINTING IN THE SCROLL WINDOW; CH INDICATES HORIZONTAL
                                      POSITION WHERE CURSOR WILL BLINK. RESULTS: A-REG CONTAINS THE INPUT CHARACTER
                                      (WHICH MAY BE ANY CHARACTER INCLUDING ANY CONTROL KEY OR ESCAPE KEY);X-REG IS
                                      UNCHANGED; Y-REG CONTAINS CONTENTS OF CH; CV CH BASL~H REMAIN UNCHANGED (A- X-
                                      Y-REGS ALTERED)
"RDKEY"    (-3247) [$F351] \SE\       INTEGER BASIC ENTRY TO ROUTINE TO READ AN INPUT FOR BASIC FROM KEYBOARD
RDRIGHT    (15815) [$3DC7] \SL\       DOS 3.2 RWTS (READ-WRITE TRACK-SECTOR) INTERIOR LABEL WHICH STARTS CODE TO
                                      DETERMINE IF ONE IS READING CORRECT TRACK SECTOR AND VOLUME
RDRIGHT    (-16964~-16916) [$BDBC~$BDEC] \SB\DOS 3.3 - INITIALIZE MAX RETRIES AT 48. READ ADDRESS FIELD VIA 'RDADR16'
                                      ($B944). IF GOOD READ BRANCH TO 'RDRIGHT' ($BDED). IF BAD TRY AGAIN
                                      DECREMENTING RETRIES. IF NONE LEFT PREPARE TO RECALIBRATE. DECREMENT RECAL
                                      COUNT. IF NO MORE THEN 'DRVERR' ($BE04). OTHERWISE RESET RESEEKS AT 4 AND
                                      RECALIBRATE ARM. TRY AGAIN
RDRIGHT    (-16915~-16893) [$BDED~$BE03] \SE\DOS 3.3 - VERIFY TRACK. IF CORRECT BRANCH TO 'RTTRK' ($BE10) OTHERWISE GOTO
                                      'SETTRK' ($BE95) AND DECREMENT RESEEK COUNT. IF ZERO RECAL OTHERWISE RESEEK TRACK
RDSP1    (-1308) [$FAE4]              MONITOR MEMORY LOCATION 'RDSP1'
READ    (-18179~-18076) [$B8FD~$B964] \SB\DOS 3.1~3.2~3.2.1 (SEE $B8DC FOR DOS 3.3 'READ') RWTS (READ-WRITE TRACK-SECTOR
                                      READ MODULE. READS A SECTOR OFF THE DISK FORMING 410 ($19A) 5-BIT
                                      RIGHT-JUSTIFIED NIBBLES
READ    (-259) [$FEFD] \SE\           READS DATA FROM CASSETTE TAPE PUTTING FIRST DATA READ INTO LOCATION POINTED TO BY
                                      A1L~H ($003C~$003D) AND CONTINUING TO READ UNTIL DATA GOES TO LOCATION POINTED TO
                                      BY A2L~H ($003E~$003F). ALSO COMPUTES A RUNNING EXCLUSIVE OR CHECKSUM IN 'CHECKSUM'
                                      ($002E)
READ16    (-18212~-18109) [$B8DC~$B943] \SB\DOS 3.3 'READ' IN RWTS (READ-WRITE TRACK-SECTOR). READS A SECTOR OFF THE
                                      DISK INTO SECONDARY BUFFER ($BC00-$BC55) HIGH TO LOW THEN INTO PRIMARY
                                      ($BB00-$BBFF) LOW TO HIGH EN ROUTE TO OVERALL PROCESS OF  FORMING $153
                                      RIGHT-JUSTIFIED 6-BIT NIBBLES
```

```
NAME  (DEC LOCN)  [HEX LOCN] \USE-TYPE\ - DESCRIPTION
------------------------------------------------------------------------------------------------

READADR (DOS 3.2)   (-18075~-17984) [$B965~$B9C0] \SB\DOS 3.1~3.2~3.2.1 (SEE $B944 FOR DOS 3.3 'READADR (DOS 3.2)')
                                        RWTS (READ-WRITE TRACK SECTOR) READ ADDRESS MODULE. READS
                                        ADDRESSES ON THE SECTORS OF CURRENT TRACK UNTIL IT FINDS A
                                        SECTOR. THEN IT RETURNS PUTTING CHECKSUM INTO $002C;SECTOR INTO
                                        $002D;TRACK INTO $002E; AND VOLUME INTO $002F.. CARRY IS SET ON ERROR
READADR-RDADR16 (DOS 3.3)  [.3)$B944~$B99F] \SB\DOS 3.3 READADR. FUNCTION SAME AS READADR-RDADR16 (DOS 3.2)
READX1    (-254) [$FF02]                HI-RES GRAPHICS - READ WITHOUT HEADER
REASON    (-11293) [$D3E3] \SE\         CHECKS FOR ENOUGH ROOM IN MEMORY; CHECKS THAT ADDR Y-REG(MSB)&A-REG(LSB)
                                        LESS THAN FRETOP. MAY CAUSE GARBAGE COLLECTIOV. CAUSE OMERR IF NO ROOM
REGDSP    (-1321) [$FAD7] \SE\          DISPLAY SAVED REGISTER CONTENTS FROM MEMORY LOCNS $0045~$0049 WITH
                                        PRECEDING CARRIAGE RETURN (SEE 'SAVE' ROUTINE AT $FF4A) (A- X-REGS
                                        ALTERED}
REGZ    (-321) [$FEBF] \SE\             MONITOR S/R TO DISPLAY REGISTERS
REL    (-2816) [$F500]                  MINIASSEMBLER MEMORY LOCATION 'REL'
REL2    (-2804) [$F50C]                 MINIASSEMBLER MEMORY LOCATION 'REL2'
REL3    (-2794) [$F516]                 MINIASSEMBLER MEMORY LOCATION 'REL3'
RELADR    (-1736) [$F938]               MONITOR MEMORY LOCATION 'RELADR' (RELATIVE ADDRESS)
REMN    (-9818) [$D9A6] \SE\            APPLESOFT - CALCULATE OFFSET IN Y-REG FROM TXTPTR TO NEXT COL(0)
REMSTK    (248) [$00F8] \P1\            APPLESOFT STACK POINTER SAVED BEFORE EACH STATEMENT
(RESET)    (-6066) [$E84E] \SE\         RESET FACEXP($009D) AND $00A2 (FACSIGN) & A-REG TO ZERO (A-REG=>0;X-
                                        Y-REG NOT ALTERED}
RESET    (-1438) [$FA62]                AUTOSTART MONITOR MEMORY LOCATION 'RESET'
RESET    (-167) [$FF59] \SE\            CALL HERE HAS SAME EFFECT AS PUSHING RESET BUTTON
RESETZ    (-2670) [$F592]               MINIASSEMBLER MEMORY LOCATION 'RESETZ'
RESTOR    (-10167) [$D849] \SE\         APPLESOFT RESTORE FUNCTION - SET DATA POINTER (DATPTR) TO BEGINNING OF
                                        THE PROGRAM
RESTORE    (-193) [$FF3F] \SE\          RESTORE 6502 REGISTERS:  ($0045)=>A-Reg; ($0046)=>X-Reg; ($0047)=>Y-Reg;
                                        ($0048)=>P-Reg;  {A- X- Y- P-REGS ALTERED}
RESTR1    (-188) [$FF44]                MONITOR MEMORY LOCATION 'RESTR1'
RESUME    (-3305) [$F317] \SE\          APPLESOFT ERROR PROC - RESTORE CURLIN FROM ERRLIN & TXTPTR FROM ERRPOS.
                                        TRANSFER ERRSTK INTO 6502 STACK POINTER
(RET W/O GOSUB)    (-9863) [$D979]      APPLESOFT - PRINT "RETURN WITHOUT GOSUB" THEN HALT AT APPLESOFT (]) LEVEL
~RETURN~    (-5979) [$E8A5] \SE\        INTEGER BASIC ENTRY TO ROUTINE FOR RETURN FROM GOSUB
RGDSP1    (-1318) [$FADA] \SE\          DISPLAY SAVED REGISTER CONTENTS FROM MEMORY LOCNS $0045~$0049 WITHOUT
                                        PRECEDING CARRIAGE RETURN (SEE 'SAVE' ROUTINE AT $FF4A) (A- X-REGS
                                        ALTERED}
RGTIM    (16094) [$3EDE] \SL\           DOS 3.2 DISK FORMATTER INTERIOR LABEL 'RGTIM'
RND    (201~205) [$00C9~$00CD] \P5\     APPLESOFT FLOATING POINT RANDOM NUMBER (5-BYTE FLOATING POINT PACKED
                                        FORMAT C9=EXP CA-CD=MANTISSA)
RND    (-4178) [$EFAE] \SE\             APPLESOFT FP - FORM A 'RANDOM' NUMBER IN FAC USING ORIGINAL VALUE IN FAC
                                        AS PARAMETER 'KEY' OR 'SEED'. MODIFIES MANY FP LOCNS
RNDL~RNDH    (78~79) [$0C4E~$004F] \P2\ 16 BIT NO. RANDOMIZED WITH EACH KEY ENTRY DONE BY MONITOR KEYIN ROUTINE
                                        (AND BY MANY OTHER ROUTINES SUCH AS SERIAL & COMM CARD WHICH ARE USED TO
                                        REPLACE KEYIN). RANDOMIZATION ACCOMPLISHED BY CONTINUOUSLY INCREMENTING
                                        WHILE AWAITING KEYBOARD INPUT. HIGH ORDER BYTE $4F
~RND~    (-4274) [$EF4E] \SE\           INTEGER BASIC ENTRY TO RANDOM NUMBER GENERATOR
RNGERR    (-4504) [$EE68] \P1\          INTEGER BASIC RANGE ERROR
RTAR    (-2947) [$F47D] \SE\            DENORMALIZE FP1 BY SHIFTING M1(&E) RIGHT 1 BIT POSN & INCREMENTING X1 (A-
                                        X-REGS ALTERED}
RTBL    (-1255) [$FB19]                 MONITOR MEMORY LOCATION 'RTBL'
RTMASK    (-2036) [$F80C]               MONITOR MEMORY LOCATION 'RTMASK'
------------------------------------------------------------------------------------------------
```

```
RTMSKZ   (-1921) [$F87F]            MONITOR MEMORY LOCATION 'RTMSKZ'
RTNJMP   (-1327) [$FAD1]            MONITOR MEMORY LOCATION 'RTNJMP'
RTNL~RTNH   (44~45) [$002C~$002D] \P2\MONITOR RETURN POINTER (POINTS TO SAVE AREA USED BY INSTRUCTION TRACE ROUTINE)
RTS1   (-1999) [$F831]              MONITOR MEMORY LOCATION 'RTS1'
RTS2   (-1695) [$F961]              MONITOR MEMORY LOCATION 'RTS2'
RTS2B   (-1041) [$FBEF]             MONITOR MEMORY LOCATION 'RTS2B'
RTS2D   (-1234) [$FB2E]             MONITOR MEMORY LOCATION 'RTS2D'
RTS3   (-1028) [$FBFC]              MONITOR MEMORY LOCATION 'RTS3'
RTS4   (-981) [$FC2B]               MONITOR MEMORY LOCATION 'RTS4'
RTS4B   (-824) [$FCC8]              MONITOR MEMORY LOCATION 'RTS4B'
RTS4C   (-571) [$FDC5]              MONITOR MEMORY LOCATION 'RTS4C'
RTS5   (-489) [$FE17]               MONITOR MEMORY LOCATION 'RTS5'
RTTRK   (15856) [$3DF0] \SL\        DOS 3.2 RWTS (READ-WRITE TRACK-SECTOR INTERIOR LABEL WHICH ASSUMES RIGHT TRACK
                                    SELECTED AND BEGINS CHECK OF CORRECT VOLUME NUMBER ON DISKETTE
RTTRK   (-16880~-16859) [$BE10~$BE25] DOS 3.3 -CHECK VOL# FOUND VS VOL# WANTED. IF NO VOL SPECIFIED NO ERROR OTHERWISE
                                    IF MISMATCH LOAD A-REG WITH $20 (VOLUME MISMATCH ERROR) AND EXIT VIA 'HNDLERR'
                                    ($BE48)
~RUN #N~   (-4110) [$EFF2] \SE\     INTEGER BASIC ENTRY TO ROUTINE TO RUN FROM LINE #N
RUN   (-10906) [$D566] \SE\         APPLESOFT - RUN THE PROGRAM IN MEMORY. THIS ROUTINE DOES NOT RETURN
RUNMODE   (217) [$00D9] \P1\        INTEGER BASIC MEMORY LOCATION 'RUNMODE' USED AS RUN MODE FLAG BYTE
RUNMODE   (217) [$00D9] \P1\        USED BY DOS TO TEST FOR DIRECT-DEFERRED MODE USAGE. IF $AAB6 CONTAINS 0 AND BIT 7
                                    OF THIS LOCATION IS CLEAR DOS ASSUMES DIRECT MODE AND WILL NOT DO OPEN OR OTHER
                                    DIRECT MODE COMMANDS
~RUN~   (-4116) [$EFEC] \SE\        APPLE INTEGER BASIC RUN ROUTINE (RUN FROM BEGINNING)
RWTS   (15616) [$3D00] \SE\         DOS 3.1/3.2 READ\WRITE A TRACK & SECTOR. UPON ENTRY A- & Y-REGS POINT AT I/O
                                    CONTROL BLOCK (IOB)
RWTS   (15616~16027) [$3D00~$3E9B] \SB\DOS 3.1/3.2 RWTS SUBROUTINE
S16PAG   (247) [$00F7] \P\          SWEET-16 MEMORY LOCATION 'S16PAG'
SAMESLOT   (15661) [$3D2D] \SL\     DOS 3.2 RWTS (READ-WRITE TRACK-SECTOR) INTERIOR LABEL - STARTS CODE TO DETERMINE IF
                                    SAME SLOT BEING USED
SAMESLOT   (-17100~-17069) [$BD34~$BD53] \SB\ENTER READ MODE AND READ WITH DELAYS TO SEE IF DISK IS SPINNING. SAVE
                                    RESULTS OF TEST AND TURN ON MOTOR ANYHOW
SAV1   (-180) [$FF4C]               MONITOR MEMORY LOCATION 'SAV1'
SAVE   (-10064) [$D8B0] \SE\        APPLESOFT CASSETTE - SAVE THE PROGRAM IN MEMORY TO CASSETTE TAPE
SAVE   (-182) [$FF4A] \SE\          MONITOR S/R TO SAVE 6502 REGISTERS: (A-REG)=>$0045; (X-REG)=>$0046;
                                    (Y-REG)=>$0047; (P-REG)=>$0048; (S-REG)=>$0049 {NONE}
~SAVE~   (-3776) [$F140] \SE\       INTEGER BASIC ENTRY TO ROUTINE TO SAVE A PROGRAM TO CASSETTE TAPE
SB   (6912~7423) [$1B00~$1CFF]      TEMPORARY LOCATION OF DOS 3.2 RELOCATION CODE DURING DOS 3.2 BOOT (SB)
SCALE   (231) [$00E7] \P1\          HI-RES GRAPHICS SCALE FACTOR
SCALE   (807) [$0327] \P1\          ON-THE-FLY SCALE FACTOR FOR DRAW~ SHAPE~ MOVE
~SCRATCH~   (-4096) [$F000] \SE\    INTEGER BASIC ENTRY TO SCRATCH EVERYTHING ROUTINE
SCRL1   (-906) [$FC76]              MONITOR MEMORY LOCATION 'SCRL1'
SCRL2   (-884) [$FC8C]              MONITOR MEMORY LOCATION 'SCRL2'
SCRL3   (-875) [$FC95]              MONITOR - CLEAR LINE (BASL~H) {WHOLE LINE} THEN SET NEW BASL~H FROM CV & WNDLFT
SCRN   (-1935) [$F871] \SE\         GET (LOAD TO A-REG) LO-RES GRAPHICS COLOR OF POINT Y-COORD = (A-REG); X-COORD =
                                    (X-REG)  {A-REG ALTERED}
SCRN2   (-1927) [$F879]             MONITOR MEMORY LOCATION 'SCRN2'
~SCRN~   (-7542) [$E28A] \SE\       INTEGER BASIC ENTRY POINT TO SCREEN X~ Y~ COLOR VALUE FUNCTION
SCROLL   (-912) [$FC70] \SE\        MONITOR S/R TO SCROLL UP 1 LINE.  {A- Y-REGS ALTERED}
SCRTCH   (-10677) [$D64B] \SE\      APPLESOFT INITIALIZATION - THE 'NEW' COMMAND. CLEARS PROGRAM VARIABLES & STACK
SECT   (45) [$002D] \P1\            DOS RWTS (READ-WRITE TRACK-SECTOR) PARAMETER FOR CURRENT DISK SECTOR
```

```
SEEK    (15948) [$3E4C] \SE\          DOS 3.2 RWTS (READ-WRITE TRACK-SECTOR) INTERIOR LABEL AT SOFT ENTRY POINT OF SEEK
                                      SUBROUTINE
SEEKABS (DOS 3.2)    (-18016) [$B9A0] \SB\DOS 3.2 'SEEKABS'
SEEKABS (DOS 3.3)    (-18016~-17924) [$B9A0~$B9FC] \SB\DOS 3.3 - MOVES DISK AREM TO DESIRED TRACK. CALLS ARM MOVE DELAY
                                           SUBROUTINE ($B9FD). ON ENTRY $0478 CONTAINS CURRENT TRACK; X-REG
                                           CONTAINS SLOT*16; A-REG DESIRED TRACK. ON EXIT X-REG UNCHANGED;
                                           A-REG Y-REG CLOBBERED; $0478 &$002A: FINAL TRACK;$27 PRIOR TRACK
                                           (IF SEEK NEEDED). USES $0026;$0027;$002A;$002B. EXITS TO CALLER
SEEKABS    (-17890~-17777) [$BA1E~$BA8F] \SB\  DOS 3.1~3.2~3.2.1 (SEE $B9A0 FOR DOS 3.3) RWTS (READ-WRITE TRACK SECTOR)
                                           SEEKABS MODULE. MOVES HEAD TO TRACK SPECIFIED BY A-REG. $0478 IS CURRENT.
                                           RWTS DOES PHASE OFF FOR ALL FOUR BEFORE CALL
SEEKCNT    (1275) [$04FB] \P1\             DOS 3.2 RWTS (READ-WRITE TRACK-SECTOR) SEEK COUNTER PARAMETER
SETAN0     (-16296) [$C058] \FF\           VALUE<>0 WHEN GAME AN0 IS SET. POKE 0 TO CLEAR GAME I/O OUTPUT AN0 (3.5V
                                           AT PIN 15)
SETAN1     (-16294) [$C05A] \FF\           POKE 0 TO CLEAR GAME I/O OUTPUT AN1 (3.5V AT PIN 14)
SETAN2     (-16292) [$C05C] \FF\           POKE 0 TO CLEAR GAME I/O OUTPUT AN2 (3.5V AT PIN 13)
SETAN3     (-16290) [$C05E] \FF\           POKE 0 TO CLEAR GAME I/O OUTPUT AN3 (3.5V AT PIN 12)
~SETBUF~    (-3796) [$F12C] \SE\           INTEGER BASIC ENTRY TO ROUTINE TO SET UP PROGRAM SAVE/LOAD PARAMETERS
SETCOL     (-1948) [$F864] \SE\            SET LO-RES COLOR TO COLOR CODE SPECIFIED BY A-REG FOR FUTURE PLOTTING
                                           {A-REG ALTERED}
SETGR   (-1216) [$FB40] \SE\               MONITOR S/R- SET GRAPHIC MODE (GR). THIS INCLUDES SETTING TO MIXED
                                           MODE;CLEARING GRAPHICS PART OF SCREEN; AND RESETTING
                                           WNDTOP~WNDLFT~WNDWDTH~WNDBTM & TABV  {A-REG ALTERED}
SETHCOL    (-2324) [$F6EC] \SE\            APPLESOFT HI-RES - SET COLOR TO CONTENTS OF X-REG (MUST BE LESS  THAN 8)
~SETHDR~    (-3810) [$F11E] \SE\           INTEGER BASIC ENTRY TO SET UP HEADER FOR SAVE/LOAD PARAMETERS
SETHRL     (-12288) [$D000] \SE\           HI-RES GRAPHICS INIT S/R CALL (ROM VERSION)
SETIFLG    (-378) [$FE86]                  MONITOR MEMORY LOCATION 'SETIFLG'
SETINV     (-384) [$FE80] \SE\             MONITOR S/R TO SET VIDEO OUTPUT TO INVERSE
SETKBD     (-375) [$FE89]                  MONITOR MEMORY LOCATION 'SETKBD'
SETMDZ     (-483) [$FE1D]                  MONITOR MEMORY LOCATION 'SETMDZ'
SETMODE    (-488) [$FE18]                  MONITOR MEMORY LOCATION 'SETMODE'
SETNORM    (-380) [$FE84] \SE\             MONITOR S/R TO SET VIDEO OUTPUT TO NORMAL (NOT INVERSE)
SETPG3     (-1367) [$FAA9]                 AUTOSTART MONITOR MEMORY LOCATION 'SETPG3'
~SETPRMPT~    (-8186) [$E006] \SE\         INTEGER BASIC ENTRY POINT TO SET UP '>' PROMPT
SETPWRC    (-1169) [$FB6F] \SE\            SET POWER CONDITION (AUTOSTART ROM ONLY)
SETTRK     (16002) [$3E82] \SM\            DOS 3.2 RWTS (READ-WRITE TRACK-SECTOR) INTERIOR LABEL - CODE SETS THE
                                           SLOT-DEPENDENT TRACK LOCATION
SETTRK     (-16747~-16722) [$BE95~$BEAE]   DOS 3.3 - SET TRACK #
SETTRK2    (16015) [$3E8F] \SM\            DOS 3.2 RWTS (READ-WRITE INTERIOR LABEL 'SETTRK2'
SETTXT     (-1223) [$FB39] \SE\            MONITOR S/R- SET SCREEN TO TEXT MODE. CLOBBERS ACCUMULATOR {A-REG ALTERED}
SETVID     (-365) [$FE93]                  MONITOR MEMORY LOCATION'SETVID'
SETWND     (-1205) [$FB4B] \SE\            MONITOR S/R- SET NORMAL LOW-RESOLUTION GRAPHICS WINDOW
SGN (FPSGN)    (-5232) [$EB90] \SE\        APPLESOFT FP - CALLS SIGN AND FLOATS THE RESULT IN THE FAC. FAC=+1 IF FAC
                                           WAS +;=0 IF FAC WAS 0;=-1 IF FAC WAS -
~SGN~    (-6308) [$E75C] \SE\              INTEGER BASIC ENTRY POINT TO GET SIGN OF A NUMBER
SHAPEL~SHAPEH    (26~27) [$001A~$001B] \P2\  HI-RES POINTER TO SHAPE LIST (ON-THE-FLY SHAPE POINTER)
SHAPEX    (81) [$0051] \P1\                HI-RES GRAPHICS SHAPE TEMP.
SHAPXL~SHAPXH    (808~809) [$0328~$0329] \P2\  START-OF-SHAPE-TABLE POINTER
SHLOAD    (-11335) [$D3B9] \SE\            HI-RES GRAPHICS SHLOAD S/R CALL
SHLOAD    (-2187) [$F775] \SE\             APPLESOFT HI-RES. LOADS SHAPE TABLE INTO MEMORY FROM TAPE ABOVE MEMSIZ
                                           (HIMEM) AND SETS POINTER AT $00E8
```

SIGN (47) [$002F] \P1\	$01 BIT SET AFTER CALL TO MULPM OR DIVPM (SIGNED 16 BIT MULT OR DIV) TO SPECIFY WHETHER COMPLEMENT NEEDED (NOTE MULPM & DIVPM IN OLD MONITOR ONLY ~ NOT IN AUTOSTART)
SIGN (243) [$00F3] \P1\	MONITOR & FLOATING POINT ROUTINES MEMORY LOC 'SIGN'
SIGN (-5246) [$EB82] \SE\	APPLESOFT FP - SETS A-REG ACCORDING TO VALUE OF FAC. ON EXIT A-REG=1 IF FAC +;A-REG=0 IF FAC=0;A-REG=$FF IF FAC - {X- Y-REGS NOT ALTERED}
SIN (-4111) [$EFF1] \SE\	APPLESOFT FP - COMPUTE THE SINE OF THE NUMBER IN FAC. RESULT TO FAC. MODIFIES INDEX CHARAC COMPTRTYP XORFPSGN & MANY OTHER FP LOCNS
SLOOP (-1351) [$FAB9]	AUTOSTART MONITOR MEMORY LOCATION 'SLOOP'
(SLOT #) (2040) [$07F8]	CONTAINS SLOT NUMBER (IN THE FORMAT $CS) OF THE PERIPHERAL CARD CURRENTLY ACTIVE - PRINT PEEK(2040)-192 YIELDS SLOT # IN DECIMAL FORMAT
SLOT (1528+S) [$C5F8+S] \P1\	DOS READ-WRITE-TRACK-SECTOR (RWTS) 'SLOT' = HOLDS SLOT NUMBER USED
SNGFLT (-7423) [$E301] \SE\	APPLESOFT - FLOAT THE UNSIGNED INTEGER IN Y-REG INTO FAC. RESETS VALTYP. {RESET Y-REG=0}
SOFTEV (1010~1011) [$03F2~$03F3] \P2\	AUTOSTART ROM RESET VECTOR USED FOR SOFT ENTRY TO LANGUAGE IN USE - DEFAULT VALUE $E003 FOR APPLESOFT
SPACE (-2631) [$F5B9]	MINIASSEMBLER MEMORY LOCATION 'SPACE'
SPDBYT (241) [$00F1] \P1\	USED FOR SPEED CONTROL OF OUTPUT & DISPLAY. SPEED 0-255 ($00-$FF) CONTROLS INSERTED DELAY)
SPKR (-16336) [$C030] \H1\	PEEK TO TOGGLE SPEAKER (PRODUCES A 'CLICK')
SPKR (-16336~-16321) [$C030~$C03F] \H1\	SPEAKER TOGGLE FLIP FLOP. READ ONLY - DO NOT WRITE TO THES ADDRESSES WHICH ARE DECODED AS SAME SINGLE BIT LOCN
SPNT (73) [$0049] \P1\	USER STACK POINTER (S-REGISTER) SAVED HERE BY MONITOR 'SAVE' ROUTINE ON BRK & DURING TRACE
SQR (FPSQR) (-4467) [$EE8D] \SE\	APPLESOFT FP - TAKE SQUARE ROOT OF FAC. RESULT TO FAC. MODIFIES CHARAC INDEX AND MANY OTHER FP LOCNS
(SQR(.5)) (-5843~-5839) [$E92D~$E931] \P5\	APPLESOFT FP CONSTANT SQR(.5) = .707..
(SQR(2)) (-5838~-5834) [$E932~$E936] \P5\	APPLESOFT FP CONSTANT SQR(2) = 1.414...
SRCH2L~SRCH2H (210~211) [$00D2~$00D3] \P2\	INTEGER BASIC MEMORY LOCATION 'SRCH2L' (SECOND VARIABLE SEARCH POINTER)
SRCHL~SRCHH (208~209) [$00D0~$00D1] \P2\	INTEGER BASIC MEMORY LOCATION 'SRCHL' (POINTER TO SEARCH VARIABLE TABLE)
STAT (2040+S) [$07F8+S] \P1\	APPLE COMMUNICATIONS INTERFACE CARD IN SLOT #S - STATUS (SEE ACIC MANUAL PG 17). E.G. POKE 2040+S~17
STATUS (72) [$0048] \P1\	USER STATUS REGISTER (P-REGISTER) SAVED HERE ON BRK TO MONITOR & DURING TRACE. WARNING: INITIALIZE BEFORE G FUNCTION TO AVOID DECIMAL MODE IF DOS HAS BEEN USED
STATUS (1400+S) [$0578+S] \P1\	EXAMPLE: APPLE SERIAL INTERFACE IN SLOT #S: PARITY CHECKSUM OPTIONS (SEE MANUAL)
STBITS (1272+S) [$04F8+S] \P1\	EXAMPLE: APPLE SERIAL INTERFACE IN SLOT #S: CONTAIN NUMBER OF STOP BITS (INCLUDING 1 PARITY BIT)
STEP (-1469) [$FA43]	MONITOR S/R- PERFORM A SINGLE STEP (NOT AVAILABLE WITH AUTOSTART ROM). EXECUTES ONE INSTRUCTION AT (PCL~H) WITH REGISTER RESTORE BEFORE; REGISTER SAVE AFTER; UPDATE OF PCL~H; DISPLAY OF INSTRUCTION & DISPLAY OF RESULT REGISTERS
STEPZ (-316) [$FEC4]	MONITOR MEMORY LOCATION 'STEPZ'
~STEP~ (-3463) [$F279] \SE\	INTEGER BASIC ENTRY TO ROUTINE TO HANDLE STEP FUNCTION FOR FOR/NEXT LOOP
STILLON (15646) [$3D1E] \SL\	DOS 3.2 RWTS (READ-WRITE TRACK-SECTOR) INTERIOR LABEL STARTS CODE WHICH SENSES IF MOTOR STILL ON
STITLE (-1179) [$FB65]	AUTOSTART MONITOR MEMORY LOCATION 'STITLE'
STKINI (-10621) [$D683] \SE\	APPLESOFT STACK INITIALIZATION - CLEARS THE STACK
STOADV (-1040) [$FBF0] \SE\	MONITOR - LOAD Y FROM CH; STORE A-REG TO SCREEN AT (BASL)~Y; AND GOTO ADVANCE ($FBF4) {A- Y-REG ALTERED}

```
NAME  (DEC LOCN)  [HEX LOCN] \USE-TYPE\ - DESCRIPTION
-----------------------------------------------------------------------------------------------------

~STOPPED AT~   (-5949) [$E8C3] \SE\ INTEGER BASIC ENTRY TO ROUTINE TO PRINT 'STOPED AT LINE #'
STOR   (-501) [$FE0B]                 MONITOR MEMORY LOCATION 'STOR'
STREND    (109~110) [$006D~$006E] \P2\APPLESOFT STORAGE END POINTER (POINTS TO TOP OF ARRAY STORAGE I.E. TO END OF
                                      NUMERIC STORAGE IN USE)
STRINI    (-7211) [$E3D5] \SE\        APPLESOFT - GET SPACE FOR CREATION OF A STRING & CREATE DISCRIPTOR FOR IT IN
                                      DSCTMP. ON ENTRY A-REG = LEN OF STRING.
STRLIT    (-7193) [$E3E7] \SE\        APPLESOFT - STORE A QUOTE IN ENDCHR AND CHARAC SO THAT STRLT2 WILL STOP ON IT
STRLT2    (-7187) [$E3ED] \SE\        APPLESOFT - BUILD DESCRIPTOR FOR STRING LITERAL WHOSE 1ST CHAR POINTED TO BY Y-REG
                                      (MSB) & X-REG (LSB). PUT INTO TEMPORARY & POINTER TO IT IN FACMO~FACLO.
STRNG1    (171~172) [$00AB~$00AC] \P2\APPLESOFT POINTER TO A STRING USED IN 'MOVINS' STRING UTILITY
STRNG2    (173~174) [$00AD~$00AE] \P2\APPLESOFT POINTER TO A STRING USED IN STRLT2 STRING UTILITY
STROUT    (-9414) [$DB3A] \SE\        APPLESOFT - PRINT STRING POINTED TO BY Y-REG (MSB) & A-REG (LSB). STRING MUST END
                                      WITH A ZERO OR QUOTE
STRPRT    (-9411) [$DB3D] \SE\        APPLESOFT - PRINT A STRING WHOSE DESCRIPTOR IS POINTED TO BY FACMO~FACLO
STRSPA    (-7203) [$E3DD] \SE\        APPLESOFT - JSR TO GETSPA. STORE THE POINTER & LENGTH IN DSCTMP.
STRTXT    (-8575) [$DE81] \SE\        APPLESOFT - SET Y-REG (MSB) & X-REG(LSB) TO TXTPTR + CARRY BIT AND FALL INTO STRLIT
STXTPT    (-10601) [$D697] \SE\       APPLESOFT INITIALIZATION - SET TXTPTR TO BEGINNING OF PROGRAM
SUBFLG    (20) [$0014]                APPLESOFT SUBSCRIPT FLAG: $00= SUBSCRIPTS ALLOWED;$80= SUBSCRIPTS NOT ALLOWED
SUBTBL    (-29) [$FFE3]               'SUBTBL' L.S.B. ADDRESS-1 OF BASCONT SUBROUTINE
SUBTBL    (-29~-23) [$FFE3~$FFE9] \PB\TABLE OF SUBROUTINE ADDRESSES -1 {INDEX PC WITH TBL ITEM FOR S/R ENTRY}: (ADDRESS
                                      MSB = $FE; LSB = TABLE ENTRY +1)
~SUBTRACTION~   (-6270) [$E782] \SE\INTEGER BASIC ENTRY POINT TO SUBTRACTION FUNCTION
SYNCHR    (-8512) [$DEC0] \SE\        APPLESOFT SYNTAX CHARACTER CHECK - CHECKS TO VERIFY TXTPTR POINTS TO SAME CHARACTER
                                      AS THAT IN A-REG. NORMAL EXIT THRU CHGET TO GET NEX CHAR FROM INPUT BUFFER OTHEWISE
                                      SYNTAX ERROR. TXTPTR NOT MODIFIED. {Y-REG RESET TO ZERO}
SYNPAGL~SYNPAGH   (254~255) [$00FE~$00FF] INTEGER BASIC SYNTAX PAGE POINTER. IF $00FF NOT ZERO THEN ERROR CONDITION
                                        EXISTS
SYNSTKDX   (253) [$00FD] \P1\           INTEGER BASIC MEMORY LOCATION 'SYNSTKDX' (SYNTAX STACK INDEX VALUE)
SYNSTKH    (88) [$0058]                 INTEGER BASIC MEMORY LOCATION 'SYNSTKH'
SYNSTKL    (128~159) [$0080~$009F]      INTEGER BASIC MEMORY LOCATION 'SYNSTKL' (SYNTAX STACK LOCATION)
~SYNTABL~    (-5120~-4609) [$EC00~$EDFF] \PB\INTEGER BASIC SYNTAX TABLE
(TABLE1 DOS 3.2.1)    (-17780) [$BA8C] \SB\DOS 3.2.1 RWTS OPERATION TIMER ROUTINE TABLE1
TABV   (-1189) [$FB5B] \SE\               PLACE CURSOR AT LINE (A-REG) COLUMN (CH) SETTING CV AND BASL~H FROM A-REG
                                          {A-REG ALTERED}
~TAB~   (-6236) [$E7A4] \SE\              INTEGER BASIC ENTRY POINT TO HORIZONTAL TAB FUNCTION
TAN   (-4038) [$F03A] \SE\                APPLESOFT FP - COMPUTE THE TANGENT OF THE NUMBER IN FAC. RESULT TO FAC.
                                          MODIFIES CHARAC INDEX XORFPSGN AND MANY OTHER FP LOCNS
TAPEIN    (-16288) [$C060]                MONITOR MEMORY LOCATION 'TAPEIN'
TAPEIN   [$C060/8] \H1\                   STATE OF 'CASSETE DATA IN' APPEARS IN BIT 7
TAPEOUT    (-16352) [$C020] \H1\          PEEK TO TOGGLE CASSETTE OUTPUT (CREATE A 'CLICK' ON RECORDING)
TAPEOUT    (-16352~-16337) [$C020~$C02F] \H1\CASSETTE OUTPUT TOGGLE FLIP FLOP. READ ONLY DO NOT WRITE TO THESE ADDRESSES
                                          WHICH ARE DECODED AS SAME SINGLE BIT LOCN
TEMP   (44~45) [$002C~$002D] \P2\         DOS RWTS (READ-WRITE TRACK-SECTOR TEMPORARY STORAGE FOR ADDRESS INFORMATION
TEMP1    (147~151) [$0093~$0097] \P5\     APPLESOFT REGISTER TEMP1 FOR FLOATING POINT MATH PACKAGE (PACKED 5-BYTE FORMAT)
TEMP2    (152~156) [$0098~$009C] \P5\     APPLESOFT FLOATING POINT MATH PACKAGE REGISTER TEMP2 (PACKED 5-BYTE FORMAT)
TEMP3    (138~142) [$008A~$008E] \P5\     APPLESOFT REGISTER TEMP3 FOR FLOATING POINT MATH PACKAGE (PACKED 5-BYTE FORMAT)
TEMPPT    (82) [$0052] \P1\               APPLESOFT TEMPORARY POINT - LAST USED TEMPORARY STRING DESCRIPTOR (SEE DSCTMP)
(TEXTLN0)   [$0400-$0427] \BB\            VIDEO SCREEN BUFFER TEXT LINE 0
(TEXTLN1)   [$0480-$04A7] \BB\            VIDEO SCREEN BUFFER TEXT LINE 1
(TEXTLN10)   [$0528-$054F] \BB\           VIDEO SCREEN BUFFER TEXT LINE 10
(TEXTLN11)   [$05A8-$05CF] \BB\           VIDEO SCREEN BUFFER TEXT LINE 11
```

```
(TEXTLN12)  [$0628-$064F] \BB\          VIDEO SCREEN BUFFER TEXT LINE 12
(TEXTLN13)  [$06A8-$06CF] \BB\          VIDEO SCREEN BUFFER TEXT LINE 13
(TEXTLN14)  [$0728-$074F] \BB\          VIDEO SCREEN BUFFER TEXT LINE 14
(TEXTLN15)  [$07A8-$07CF] \BB\          VIDEO SCREEN BUFFER TEXT LINE 15
(TEXTLN16)  [$0450-$0477] \BB\          VIDEO SCREEN BUFFER TEXT LINE 16
(TEXTLN17)  [$04D0-$04F7] \BB\          VIDEO SCREEN BUFFER TEXT LINE 17
(TEXTLN18)  [$0550-$0577] \BB\          VIDEO SCREEN BUFFER TEXT LINE 18
(TEXTLN19)  [$05D0-$05F7] \BB\          VIDEO SCREEN BUFFER TEXT LINE 19
(TEXTLN2)  [$0500-$0527] \BB\           VIDEO SCREEN BUFFER TEXT LINE 2
(TEXTLN20)  [$06=0-$0677] \BB\          VIDEO SCREEN BUFFER TEXT LINE 20
(TEXTLN21)  [$06D0-$06F7] \BB\          VIDEO SCREEN BUFFER TEXT LINE 21
(TEXTLN22)  [$0750-$0777] \BB\          VIDEO SCREEN BUFFER TEXT LINE 22
(TEXTLN23)  [$07D0-$07F7] \BB\          VIDEO SCREEN BUFFER TEXT LINE 23
(TEXTLN3)  [$0580-$05A7] \BB\           VIDEO SCREEN BUFFER TEXT LINE 3
(TEXTLN4)  [$0600-$0627] \BB\           VIDEO SCREEN BUFFER TEXT LINE 4
(TEXTLN5)  [$0680-$06A7] \BB\           VIDEO SCREEN BUFFER TEXT LINE 5
(TEXTLN6)  [$0700-$0727] \BB\           VIDEO SCREEN BUFFER TEXT LINE 6
(TEXTLN7)  [$0780-$07A7] \BB\           VIDEO SCREEN BUFFER TEXT LINE 7
(TEXTLN8)  [$0428-$044F] \BB\           VIDEO SCREEN BUFFER TEXT LINE 8
(TEXTLN9)  [$04A8-$04CF] \BB\           VIDEO SCREEN BUFFER TEXT LINE 9
(TEXTMACROLINE2)   (1280~1399) [$0500~$0577] \HB\TEXTVIDEO DISPLAY - SUBPAGE 2. CONSISTS OF TEXT LINES 2~ 10 & 18
                                        FOLLOWED BY AN 8-BYTE BLOCK FOR I-O PERIPHERALS
TEXTTAB   (103~104) [$0067~$0068] \P2\  APPLESOFT TEXT TABLE POINTER (POINTS TO TO BEGINNING OF PROGRAM TEXT . DEFAULT
                                        VALUE $0801
(TIMER DOS 3.1~3.2)   (-17793) [$BA7F] \SB\DOS 3.1~3.2 RWTS OPERATION TIMER ROUTINE
(TIMER DOS 3.2.1)   (-17797) [$BA7B] \SB\DOS 3.2.1 RWTS OPERATION TIMER ROUTINE
TITLE   (-1271) [$FB09]                 AUTOSTART MONITOR MEMORY LOCATION 'TITLE'
~TO/FOR~   (-5808) [$E950] \SE\         INTEGER BASIC ENTRY POINT TO ROUTINE TO HANDLE LOOP COUNTER # TO # STEP #
TOKNDX   (241) [$00CF1] \P1\            INTEGER BASIC MEMORY LOCATION 'TOKNDX' (TOKEN INDEX VALUE)
TOKNDXSTK   (209~240) [$00D1~$00F0]     INTEGER BASIC MEMORY LOCATION 'TOKNDXSTK' ('TOKEN INDEX STACK?)
(TOOCOMPLEX)   (-7120) [$E430] \SE\     APPLESOFT - PRINT "FORMULA TOO COMPLEX" THEN HALT AT APPLESOFT (]) LEVEL
TOSUB   (-66) [$FFBE]                   MONITOR & MINIASSEMBER MEMORY LOCATION 'TOSUB'
TRACE   (-318) [$FEC2] \SE\             CALL TO PERFORM MONITOR TRACE
~TRACEIT~   (-3715) [$F17D] \SE\        INTEGER BASIC ENTRY TO ROUTINE TO EXECUTE THE TRACE FUNCTION
~TRACE~   (-3727) [$F171] \SE\          INTEGER BASIC ENTRY TO ROUTINE TO SET TRACE MODE FOR EXECUTION
TRACK - TRKN   (46) [$002E] \P1\        DOS RWTS (READ-WRITE TRACK-SECTOR) TRACK NUMBER
TRKCNT   (65) [$0041] \P1\              DOS DISK SYSTEM FORMATTER SPECIAL TRACK COUNTER
TRKDON   (16243~16340) [$3F73~$3FD4] \SB\DOS 3.2 DISK FORMATTER CHECK TRACK FORMATTING ROUTINE
TRKDON   (-4237) [$EF73] \SE\           DOS 3.2 DISK FORMATTER INTERIOR LABEL AT POINT WHERE TRACK FORMATTING IS DONE
                                        AND CHECKING OF THAT FORMATTING BEGINS
TRKFRM   (16046) [$3EAE] \SL\           DOS 3.2 DISK FORMATTER LABEL AT POINT WHERE TRACK FORMATTING BEGINS
TRYADR   (15776) [$3DA0] \SL\           DOS 3.2 RWTS (READ-WRITE TRACK SECTOR) INTERIOR LABEL 'TRYADR'
TRYADR2   (15784) [$3DA8] \SL\          DOS 3.2 RWTS (READ-WRITE TRACK SECTOR) INTERIOR LABEL 'TRYADR2
TRYNEXT   (-2724) [$F55C]               MINIASSEMBLER MEMORY LOCATION 'TRYNEXT'
TRYTRK   (15754) [$3D8A] \SL\           DOS 3.2 RWTS (READ-WRITE TRACK-SECTOR INTERIOR LABEL - TRY DISK TRACK AS PART
                                        OF LOCATING CORRECT SECTOR FOR READ
TRYTRK   (-16981~-16965) [$BDAB~$BDBB] \SB\DOS 3.3 - GET COMMAND CODE.  IF NULL EXIT VIA 'ALLDONE' ($BE46) TURNING OFF
                                        DRIVE & RETURNING TO CALLER. IF COMMAND CODE=4 BRANCH TO 'FORMDSK' ($BEOD);
                                        OTHERWISE MOVE LOW BIT INTO CARRY (SET=READ;CLEAR=WRITE) AND SAVE VALUE ON
                                        STATUS REG. IF WRITE OPN DATA IS PRENIBBILIZED VIA 'PRENIB16' ($B800)
TRYTRK2   (15771) [$3D9B] \SL\          DOS 3.2 RWTS (READ-WRITE TRACK-SECTOR INTERIOR LABEL 'TRYTRK2'
```

```
(TWO PI)    (-3989~-3985) [$F06B~$F06F] \P5\APPLESOFT 5-BYTE FLOATING POINT CONSTANT 2*PI = 6.2832...
TXTCLR    (-16304) [$C050] \H1\        POKE TO 0 TO SET FROM TEXT TO GRAPHICS MODE W/O CLEARING SCREEN
TXTNDX    (200) [$00C8]                INTEGER BASIC MEMORY LOCATION 'TXTNDX' (TEXT INDEX VALUE)
TXTNDXSTK    (168~199) [$00A8~$00C7]   INTEGER BASIC MEMORY LOCATION 'TXTNDXSTK' (TEXT INDEX STACK)
TXTPTR    (184~185) [$00B8~$00B9] \P2\ TXTPTR - POINTS AT NEXT CHAR OR TOKEN FROM PROG (C/A DEC 78)
TXTSET    (-16303) [$C051] \H1\        POKE TO 0 TO SET FROM GRAPHICS TO TEXT MODE W/O RESETTING SCROLLING WINDOW
(UNDEF'D STMT PRT)    (-9860) [$D97C]  APPLESOFT - PRINT "UNDEF'D STATEMENT" THEN HALT AT APPLESOFT (]) LEVEL
~UNPACK~    (-8083) [$E06D] \SE\       INTEGER BASIC ENTRY POINT TO UNPACK TOKENED CODE TO MNEMONICS
UP ~ CURSUP    (-998) [$FC1A] \SE\     MONITOR S/R TO MOVE CURSOR UPWARD (IF POSSIBLE) {A-REG ALTERED}
USR    (-310) [$FECA]                  MONITOR MEMORY LOCATION 'USR'
USRADR    (1016) [$03F8]               IN MONITOR MODE KEYBOARD ENTRY OF CTL-Y WILL CAUSE JSR HERE
V2    (45) [$002D] \P1\                BOTTOM PT OF LO-RES VERT LINE DRAWN BY VLINE. RANGE: 0-19(~$21) FOR MIXED SCR;
                                       0-23(~$17) FOR FULL SCR
~VALGETL~VALGETH~    (206~207) [$00CE~$00CF] \P2\INTEGER BASIC PRIMARY EVALUATOR TEMPORARY LOCATION
~VALL~VALH~    (206~207) [$00CE~$00CF] \P2\INTEGER BASIC 16-BIT TEMPORARY VALUE FOR MATHEMATICAL OPERATIONS
VALTYP    (17) [$0011]                 APPLESOFT FLAG FOR LAST FAC (FLOATING ACCUMULATOR) OPERATION: $00 = NUMBER;
                                       $FF=STRING
VARPNT    (131~132) [$0083~$0084] \P2\ APPLESOFT POINTER TO THE LAST-USED VARIABLE'S VALUE (USED BY PTRGET)
VARTAB:    (105~106) [$0069~$006A] \P2\ APPLESOFT VARIABLE TABLE POINTER - POINTS TO TO START OF SIMPLE VARIABLE SPACE
                                       (AT END OF APPLESOFT PROGRAM TEXT)
VARTIO    (-10000) [$D8FC] \SE\        APPLESOFT CASSETTE - SET UP A1 & A2 TO SAVE 3 BYTES ($0050~$0052) FOR LENGTH
~VERBADL~    (-5616~-5497) [$EA10~$EA87] \PB\INTEGER BASIC VERB DISPATCH TABLE LOW BYTE
~VERBADRH~    (-5496) [$EA88] \PB\     INTEGER BASIC VERB DISPATCH TABLE HI BYTE
VERBNOW    (214) [$00D6] \P1\          INTEGER BASIC MEMORY LOCATION 'VERBNOW' (VERB CURRENTLY IN USE)
VFY    (-458) [$FE36] \SE\             MONITOR S/R TO PERFORM A MEMORY VERIFY (A1-A2 TO A4)
VFYOK    (-424) [$FE58]                MONITOR MEMORY LOCATION 'VFYOK'
VIDOUT    (-1027) [$FBFD] \SE\         MONITOR S/R- OUTPUT A-REGISTER AS ASCII ON TEXT SCREEN OR PROCESS CONTROL
                                       CHARACTER. IF (A)<$80 GOTO STOADV;  =$87 SOUND BELL; =$88 GOTO BS; =$8A GOTO
                                       LF; =$8D GOTO CR; >$9F GOTO STOADV; OTHERWISE IGNORE ENTRY SCREEN RTS 1
VIDWAIT    (-1160) [$FB78]             AUTOSTART MONITOR MEMORY LOCATION 'VIDWAIT'
VLINE    (-2008) [$F828] \SE\          LO-RES PLOT VERT LINE AT X-COORD = (Y-REG) AND Y-COORD FROM (A-REG) THRU
                                       ($002D) {A-REG ALTERED}
VLINEZ    (-2010) [$F826] \SE\         LO-RES PLOT VERTICAL LINE AT X-COORD = (Y-REG) AND Y-COORD FROM
                                       (A-REG)+1+CARRY THRU ($002D) {A-REG ALTERED}
~VLIN~    (-4410) [$EEC6] \SE\         INTEGER BASIC ENTRY POINT TO DRAW A LO-RES VERTICAL LINE
VOLUME    (47) [$002F] \P1\            DOS RWTS (READ-WRITE TRACK-SECTOR) DISK VOLUME NUMBER
VTAB    (-990) [$FC22] \SE\            PERFORM A VERTICAL TAB TO ROW SPECIFIED IN A-REG ($0~$17). SET BASL~H FROM CV
                                       (AND WNDLFT) {A-REG ALTERED}
VTABZ    (-988) [$FC24] \SE\           SET BASL~H FROM (A-REG) AND WNDLFT WITHOUT REGARD TO CV {A-REG ALTERED}
~VTAB~    (-4521) [$EE57] \SE\         INTEGER BASIC ENTRY TO VERTICAL TAB FUNCTION
WAIT    (-856) [$FCA8] \SE\            CALL FOR WAIT LOOP. WAIT ESTIMATED AT 2.5A~2+13.5A+13 WAIT CYCLES OF 1.02
                                       MICROSECONDS WHERE A IS CONTENTS OF A-REG WHEN S/R CALLED
WAIT2    (-855) [$FCA9]                MONITOR MEMORY LOCATION 'WAIT2'
WAIT3    (-854) [$FCAA]                MONITOR MEMORY LOCATION 'WAIT3'
WBYTE    (16315) [$3FBB] \SL\          DOS 3.2 DISK FORMATTER INTERIOR LABEL AT BEGINNING OF TIGHT TIMING ROUTINE
WINBLB2    (16331) [$3FCB] \SL\        DOS 3.2 DISK FORMATTER INTERIOR LABEL 'WINBLB2'
WINBLC    (-4147) [$EFCD] \SL\         DOS 3.2 DISK FORMAT INTERIOR LABEL 'WINBLC'
WLOOP    (16256) [$3F80] \SL\          DOS 3.2 DISK FORMATTER INTERIOR LABEL AT BEGINNING OF 26 MICROSECOND WAIT LOOP
WNDBTM    (35) [$0023] \P1\            BOTTOM LINE OF SCROLL WINDOW: RANGE (WNDTOP)+1 TO 24($18).
WNDLFT    (32) [$0020] \P1\            LEFT COLUMN OF SCROLL WINDOW: RANGE 0-39 OR $0~$27. USED ONLY IN VTABZ.
WNDTOP    (34) [$0022] \F1\            TOP LINE OF SCROLL WINDOW: RANGE 0-22($16) FOR FULL TEXT SCREEN 20-22($14~$16)
                                       FOR MIXED SCREEN
```

```
WNDWDTH   (33) [$0021] \P1\              WIDTH OF THE SCROLL WINDOW: RANGE:1 TO 40-(WNDLFT) OR $1 TO $28 - (WNDLFT)
WNIBLA   (16330) [$3FCA] \SL\            DOS 3.2 DISK FORMATTER INTERIOR LABEL 'WNIBLA'
WR1   (-300) [$FED4]                     MONITOR MEMORY LOCATION 'WR1'
WRBIT   (-810) [$FCD6]                   MONITOR - WRITES A BIT TO CASSETTE TAPE (CALLED BY WRBYTE AND HEADR)
WRBYT2   (-273) [$FEEF]                  MONITOR MEMORY LOCATION 'WRBYT2'
WRBYTE   (-275) [$FEED]                  MONITOR - USES WRBIT TO WRITE 10 BITS  TO CASSETTE TAPE
WRIT   (15922) [$3E32] \SL\              DOS 3.2 RWTS (READ-WRITE TRACK-SECTOR) INTERIOR LABEL AT START OF CODE TO WRITE
                                         NIBBLES TO DISK IF NOT WRITE PROTECTED
WRIT   (-16815~-16807) [$BE51~$BE59]     DOS 3.3 - WRITE A SECTOR USING 'WRITE16' ($B82A); IF GOOD WRITE EXIT VIA
                                         'ALLDONE' ($BE46) OTHERWISE LOAD A-REG WITH $10 (WRITE PROTECT ERROR) AND EXIT
                                         VIA 'HNDLERR' ($BE48)
WRIT2   (16098) [$3EE2] \SL\             DOS 3.2 DISK FORMATTER INTERIOR LABEL 'WRIT2'
WRIT3   (16103) [$3EE7] \SL\             DOS 3.2 DISK FORMATTER INTERIOR LABEL 'WRIT3'
WRITE   (-18326~-18180) [$B86A~$B8FC] \SB\DOS 3.1~3.2~3.2.1 (SEE $B82A FOR DOS 3.3 'WRITE') RWTS (READ-WRITE
                                         TRACK-SECTOR) WRITE MODULE. WRITES A BUFFER OF 410 ($19A) 5-BIT
                                         RIGHT-JUSTIFIED NIBBLES ONTO THE DISK SURFACE AS A SECTOR CONVERTING THEM TO
                                         A 8-BIT 'DISK BYTE' FORMAT FIRST
WRITE   (-307) [$FECD] \SE\              MONITOR S/R TO WRITE DATA FROM MEMORY TO CASSETTE TAPE - FIRST MEMORY LOCATION
                                         POINTED TO BY A1L~H ($003C~$003D); LAST BY A2L~H ($003E~$003F).  CASSETTE TAPE
                                         GETS 10 SECONDS OF TONE HEADER THEN THE DESIGNATED DATA BITS AND ONE CHECKSUM
                                         BYTE
WRITE16 (DOS 3.3)   (-18390~-18249) [$B82A~$B8B7] \SB\DOS 3.3 'WRITE'. WRITES PRENIBBILIZED DATA FROM PRIMARY &
                                                 SECONDARY BUFFERS TO DISK; CALLS WRITE-A-BYTE S~R; WRITES 5 BYTES
                                                 AUTSYNC~ STARTING DATA MARKS ($D5~$AA~$AD)~ 342 BYTES DATA~ ONE
                                                 BYTE CHECKSUM~ AND CLOSING DATA MARKS ($DE~$AA~$EB). USES WRITE
                                                 TRANSLATE TABLE ($BA29). ON ENTRY X-REG CONTAINS SLOT#*16. ON
                                                 EXIT X-REG UNCHANGED;Y-REG $00; CARRY CLEAR. USES $0026~ $0027~ $678
WRITSF   (16102) [$3EE6] \SL\                    DOS 3.2 DISK FORMATTER INTERIOR LABEL 'WRITSF'
WRNIBL   (-4146) [$EFCE] \SL\                    DOS 3.2 DISK FORMAT INTERIOR LABEL 'WRNIBL'
WRTAPE   (-795) [$FCE5]                          MONITOR MEMORY LOCATION 'WRTAPE'
WRTRK   (16068) [$3EC4] \SL\                     DOS 3.2 DISK FORMATTER - LABEL AT POINT WHERE WRITE OF FORMATTING INFO
                                                 ONTO TRACK BEGINS -- A HIGHLY TIMING-SENSITIVE AREA OF CODE
XOL~XOH   (800~801) [$0320~$0321] \P2\           HI-RES GRAPHICS- PRIOR X-COORD SAVE AFTER HLIN OR HPLOT
X1   (248) [$00F8]                               OLD (NON-APPLESOFT) FLOATING POINT ROUTINES FLOATING POINT ACCUMULATOR
                                                 FP1 MEMORY LOC 'X1' (EXPONENT)
X2   (244) [$00F4] \P1\                          MONITOR & OLD (NON-APPLESOFT) FLOATING POINT ROUTINES FLOATING POINT
                                                 ACCUMULATOR 2 MEMORY LOC 'X2' (EXPONENT)
XAM   (-589) [$FDB3] \SE\                        MONITOR S/R TO EXAMINE CONTENTS OF MEMORY FROM (A1L~A1H) TO(A2L~A2H).
                                                 Y-REG=0 BEFORE CALL {A-REG ALTERED}
XAM8   (-605) [$FDA3] \SE\                       MONITOR S/R TO EXAMINE 8 MEM LOCNS. PRINTS HEX OF MEMORY FROM XXXX TO
                                                 XXX7 WHERE XXXX IS CONTENTS OF A1L~A1H; Y-REG MUST =0 ON ENTRY {A-REG
                                                 ALTERED }
XAMPM   (-570) [$FDC6]                           MONITOR MEMORY LOCATION 'XAMPM'
XBASIC   (-336) [$FEB0] \SE\                     MONITOR S/R TO JUMP TO BASIC
XBRK   (-1380) [$FA9C]                           MONITOR MEMORY LOCATION 'XBRK'
XDRAW   (-2467) [$F65D] \SE\                     APPLESOFT HI-RES - DRAW SHAPE POINTED TO BY Y-REG(MSB)&X-REG(LSB) BY
                                                 INVERTING EXISTING COLOR OF DOTS SHAPE DRAWS OVER. A-REG = ROT FACTOR
XJMP   (-1340) [$FAC4]                           MONITOR MEMORY LOCATION 'XJMP'
XJMPAT   (-1339) [$FAC5]                         MONITOR MEMORY LOCATION 'XJMPAT'
XJSR   (-1351) [$FAB9]                           MONITOR MEMORY LOCATION 'XJSR'
XQ1   (-1416) [$FA78]                            MONITOR MEMORY LOCATION 'XQ1'
```

NAME (DEC LOCN) [HEX LOCN] \USE-TYPE\	- DESCRIPTION
XQ2 (-1414) [$FA7A]	MONITOR MEMORY LOCATION 'XQ2'
XQINIT (-1458) [$FA4E]	MONITOR MEMORY LOCATION 'XQINIT'
XQT/XQTNZ (60~67) [$003C~$0043] \PB\	8 BYTE WORK AREA FOR INSTRUCTION STEP/TRACE. NEXT INSTRUCTION SOMETIMES MOVED HERE
XREG (70) [$0046] \P1\	USER X-REG SAVED HERE ON BRK TO MONITOR & DURING TRACE
XRTI (-1371) [$FAA5]	MONITOR MEMORY LOCATION 'XRTI'
XRTS (-1367) [$FAA9]	MONITOR MEMORY LOCATION 'XRTS'
XSAVE (216) [$00D8] \P1\	INTEGER BASIC MEMORY LOCATION 'XSAVE' (TEMPORARY STORAGE FOR CONTENTS OF X-REGISTER)
XTNDL~XTNDH (82~83) [$0052~$0053] \P2\	OLD MONITOR (NOT AUTOSTART) - USED IN 16-BIT MULT & DIVIDE AS ACCUMULATOR EXTENSION (TO 32 BITS)
XTOY (15995) [$3E7B] \DL\	DOS 3.2 RWTS (READ-WRITE TRACK-SECTOR) INTERIOR LABEL 'XTOY'
XTOY (-16754~-16748) [$BE8E~$BE94]	DOS 3.3 - X-REG/16 =>Y-REG. USED TO PUT SLOT INTO Y-REG
YO (802) [$0322] \P1\	HI-RES GRAPHICS YO - MOST RECENT Y-COORDINATE
YCNT (71) [$0047] \P1\	DOS DISK SYSTEM FORMATTER NYBBLE COUNTER (ALSO COUNTER FOR DISK-DRIVE MOTOR-ON TIME?)
YREG (71) [$0047] \P1\	USER Y-REG SAVED HERE ON BRK TO MONITOR & DURING TRACE {Y-REG SAVED HERE ON BRK}
YSAV (52) [$0034] \P1\	USED BY MONITOR COMMAND PROCESSOR TO SAVE CONTENTS OF Y-REGISTER DURING PROCESSOR {Y-REGISTER SAVE LOCN FOR MONITOR}
YSAV1 (53) [$0035] \P1\	USED TO SAVE CONTENTS OF Y-REGISTER ACROSS A CALL TO SCREEN OUTPUT ROUTINES. {Y-REGISTER SAVE LOCN FOR COUT1}
YTEMP (201) [$00C9]	INTEGER BASIC MEMORY LOCATION 'YTEMP' (TEMPORARY STORAGE FOR Y-REGISTER)
ZERDLY (-805) [$FCDB]	MONITOR MEMORY LOCATION 'ZERDLY'
ZMODE (-132) [$FF7C]	MONITOR & MINIASSEMBLER MEMORY LOCATION 'ZMODE'
ZMODE (-57) [$FFC7]	MONITOR MEMORY LOCATION 'ZMODE'
ZPGBM3 ZPGFCB (67~67) [$0043~$0043]	DOS - USED AS GENERAL PURPOSE POINTER BY SECOND-LEVEL DOS ROUTINES

Other Works on the Apple Computer from MICRO INK

MICRO

Our monthly journal, **MICRO**, has covered the Apple in depth since 1977. It is edited for users of the Apple and users of other 6502- or 6809-based microcomputers who want to get the most out of their machines. Those who want to go beyond canned software, use computers for more than games, learn advanced programming techniques, and understand the inner workings of their machines, will profit by reading **MICRO.**

Subscription: $18.00 per year in the U.S.; $21.00 per year by surface mail elsewhere.
Airmail rates are available on request.
(Subscription rates subject to change.)

MICRO on the Apple
A series of books for Apple users

The first two volumes in this series present the best Apple articles from MICRO in an integrated collection. Articles and programs have been updated by the original authors or MICRO's staff. All programs have been tested and entered on a diskette which comes with the book (13 sector, 3.2 DOS format, convertible to 3.3). Each volume in the series is 6 × 9 inches, with approximately 224 pages, and includes a pocket for storing the diskette. A Wire-O binding allows the book to lie flat when open. Subsequent volumes in the series may contain previously unpublished material.

Volume 1 (published in April 1981) contains 30 articles and 38 tested programs which enable users to speed up programming in Applesoft and Integer BASIC; add Apple II Plus editing features (at no cost); round and format numbers accurately in business applications; get lowercase letters and punctuation into Applesoft strings (at no cost); do a shape table easily and correctly; play the hit game "Spelunker"; and more.

Volume 2 (to be published in the fall of 1981) contains over two dozen articles and tested programs which will enable users to sort larger arrays quickly and easily in Applesoft, speed up machine language and BASIC programming and interfacing, write music on the Apple, understand DOS and Applesoft routines more thoroughly, compress high-resolution pictures, manipulate cassette tapes efficiently, and more.

At your computer store, volumes 1 and 2 (with diskette) are each **$24.95** (in 1981).

For shipping and handling on mail orders, add $2.00 for surface shipping
Massachusetts residents add 5% for sales tax.

MICRO INK, Inc.
34 Chelmsford Street
P.O. Box 6502
Chelmsford, MA 01824
Telephone: (617) 256-5515

VISA and Mastercard accepted.